The Two Majorities and the Puzzle of
Modern American Politics

The Two Majorities
and the Puzzle of
Modern American Politics

Byron E. Shafer

University Press of Kansas

Published by the University Press of Kansas (Lawrence, Kansas 66049), which
was organized by the Kansas Board of Regents and is operated and funded by
Emporia State University, Fort Hays State University, Kansas State University,
Pittsburg State University, the University of Kansas, and Wichita State University

Library of Congress Cataloging-in-Publication Data

Shafer, Byron E.
    The two majorities and the puzzle of modern American politics/ Byron E.
Shafer.
        p.   cm.
Includes bibliographical references and index.
    ISBN 0-7006-1235-1 (cloth : alk. paper) —
ISBN 0-7006-1236-X (pbk. : alk. paper)
    1. Political parties—United States.   2. Political
participation—United States.   3. United States—Politics and
government—20th century.   I. Title.
    JK2261. S4298 2003
    320.973—dc21   2002154106

British Library Cataloguing in Publication Data is available.

Printed in the United States of America

10 9 8 7 6 5 4 3 2 1

The paper used in this publication meets the minimum requirements of the
American National Standard for Permanence of Paper for Printed Library
Materials Z39.48-1984.

I have had the opportunity over the years to work with
four remarkable teachers, remarkable for their intellectual
abilities but also for their ability to impart a way of
thinking without insisting on a template to go with it.
I recognize their influence in the essays that follow,
even as I continue to guarantee them total deniability.
This book is dedicated to them:

Robert K. Merton
Nelson W. Polsby
David B. Truman
Aaron B. Wildavsky

CONTENTS

ACKNOWLEDGMENTS

A collection like this requires three levels of acknowledgment. There are those who suggested, and then supported, creation of the volume itself. Without their initiatives, there would be no book. Every bit as integral, however, are those who agreed to be part of the larger projects from which these pieces are taken. It was the willingness of these individuals to participate—and to participate in certain structured ways—that made my own part in such projects possible. Last, there are those who shaped my thinking about American politics. Their influence is perhaps least obvious to others, so I will start with them.

My own approach to the search for influences on American politics has become a self-conscious strategy of inquiry. It did not start out that way. This evolution began with an early set of scholarly influences—two sets, really—that weighted the balance between strategic actors and a structuring environment in different ways. Nelson W. Polsby and Aaron B. Wildavsky at the University of California at Berkeley first focused my attention on the *strategies* of American politics: on what political actors do and why they do it. Later, Robert K. Merton and David B. Truman at the Russell Sage Foundation in New York emphasized the *constraints* of American politics: the contours of the recurring landscape within which actors (must) act and thus the recurring influences on the world in which they operate.

Neither side was doctrinaire. That is, neither offered an enduring social structure that determined political outcomes regardless of the context of the day; just as neither tolerated any simple strategic calculation independent of social structuring—independent of *multiple* structuring devices in the nature of American politics. As a result, each of these individuals could be hugely influential while differing on the balance, not the centrality, of both elements in the equation.

This general intellectual focus acquired the bite characterizing its application in the articles herein from a different sort of "educational" experience. All were products of time spent in the Andrew W. Mellon Professorship of American Government at Oxford University. I discuss, in the introduction, some implications of this scholarly site: a focus on continuity rather than change, a need for at least implicit comparison. Yet the articles presented here are also the product of different incentives associated with the Mellon chair—incentives, at the very least, to paint with a broad brush. Students, colleagues, journalists, and even practitioners had much more use for the resulting picture. Students tended to have many disparate bits of information about American politics but real difficulty fitting them together. Professional observers needed recurrent patterns to help adjust their own behavior to what they could reasonably expect American politics to be like.

Finally, some disciplinary channels of a different sort—more exactly, some encouragement toward ignoring the conventional borders in scholarly disciplines—also contributed to the pieces assembled here. I hope that these articles are still reliably the product of a self-conscious political science. Nevertheless, it is a political science heavily shaped by what should be called sociological approaches, which Berkeley, Russell Sage, and especially Nuffield College, Oxford, powerfully reinforced. It is a political science shaped by a joint appointment to the Politics and Modern History faculties at Oxford, where political history has a security and a standing—an essential quality—that it lacks at the moment in the United States. It is a political science shaped, especially in its concern with the substance of policy conflict, by the interest in political theory so traditionally central to the study of politics at Oxford: what the struggle is actually about should never be allowed to disappear from its portrayal. And it is a political science shaped in crucial ways—though here, the main shapers might deny it—by my economics colleagues at Nuffield, who (mostly) endured my efforts to get an education in their subject matter with bemusement and even grace.

That is the biggest picture, the most grand and general description of where these pieces (and this volume) came from. Yet each individual piece has not only its own story but also its own cast of supporting characters. And in the case of many of them, it is the coordinated contribution from these individuals that made my own contribution possible.

Chapter 1, "Economic Development, Issue Evolution, and Divided Government, 1955–2000," was originally subtitled "The Two Majorities and the Puzzle of Modern American Politics" and appeared in Byron E. Shafer and Anthony J. Badger, eds., *Contesting Democracy: Substance & Structure in American Political History, 1775–2000* (Lawrence: University

Press of Kansas, 2001). It was the final chapter in that grand, overlapping, and argumentative survey energized by Peter H. Argersinger of Southern Illinois University, Ronald P. Formisano of the University of Florida, Michael F. Holt of the University of Virginia, Richard Jensen of the University of Illinois at Chicago (emeritus), James T. Patterson of Brown University, Joel H. Silbey of Cornell University, David Waldstreicher of Yale University, and, of course, the two editors and Mellon professors of Oxford and Cambridge, respectively.

Chapter 2, "The Search for a New Center," was originally subtitled "Substance and Structure, 2001" and appeared in Byron E. Shafer, ed., *The State of American Politics* (Lanham, Md.: Rowman & Littlefield, 2002). This essay and its original volume, like several others in the roster below, began as a lecture series and migrated into print, thereby underlining the way that the entire project was dependent on the collaboration and coordination of a set of supportive colleagues. In this case, they were a mix of journalists and scholars, including Michael Barone of *U.S. News & World Report*, James A. Barnes of *National Journal*, Richard G. C. Johnston of the University of British Columbia, Charles O. Jones of the University of Wisconsin at Madison, David R. Mayhew of Yale University, William Schneider of CNN, and Martin M. Shapiro of the University of California at Berkeley.

Chapter 3, "Are There Any New Democrats? And by the Way, Was There a Republican Revolution?" originally appeared in Colin Campbell and Bert A. Rockman, eds., *The Clinton Legacy* (New York: Seven Bridges Press, 2000). Besides chapters from Colin (of Georgetown University) and Bert (of the University of Pittsburgh), the piece was joined by essays from Joel D. Aberbach of UCLA, George C. Edwards III of Texas A & M, Emily Goldman and Larry Berman of the University of California at Davis, David O'Brien of the University of Virginia, Mark A. Peterson of UCLA, Paul J. Quirk and William Cunion of the University of Illinois at Urbana-Champaign, Virginia Sapiro and David Canon of the University of Wisconsin at Madison, Barbara Sinclair of UCLA, and Graham Wilson of the University of Wisconsin at Madison.

Chapter 4, "We Are All Southern Democrats Now," was originally subtitled "The Shape of American Politics in the Very Late Twentieth Century" and appeared in Byron E. Shafer, ed., *Present Discontents: American Politics in the Very Late Twentieth Century* (Chatham, N.J.: Chatham House Publishers, 1997). That volume followed from a lecture series featuring talks, and subsequent chapters, by another mix of journalistic and scholarly interpreters—journalists who pay some attention to the political science literature, and scholars who believe in speaking to an intelligent lay public—including Joel H. Silbey of Cornell University, Michael Barone of *U.S. News & World Report*, Charles O. Jones of the University of Wisconsin at Madison, Alan Ehrenhalt of *Governing Magazine*, Edward G. Carmines and Geoffrey C. Layman of Indiana University, and Thomas B. Edsall of the *Washington Post*.

Chapter 5, "The Changing Structure of American Politics," began life as that curious Oxford creature called an inaugural lecture, in which a new professor introduces at least himself and often his field to the wider university audience. Mine was hugely encouraged by Michael Brock, then warden of Nuffield, and by Robert Merton and Nelson Polsby. Its train of argument was subsequently encouraged—or occasionally challenged—by my Oxford colleagues, especially Nigel Bowles of St. Anne's College, Desmond King of St. John's College, and Alan Ware of Worcester College, along with the late Leslie Stone, then chief commentator of the BBC World Service.

Chapter 6, "The Circulation of Elites, 1946–1996," appeared originally as "Partisan Elites, 1946–1996" in Byron E. Shafer, ed., *Partisan Approaches to Postwar American Politics* (Chappaqua, N.Y.: Chatham House Publishers, 1998). This volume followed from a panel at the annual meetings of the American Political Science Association, which became a second lecture series featuring talks (and subsequently chapters) by Randall W. Strahan of Emory University, Nicol C. Rae of Florida International University, John F. Bibby of the University of Wisconsin at Milwaukee, William G. Mayer of Northeastern University, and Harold F. Bass, Jr., of Ouachita Baptist University. Anyone who has looked into that volume will know how remarkably willing these scholarly collaborators were to coordinate their work around a central approach.

Chapter 7, "Reform in the American Experience," was ultimately published in *Corruption and Reform* 6, no. 1 (1991): 1–24. It began life, however, as the keynote lecture from the American side in a conference between American and (then) Soviet political scientists under the auspices of the Soviet Academy of Sciences. It was a portentous historical moment—the hinge years between the old Soviet Union and the new Russia. Delegation colleagues included Alexander Dallin of Columbia University, Richard F. Fenno of the University of Rochester, Samuel P. Huntington of Harvard University, Gail W. Lapidus of the University of California at Berkeley, Seymour Martin Lipset of Stanford University, Lucian W. Pye of Harvard

University, Catherine E. Rudder of the American Political Science Association, and Kenneth N. Waltz of the University of California at Berkeley.

Chapter 8, "From Social Welfare to Cultural Values in Anglo-America," was ultimately published in the *Journal of Policy History* 10, no. 4 (1999): 1–44. It had its roots, however, in panels on political history at the annual meetings of the Organization of American Historians and the American Historical Association, organized by Hugh Davis Graham of Vanderbilt University and Anthony J. Badger of Cambridge University, respectively. It achieved its current form—becoming a "real article"—thanks to the dedicated efforts of its coauthor, Marc D. Stears of Cambridge University. I dare say that neither of us would have attempted such an interpretation of recent political history in the two nations (an even more obviously contrarian interpretation in Britain than in the United States), without encouragement from the other.

Chapter 9, retitled here as "Issue Evolution, Institutional Structure, and Public Preferences in the G-7," was originally the "Synthesis" in Byron E. Shafer, ed., *Postwar Politics in the G-7: Orders and Eras in Comparative Perspective* (Madison: University of Wisconsin Press, 1996). This one too began as a panel at the annual meetings of the American Political Science Association, where six panelists covered the other six G-7 countries in presentations that evolved into chapters: Andrew Adonis of the *Financial Times* on Britain; Stephen J. Anderson of the International University of Japan on Japan; Miriam Feldblum of the University of San Francisco on France; J. Jens Hesse of Nuffield College, Oxford, on Germany; Richard G. C. Johnston of the University of British Columbia on Canada; and Carol A. Mershon of the University of Virginia on Italy.

Finally, chapter 10, "What Is the American Way? Four Themes in Search of Their Next Incarnation," appeared originally as the conclusion to Byron E. Shafer, ed., *Is America Different? A New Look at American Exceptionalism* (Oxford: Clarendon Press, 1991). This piece followed a conference addressing the title question in a variety of grand realms and featured related essays from Seymour Martin Lipset of Stanford University with an overview, Daniel Bell of Harvard University on government, Peter Temin of the Massachusetts Institute of Technology on the economy, Andrew Greeley of the University of Arizona on religion, the late Aaron Wildavsky of the University of California at Berkeley on culture, Martin Trow of the University of California at Berkeley on higher education, and Richard Rose of Strathclyde University on public policy.

If those are the influences, such as I understand them, that shaped my own approach to American politics and the particular examples herein, there is of course another, final, proximate set of contributors. The general idea for this volume grew out of discussions with Charles O. Jones. He has reminded me of more missing aspects to my analysis than I care to remember. The specifics of that idea then became concrete in conversation with Fred Woodward, director of the University Press of Kansas. This has become an ongoing conversation that ranges reliably from the professional—the state and evolution of political science and political history—to the deeply philosophical—the appropriate life stages for various types of work and the appropriate breeds of companion dog to support those life stages. The resulting book was also critically supported at Kansas by Melinda Wirkus, production manager, and Susan Schott, marketing director. Last, David R. Mayhew of Yale University provided decisive advice on the organization and ordering of the individual pieces. I hope he sees his larger influence reflected here as well.

The Two Majorities and the Puzzle of
Modern American Politics

INTRODUCTION

In a world in which professional students of politics are increasingly accused of knowing more and more about less and less, the chapters that follow aspire to be different. All focus on major aspects of American politics; there are no political miniatures here. At their most restrained, these analyses focus on a specific set of recent policy conflicts and institutional combatants, though even then the goal is to illuminate the *ongoing* substance and structure that determine their character. These analyses are equally likely to range across time, searching for continuing issues and influences, or even across nations, searching for the same things in a different locale.

All these chapters search additionally for the patterned relationships, the recurrent behaviors, that characterize these realms. Such behaviors are perhaps most easily accessed—and most likely to come together—on the curiously understudied terrain of political intermediaries. There, they can involve relationships between the politically active and their putative rank and file. Or they can involve the overall character of the intermediary institutions that link a mass public with its formal government. Note, however, that a focus on intermediaries, at least here, is not an assertion about the autonomous influence of political parties, interest groups, or the mass media—to take only the most obvious examples. Rather, such a focus achieves its main value through the linkage of these institutions to theoretically fruitful processes and phenomena.

All these chapters thus seek to live in the hallowed land of "middle-level theory." This is the elusive territory that lies between the simple accumulation of observations, resulting in nothing so much as a kind of high-grade journalism, and the pursuit of deliberate abstraction, which results in a political science in which the guts of politics as we normally understand it—public policies, partisan coalitions, and strategic conflicts—essentially disappear. Such a focus assumes that we can in fact go on to isolate major and recurrent influences shaping American politics. And it implies that that is *all* we can do: we cannot specify their precise weights, much less their precise implications, in specific contexts yet to come.

Beyond that, all these chapters are self-consciously interpretive, because a professional political science ought to be able to speak to an intelligent public without abandoning the tenets of its profession. This approach requires hunting consciously for the diagnostic detail, just as it requires squeezing such details for their larger structural implications. And it requires wrapping the result in the "big picture." This was once a central secondary purpose of having a political science. It ought to be recaptured.

All these chapters, as a result, attempt to constrain possible explanations for major political developments, without pretending that they could have been predicted—and without believing that much more than this kind of intellectual constraint is ordinarily possible. The search for some general theory of political action is eternally tempting. The temptation to collapse into mere accumulation of factoids is its opposite number. Either would destroy the prospect of an empirically grounded political science that can contribute to an understanding of political life as it unfolds.

Finally, all these chapters share the otherwise superficially untheoretical trait of having been written outside the United States: they are "the Oxford essays" in my own analytic progression. That fact seems worth mentioning because it has two more directly substantive implications. First, the demands of political interpretation "done from outside" are critically different. And second, any such efforts are always at least implicitly comparative. Let me say a further word about each.

Inside the United States, a scholarly framework has practical application if it helps explain the daily flux of politics: who or what is up or down in politics today. Outside the United States, by contrast, a scholarly framework has practical application if it provides an essential *continuity* to the latest developments. Moreover, some things just look different from a distance. From within, enduring contours are always less striking in the midst of real and daily change. From without, change is less evident, while the contours endure. There is inevitably a further incentive toward comparative treatment when this approach is applied abroad—this is not "home politics" when done in Britain, after all—but the fact of doing such work from outside still has an influence quite apart from this incentive.

Sometimes, this implicit comparativist drive is, in truth, little more than an effort at "translation," an effort that nonetheless imposes some further analytic demands. Other times, it goes on to imply a different focus, one carried into American politics from a different locale. And sometimes the comparativist drive goes all the way to the explicit search for similar—and dissimilar—dynamics, in a process more conventionally recognized as "comparative politics." Which is to say that we can hope to make sense of political behavior by searching for recurrent patterns, even though we know that these patterns will produce different ultimate outcomes depending on what else is on the policy agenda and what other structural influences are simultaneously in play.

Such a search can proceed in one of two grand ways, and these contribute the two major divisions in this collection. First, the search can jump to the immediate confrontation of a middle-level framework, even middle-level generalizations, with specific events of the day. If there are two great methodological questions in the social sciences—What is this a case of? and Compared to what?—then this is a case of asking the first question. It is also a way of proceeding in which the working political scientist borrows most directly from existing generalizations about the process of politics. Alternatively, the search for recurrent patterns can move to explicit comparison, using the second question to help generate findings that cast some original perception in a different light. In this effort, one can use a longer historical sweep both to look for generalizations and to confront them with events over time, comparing present and past within the same nation. Or this approach can turn to a comparison with other nations, using national differences both to generate political patterns and to confront their alleged generality or idiosyncrasy.

In the first case—direct confrontation with some middle-level framework—the point here is that there is a new pattern to American politics. It dominates much of the surface flux of contemporary politicking, and it contributes the title to this volume. This pattern is distinctively modern in the sense that it continues to characterize our day. But it is getting on to half a century of political life, so it is surely modern without being new.

Chapter 1 sets out the continuing contours of this pattern, that is, its policy substance and its social structure. Chapters 2, 3, and 4 then apply this pattern—this theoretical framework—to the creation of the second Bush presidency, to the vicissitudes of trying to create "New Democrats" (as well as "Republican Revolutionaries"), and to major policy conflicts in the first Bush and early Clinton administrations. Chapter 5, the oldest of these essays, summarizes the lay of the intellectual and practical landscape at the point when the need for some new understanding of American politics was becoming widely recognized.

The pattern looks different when it is framed in terms of the second main way of proceeding, framed by comparison to its own historical context or to the evolving politics of different developed nations. In historical perspective, the new framework of American politics in our time—the political order to go with a modern political era—appears more as a reshuffling of major elements and aspects of a long-established American politics than as something discontinuous. Or, perhaps better stated, it appears as an evolution within a set of larger contours—contours that constrain its novelty while giving that novelty form. Chapter 6 does this with elite politics and the profoundly sociological concept of a "circulation of elites." Chapter 7 does it with institutional structures and the politics of self-conscious reform.

The pattern looks different yet again if it is framed in terms of the contemporary or recent experience of other nations. Seen in this more deliberately comparative perspective, the current shape of American politics becomes more a story of common stimuli to political action, encountering distinctive means by which to respond and producing notably different outcomes as a result—recognizable, but with the dials adjusted in consequential fashion. Chapter 8 begins this comparison using postwar Britain as the template. Chapter 9 moves out to the full complement of G-7 nations. Chapter 10 then brings the two approaches—the historical and the comparative—back together, closing with the classic implicit comparison in the argument over "American exceptionalism": whether its key putative ideological and structural elements did exist or do exist, and where they are likely to go.

Happily, the effort to provide such a picture in both ways is just a further goad to middle-level theorizing and thus to staking the results in territory where professional social scientists and applied political observers intermittently meet. If this gives the subject further life for students and intermittent relevance for practitioners, so much the better. If it also helps to constrain potential explanations for the outcomes of American politics by giving some order to the factors that *shape* those outcomes, I will be satisfied.

Part I

In Our Time

CHAPTER ONE

Economic Development, Issue Evolution, and Divided Government, 1955–2000

In their own time, the surface upheavals of American politics during the immediate postwar years might reasonably have suggested a major political shift, the coming of a new political era with different issue contents and different supporting arrangements. Yet with hindsight, the immediate postwar period, for all its undeniable fluctuations, still appears politically of a piece with the ongoing New Deal era. Elite partisan combatants of the day variously hoped or feared that 1956 would mark an effective end to this era. The election of 1956 would instead confirm its continuation, albeit in a form modified from its substantive and structural heyday. Participants could not know that the central substantive concerns of that era had a full postwar generation to run, nor that its central structural supports had a full postwar generation in which to be key shaping influences. Nevertheless, it would be a full generation after the end of the Second World War before evident and dramatic issue shifts would come together with glacial but irresistible social changes, explosively, to demand a different political dynamic.

Similarly, when that explosion finally arrived in the late 1960s, few participants could be confident that it represented lasting change. Both the fearful and the hopeful were naturally inclined to focus on surface manifestations of disruption that almost could not, in principle, form the underpinnings of an extended era. Few observers at the time failed to notice the extensive anomalies of the 1968 election—anomalies, that is, when viewed within the confines of the New Deal order. None missed the fact that these led to Richard Nixon's narrow victory as president, while the Democratic Party retained solid control of both houses of Congress. Yet none could know that the latter was to become the diagnostic partisan outcome for a new political era. And none could know that the surface anomalies of 1968

were best seen not as idiosyncratic events in their own right but as crystallizing vehicles for the emergent issues and long-term forces that would termi-
nate the late New Deal.

The Era of the Late New Deal

None of this seemed inevitable when the postwar era began. Indeed, a
reasonable reading of immediate postwar politics would have suggested that
some new era was already in the process of being born. In the first fully
postwar election, that of 1946, the chaos of economic and social reconver-
sion produced the first Republican Congress since 1928. Harry S. Truman
then spiked hopes (or fears) that the New Deal era had been just a Roosevelt
interregnum when Truman held the presidency in his own right in 1948
and regained control of Congress. But the Republicans were back in 1952, in
control of both the presidency and Congress this time, making that a potential turning point in their hopes for a new political order. By 1956, however,
what Dwight D. Eisenhower, his voters, and Americans in general could
deduce from all this superficial upheaval was only that they were living in a
modified extension of the existing political world, in what can rightfully be
called the "late New Deal era."

Afterward, the world of the 1950s would be widely understood as an
extension of the political world of Franklin D. Roosevelt and the New Deal.
And in fact, the main issues and influences underpinning the late New Deal
era—the substantive and structural foundations for it—were widely recognized both now and then, though without the hindsight of history, it was
difficult to connect them up to suggest the political dynamic that more or
less inevitably occurred within them.

The late New Deal era was characterized by one dominant and one
major secondary cluster of political issues, and these gave a structure to
policy conflict throughout its remaining years. The great and dominating
substantive concern of both ends of this era was social welfare, as befitted an
agenda called into being by economic catastrophe (Schlesinger 1959; Leu-
chenterberg 1963; Hamby 1973; Sundquist 1968). The great and dominating secondary concern of this period was foreign affairs, again befitting an
era forced within a painfully few years to confront the catastrophe of total
war (Burns 1973; Blum 1976; Gaddis 1972; Brown 1968).

The late New Deal era was similarly characterized by three continuing structural influences—social coalitions, organized interests, and party machinery—that likewise gave shape to its policy conflicts into the 1960s. A blue-collar coalition, aligned with the national Democratic Party, featured working-class Americans generally, a few key multiclass minorities (especially Jews), and the entire (the "solid") South. A (smaller) white-collar coalition, aligned with the national Republican Party, was essentially reliant on middle-class Americans (Sundquist 1973; Ladd with Hadley 1975; Burner 1968).

Union labor, enjoying its all-time American heyday in terms of membership, finance, and organizational coherence, became an increasingly important adjunct to the Democratic Party. Although corporate management was also enjoying a great postwar expansion, the real counterpart to organized labor among Republican interest groups remained small, not big, business (Zieger 1986; Rae 1989; Shafer 1998b, chap. 3). And by 1956, the Democrats were otherwise an amalgam of urban machines in the North, courthouse rings in the South, and volunteer activist branches scattered throughout the country. The Republicans, by contrast, had already moved to become the kind of organizationally amorphous, activist-based political party that both would become in the second postwar era, relying on ideology and issues to motivate party workers (Ware 1985; Mayer 1964; Mayhew 1986).

That was—or at least it should have been—a familiar picture of the foundations of the late New Deal era. Yet there was also, in consequence, a diagnostic partisan dynamic to this mix of policy conflicts, social coalitions, and organized intermediaries, and it was (and is) less commonly recognized for being the central character of its politics. Seen by way of ongoing policy conflicts, the party on the Left, the Democrats, was widely perceived as being more in tune with public preferences on social welfare. By contrast, the party on the Right, the Republicans, was widely perceived as being more in tune with public preferences on foreign affairs. The crucial fact was that the public ordinarily gave a much higher priority to social welfare.

Seen by way of ongoing social coalitions instead, the dominant fact about partisan politicking from 1932 through 1968 was that the unity and vitality of the Democratic coalition remained the central story of electoral and institutional politics (Campbell et al. 1960, chap. 5; Wildavsky and Polsby 1964; Campbell 1960). The election of 1946 had signaled an adjustment to this dominant fact. Before 1946, Democrats won, full stop. Afterward, Republicans could win if Democratic policy assets were devalued, as they were in 1946, or if Republicans had special assets of their own, as they would in 1952. But this was still an adjustment, not a change.

As happened so often in American history, the basic institutional structure of American government channeled this partisan dynamic in important ways. Because president and Congress were separately elected, there had to be, in effect, *four* institutional parties within the American two-party system: a presidential and a congressional Democratic and Republican Party. But here, the response of the minority Republicans was most revealing. In a presidential contest, all the state Republican Parties that found themselves in either competitive or Democratic states—at the time, the states representing the majority of Americans—needed an economic moderate as their nominee. Which is to say, the presidential Republican Party did accept the social welfare consensus.

In congressional contests, however, the situation—with its incentive structure—was strikingly different (Eidelberg 1968, chaps. 4, 5, 9; Binkley 1937; Jones 1965). Many seats remained reliably Republican, thus obviating the need for social welfare accommodation. Many of the rest were reliably Democratic, such that accommodation (or not) was irrelevant. Lacking much incentive, then, few successful Republican Parties moderated at the congressional level. Moreover, just to make the partisan picture more stark (and Republican problems more severe), it should be noted that an institutional arrangement that helped hobble a minority Republican response to party competition presented no difficulties for the majority Democrats. For them, differing presidential and congressional parties, both dominant, could comfortably go their separate ways under the Democratic label. If they needed to reconcile for policy purposes, they could always do so in government, in Washington.

Those facts make the Eisenhower interlude especially good at showing the political dynamic of the late New Deal in its full complexity. Eisenhower, the Republican presidential candidate in 1952, was the most popular living American. If Roosevelt had beaten the depression, "Ike" had won the war—and Roosevelt was dead. Yet Eisenhower largely accepted the strategic imperatives that FDR had bequeathed him, featuring foreign policy issues but emphasizing that he was a "modern Republican," at home with popular social welfare programs. This was sufficient not just to earn him the presidency but also to draw a Republican congressional majority into office with him. His fellow officeholders, however, those Republican beneficiaries of his presidential coattails, had not begun to make their peace with the New

Deal. Accordingly, the public threw them out at its first opportunity, in the midterm elections of 1954, and even Eisenhower could not drag them back with him when he was reelected (by a landslide) in 1956 (Ambrose 1990; Thomson and Shattuck 1960).

More lastingly, Eisenhower would accomplish one great partisan task and fail at another, and the two together would influence party competition until after 1968. In the first, Eisenhower ended the Korean War while simultaneously cementing his fellow Republicans into the Cold War consensus. This was one policy realm he really cared about, and he would be lastingly successful in it. What he failed to do was bring the Republican congressional party into the social welfare consensus too. Indeed, Eisenhower himself actually moved closer to Republican dissidence on these issues as his administration aged. As a result, the human icon could still be comfortably reelected; there was no counterpart figure on the political landscape. But his party, despite the fact that it increasingly was his party, could not.

The Foundations Crumble

The year 1956 was noteworthy for a much less obvious fact about American society, albeit a fact with substantial implications for American politics. This was the first year in American history that the Census Bureau declared a white-collar majority for the nation as a whole (Freeman 1980; Chafe 1991, 114; *Statistical Abstract,* various years). The political implications of this massive subterranean fact were indirect and complex. Indeed, the next round of elections, the congressional elections of 1958, would bring one of the largest Democratic gains of the postwar years; it would be almost two generations before the Democratic Party gave these back. Yet American society was changing in glacial but irresistible ways that were utterly uncharacteristic of the world of the depression and the Second World War and hence unlikely to underpin a continuing New Deal order.

The great if undifferentiated engine for this change was the postwar economic boom. From the late 1940s through the mid-1960s, the American economy provided explosive growth. Initially appearing all the more remarkable from the viewpoint of the other developed nations, each seriously damaged by the Second World War, economic growth in postwar America remained remarkable in its own right, and it represented a complex of further changes. It was not just total income—and median income and average income—that grew apace in the postwar years. Such wealth was the product of a hugely different economy in which a long-term trend away from agriculture became a huge movement into manufacturing and industry and then eventually into service provision and information technology. A different structure to the economy also meant, by definition, a different occupational structure for American society. And a different occupational structure meant a different class structure as well (Freeman 1960; Feldstein 1980; Easterlin 1998).

The partisan implications of this change, as it moved closer to an impact on politics and public policy, were not straightforward. The great decline in national economic fortunes of the late 1920s and 1930s *had* shifted the social base for American politics from a geographic to a class alignment. By the end of the Second World War, there was one party rooted in the working class facing another party rooted in the middle class, with many cross-currents but with a clear societal majority for the former. Had these sharpened class lines held in anything like their midcentury incarnation, the implication of postwar economic change would have been obvious: as the middle class grew, so should the Republicans. Yet the hidden breakpoint of 1956 was early evidence that this was not to be the case. The middle-class majority had already arrived; Republican prospects continued to lag. Indeed, the share of society that identified with the Democratic rather than the Republican Party continued to grow. And very little of this further partisan drift resulted from any additional working-class increment to the Democrats (Miller and Traugott 1989, as updated in National Election Studies 1998; Manza and Brooks 1999).

What was happening instead was a major change in the class base of both parties, but especially of the Democrats, with powerful implications for subsequent politics. By inexorable extension, the Democrats too were becoming a more middle-class party. One implication of this change was that a growing segment of the party would be less concerned with the old redistributional issues that had underpinned the New Deal Democratic coalition and more concerned with an aggregate of social, cultural, and behavioral issues—less with the "quantity of life" and more with the "quality of life" (Barone 1990, pt. 4; Patterson 1996, chaps. 19–24; Diggins 1989; Blum 1991). Middle-class Democrats, representing the more liberal elements of the American middle class, would never turn their backs on the social welfare gains of the New Deal, and this fact would remain important.

But new priorities almost had to follow from their new and growing partisan presence.

Because the Republicans would remain the minority party throughout the ensuing generation, their story was less consequential to American politics as a whole. Once, they would have acquired the liberal middle class by means of class identification. If they no longer did, this party too was becoming a very different social coalition (and ideological vehicle) just under the surface. If anything, its commitment to economic and welfare conservatism was being strengthened, but so was the potential for a newly fashioned conservatism on those quality-of-life issues. This particular subterranean fact would be masked for another generation, while the liberal Republicans of the Northeast, the industrial Midwest, and the West Coast remained an important minority faction within the minority party. But by 1956, these liberal Republicans were already (had they known it) an endangered species.

Such grand and gross partisan transitions were hardly the end of the roster of political impacts from economic development. The major interest groups of American politics were being reshaped as well, again indirectly but forcefully. One of the great stories of the New Deal era had been the rise of organized labor generally, and then its integration into the Democratic coalition. Economic decline and resurgent class conflict would have been stimuli toward union resurgence on their own. But this time, the government had been actively supportive of labor organization, union recognition, and collective bargaining, and this legislative support was a powerful contributor to the explosive growth of the labor movement in the immediate postwar years. Unlike earlier periods of union growth, however, organized labor this time came quickly to establish a huge overhead agency, the AFL-CIO, and to affiliate it, informally but effectively, with the national Democratic Party (Vale 1971; Wilson 1979; Bok and Dunlop 1970). The result was important for keeping social welfare issues at the center of American politics and for forging the policy link between welfare liberalism and Cold War anticommunism.

There had been a parallel development on the other side of the organizational aisle, for the immediate postwar years were also the heyday of the giant corporations, massive corporate entities characteristic of a booming postwar economy. The form itself had emerged by the 1920s, before the Great Depression choked off its spread. Its growth merely resumed in the immediate postwar years. Yet this was to be the era of corporate gigantism, and that fact too had implications for the New Deal order. Much more than small business, big business was prepared to make its peace both with union labor as an organized interest and with the main policy substance of the New Deal. This remained a practical, not a principled, peace; the great corporations would hardly become another element of the Democratic coalition. Yet they did accept labor-management relations as a normal part of economic life. Moreover, because they tended to be concentrated in states where big labor was also particularly strong, corporate Republicans came to accept basic social welfare programs as a normal element—that is, a normal imperative—of the political landscape (Chandler 1977; Jacoby 1991; Epstein 1969).

The postwar economic boom then undermined both these developments. Which is to say, in undermining both these great organized interests, economic change undermined their policy contribution as well. The membership of organized labor peaked in the early 1950s and declined gradually from then on. It peaked as the sectors of the economy that were most easily unionized—those same great corporate manufacturing sectors—peaked themselves as a share of the economy. Thereafter it declined, as manufacturing gave way to service provision as the growth sector of the economy. Labor remained a crucial element of the Democratic coalition, in triumph through the mid-1960s and in adversity thereafter. But it would never again walk the halls of Congress, much less the corridors of the White House, with the confidence it had in the 1950s and early 1960s (Price 1980; Kochan, Katz, and McKersie 1986).

Once more, there were parallel developments on the other side of the labor-management divide, for corporate gigantism also peaked in the 1950s. Ironically, just when social thinkers were beginning to set out the character of an organizational world built around these giant economic units, they began to recede (Galbraith 1967; compare Feldstein 1980). This too was a response to the growth of the service and knowledge sectors of the economy, as opposed to the industrial and manufacturing sectors. It meant that a number of other social phenomena associated with the rise of what Eisenhower designated "Modern Republicanism"—accepting organized labor, being at ease with social welfare—also began to change. Eventually, this more liberal wing of the Republican Party would be folded into the regular party structure.

These economic changes, in their final indirect contribution to politics, naturally began to affect the structure of the political parties. Among Democrats, the result was huge policy tensions within the dominant Democratic coalition, followed by extensive procedural reform. The key impetus to both was the explosive rise in the share of college-educated Democratic identifiers. At the end of the Second World War, although there was an unavoidable "intellectual wing" to the Democratic coalition, the share of college graduates was minuscule. During the 1950s, courtesy of the economic boom generally but also of the GI Bill as a conscious policy intervention, not only the share of college-educated Americans but also the share of college-educated Democrats grew apace.

There were problems as well as prospects in this growth. The new (middle-class, college-educated) Democrats were not normally members of the main organized constituency groups of the national Democratic Party, namely, organized labor and the growing civil rights organizations (Shafer 1983a; Ladd 1976–1977). They resided in areas where the orthodox party organization, the "regular" Democratic Party, was frequently enfeebled, namely, the burgeoning suburbs. They were also equipped and inclined to participate in politics as independent actors, often motivated by specific causes, rather than as devoted members of basically partisan organizations. Eventually, they would have their way through a stream of participatory procedural reforms, from extending the reach of primary elections into presidential politics to extending a bill of rights for individual members of Congress.

The Republican version of this story was inevitably related, though with the main elements reversed. The Republican Party had long since achieved the organizational character that the Democrats were only just approaching, courtesy of the death of the old Republican machines and the debilitating effect of protracted minority status. More to the practical point, as the New Deal era aged and as the Democratic Party grew but became more internally divided, the Republicans at first appeared to shrink and become more homogeneous. Liberal Republicans, the main dissident faction, had always been heavily dependent on deference from the regular party. When corporate gigantism receded and the party structure became more skeletal and hence more dependent on the Old Guard, this more liberal faction just disappeared into that regular party structure.

As the liberal middle class also became more Democratic, there was a more evidently homogeneous social base left to be reflected in this more skeletal Republican Party structure, a more socially but especially a more economically conservative social base. What prevented this from becoming a long-running extension of the old order was a different and even more indirect fallout from economic growth, capped by a conscious elite reaction to developments inside the Democratic Party. Said differently, as an important slice of highly educated Americans began to secure their policy wishes within the Democratic Party, a less-educated segment of society, reacting against these policies, became increasingly available to the Republicans. And this development brought both counterpart opportunities and counterpart tensions to the other side of the partisan aisle.

This new target population came to be recognized (and even symbolized) most clearly in the evangelical—the pietistic—Protestants, who were strong conservatives on the very cultural and national questions that were central to the rise of middle-class Democrats (Soper 1994; Marsden 1980; Hunter 1983). Economic development contributed to their leadership too, producing new seminaries that paid special attention to the latest technology for reaching their followers. It was these leaders who would forge an informal but strong relationship with the Republican Party. As with the coming of corporate Republicans in an earlier era, however, this potential for numerical gain came at the cost of increased intraparty tensions. From one side, the evangelicals were much more socially conservative than the remainder of the party. From the other, they were much less economically conservative, resting well inside the national consensus on social welfare.

Flash Fires and Crystallizing Issues

The issue substance of American politics was likewise undergoing an evolution during the late New Deal years. But here, the surface manifestations of change were insistent, even intrusive. Each great underlying dimension to public policy—social welfare and foreign affairs—generated a dramatic and extended substantive conflict. Although both these conflicts were inevitably shaped by the changing contours of the society in which they occurred, neither was directly a product of these changes. Rather, both grew logically out of the policy positions and social coalitions of the New Deal era. By the time they played out, however—and both were not just dramatic but also long running—they had helped refashion the entire nature of substantive conflict in American politics.

The greatest and most dramatic of these new issues was civil rights, culminating in a veritable civil rights revolution. In playing his part in constructing the New Deal order, Franklin Roosevelt had consciously avoided this issue. For him, a central task in building a liberal coalition behind the social welfare programs of the New Deal had been attracting and then holding southern Democrats. The problem was that they were both numerically essential and the most conservative elements in this aspiring coalition. What made the American South "solid" in the Democratic coalition, despite this instinctive conservatism, was a multiclass white majority united by racial segregation as public policy. Roosevelt recognized that civil rights as a policy priority would challenge this arrangement, stress his coalition, and thus potentially imperil his economic and welfare gains. He chose social welfare and allowed civil rights to languish (Friedel 1947; Sitkoff 1978).

In partisan terms, not much changed with the passing of Roosevelt: a focus on civil rights still seemed likely to reduce the policy advantage that the national Democratic Party derived from economic and welfare issues, perhaps in a major way. Nevertheless, liberal activists in the postwar years set about redressing this otherwise curious hole in their overall policy program, a move in which they were powerfully reinforced by an increasingly aggressive and mobilized civil rights movement. The Civil Rights Act of 1957 and then the far more consequential Civil Rights Act of 1964 and Voting Rights Act of 1965 were the main substantive products. Huge new constituencies for the Democratic Party were their most immediate structural result, in the form of newly mobilized black voters in the South but also in the North. Huge new stresses in the northern Democratic coalition and major cracks in its southern counterpart also followed (Brooks 1974; Sitkoff 1981; Graham 1989).

The other great, partially autonomous, substantive contribution of the late New Deal era, one that had a curious parallel to that of civil rights, involved what was to become the Vietnam War. There had been an earlier attempt to draw the United States into combat in Southeast Asia, when the French were defeated at Dien Bien Phu and Vietnam was partitioned. But President Eisenhower, with Korea as a powerful recent analogy—that is, mindful of the fact that ending the Korean War remained a major policy asset for the Republican Party—failed to respond. By contrast, John F. Kennedy, an orthodox product of a Democratic coalition that melded pursuit of social welfare with prosecution of the Cold War, and needing personally to neutralize foreign policy issues by appearing no less firm than his Republican opponents, took the opposite tack (Herring 1979; Berman 1982, chap. 2).

Lyndon Johnson then brought both aspects of the Democratic policy inheritance from the New Deal to their postwar zenith. He launched the Great Society, including Medicare, Head Start, and the War on Poverty. And he escalated the war in Vietnam by means of a manpower draft that ultimately reached into the collegiate middle class. The partisan consequences, by way of stresses inside the Democratic coalition, were cataclysmic. The new college-educated Democrats were not stressed by the Great Society; it was not what principally motivated them, but they were supportive. They were, however, deeply unhappy with the Vietnam War, and the baby-boom generation, in college at the time, would provide them with expressive "shock troops" for their unhappiness (Goldman 1968; Kearns 1976; Easterlin 1980; Miller1994). In the process, dramatic public protests also elevated the issue realm of foreign affairs in the public mind, a realm where Republicans retained the policy advantage.

These two issue areas, separately and together, would draw an array of others onto the substantive agenda of American politics. The violent aftermath of the civil rights revolution, along with the extensiveness of student protest, fueled an associated concern with public order. More tellingly, so did an explosion of crime in general within American society. Murder, robbery, burglary, rape, and assault all jumped alarmingly in the 1960s, most with the greatest decadal increase since statistics were collected. If legal desegregation was the most intensive substantive development of the time, and if student protest was the most symbolically dramatic, increased criminal activity was both more extensive than the former and more tangible than the latter. No party would be able to seize any continuing advantage from being better able to handle crime, but thereafter, the perception of being tolerant of it would always be extremely harmful (Scammon and Wattenberg 1970; Wilson 1975; Gaubatz 1995).

A cluster of other, lesser concerns also claimed their place on the policy agenda, and though most of these had been seen before in earlier historical incarnations, they inevitably reappeared in a manner appropriate to the structural character of contemporary politics. Thus the natural environment came back as a matter for political debate, but in a way that reflected the postwar boom and the new social composition of the political parties. Historically, the more middle-class Republican Party had been the vehicle for conservation and environmental concern, while the Democrats focused on redistribution and concrete benefits. Now, it was the middle-class wing of the Democratic Party—the liberal middle class—that focused on conservation and environmental activism. Feminism moved onto the agenda as well, with the same social and partisan relationships. Historically, feminism had fit most comfortably with the progressivism of the Republican Party. Now, it fit most comfortably in the college-graduate wing of the Democratic Party instead (Lacey 1993; Hays 1990; Chafe 1992; Harrison 1989).

It jumps ahead of the story to note that all these latter concerns—Richard Nixon would summarize them simply as "permissiveness"—fueled a backlash by Protestant evangelicals to what they viewed as inescapable evidence of moral and cultural decline. But what was already much in evidence by the early 1960s was the role of one particular institution of American national government in further propelling and then holding these cultural and social concerns at the center of the American policy agenda. That role was to be large and recurrent. It was also a particularly good example of the way in which partially autonomous (and thoroughly unintended) structural changes could shape the substantive content of a national policy agenda.

This institution was, of course, the U.S. Supreme Court. The Court under Chief Justice Earl Warren had already, in the 1950s, been a critical actor in vastly upping the importance of civil rights as a policy realm. Beginning in the 1960s, the Court then turned to a string of essentially cultural conflicts, once more elevating their public importance as it did so. Moreover, the Warren Court, ending an era in which economic regulation dominated the Court's agenda and beginning an era characterized by civil liberties instead, reliably offered one side, the progressive position, on cultural issues such as busing, school prayer, abortion, capital punishment, criminal justice, homosexual rights, and so on, often in clear contraposition to public preferences (Pacelle 1991; O'Brien 1986).

The key point, however, did not involve the individual substance of any of these issues, great or small. The key point was that civil rights as a new twist on social welfare, along with Vietnam as the latest twist on foreign affairs, was only the flash point, however dramatic, for a much larger evolution in the central substance of American politics. There are many ways to distinguish the substantive core of the new era. But at bottom, the old political world had featured partisan division and issue conflict over the (re)distribution of material goods, around economics and social welfare. The new political world added—and often featured—partisan division and issue conflict over the character of national life, over the behavior operationalizing a national culture, from the family hearth to the international stage.

This first set of concerns was essentially distributional, involving the proper share of divisible goods allocated to various sectors of society. The second set was essentially valuational, involving the proper behavioral norms within which social life should proceed. The older economic-welfare concerns hardly went away, and their continuing presence remained central to the substantive character of the new era. But they were joined by the new cultural-national concerns on secondary, equal, or superior footing, depending on the context of the day. In that sense, the key substantive characteristic of this successor era was the vigorous presence of two great (and crosscutting) dimensions to political conflict.

Given that its substantive and structural foundations were shifting—crumbling over much of the postwar period—the New Deal era managed to last and last. Nevertheless, it could not last forever, and it came apart, with an explosion, in one disruptive year. At the time, it was possible to chalk up the disruptions of 1968 to peculiar—horrible—acts of fortune, such as the assassination of Robert Kennedy, or to dramatic but idiosyncratic personalities, such as the quixotic emergence of George Wallace. For some years afterward, it was still possible to chalk up the presidency of Richard Nixon to the specific events of 1968, events disastrous enough to bring a defeated former vice president to power with only a plurality vote, and an exceedingly narrow one at that (White 1969; Chester, Hodgson, and Page 1969). In such a context, it was still reasonable to believe that the American political sequence might feature a Nixon interregnum, as it had earlier featured an Eisenhower interregnum, followed by restoration of unified Democratic control of national government.

Yet with hindsight, what those disastrous events did was to crystallize a set of long-running developments that had been undermining the late New Deal era since at least the mid-1950s. The crystallizing events would, of course, go away. Their underlying developments would not. Said differently, the constituent elements of a new political era, in both its substance and its structure, were all incipiently present by the time of the 1968 election. It may have *seemed* that some simple strategic correction could neutralize that fact, but when political orders shift, this is a common (temporary) misperception. In the nature of politics, the passage of time is required for a new political dynamic, appropriate to these substantive and structural contours, to be consolidated. And this dynamic necessarily acquires its operational impact through the details of politicking on particular events. But all that would not just occur. It was effectively prefigured by 1968.

The Era of Divided Government

When it first arrived, the substantive breakup of the old era was easiest to recognize in foreign affairs, where the Cold War consensus disintegrated. Now, nationalists who continued to support the containment of communism faced off against accommodationists who felt that containment was an increasingly sterile doctrine and that it was time to move on to acceptance and engagement. Although the Vietnam War gave this division its initial edge, a panoply of security issues, from arms control through defense budgets, would be available to keep the division alive (Holsti and Rosenau 1984; Ladd and Hadley 1973). And foreign affairs was now to be joined with a much broader array of essentially cultural concerns, helping to bring them to the fore while simultaneously reducing its own role within this evolving cluster.

Vietnam protest was still a useful route into the remainder of this valuational dimension, within which foreign affairs was only one large but supporting element. Antiwar protest as behavior had been borrowed, most centrally, from civil rights protest. And antiwar protest was to lead to a general round of reform agitation in politics. But from the start, protest was linked in the public mind to other, essentially cultural divisions—over the burgeoning crime wave, for example, where the question was whether crime was a socioeconomic product to be understood (the progressive position) or a moral breakdown to be countervailed (the traditional view) (Lipset and Rokkan 1967; Inglehart 1977).

In one sense, the structure of politics at the social base for any era characterized by ongoing dual concerns—the social coalitions to go with substantive divisions over both social welfare and, now, cultural values—had long been incipiently familiar. At least it had long been understood that economic liberals, those most concerned with the welfare essence of the New Deal program, were often social conservatives, emphasizing family, neighborhood, community, and country, just as it had long been known that economic conservatives, especially the highly educated and occupationally prestigious among them, were often cultural liberals, emphasizing the autonomous management of social life—their own and others' (Adorno

1950; Lipset 1960, chap. 4). What changed, then, was only the arrival—some would say the reappearance—of a second great dimension, the cultural dimension, to a position of equal prominence in national politics.

This seemed surprising only because the presence of these relationships, especially the presence of a traditionalist cultural majority within them, had previously been accepted intuitively by party operatives and candidates for public office, had indeed been understood to be so overwhelming as to make this dimension the "third rail" of American politics. Events of the late 1960s made this no longer so self-evident. At a minimum, a huge postwar generation had grown up without the need to consider economic security. For them, there was mainly the long postwar boom, and then the social insurance programs of the New Deal whenever it hesitated. In that light, cultural traditionalism and orthodox social controls could seem to be not the glue holding society together but the residue of a time lag in social thinking.

Changes in the structure of political parties then institutionalized these divisions. In fact, both American political parties now shared the dominant structural characteristics of the immediate postwar Republicans. That is, both were now effectively networks of issue-oriented political activists, not individuals for whom partisan solidarity displaced ideology (Ware 1985; Wilson 1973, chaps. 1–6). The New Deal program had sustained the organized Democratic Party for another generation after the inception of that program, actually funneling some fresh resources through party channels. Yet the institutionalization of these benefits had been principally through formal governmental machinery even then. Beyond that, continuing civil service reform was joined by the gradual unionization of government—the greatest success of a union movement in decline—taking far more resources out of the hands of either party than the government had given back. The gradual passing of a New Deal generation of partisans, with no subsequent generation able to achieve the same programmatic fervor, was topped off by institutional reform of presidential selection, the last holdout against reform generally. And the old structure of the political parties was gone.

In its place were individual activists whose support was now essential to mounting campaigns and gaining public office: they *were* the party in the operational sense. More to the practical point for a new political order, they were also the key to institutionalizing a partisan connection between the economic-welfare and cultural-national dimensions. They had not abandoned the old social welfare basis of the party system, and they had not moderated it. They had merely expanded the foreign affairs dimension to cultural issues more generally, in a way that they found to be ideologically consistent. Republican activists were thus traditionalist in social matters and nationalist in foreign affairs; Democratic activists were progressive in social matters and accommodationist in foreign affairs (Davies 1996; Matusow 1984).

Had these increasingly consequential activists not been naturally inclined toward this particular combination of positions, they might have been driven to it anyway by the nature of the new (ideological and issue-oriented) organized interests that joined one or the other party coalition. For the Democrats, these included environmentalists, peace groups, feminists, and homosexuals. For the Republicans, they included antiabortionists, gun owners, tax reformers, and religious fundamentalists. But in truth, there was no need for "pressure" from these groups to secure the two opposing partisan programs. Party activists were now the natural product of membership in precisely these organizations (Schlozman and Tierney 1985; Walker 1991).

Once again, there was a characteristic political dynamic to go with this mix of issue conflicts, social cleavages, and altered intermediaries, a dynamic to characterize partisan competition in the era of divided government. There was not just a heightened interparty conflict inherent in this tension, between what had become consistent liberals and consistent conservatives among those who did the work of the political parties. Now, there was an intraparty conflict, an elite-mass conflict as well, between these activists and their own rank and file. Among Republicans, this latter conflict was at its most intense between economically conservative but culturally liberal identifiers and their leaders. Among Democrats, it was most intense between economically liberal but culturally conservative identifiers and their leaders (Shafer and Claggett 1995; Ladd and Hadley 1973).

Yet the institutions of American government again provided a simple resolution for these tensions, and it was this resolution that would provide the context for public policy making in our time. At bottom, there were now two opposing majorities simultaneously present in the general public— more liberal than the active Republican Party on economic and welfare issues, more conservative than the active Democratic Party on cultural and national concerns. The obvious solution was to colonize one elective branch of national government with one majority and one elective branch with the other. Split partisan control was what this solution contributed practically.

"Divided government" was what it came to be called, and the era of divided government had been born.

Afterword

There was only one serious effort to configure this era differently, to make it work differently rather than just to triumph within it, and that effort came right at the start. Having arrived at the White House courtesy of the social upheavals of the 1960s, Richard Nixon attempted, in effect, to make the new political order a Republican counterpart to the old, with Republican majorities in the general public and Republican control of all the main institutions of national government, presumably to be punctuated by the occasional Democratic interlude. In order to do this, he needed not just to capitalize on foreign affairs and cultural values, areas where the Republican Party already possessed major latent assets. He needed also to neutralize party disadvantages on economics and social welfare, which meant accepting Keynesian fiscal interventions and making some final peace with the welfare state (Mason 1998; Moynihan 1969).

Once more, however, though this made great sense for the presidential Republican Party, it had few obvious attractions for sitting congressional Republicans, who were already successful without any such adjustment. Worse still, it had little attraction to the active Republican Party in states and localities, whose volunteers were increasingly active in politics precisely because they were conservative on both major dimensions; that was the point of their participation. As a result, Nixon failed to transform the era of divided government into a period of unified Republican dominance, an opposite partisan successor to the New Deal era. His efforts, always powerfully constrained by his own party, crashed completely with the Watergate crisis. His successors, Ronald Reagan and George Bush Sr., albeit hugely successful in other respects, never really tried.

In the particular sequence in which this era initially arrived—led off by Vietnam, race, public order, and countercultural protest—the logical opening resolution was a Republican presidency stapled onto a Democratic Congress. Yet other issue sequences were easily capable of other results in a political dynamic with these enduring characteristics. All that reliably followed was that unified partisan control of national government had become the deviant outcome, in effect requiring strategic disasters or public miscalculations.

One of these happened immediately after Nixon, when circumstances allowed Jimmy Carter to re-create unified partisan control (Glad 1980; Jones 1988). Another returned sixteen years later, with the initial election of Bill Clinton. The political contours that had generated the notion of an *era* of divided government, however, hardly went away in either case. The Carter exception could not stretch into a second term. The Clinton exception could not stretch into even a second Congress of his first term. The substantive and structural preconditions for split partisan control thus appeared to continue, inescapably, relentlessly. Actual divided government continued as well, in all but the six years of Carter and Clinton exceptions.

Accordingly, there was an established political dynamic, developing gradually and indirectly during the late New Deal, crystallizing explosively in 1968, and running relentlessly through politics thereafter. This dynamic was in turn the product of an ongoing interaction between continuing substantive conflicts and continuing structural influences. These continuing contours favored split partisan control of American national government, though they did not insist on a particular mix. They tolerated the occasional drift into unified partisan control, though not for very long. Yet these partisan mixes were merely one outcome, really just the surface "marker" for the structure of the American politics underneath them.

More consequentially, these substantive clusters and structural influences were the contours within which both electoral and legislative politics played out during an extended period—from 1968 and counting—in American political history. Which is to say, it was their composition, not the partisan pattern they produced, that truly mattered. Active Democrats remained very liberal on both major substantive dimensions of American politics, and active Republicans remained very conservative on both. The general public remained left of those active Republicans on economics and social welfare and right of those active Democrats on cultural values and foreign affairs. And the institutions of American government accommodated these divisions easily, through the device of split partisan control.

The era of divided government was no doubt being undermined by changing social structures and emerging substantive concerns while all this occurred. The late New Deal era, after all, was being seriously undermined even while Lyndon Johnson brought it to one more diagnostic peak. Yet the era of divided government was also safely enough ensconced to extend into the new millennium as the framework for American politics and policy making.

CHAPTER TWO

The Search for a New Center

The presidential administration of William Jefferson Clinton ushered in a recognizably new phase of an ongoing political order. The underlying order had begun with a bang in 1968. The new phase began less dramatically in 1992 with the election of Clinton, when the contours characterizing American politics for the previous quarter century came under renewed stress. Nevertheless, it was destined to run on to include the election of George W. Bush, son of Clinton's defeated 1992 opponent, in 2000. As a result, this new phase crucially subsumed not just another presidential election, Clinton's reelection in 1996, but also the major legislative events of the intervening eight years. And it will surely provide at least the opening context for the main legislative events of the Bush administration, however long that may be.

The distinguishing feature of this new political phase was not an attempt to break new ground by capturing some great emergent issue for one or the other political party. That sort of change was last seen in its pure form in the 1930s and in dilute form in the 1960s. Rather, this new and distinguishing feature was more a strategic attempt to break old ground. Which is to say, the distinguishing feature of this new political phase was a strategic effort by the successful presidential candidates of both parties to find a way to distance themselves from their respective liabilities. Their main motivating goal was thus not innovation but reconstitution: to redress the main drawbacks inherited with their party attachments and thereby allow their existing advantages to register more fully.

It is most common—and certainly simplest—to talk about such an effort in terms of parties or party systems. In these terms, this was an effort, structurally, to rebalance partisan identifications in the general public, as well as an effort, substantively, to move the active party back toward a winning position. Seen the first way, Democrats concentrated on shoring up public attachments forged originally in the 1930s, while Republicans concentrated on harvesting a Republican drift recognized initially in the 1960s. Seen the second way, both parties sought to return to the ideological and policy center, in effect, modernizing their appeals by adapting them to a changed social world. Seen either way—and this is the important point—both notions of how a conscious new political phase arrives are actually more misleading than helpful in understanding the current moment.

Instead, it is necessary to think about the *social coalitions* that underpin policy conflict at any given point in time. And it is necessary to think about the *issue context* that goes with those social coalitions. A focus on *party systems* may still be the most efficient way to gather these two key elements into a coherent whole: parties remain the leading intermediaries to American politics, however strong or weak, reflective or distorting they may be. Yet a move to structural influence and policy substance, and within them to social coalitions and issue contexts most especially, is what is necessary to understand the current moment.

The Old Order

This bedrock distinction—among social coalitions, issue contexts, and party systems—is central to understanding the current moment precisely because the last of these elements, the party system, continues from a much older time, shorn increasingly of both the social coalitions and the issue contexts that arrived with it. That time was the 1930s. Its issue context was forged by the Great Depression and secondarily by the World War that followed. Its social divisions were built around social class, though they retained important ethnic, racial, and especially regional twists. Its party system featured new majority and minority parties, a new sun and moon to anchor the tides and seasons of American politics, recasting the roles of the Democratic and Republican Parties, respectively.

The Great Depression initially roiled the partisan waters of American politics without calling forth strategic adaptations capable of institutionalizing a new order. A solid and substantial Republican triumph in the presidential election of 1928 was followed by the stock market crash of 1929 and then by equally solid and substantial Democratic gains in the midterm election of 1930. The latter were still mainly a protest against existing conditions, however, rather than an incipient definition of the alternative. Indeed, the presidential election of 1932, won crushingly by the Democrats, contained as many promises of "out-Republicaning the Republicans"—slashing spending, cutting taxes—as major new policy directions.

But from 1933 onward, with the inauguration of the new Roosevelt administration, the programs that would constitute the New Deal—unemployment insurance, old-age pensions, farm price supports, rural electrification, public works, and on and on—came to acquire a basic social welfare character and brought the welfare state to the American people. Inevitably, the social coalitions that formed around them acquired a distinctive character as well. These too were initially amorphous, as the vast majority of Americans reacted against unhappy economic and social developments. But as an aggressive welfare state became the clear policy response to these developments, a clear if moderate class division, pitting blue-collar against white-collar Americans, came to be the obvious coalitional result (Schlesinger 1957; Leuchtenberg 1963).

The key programmatic divide retained some anomalies, the largest of which was civil rights. In this, an interventionist governmental program on behalf of the less advantaged only indirectly challenged the place of the Republican Party as the champion of black Americans and the place of the Democratic Party as their oppressor. The key coalitional divide retained major anomalies as well, the largest being related to this programmatic twist. Class politics did not realign the "solid South," because a new social welfare emphasis reinforced the Democratic loyalties of less-advantaged white southerners, while a multiclass one-party system—reinforcing the civil rights anomaly—reinforced the attachments of the more advantaged, so long as the Democrats were so clearly ascendant nationwide.

The political parties that pulled all this together and linked it to the institutions of national government were pale counterparts to the historic parties that had once given much stronger definition to a party system (Silbey 1991, chaps. 1, 13; Sundquist 1973, chaps. 10–12; Ladd with Hadley 1975, pt. 1). Both drew their strength principally from psychological attachments by individual voters rather than from organized party machinery. Nevertheless, they did have consequential characteristics of their own. Although these were not the great statewide patronage machines of the late nineteenth century, they did reserve substantial authority to party officeholders, and this reserve allowed party elites to calculate partisan strategy within the overall context in which they found themselves—adding some partially autonomous, further contributions of their own.

For the Democrats, this implied a focus, front and center, on social welfare. It was, after all, the New Deal program that had brought them to majority status. The evident majority of Americans supported the main planks in that program, and party leaders did not miss this foundational strategic fact. An electoral contest focused on social welfare would return the maximal share of Democrats to office. They could then turn to protecting and extending that economic-welfare program. At the very least, whether legislatively successful or not, they could use the institutions of government to keep policy debate focused on welfare policy.

In the aftermath of the Second World War and in the face of an exploding Cold War, it seemed equally obvious—it would seem much less obvious thirty years later—that a new international engagement, centered around the containment of communism, would be a major secondary focus. This concept was arguably new to American politics as a whole. A nation that had maintained only a derisory standing army, along with a palpable dislike of "entangling alliances," was now being transformed. And the process of transforming it, presumably into a more normal "great power," took a great deal of time, energy, and conflict in the immediate postwar years (Kennedy 1999; Gaddis 1972). Moreover, this was not just a struggle internal to the dominant Democratic Party.

Republicans had their own version, and internal Republican conflicts over a response to the Cold War were critical to cementing what would ultimately become a bipartisan consensus on foreign policy, one destined to last into the 1960s. For a while, the Republican outcome itself was unclear. But the party retained substantial public credibility in foreign affairs, and after Dwight Eisenhower used his Republican presidency to solve the problem of its Cold War positioning, that asset would remain available to party leaders in their quest for electoral majorities nationwide. A public priority for foreign affairs could propel a Republican candidate with obvious foreign policy credentials into office, and he could attempt to use that office to reinforce public attention to foreign affairs.

Yet the main public priority remained stubbornly elsewhere, on social welfare, so the main need for Republican Party officials, at least in national contests, was for candidates who could accommodate that dominant issue context. In their successful local contests, Republican Party leaders felt much less need for welfare moderates and in fact were actively *not* enamored of them. Yet they needed them nationally in order to be competitive. The party structure retained authority sufficient to address this strategic need. And for more than a generation, the national party found the candidates capable of addressing it: Wendell Willkie in 1940, Thomas Dewey in 1944, Dewey again in 1948, Dwight Eisenhower in 1952, Eisenhower again in 1956, and Richard Nixon in 1960.

Lest these party leaders award themselves too much leeway in deviating from the dominant preference inside their party coalitions, there were also major interest groups affiliated with each of the two major parties, themselves anchored centrally in the dominant issues of their time (Zieger 1986; Rae 1989; Shafer 1996, chap. 3). For the Democrats, this meant organized labor. The New Deal had revolutionized labor-management relations, and the immediate postwar years were the zenith of organized labor's membership (and political clout) in all of American history. The labor leadership was focused centrally on social welfare policy: on labor-management relations most centrally, but on extension of the welfare state in general. It had no problem with the Cold War consensus, styling itself as the main voice of "free labor" in the world at large.

For the Republicans, this dominant and reinforcing organized interest was actually small business rather than big business. The times may have been a diagnostic era of corporate growth, perhaps the dominant period of employment in the biggest corporations in all of American history. That meant serious corporate constituencies in some local areas. It meant serious financial support for national campaigns. It meant occasional "blue-ribbon" candidates from the corporate sector. And it meant, most importantly, constituencies, supporters, and candidates who could make their peace with the welfare state. But the bulk of the work of the party was still done in most areas, and especially in more successful areas, by small-business leaders. They accepted the bipartisan Cold War consensus, just as they made sure that the party did not stray too far toward moderation on issues of social welfare.

A New Order

That composite strategic environment—an issue context, two social coalitions, and a party system—came apart in the 1960s. Yet the ostensible connecting element to this environment, the party system itself, initially continued. And in that disjunction lay the critical aspect of the new strategic world. There was no obvious single counterpart to the Great Depression in this successor break. The class basis of opposing social coalitions remained roughly the same. Partisan loyalties in the mass public moved only gradually. Yet the resulting composite was so substantially different after 1968 as to be appropriately dubbed a new political order.

If there was no single counterpart to the Great Depression—and hence no obvious counterpart to the New Deal that followed—there certainly was a large cluster of new issues for American politics of the 1960s and a new set of policy conflicts for the years afterward. Some of these reduced the force of existing social welfare issues. The emergent issue of civil rights, for example, which in some theoretical sense constitutes a subdomain of civil liberties, was perceived by most Americans, white and black, as a subdomain of social welfare—as a request for benefits much more narrowly targeted than those associated with the social insurance programs of the old order.

More of these new issues, however, fell in the realm of what came to be called "social issues" in their time but might more appropriately be designated "cultural issues" in ours (Scammon and Wattenberg 1970; Hunter 1991). Racial rioting, the unhappy face of the civil rights revolution, was part of this cluster. So was widespread campus unrest, the fallout from opposition to the increasingly unpopular Vietnam War. But so, and much more lastingly, was criminal justice—crime and punishment—a core element in a newly emergent issue context. In their immediate time, these issues could all be grouped as concerns about the social order, about the reconstruction (or fraying) of a basic social fabric, pitting an emphasis on personal liberty against an emphasis on social control. Hence the nomenclature of that time: "social issues."

But in a longer perspective, and certainly when viewed as part of an issue context that was destined to last, they were probably better seen as an important subdomain of "cultural issues" more generally. Here, the distinction between personal liberty and social control became a larger difference between the protection and extension of individual expression versus the fostering and enforcement of collective norms of behavior. Cultural "progressives"—the liberals—took the former position, emphasizing rights and liberties. Cultural "traditionalists"—the conservatives—took the latter, emphasizing norms and responsibilities instead. In the 1960s and 1970s, society provided incentives for the former and incitements to the latter in disproportionate terms, and this imbalance was critical to the partisan impact of these concerns. By the 1990s, a change in this balance would have much to do with their changing impact and hence with the changing phases of a new political order.

The most pointed and dramatic of these incentives or incitements was the rise of a self-conscious (and vociferous) counterculture, deliberately attacking traditional norms in the name of the reconstitution of society. Nevertheless, there was a major institutional contribution as well, for this was the time when the Supreme Court confirmed the shift in its own substantive focus away from the economic and welfare concerns of the New Deal era and toward the rights and liberties concerns of what would be recognized as the era of divided government. Which is to say that the Court was also extremely important in propelling these same issues (and their same divisions) to the center of partisan politics through a controversial series of decisions on school prayer, abortion rights, and, once again, criminal justice (Gitlin 1993; Pacelle 1991).

Ironically, the basic social coalitions associated with opposite views on these newly salient issues did not, in principle, have to change at all. The existing division between a white-collar and a blue-collar coalition could, in some abstract sense, have slotted comfortably into a fresh division between cultural progressives and cultural traditionalists. It had long been recognized that the economically wealthier, socially advantaged, and, especially, better educated tended to be more liberal on these cultural issues, just as the poorer, disadvantaged, and undereducated were more conservative— this was the basis of those immediate postwar studies that fretted over "working-class authoritarianism" (Adorno 1950; Lipset 1960, chap. 4).

What kept this otherwise "natural" affinity from becoming merely a new phase in the New Deal era, an extension of the social coalitions of that era to an expanded issue context, were developments within its party system. In some sense, the disproportionate party of Catholics, the Democrats, should naturally have been antiabortion. The disproportionate party of social traditionalists, the Democrats, should naturally have been pro-family. And the disproportionate party of victims, the Democrats, should naturally have been anticrime. Yet changes within the party system, as reinforced by changes in the social and economic composition of society, produced the reverse.

These were not principally changes at the mass base of the party system, in the party identifications of rank-and-file Democrats and Republicans. There was, in truth, a sharp uptick in the share of the public abjuring identification with either party and calling itself independent. But even this was in many ways an artifact of, a response to, changes in a different element of the party system. This element was the strategic behavior of party elites, and the changes were rooted in *their* policy preferences—the rank and file be damned. Those preferences resulted in an exaggerated tension between party activists and their own mass identifiers, a tension that became the central aspect of the era of divided government when seen through its social coalitions.

What motivated those who did the active work of both political parties were principally cultural rather than economic issues (Barone 1990, pt. 4; Chafe 1991, chaps. 12–15). Active Democrats became antiwar and thereafter reliably accommodationist in foreign affairs. They became pro-abortion, as one lead element of being culturally progressive. They hardly became pro-crime, but they were much more concerned than were active Republicans with procedural guarantees for the accused and with constraints on the police. They came to champion dissident minorities on gender issues—first feminists, then homosexuals. Overall, they supported individual liberties over social controls, especially when the latter were backed up by institutional coercion.

Active Republicans, of course, became the reverse. Moreover, all this mattered because of a second major change in the American party system. The parties themselves, as organizational machinery, had been in long-term historic decline, beginning in the late nineteenth century. The coming of the New Deal had reinvigorated individual attachments, both for and against, and this reinvigoration masked the ongoing organizational decay. Yet New Deal programs ultimately accelerated that decay by making parties less relevant as channels to (and distributors of) the largesse of government. What those parties retained through the New Deal era, however skeletal their structure, was a great strategic reserve for party officeholders.

These party officeholders had been recruited by social welfare issues and had been extended in office by the quasi-private character of parties as organizations, so that external challenges were not easy to mount, and temporally extended work on behalf of the party was the key to gradual progression in party office. This arrangement was critical to extending the issue focus of the New Deal era, and it was finally swept away in the 1960s and 1970s (Shafer 1983a; Ware 1985; Mayhew 1986). An increasingly educated citizenry desired to participate in politics—inescapably, still through political parties—in an individual manner in response to issues of the day.

Reforms of party structure in the 1960s and 1970s, again for both parties, provided them the means to do so. The result was political parties that were now networks of issue activists, not machinery dedicated to their own survival.

Not surprisingly, these activists were generated essentially by the new *cultural* interest groups now populating the political landscape. Peace advocates sought out the Democratic Party; military traditionalists sought out the Republican. Abortion activists sought out the Democratic Party; pro-life advocates sought the Republican. Organized feminists became increasingly consequential and sought a home within the Democratic Party structure; gender traditionalists looked instead to the Republican counterpart. Organized homosexuals looked to the Democrats; supporters of traditional "family values" turned to the Republicans. Gun owners, feeling increasingly under attack, sought a home within the Republican structure; controllers of gun violence looked to the Democrats. The religiously observant, feeling the same threat, looked likewise to the Republicans; organized secularists focused on the Democrats. And on and on.

New Strategic Implications

This new division at the elite level was critically facilitated by aspects of the party system, especially by a reformed party structure. But it was ultimately underpinned by grand and gross social changes, especially in the class composition of American society, and these had inescapable implications for the social coalitions in American politics. Or rather, these changes were grand enough to demand some change in their associated political order. Conversely, they were gross—undifferentiated—enough that they did not have specific and pointed implications for the partisan character of that order. Rather, their interaction with a changing party system would determine this crucial applied impact.

As the postwar economic boom rolled across these years, American society became wealthier, better educated, and more white collar and middle class. Other things remaining equal, this should have meant rising Republican identification within the New Deal party system from the 1950s onward. Yet as the New Deal era extended into the postwar years, it was actually the Democratic Party that continued to be numerically dominant. Across the 1950s and into the 1960s, it was another element of demographic change—the replacement of pre–New Deal generations with those achieving their political consciousness in the New Deal era—that effectively kept the Democrats dominant at the mass public level (Shafer and Badger 2001, chap. 9; Abramson 1975).

One major, obvious implication was that the Democratic Party too became increasingly middle class. One key result was that, by the time the new cultural issues could claim a share of a new and dominant issue context, the Democratic Party had a substantial minority within its mass base that was actively attracted to these concerns. There was thus a changing issue context for American politics. There was a changing social base for its pursuit. And there was a party system that continued in its main rank-and-file outlines but changed substantially at the elite level, especially in its strategic potential.

In the New Deal era, that party system had reserved substantial powers to long-serving party officials to make strategic judgments based on electoral necessities. They were hardly lacking in individual policy preferences, but they normally accepted the notion that these could best be maximized through a concern with overall party fortunes. In the era of divided government, the party system shifted those powers to party activists who were energized more directly by policy issues. They too would make strategic judgments, but those judgments were much more likely to be aimed at maximizing returns from the specific issues (increasingly cultural) that had originally recruited them. The result, inevitably, was a new political order with a new strategic environment.

In terms of the changed character of this strategic environment for American politics, the key point was that there was now a new—and institutionalized—tension between party activists and their own putative rank and file. In other words, *four* key party sectors, not two, now had to be considered in order to make sense of partisan conflict (Shafer and Claggett 1995; Ladd 1976–1977; Ladd and Hadley 1973):

1. *Democratic activists* were reliably liberal. They remained liberal on social welfare—that did not change—and they added a strident liberalism on cultural values.
2. *Democratic mass identifiers* retained a huge body of supporters who remained liberal on social welfare but had never been liberal on cultural values, and they did not become so.
3. Likewise, *Republican activists* were reliably conservative. They remained

conservative on social welfare—perhaps becoming even more so—and they added conservatism on cultural values.

4. By contrast, *Republican mass identifiers* retained a huge body of supporters who also remained conservative on social welfare but had never been conservative on cultural values, and they did not become so.

In the longer run, that is, by the time of George W. Bush, these latter individuals—the economically conservative but culturally liberal—who were among the most capable in American society of understanding their options and taking action in response, would constitute as much of a problem for Republican strategists as internal dissidents would for the Democrats. In the shorter run, however, in the 1960s and 1970s when the era of divided government became established, it was dissident Democrats—economic liberals but cultural conservatives—who provided an immediate and distinctive change in character to this first phase of the new order.

That order would be consolidated in the 1970s and 1980s, and its strategic constraints would be a problem that Bill Clinton had to address in the 1990s. His arrival would mark the second distinguishable phase of the new political order, such that, by then, the Republicans would have developed their own version of the same basic environmental and strategic problems. Needless to say, when George W. Bush arrived in 2000, he would face his own version of the same challenge that had confronted Clinton. Their effectively similar responses are the story of the rest of this essay.

Before that, however, two other key facts about the structure of this changed—and increasingly problematic—political order must be noted. First, the general public did not necessarily desire split partisan control of the institutions of national government. It simply had clear preferences on the two main substantive dimensions of policy conflict in its time, social welfare and cultural values. Faced with a party system that would not cater to those preferences—one party liberal on both, the other party conservative on both—it proceeded to choose accordingly. The public would, over time, get consciously comfortable with this initially anomalous partisan outcome, with divided government, but it did not have to desire it actively in order to vote consistently for split partisan control.

Second, nothing in this pattern implied that the voting public was becoming more conservative on cultural values or more liberal on social welfare. In fact, survey evidence suggests the reverse (Mayer 1992; Smith

1990). On the one hand, the public was becoming more cautious about adding major programs to the American welfare state, though it would never back away from the main existing lineaments. On the other, the public was becoming considerably more liberal on cultural values, tolerating a wider array of social behaviors and refusing to tolerate deeds or words that had been far more common when the postwar world began. At least for 1968, however, the public remained well right of the active Democratic Party on cultural values and well left of the active Republican Party on economic welfare.

The founding father of this new political order, Richard Nixon—happy to be president but disappointed to be so far from controlling Congress— actually struggled *against* its strategic contours. He continued to emphasize cultural issues, especially traditional values and "law and order," where the Republican Party looked capable of expanding an existing partisan advantage. But he tried simultaneously to shift the party away from its disadvantage on the main lineaments of the welfare state. Thus he attempted to make his peace with Keynesian management of the economy while accepting a priority for full employment rather than price stability, and he tried to think of Republican ways to pursue popular Democratic programs: block rather than categorical grants for some, tax credits rather than public bureaucracies for others, formulaic disbursements rather than institutionalized programs for still others (Mason 1998; Hoff 1994).

The Watergate crisis ultimately wrecked any possibility of success for this larger strategic initiative, and Nixon's immediate successors would not even try. In failing to implement either economic liberalism or cultural conservatism, Nixon's accidental successor, Jimmy Carter, was undone by the larger strategic environment and left it essentially as he found it. Carter's Republican successor, Ronald Reagan, would have much more lasting impact, though what worked for him in the narrow tactical sense—stiffly conservative economics and expanded cultural conservatism—would ultimately endow the Republicans with their own version of the main Democratic dilemma.

Reagan bested Carter on both major dimensions of ongoing policy conflict, and it was this dual triumph that brought him to office. On cultural values, what he emphasized most in the 1980 campaign was defense and rearmament, and the Iran hostage crisis proved an especially effective foil for those arguments. But what he really did was to concentrate on making the election a referendum on Jimmy Carter's economic steward-ship, from a dramatic energy crisis to galloping stagflation, thereby at-tempting to defuse any residual Democratic advantage in that domain.

The Reagan reelection of 1984 then reaffirmed, if such affirmation was still necessary, that the main contours of the era of divided government remained solidly in place. When Reagan had secured his surprisingly strong upset of Carter in 1980, he had actually picked up control of the Senate and shaved the Democratic margin in the House. A classic electoral realignment of the sort that had accompanied the New Deal era, perhaps aborted by Nixon and the Watergate crisis, might have been under way again. When Reagan was powerfully returned to office in 1984, however, this notion effectively disappeared. He managed to lose seats in both houses of Con-gress; he would go on to lose the Senate itself in 1986. The initial phase of the era of divided government, born in the election of 1968, was obviously still institutionalized as the election of 1988 approached.

The Democrats' Dilemma

That was the context under which Reagan's vice president, George Herbert Walker Bush—George Bush Sr.—would try to succeed him. But it was al-ready a context that had generated substantial, ongoing, and heated debate within the *Democratic* Party about how best to address its strategic require-ments. Al Gore was central to this debate. Bill Clinton would be even more so. The Democratic Leadership Council was the main vehicle for trying to impose a self-conscious alternative approach for Democratic candidates to the issue context and social coalitions of their era. And the attempt to create—to publicize and expand—a cadre of "New Democrats" would be at the heart of this (Baer 2000).

In the aftermath of Reagan's triumph in 1980, many Democrats were still willing to treat their national problems as happenstance, with a Johnson implosion in 1968 and a Carter "accidency" in 1980. Reagan's substantial reelection in 1984 made this line of argument much more difficult, and this time, a new organization with national strategic concerns at its core re-sulted. This was the Democratic Leadership Council (DLC), which aimed specifically to reposition the national party, with an eye on a majority social coalition.

On economic welfare, the DLC argued for more cautious programs with a larger role for the market, while it sought to escape the tax-and-spend and big-government charges of Republicans. On cultural values, the new organization argued for a reinvigorated military with nationalist intentions, and it aimed to put the party very visibly back on the side of middle-class family values, while escaping the charge that it was the logical home of the socially deviant and demonstrating that it was not the prisoner of its own organized interests in either the economic or the cultural realm.

Senator Al Gore of Tennessee carried the New Democratic banner into the nominating contest, though he shared it, that year, with Congressman Richard Gephardt of Missouri, who would ultimately become a leading spokesman for the "Old Democrats." Regardless, it was Michael Dukakis, governor of Massachusetts, who ended up with the presidential nomination and who was destined, once again, to be undone by the existing political order. The defeat of Dukakis would lead, most directly, to the triumph—temporary, lasting, or transitional—of the self-styled New Democrats.

The 1988 contest was noteworthy among postwar elections for the absence of pressing issue concerns on either the economic or the cultural dimension. In this environment, Dukakis moderated his party's social welfare positions, arguing for fiscal common sense and neutral managerial competence, though he remained an outspoken cultural liberal. But because the opposition preferred to play on cultural terrain anyhow, this implicit downgrading of social welfare only played into its strategy. The campaign of George Bush Sr. did not miss its opportunity and relentlessly emphasized cultural concerns: defense, the environment, education, and crime, crime, crime (Elshtain 1989; Germond and Witcover 1989).

The outcome was another Democratic defeat. One secondary result was a shuffling of the formal leadership of the DLC, which brought Governor Bill Clinton of Arkansas to the chairmanship of that body. Clinton was already an influential figure in the rethinking of Democratic approaches to public policy, just as he was already a long-shot possibility for the Democratic nomination in 1992. Chairmanship of the DLC would provide him not just with policy support but also with an initial constituency and, joining the two, a nationwide organizational network to introduce the proto-candidate around the country and to underpin a nominating effort, if one occurred.

In the event, he did run. He did front New Democratic themes. And he did secure the nomination, though that sequence hardly ran in a straight line. Nevertheless, refusing to balance his ticket in the classic fashion, he went on to choose another New Democrat, Al Gore, as his running mate. And he began the campaign with explicit New Democratic themes.

The issue context of the campaign itself, that is, the issues of the day as they were forced in from the outside world, would have been equally fortuitous for an Old Democrat. The main issue was the ongoing recession, a major economic downturn. The main subsidiary concern was health care, as unemployment removed many Americans from job-based health insurance and appeared to threaten many more. The main cultural concern of the campaign proved to be not work incentives, resurgent nationalism, or family values but Clinton's personal character.

It was a world with the orthodox pattern of costs and benefits from the era of divided government: Democrats benefiting from economic issues, Republicans benefiting from cultural concerns. For 1992, however, it was also a world where welfare topped culture in public priorities, and Clinton was narrowly but duly elected (Pomper 1993, chap. 5; Abramson, Aldrich, and Rohde 1994). If the new president were to govern as a New Democrat, he would obviously have to reassert his priorities *against* an existing environment. Yet because the environment he was entering—a national legislative environment where the Democrats retained control of both houses of Congress—was one dominated by old elites schooled in the existing programs and by organized constituencies of an ongoing party system, the incentives were clearly stacked toward continuity rather than change.

In hindsight, his choices may have been inevitable. The middle-class tax cut was eliminated, and a major economic stimulus plan was offered instead. Welfare reform was suspended, and medical care moved to the number-one policy priority—where it then received an Old Democratic solution the likes of which probably could not have been delivered even during the New Deal era. Yet the symbolic item that probably made the greatest single contribution to a policy identification for the new administration was "gays in the military," the Clinton attempt to make open homosexuality an acceptable concomitant of military service.

Within one congressional term—indeed, even before the midterm election of 1994—White House strategists had concluded that the resulting combination of stiff economic and cultural liberalism was a dangerous mistake (Idelson 1995). Their analysis, however, was not shared by the congressional Democratic Party, which was of course the body actually contesting the midterm election of 1994. The immediate result was devastating. The Republicans seized control of both the Senate and the House, the first time they had done so since 1952, the first time they had done so without a presidential candidate at their head since 1946, and only the third time they had done so at all since 1928—three successes in thirty-three attempts.

In the short run, the surface drama continued along exactly these lines. A remarkable share of these new Republicans had signed on to a conservative manifesto, the "Contract with America" (Gillespie and Shellas 1994), which was militantly conservative on both economic and cultural matters. Their spokesman, Congressman Newt Gingrich of Georgia, who became the new Speaker of the House, actually managed to use that document to set the policy agenda for national government for the next two years. But that is a story that must be temporarily deferred to concentrate on a Democratic, not a Republican, dilemma.

Few successful Republicans doubted—and in truth, many analysts believed—that Republican control of the presidency would follow more or less naturally two years later, creating unified Republican control of the national government to contrast with the unified Democratic control of the opening Clinton years. In the longer run, however, there were two deeper results of this upheaval, results that proved to have more direct strategic impact.

In the first, this upheaval forced President Clinton to return to his New Democratic themes. This approach would be fully in place by his reelection campaign of 1996, and he would never deviate in major ways thereafter. And in the second deeper result of the 1994 upheaval, the new Republican Congress actually took the Republican Party farther to the right on both major policy dimensions, establishing the issue context that any Republican nominee in 2000 would have to address.

Clinton did endure a period of obvious strategic uncertainty in the aftermath of the 1994 election, being forced to assert at one point that "the President is relevant here" (Ceaser and Busch 1997, 42). But in relatively short order, he had not just retreated to economic moderation in its own right but also effectively converted himself into the defender of *existing* social insurance programs, especially Social Security and Medicare, such that he would be able to run for reelection in 1996 as the champion of those (vastly popular) programs without having to spend anything on them and without having to promise to do so.

At the same time, the president, no longer encumbered by orthodox Democratic elites in control of Congress, set to work refashioning his own image. This time, he actually did achieve welfare reform—not the moderate version he would have offered in 1993, but a more conservative program with stiffer time limits and greater autonomy for individual states that resulted from dealing with Republican majorities. By 1996, Clinton would be touting school uniforms, teen curfews, antismoking initiatives, family protection, and police, police, police. (By 1996, even First Lady Hillary Clinton would be championing social control in her newly published book *It Takes a Village.*) Clinton was thus in position to argue that the national Democratic Party had in effect reclaimed the American center.

New Democrats and Old Republicans

The Republican story was by then very different—or, rather, it was a different incarnation of the *exact same* underlying dynamic. Whereas years of Democratic success, courtesy of the New Deal era, had set the stage for a disadvantageous repositioning of the party in the 1960s, especially on cultural matters, years of Republican success in the opening phase of the era of divided government had done precisely the same for the Republicans. For them, however, the impact was still below the surface, in the ability of organized party constituencies to demand increasingly extreme policies, so that the debate over an alternative strategy—a Republican counterpart to the New Democrats—was still to come.

For the Republicans, the Reagan years, otherwise a time of partisan triumph, had seen an important shift in the composition of the cultural dimension, a shift with important incipient consequences. Perceived capabilities on defense and foreign affairs were to remain an asset for Republican candidates throughout the Reagan administration, as they had been since polling first revealed that status during the Eisenhower years. In contrast, the partisan value of "law and order" as a matter for policy conflict declined as racial rioting disappeared and the Vietnam War was liquidated. The Reagan administration made a serious effort on criminal justice, appointing judges who were "tough on crime," but it would always be difficult to secure reliable partisan advantage in a realm where neither side wanted to be the "pro-crime" party.

Instead, a whole array of even more explicitly cultural issues came to the fore. Reagan emphasized the virtues of religiosity, consistently attacking court policy on the separation of church and state, albeit without much concrete impact. He helped develop the theme of "family values," of support for the traditional family and for the responsibilities it entailed, which subsequent candidates would emphasize even more strongly. He kept abortion policy—in his case, antiabortion policy, the right to life—at the center of his public persona, and here, there were legislative victories. Government health programs stopped funding abortions where they had previously done so; the United States refused to support international agencies that followed pro-abortion policies.

This shift was powerfully underpinned by a change in social coalitions. If the postwar years had been characterized by the growth of educated, middle-class Democrats who were culturally liberal, those years had also been characterized by the growth of religious evangelicals, the culturally conservative wing of Protestantism (Hunter 1983; Soper 1994; Reed 1995). This growth went hand in glove with the increasing sophistication of an evangelical ministry concerned with the moral decay that cultural progressivism represented and skilled at applying new technologies—mass mailing, televangelism—to fight that decay. The 1970s then saw conservative Christianity spinning off explicitly political organizations to help in that fight.

The ideological consistency and social ease with which Ronald Reagan addressed this movement brought cultural conservatives into partisan politics on the Republican side. Reagan's reelection in 1984 then both confirmed the place of a plethora of new socially conservative groups in the organized councils of the Republican Party (this was the outcome that analysts trumpeted at the time) and began to confirm their limitations, the outcome of which would eventually prove critical to the fortunes of George W. Bush.

But the presence of a growing Republican problem, precisely parallel to that which the Democrats had experienced after 1968, was masked by the electoral success of George Bush Sr. against Michael Dukakis. If the Nixon-Reagan era continued unabated, how could there be a problem? Again there was evidence (parallel to what would become the experience of Bill Clinton), if analysts had wanted to process it. George Bush Sr. managed to succeed Reagan, but his efforts to loosen the bonds of cultural conservatism that Reagan had bequeathed him proved ineffectual and often harmful.

Bush Sr. offered some educational initiatives, in a major policy realm that was open to capture by either of the political parties, only to see his own congressional party disavow them. If he was to have any fresh educational policy, he actually had to let congressional *Democrats* establish its basic outlines and then bargain with them over the details. The need to reauthorize the Clean Air Act provided another opportunity to reposition the party culturally on environmental issues. But again, Bush Sr. lost the support of his own party and was forced to respond to Democratic initiatives. Even his attempt to address an impending recession, which White House analysts saw clearly by 1990, resulted in attacks from within his own party over abandonment of his pledge of "no new taxes" (Zuckerman 1990; Pytte 1990; Hayer 1990a).

Clinton's election might, in principle, have promoted some Republican soul-searching. But within two years, the party had engineered the stunning recapture of Congress. Again, how could there be a problem? And in truth, the main planks of the "Contract with America," most of which did not become national law even after passage in the House of Representatives, did not actually appear to hurt the party nationwide. All had been carefully poll-tested before being enunciated, and most of them worked as that testing had suggested.

The inescapable turning point (once more in the full glare of hindsight) came instead at the end of the first year of the new Republican Congress, at the end of 1995 and the beginning of 1996, when these new congressmen attempted to fulfill their promise to balance the federal budget. To that end, they needed to control expenditures on the major social insurance programs, especially Social Security and Medicare. And to that end, they shut down the government twice over the Christmas–New Year's holidays to force the president to negotiate with them.

They were never to recover. A sign of Clinton's potential vulnerability in 1996 was the fact that Senate Majority Leader Robert Dole of Kansas, frontrunner for the Republican nomination, had always run close to him and had intermittently run ahead in trial heats during 1995. From the period immediately after the second governmental shutdown, however, the candidates' support lines diverged, and Dole was never a serious threat thereafter (Shafer 1997). Worse yet, with Dole running so far behind the incumbent president during the nominating season, he was sharply constrained in what he could do, strategically, during the fall campaign.

The Republican Party of 1996, like the Democratic Party of 1992, presented an established—and strong—pattern of constraints on general election strategy. Just as the active Democratic Party was strongly liberal on both economic and cultural issues, the active Republican Party was strongly conservative. Where Clinton worked to relax these positions in the aftermath of the 1994 Republican triumph, however, congressional Republican elites worked, actively and naturally, to extend and institutionalize them. And the specifics of their effort also mattered.

Two dramatic speeches at the 1992 Republican Convention from the two Pats, Pat Buchanan and Pat Robertson, had put an apparent symbolic seal on the party's cultural positioning. Then, attempts by "Contract" Republicans to balance the budget while restraining social insurance programs had put an equally evident symbolic seal on the party's economic positioning. So the weak 1996 nominee, Senator Bob Dole, found himself in a serious strategic box. It was actually this box that George W. Bush would inherit and that he would have to try to escape in 2000.

Lacking policy credentials as a serious cultural conservative but needing the support of culturally conservative activists in order to be nominated, Dole's best available choice was to let policy repositioning alone and hope to benefit by emphasizing concerns about presidential character. Needing to counter Clinton's obvious advantage on social welfare (just reinforced by the Republican Congress), Dole sought a policy initiative in the economic realm and came up with a huge tax cut in the face of a huge budget deficit, despite his own political history as a fiscal moderate with a concern for economic responsibility.

The Republicans' Dilemma

Neither strategy was of much use. Presidential character remained an issue, and those who gave it priority voted disproportionately for Dole. But Clinton had otherwise succeeded in putting the cultural-values cluster to sleep, neutralizing Democratic disadvantages within it. The economy continued to perform robustly, on top of the huge advantages ceded by the Republican Party on basic social insurance programs (Ceaser and Busch 1997). And Dole, long a voice for fiscal responsibility in the Republican Party, was only marginally credible as the advocate of a tax cut during a period of economic expansion.

The result was a solid reelection for President Clinton coupled with the narrow retention of divided government, with Republicans holding their substantial advantage in the Senate and a marginal edge in the House. The result was also a familiar policy ballet for the remaining term of the Clinton presidency. The first Congress of this presidency featured continued pursuit of the character issue by congressional Republicans, culminating in impeachment. It also featured continued emphasis on social insurance by congressional Democrats, in a crusade to "fix" a Social Security system that actuaries could foresee going into deficit early in the twenty-first century.

The second Congress of this reelected presidency featured a dispute that no one had foreseen, over how to allocate an actual budget surplus. At bottom, this surplus was a classic product of divided government. Although the economy had been growing, Republicans were unable to offer tax cuts, and Democrats were unable to offer fresh spending. In any case, Republicans favored large tax cuts, "giving the people their money back." Democrats favored only targeted tax breaks, "extending the prosperity of the 1990s," while addressing some new programmatic needs. Neither side was able to secure its wishes. Deficit reduction became the only alternative.

Both sides, of course, made continuing efforts to take credit for the surplus, with President Clinton achieving a mild edge in the credit-claiming department (Another Paradigm Shift 1999; Budget Making 2000). Although neither side secured its policy wishes, the Democrats again gained a public-relations edge more or less by default by paying down the national debt when neither tax cuts nor new programs could be passed. They thus managed to enter the 2000 campaign with almost the ideal partisan scenario: economic prosperity, international peace, and an experienced candidate apparently well suited to their extension.

Enter "compassionate conservatism" (Bush 2000). The strategic team around Texas Governor George W. Bush as he considered whether to run for president in the apparent vacuum of attractive Republican candidates—whether he could get the nomination, whether it was worth having—was well aware of the national Republican dilemma. In a mirror image of the problems that Clinton had faced (and addressed only under eventual compulsion), the Bush team saw that the Republican Party risked inheriting a public perception of being out of the mainstream on social welfare and now out of the mainstream on cultural values to boot.

They had come a long way from the change of 1968, when the Democratic Party had evidently been out of the mainstream on cultural values and had tottered on the brink on social welfare, too. That strategic disaster had led to a quarter century of Republican government, unbroken but for the Carter "accidency." Now, however, the Republicans appeared to be even more severely handicapped at the national level. Congress represented a bright spot, a vastly improved situation, though still not approaching the one the Democrats had likewise enjoyed until 1994. But the presidency appeared to have lost the middle ground to the New Democrats, to Bill Clinton, and now to Al Gore.

"Compassionate conservatism" was to be the gathering concept for a response, an argument that Republican ways of proceeding could realize the same values dominating the center in American politics. Republicans were not punitive economically; they were not punitive socially. Indeed, they had programs that were better at realizing common values. In the process of setting out these claims, they almost could have been stealing the play book from the New Democrats in the years leading up to the Clinton presidency: "opportunity, responsibility, and community" as the themes; "the importance of work, the need for faith, and the centrality of family" as their abstract embodiment (Baer 2001).

Those themes were, however, blown off course almost immediately by the nature of the nominating contest. With a bevy of economic and cultural conservatives to challenge him and potentially chop up his front-runner status—Steve Forbes, Pat Buchanan, Gary Bauer, Alan Keyes—Bush needed to move right to avoid being isolated from the ongoing conservatism of the active Republican Party. When John McCain instead became his major challenge for the nomination—a maverick candidate appealing to those within the party who were outside its organized constituencies—Bush was planted solidly on the right. By supporting campaign finance reform and not appeasing the religious conservatives, it was McCain who became the default candidate of moderate Republicans.

With moderate Republicans going to McCain, Bush had to have the solid support of conservatives to secure the nomination. There were further fillips to this strategy, twists along the way that were unhelpful to the aspiring candidate of compassionate conservatism. For example, the key contest after McCain upset Bush in New Hampshire was in South Carolina, where the active Republican Party was especially conservative on both major dimensions. Bush triumphed there and went on to secure the nomination, but he was no longer the evident "centrist Republican" he had set out to be, the logical counterpart to the "centrist Democrat" that Clinton had been banged into becoming (Ceaser and Busch 2001, chaps. 3–4).

Bush's next opportunity to return to these themes was the Republican National Convention, and he seized upon it with a vengeance. This gathering raised the tightly scripted character of modern televised conventions to perhaps the most extreme point in their history. Yet the script itself was more noteworthy for its deviations. The official party was nearly banished from the podium. Instead of the senators, congressmen, and governors, which the national Republican Party now possessed in abundance, there were only "real people," private citizens who embodied some aspect of the Bush approach, whether it be a voluntary organization, a faith-based program, or, most commonly, an educational initiative (Cannon 2000; Von Drehle 2000; Barnes 2000).

Indeed, the whole "Anglo" party was in short supply. In previous presidential contests, national Republicans had actively flirted with an anti-immigrant and antiminority stance to help firm up the support of Americans of European origin. The Bush convention instead featured numerous black spokespersons and an absolute plethora of Hispanics. Some of this was aimed at members of these groups themselves: the Bush team felt that it needed more than a third of the Hispanic vote in order to win an election, and two Texas campaigns had provided substantial experience in seeking it. Bush strategists were less hopeful about cracking the black vote, but an evident willingness to seek it had additional benefits: it signaled to moderate Anglos, as forcefully as anything in their arsenal, that they intended to be policy moderates, not extremists.

It would have been possible, in principle, to do all this in prime (tele-vised) time and feature the alternative—party officials and Anglos—in off hours. Instead, the Bush team seemed to be not only sending a national message via television but also running a partisan tutorial about the shape of a successful party campaign. The audience for this tutorial was, of course, the party activists gathered in the hall. If they went home willing to give the new strategy a try, that would be a major secondary gain from the convention. If the new strategy failed, it might be a long time before it got another chance.

Back in from the Cold?

The subsequent campaign for the general election, like all general election campaigns, generated peculiar incidents all its own, incidents that the candidates' operations had to address apart from any overall strategy. The "rats" advertisements early in that campaign—televised ads that were said to have negative subliminal messages embedded in them—were a particular trial for the Bush operation. The erratic performance of nominee Gore in the televised debates—changing in each debate, unsuccessful in all—was a particular trial for their Democratic counterparts (Berke 2000a, 2000b). Yet both campaigns basically followed their strategic intentions from September to November.

In this, the Bush campaign eschewed conventional Republican wisdom about avoiding social welfare and emphasizing cultural values. The campaign did, however, use the traditional Republican riposte on social welfare, involving the promise of tax cuts, repeatedly and in a big way. But it also tackled the question of social insurance programs head-on, with its own plan for "saving" Social Security by providing individual retirement accounts to help people structure their own pension programs (Nelson 2001; Pomper 2001; Abramson, Aldrich, and Rohde forthcoming).

Likewise, the campaign did not shy away from that old standby, the character issue, attempting to tar Al Gore with the sins of Bill Clinton in geographic areas where the latter was notably unpopular. But it also made a major effort to acquire "the education issue" for Republicans. A generalized anxiety about the quality of public education in the United States—for 2000, this was the number-one issue in opinion polls—gave Bush the chance to present himself (as his father had done) as "the education president." School vouchers were the more controversial aspect of this issue, national testing standards less so, though neither was consensual, and both were opposed by the Democrats.

From the other side, Gore retained substantial assets, though most had strategic liabilities attached. The obvious strategic task for Gore was to blend New Democratic themes, which he had helped pioneer and from which Clinton had so clearly benefited, with an appeal to the main organized constituencies of the national Democratic Party, and as a sitting vice president who had done policy business with these organizations for eight years, he was in a unique position to do so. The former would hold on to the ideological center; the latter would boost turnout among reliable Democratic votes. Gore pursued both tasks throughout the fall, accepting the risk that he would fully accomplish neither.

The campaign was also noteworthy for the disappearance of some ongoing "hot-button" concerns, and here, abortion policy is an excellent example. Neither candidate deviated from what had become established party positions: Bush was solidly pro-life, Gore solidly pro-choice. Both emphasized these positions in the nominating campaign, and both reiterated them in their acceptance speeches at the national party conventions. The issue then disappeared from general election radar, and it was not hard to see why. CNN, which supported its convention coverage with focus-group analyses of major speeches, found that the low point in public attractiveness of the Bush acceptance speech came with his endorsement of the right to life, just as the low point in the Gore acceptance speech came with his endorsement of the right to choose.

The final result was as ambiguous as such results can be. Gore won the popular vote nationwide, very narrowly. Bush won the electoral vote as narrowly—and as protractedly—as possible. For Bush, however, even the popular vote was a great improvement over the last two presidential outings, though the electoral vote was of course the ultimate improvement. However, Republicans dropped a small number of seats in the closely balanced House, and they dropped a large number of seats in the less closely balanced Senate.

Democrats had gone into the campaign believing that they had already found the great American center. Regardless, the American public surely returned to that center: 49 to 48 percent in the presidential vote, 50+ to 50– percent in the electoral vote, 50 to 50 percent in the Senate, and 51 to 49 percent in the House. But had the Republicans found the center too? And was the result thus a confirmation of a new phase in the era of divided government, with the initial phase of opposite extremes being replaced by a subsequent phase of centrist alternatives?

The evolution of Bill Clinton, his policy program and his personal presentation, was warning against any easy, early answer. George W. Bush certainly faced the same risky prospect that Clinton had faced, in which a congressional party wedded to the ongoing policy positions of an established order was disinclined to move to any "new centrism." In a perverse sense, the equal party balance that Bush encountered in Congress could actually be an asset in this regard, making it less apparently possible to govern through a consistent blend of conservative economics and conservative culture.

The Bush team had thought carefully about all this. But then, so had the Clinton team in its time. The new president actually appeared more inclined to tack with the partisan environment than to impose a self-consciously new and centrist vision on it. But then, so had the outgoing president when he arrived in office. The Bush team arrived touting the virtues of bipartisanship while simultaneously bristling at the preferences of their partisan opponents. The Clinton team had arrived denigrating the virtues of bipartisanship while simultaneously complaining about the behavior of their opposite numbers.

Major external events could shape the fate of the new Bush presidency, quite apart from all such calculations. Otherwise, the Bush team could obviously fail by appearing to abandon the compassionate conservatism of the election campaign, just as it could obviously fail by being deserted by its own partisans in Congress. Both failings had indeed cursed the presidency of George Bush Sr. From the other side, the Democrats could hope to succeed only by hamstringing this Bush presidency and retaking both houses of Congress in the 2002 midterm election, just as they could hope to succeed only by avoiding the perception that they were the problem in securing successful governance over the next two years. The outcome, either way, would be major evidence toward the character of a new phase in the ongoing era of divided government—or not.

CHAPTER THREE

Are There Any New Democrats? And by the Way, Was There a Republican Revolution?

We offer our people a new choice based on old values. We offer opportunity. We demand responsibility. We will build an American community again. The choice we offer is not conservative or liberal. In many ways it's not even Republican or Democratic. It's different. It's new. And it will work.
    —Bill Clinton, acceptance speech, Democratic Convention, July 16, 1992

What is ultimately at stake in our current environment is literally the future of American civilization as it has existed for the last several hundred years. I'm a history teacher by background, and I would assert and defend on any campus in this country that it is impossible to maintain civilization with twelve-year-olds having babies, fifteen-year-olds killing each other, with seventeen-year-olds dying of AIDS, and with eighteen-year-olds ending up with diplomas they can't even read. What is at issue is literally not Republican or Democrat or liberal or conservative, but the question of whether or not our civilization will survive.
    —Newt Gingrich, Washington Research Group symposium,
      November 11, 1994

The Clinton years were nothing if not a period characterized by *claims* about major partisan change. Two of these, however, crowd out all the others. The first involved the coming of the New Democrats, self-described. The second involved a putative Republican revolution. Both were on a grand scale in terms of their purported impact. Each only gained emphasis from the fact that it ran directly opposite to the other. If either was true, it defined the partisan legacy of the Clinton presidency. If neither was accurate, the Clinton presidency was, in partisan terms, a period of struc-

52

tural drift and opportunistic response—a time when no one could find the key to shaping an era, or when the nature of that era did not permit systematic success.

The Clinton years suffered no lack of superficially compelling individual events with partisan implications. Yet for such events to have any lasting partisan effect, they needed to register in one of two ways: they needed to shift the *social coalitions* associated with the two main political parties, or they needed to shift the *programmatic positions* that party candidates offered the general public. These two elements are normally united in a more or less seamless fashion in practical politicking. They can be separated for analytic purposes, however, and in fact, the two main claims about a partisan legacy for the Clinton years spoke explicitly to both.

The first of these claims involved the ascension to national leadership of the "New Democrats." That moniker was intended to distinguish them from party predecessors in both critical regards. From one side, they were to offer a new programmatic focus, one more attuned to contemporary fiscal constraints and more connected—or, in their view, reconnected—to public values. From the other side, they were to champion a new social constituency in the form of (in their rhetoric) the "forgotten middle class." The fate of Bill Clinton was intertwined with these goals well before his actual election. Because he was elected and, especially, reelected using precisely these campaign thematics, his fortunes put the issue of the existence, content, and consequence of a New Democracy at the center of any Clinton legacy in partisan affairs. In European terms, Clinton was cast as the key party "modernizer" of his time. The question is whether he succeeded.

The fortunes of a putative New Democracy were not alone at the contentious center of any Clinton legacy. Indeed, right beside them, jostling for legacy status, was a development on the opposite side of the partisan aisle. For the first time in either forty or seventy years, depending on how you count, the Republicans resumed control of Congress at the first midterm election of the Clinton presidency. And they too asserted both critical elements of a lasting partisan change. Programmatically, they promised to reconfigure existing policies in line with modern fiscal reality, while turning governmental machinery to the active support of public values. Coalitionally, they were less pointed than the Democrats, but that was because they promised that even more of the broad and amorphous American middle class would find its natural home in the newly invigorated Republican Party. Otherwise, they were even less abashed in proclaiming a change. Newt

Gingrich, the Georgia congressman who would become Speaker of the newly Republican House, heralded their arrival as nothing short of a "Republican revolution."

The Old Order and the New Politics

I was born in a little town called Hope, Arkansas, three months after my father died. I remember that old two-story house where I lived with my grandparents— they had very limited income. It was in 1963 that I went to Washington and met President Kennedy, at the Boys Nation program. And I remember just thinking what an incredible country this was, that somebody like me, you know, had no money or anything, would be given the opportunity to meet the President. That's when I decided that I could really do public service, 'cause I cared so much about people. I worked my way through law school, with part-time jobs, anything I could find. And after I graduated, I really didn't care about making a lot of money. I just wanted to go home and see if I could make a difference. We've worked hard in education, in health care, to create jobs, and we've made real progress. Now it's exhilarating to me to think that as president, I could help to change all our people's lives for the better, and bring hope back to the American dream.
—Democratic commercial, 1992 general election campaign

The party system within which these competing claims surfaced, and which they had to transform in order to prove accurate, had been in existence for sixty years by the time Bill Clinton was elected president. Indeed, the course of his life is a reasonable introduction to critical moments in this "New Deal party system." Clinton was born on August 19, 1946, only weeks before the first serious challenge to the system, when Republicans first reseized control of Congress and announced their aspirations to bring the system to an end. They failed, and the New Deal era would run for another generation. By the time this era finally ended in 1968, Clinton was in college, preparing to enter politics. He did, and one of his initial tasks was—presciently—to adapt the local Democratic Party to an emerging new politics in a new period known nationally as the era of divided government. Twenty years later, he would acknowledge the same goals and trumpet the same skills for a potential Clinton presidency.

But that is getting ahead of the story. The New Deal era, the old order into which Clinton was born, had been sparked by the stock market crash of 1929, fanned by the Roosevelt landslide of 1932, and fed by the New Deal program that followed. The great and dominating substantive concerns of this era were economics and social welfare, as befitted an agenda called into being by economic catastrophe. By the time Clinton was born, the policy content of this dominant economic-welfare dimension included all the hallmark programs of the Rooseveltian New Deal. In the years after Clinton's birth, the policy content of the same dimension would expand to include full employment plus the remainder of the original New Deal agenda: health care, housing assistance, poverty amelioration, higher education, and, last but not least, civil rights. The staying power of these programs, as items for partisan conflict, would prove remarkable (Leuchtenberg 1963; Burns 1973; Sundquist 1968; Brown 1968).

The great and continuing secondary concern of this period was foreign affairs, again befitting an era forced to confront the catastrophe of total war. In the years before Clinton's birth, this involved proper pursuit of World War II through a huge buildup of defense manpower and industry. In the years after, it involved proper pursuit of the Cold War, with its mixture of international alliances, military support, and conventional foreign aid. The United States had been drawn reluctantly into the worldwide conflicts capped by the Second World War; it was to be a principal architect of the succeeding international environment. Both tasks would belong largely to the Democratic Party.

As ever, there were social coalitions to go with these programmatic directions, coalitions that were in fact integral to them. By 1946, two of these, robustly constructed, dominated the political landscape. Both were built principally on social class, unlike the geographic basis of the previous party system, albeit with important ethnic and regional twists. The larger was a blue-collar coalition, aligned with the national Democratic Party, that featured working-class Americans generally, a few key multiclass minorities, and the entire (the "solid") South. The smaller was a white-collar coalition aligned with the national Republican Party and confined essentially to middle-class Americans, plus farmers outside the South (Sundquist 1973, chaps. 10–12; Ladd with Hadley 1975, pt. 1; Shafer 1998b, chap. 3).

These coalitions were then crucially buttressed by the main division among the interest groups of its time, essentially a business-labor divide. Organized labor became an increasingly important adjunct to the Democratic Party, first in legislative and then in electoral politics. By contrast, although corporate management provided some funding and the occasional "blue-ribbon" candidate for the Republicans, it was really small business—the Chamber of Commerce, not the National Association of Manufacturers—that carried the load for the Republican Party among the organized interests.

Policy positions and social coalitions were then knit together and connected to the institutions of national government by the political parties. Already by 1946, however, these were not just mirror images within the party system of the late New Deal. The Democrats were an amalgam of urban machines in the North, courthouse rings in the South, and volunteer activist branches scattered throughout the country. The Republicans, still paying a high price for incumbency when the Great Depression hit, had instead moved to become the kind of organizationally amorphous, activist-based political party that both would become in the second postwar era, relying on ideology and issues to motivate party workers. For the Republican Party, in truth, this was not so much modernization as simple survival.

There was, finally, a diagnostic partisan dynamic to go with this mix of policy conflicts, social coalitions, and partisan intermediaries, a distinctive character to party competition in the long-running New Deal era. Seen by way of ongoing policy conflicts, the party on the Left, the Democratic Party, was widely perceived as being more in tune with public preferences on social welfare. By contrast, the party on the Right, the Republicans, was widely perceived as being more in tune with public preferences on foreign affairs. The crucial fact, then, was that the public ordinarily gave a much higher priority to social welfare.

Seen by way of ongoing social coalitions instead, the dominant fact of partisan politicking from 1932 through 1968 was that the unity and vitality of the Democratic coalition remained the central story of electoral *and* institutional politics. After 1946, however, Republicans could win if Democratic policy assets were devalued and if Republicans had special assets of their own, as they would in 1952 with Dwight Eisenhower as their nominee. Eisenhower brought remarkable personal assets to help produce the one great exception to Democratic dominance in this era. When he did, the Republicans too were entitled to assume unified partisan control of American national government (Campbell et al. 1960; Campbell 1960).

The New Deal era came to an end in 1968, but the New Deal party system continued—and in that distinction lay much of the story of partisan politics from 1968 through the arrival of Bill Clinton as president in 1992. At the time of the 1968 presidential election, Clinton was consolidating an interest in politics while dramatically broadening his social horizons. As a Rhodes scholar at Oxford University, he was old enough to engage seriously with the political currents and social trends of his time, some of which would return to haunt him as lesser issues when he ran for president. He would come back to pick up a law degree and then enter politics in Arkansas, where he would inevitably have to adapt to the changes producing a new political era.

Dramatic surface indications of change were everywhere in 1968: in the domestic social realm, through race riots and campus unrest; in the international realm, through the omnipresent if faltering Vietnam War; and in the political process itself, through political assassinations and the implosion of the national Democratic Party in convention. Explicit partisan change followed closely on these. Richard Nixon was narrowly elected president, while the Democratic Party retained solid control of both houses of Congress. On the one hand, then, it remained possible to believe that unhappy surface events had produced peculiar, temporary partisan outcomes, to be followed by restoration of unified Democratic control of national government. On the other hand, the constituent elements of a new era and order, especially their programmatic divisions and social coalitions, were all incipiently present.

As the new order arrived, the substantive breakup of the old era was easiest to recognize in foreign affairs, where the Cold War consensus disintegrated. Now, there were nationalists who continued to support the containment of communism, opposed by accommodationists who felt that containment was an increasingly sterile doctrine. The Vietnam War gave this division its cutting edge, and Clinton's relationship to it would put him on one side, and come back to haunt him, a generation later. But more to the practical point, Vietnam *protest* was a key route into the rest of a newly augmented set of valuational conflicts, within which foreign affairs was only one large but supporting element. Indeed, Vietnam protesters themselves often underlined this link by insisting that they were part of a "counterculture." This was as good an introduction as any to the larger valuational division that eventually included such socially central matters as public deportment, national integration, educational standards, criminal justice, religious observance, family structure, and even the proper attitude toward human life itself (Davies 1996; Scammon and Wattenberg 1970).

The social coalitions that went with these substantive divisions—the social coalitions that went with *dual* concerns for social welfare and (now) cultural values—had long been incipiently familiar. Or at least it had long been understood that economic liberals, those most concerned with the welfare essence of the New Deal program, were often social conservatives, emphasizing family, neighborhood, community, and country. Conversely, it had long been known that economic conservatives, especially the highly educated, occupationally prestigious, and financially prosperous among them, were often cultural liberals, emphasizing personal choice and the individual construction of social life. These background alignments were not themselves new. What had changed was merely the relative importance—the weight—of this second set of (essentially cultural) concerns (Shafer and Claggett 1995; Lipset and Rokkan 1967).

Yet while this was occurring, the political parties had also changed in their basic structure. At bottom, both political parties now shared the dominant characteristics of the immediate postwar Republicans. That is, both were now effectively networks of issue-oriented activists. Especially for the Democrats, gone was the reliable party "machinery," built on control of the divisible rewards of government and buttressed by an unreformed hierarchy of party offices and by the loyalty of a New Deal generation of partisans, who were gradually passing from the scene. In its place were individual issue activists whose support was now essential to mounting campaigns and gaining public office: they *were* the party in the operational sense.

More to the practical point for a new political order, these individuals were also the key to institutionalizing a partisan connection between economic-welfare and cultural-national issues. They had hardly abandoned the old social welfare basis of the party system. Republican activists remained very conservative and Democratic activists very liberal on these matters. What they had done was vastly expand the foreign affairs dimension, to cultural issues more generally, in a way that *they* found ideologically consistent. Republican activists were thus traditionalistic in social matters, nationalistic in foreign affairs; Democratic activists were now progressive in social matters, accommodationist in foreign affairs (Ware 1985; Mayhew 1986).

Moreover, it was really the ascendant cultural and national concerns that mobilized these activists as individuals and energized the new interest groups from which they collectively sprang. For the Democrats, these included environmentalists, peace groups, feminists, and homosexuals. For the Republicans, they included antiabortionists, gun owners, tax reformers, and religious fundamentalists. And on and on in both cases. As a result, there was no need for "pressure" from these groups to secure two opposing partisan programs. Party activists were now the natural products of membership in precisely these organizations.

This development implied a heightened interparty conflict—Democrat versus Republican—between consistent liberals and consistent conservatives. Yet it also implied a further intraparty conflict—Democrat versus Democrat and Republican versus Republican—between party activists and their own rank and file. At bottom, there were now two opposing majorities simultaneously present in the mass public: more liberal than the active Republican Party on economics and social welfare, more conservative than the active Democratic Party on culture and foreign affairs.

The obvious solution in the United States was to colonize one elective branch of national government with one majority, and one elective branch with the other. Split partisan control of national government was what that solution contributed practically, and in the particular historical sequence in which this new partisan dynamic arrived, it implied a Republican presidency coupled with a Democratic Congress. "Divided government" was what it came to be called, and the era of divided government was thus at hand. Indeed, if the one-term, idiosyncratic presidency of Democrat Jimmy Carter is chalked up to the Watergate crisis—it is hard to imagine Carter as a plausible candidate in 1972, and he was defeated for reelection in 1980—then the entire period between the election of Richard Nixon in 1968 and the arrival of Bill Clinton in 1992 featured Republican control of the presidency and Democratic control of Congress.

The Rise of the New Democrats?

They're a new generation of Democrats, Bill Clinton and Al Gore, and they don't think the way the old Democratic Party did. They've called for an end to welfare as we know it, so welfare can be a second chance, not a way of life. They've sent a strong signal to criminals, by supporting the death penalty. And they've rejected the old tax-and-spend politics. Clinton's balanced twelve budgets, and they've proposed a new plan investing in people, detailing $140 billion in spending cuts they'd make right now. Clinton-Gore. For people. For a change.
    —Democratic commercial, 1992 general election campaign

The background contours of a new political order were not obvious even to its main participants at the time of its arrival. Crosscutting policy conflicts and crosscutting social coalitions, with an overlay of recurring tensions between active members and the rank and file of both parties, would become the ongoing context for electoral and institutional politics in the quarter century after 1968. Such a context did not lack strategic imperatives, implicit advice that party leaders ignored at their peril. For the Republicans, this new political context counseled an emphasis on cultural-national issues and neutralization of economic-welfare concerns. For the Democrats, the opposite advice applied: emphasis on economic-welfare concerns, neutralization of cultural-national issues. But because the new order was both complex and different, the strategic imperatives that came with it were learned only in a kind of trial and error.

In contrast, the direct partisan outcomes of the new order were inescapable. Split partisan control of the institutions of national government now reliably occurred. Moreover, for almost a quarter century, this split had a further partisan patterning: Republicans captured the presidency, while Democrats captured—held, really—Congress. Divided government as an outcome was frustrating for both parties, but this further pattern also colored their thinking about how to address it. For their part, Republicans did not celebrate their return to the presidency after nearly sixty years in the partisan wilderness. Instead, they resented their inability to "complete" the return and add control of Congress. Most often, they assigned this failure to a massive superstructure of pork-barrel corruption put in place over sixty years by way of the old divisible goods of government, the new distributive formulas of politics, and the directly personal rewards of office.

Republican dismay, however, was fully matched among Democrats, who lamented their failure, for more than a generation, to hold on to the presidency when "nothing else had changed." Their congressional margins rose and fell, but only slightly. Ronald Reagan appeared to threaten these when he captured the Senate in 1980, but his gains disappeared at the end of the first full cycle for this new crop of senators, returning the Senate to Democratic control in 1986. In any case, the House of Representatives remained Democratic throughout. At the beginning of this twenty-year run, neither the initial Nixon election of 1968 nor the landslide reelection of 1972 shook this control. At the end, the House was solidly Democratic even before the Democrats regained the Senate in 1986, and it remained solidly Democratic afterward, when George Bush defeated Michael Dukakis for president, solidly, in 1988. Which is to say, year in and year out, there was a Democratic House, and year in and year out, it looked basically the same.

One of the earliest responses to the Democratic side of this puzzle was the formation, by the House Democratic Caucus after the 1980 election, of the Committee on Party Effectiveness. Jimmy Carter, incumbent Democratic president, had just been resoundingly defeated for reelection, so that it was not as easy to argue that Democratic misfortunes were only some Nixonian interlude. Regardless, without a Democratic president to represent the national party, and in the face of a confusing new partisan landscape, congressional Democrats felt the need to increase their influence. There was some incipient conflict behind this aspiration, since that influence was to be exercised in implicit opposition to the activist base of the party, including the Democratic National Committee, which congressmen viewed as insufficiently attached to the practical needs of gaining and holding public office. Otherwise, however, the programmatic and coalitional implications of this new committee were left intentionally vague (Baer 1998; Hale 1995).

Both implications edged closer to becoming explicit with the creation of an extraparty organization, the Democratic Leadership Council (DLC), after the 1984 election. The Reagan reelection was disastrous for the Democrats in the same puzzling way its predecessor had been. In response, the DLC aspired to be a more effective voice for successful Democratic officeholders, of whom there were still many, by moving beyond the House Democratic Caucus to include senators, governors, and other key state-level officials. In terms of a policy program, DLC members continued to be more likely than the active party as a whole to favor economic moderation and cultural traditionalism, and hence more likely to be moderates and conservatives than liberals. In terms of a social coalition, they continued to be more likely to be southern and western than northeastern and midwestern, more likely to come from middle-class than working-class areas, and more likely to represent suburban than urban districts. Otherwise, the new organization remained hesitant about drawing lines that would inevitably set "New Democrats" against their predecessors.

The 1988 election changed all that. It proved to be another disaster on the same template, despite the careful and conscious efforts of nominee Michael Dukakis to emphasize neutral competence. But this time, the outcome, so disappointing after early leads in the polls, altered the orientation of the DLC and put definition into an incipient New Democracy. Line-drawing did occur, dissident members exited, and a redrawn organization became the single clearest embodiment of what it meant to be a New Democrat. The idea was to recast the Democratic Party coalition so as to restore it to enduring majority status under changed social conditions, a general goal that could be saluted by most Democrats. But once it had to be given specifics, even the definition of "changed social conditions," much less of a changed policy program and a changed social coalition, was bound to be highly conflictual. Despite that, two key documents set out what it meant, thereafter, to reside on the New Democratic side of the line.

The first was an analysis entitled "The Politics of Evasion: Democrats and the Presidency," focusing on three alleged myths that were recurrently defeating the national party (Galston and Kamarck 1989):

1. The myth of mobilization, which excused defeat through declining turn-out and suggested that victory would return if the party worked harder. Careful statistical reanalysis, said the DLC, made this claim simply false.
2. The myth of liberal fundamentalism, which argued that policy change, if any, needed to emphasize the *distance* between Democrats and Republicans. This led, in the DLC analysis, to programmatic positions wildly discordant with general public values.
3. The myth of the congressional bastion, which argued that repeated partisan defeats were nevertheless transitory, as evidenced by the fact that Democrats continued to do well in Congress. The DLC countered that gradual destruction of this congressional advantage must follow continual loss of the presidency.

Published in September 1989, "The Politics of Evasion" was the most systematic analysis of the problem from a New Democratic perspective. The solution, and the other key substantive document in the evolution of a New Democracy, was the policy statement ratified at the DLC annual convention in May 1991 and published as "The New American Choice: Opportunity, Responsibility, Community" (Democratic Leadership Council 1991). Its "New American Choice Resolutions" ranged widely to include governmental structure, environmental policy, educational reform, foreign trade, military reorganization, child support, and equal opportunity. But they could be gathered into four main initiatives, two in the realm of economics and social welfare, and two in the realm of culture and foreign affairs.

The economic-welfare planks were premised, first, on addressing social welfare needs through accelerated economic growth and, second, on restoring the reputation of the party as a governing instrument by emphasizing spending cuts. The cultural-national planks were premised, first, on putting the party back on the side of "the moral and cultural values that most Americans share" and, second, on coupling this with a strong national defense for a dangerous world.

The Old Democracy, in the form of the issue activists who generated presidential campaigns and did the work of the party at state and local levels, could be characterized as strongly liberal on both these two main dimensions of public issues and policy conflict, with a particular attachment to the newer cultural and national concerns. The New Democrats now had a counterpart position. They could be characterized as self-consciously *moderate* on both dimensions, in full understanding that cultural and national moderation would seem especially controversial within the active Democratic Party of its day.

Although "The New American Choice" did not set out the social coalitions that went with these programs, its framers, and active members of the DLC generally, knew the content of these coalitions. For them, the party needed to escape the geographic locus of its reliable strength, the Northeast and industrial Midwest, for the growing West and South. It needed to escape the spatial locus of its reliable strength, urban America, for the growing suburbs. And it needed to escape the social locus of its reliable strength, the working class and the poor, for the growing middle class.

One other important change occurred while the DLC was abandoning its amorphous content in order to define the "New Democrat." Bill Clinton, incumbent governor of Arkansas, became its chairman in March 1990. Clinton had thought about a presidential run in 1988, and he was thinking even more seriously about one in 1992. The DLC chairmanship would provide him not just with a prepackaged program but also with organizational connections around the country. His actual campaign, both for the Democratic nomination and in the general election, would thus be the first successfully national campaign by a New Democrat, strictly defined. It would also be a classic example of the way intendedly strategic definitions become blended with the actual events and demands of practical politics, as well as of the way such a blend has to conform to the larger structure of the political order around it (Abramson, Aldrich, and Rohde 1994; Pomper et al. 1993; Nelson et al. 1993).

It was widely noted at the time that a weak field of alternative contenders for the Democratic nomination in 1992 facilitated Clinton's march to the nomination. At the point when entry decisions for the nominating contest had to be made, George Bush, an incumbent president fresh from victory in the Gulf War, looked extremely difficult to unhorse. Yet it was less widely noted that the character of this field meant that Clinton did not need to define himself diagnostically as a New Democrat, because he had no strong and serious opposition from an archetypal Old Democrat to overcome. Likewise, it was widely noted that the issue agenda of the campaign changed radically between the time of entry decisions and the time of actual delegate selection, with the Gulf War victory unceremoniously pushed aside by national economic recession. But it was again less widely noted that this led the Democratic nominating and electing campaigns to look like archetypal responses to the existing—the ongoing—political order.

In his own nominating campaign, Clinton was encouraged to concentrate on economics and social welfare and to slight cultural and national issues. From one side, the economic situation had deteriorated seriously, and *any* Democratic nominee had to demonstrate his potential for dealing with that issue. Yet the prominence of such a need also encouraged any potential nominee to sound very much like an Old Democrat. So did the related emergence of health care as the major social welfare issue of the campaign. All Democrats, Old and New, could be united on this, and it was quickly seized by the Clinton campaign as a central plank in its program.

From the other side, the Clinton nominating campaign was dogged by personal revelations and character attacks that almost undid him at the start. So the cultural dimension, when it was receiving emphasis from the environment, was doing so in a very unhelpful way. Clinton was nevertheless careful to eschew cultural progressivism, and he offered some specific programs with strong traditional themes: his promise of a National Service Corps, for example, and the one that would come back to haunt him, his promise to "end welfare as we know it." But an emphasis on economics and social welfare, plus the risk of harm from cultural and national issues, made Clinton look very much like the logical next link in a chain of Democratic nominees stretching back to 1968.

So, in essence, did the general election campaign. The Republicans needed to talk about foreign affairs in 1992, with a sitting president who had won the Gulf War (over both the Iraqis and the Democratic Congress). The Republicans also needed to talk about experience and character; a sitting governor of Arkansas could not possibly match the former and had not fared well on the latter. By contrast, the Democrats needed to talk about the economy—"Stupid!"—and they did so in their televised commercials, ad nauseam. They also needed to talk about social welfare, especially health care in a year when recession was canceling job-based insurance, and they did not fail to meet that imperative either.

At the end, the result looked very much like the standard product of the era of divided government, in all but one of its key details, rather than the opening embodiment of a New Democracy. Bill Clinton secured slightly less of the aggregate vote than Michael Dukakis had before him: 43.0 percent for Clinton, versus 45.6 percent for Dukakis. But in a year in which Ross Perot took 18.9 percent as an independent candidate, a slight decline was sufficient to carry thirty-two states and win 370 electoral votes for Clinton, versus ten states and 112 electoral votes for Dukakis.

That converted painful defeat into substantial victory, so it could hardly be argued that the coming of the first self-conscious New Democrat to the White House had been constrained by the thematics of the New Democracy. However, it was hard to find much impact from those thematics in the specifics of the vote, that is, in Clinton's social coalition. Clinton did improve the Democratic presidential vote in the South, but the West was simultaneously down, and both effects were marginal.

Exit polls echoed these results for the other target constituencies of the New Democracy. Thus Clinton ran a little better than Dukakis in the suburbs and small cities and a little worse in the big cities and rural areas. He ran a little better with the white middle class and a little worse with the white working class. He ran a little better than Dukakis among self-described moderates and a little worse among both conservatives and liberals. Yet these increments were tiny—one or two percentage points—and an analyst unconcerned with the New Democracy could be excused for not noticing. They might just as easily have been evidence that *any* campaign had to have some effect (Butler 1993).

The Coming of a Republican Revolution?

[The Blue Danube *plays in the background, under a legend proclaiming "The Clinton/McCurdy Crimefighter Follies," as rough-looking men in tutus waltz with each other.] Dance lessons. Midnight basketball. New restrictive gun controls. Just some of the ways Bill Clinton and Dave McCurdy think their new*

$30 billion crime bill will make our streets safer. No wonder the Oklahoma
Fraternal Order of Police endorsed Jim Inhofe for Senate. [Fade out around the
legend "Feel Safer Yet?"]
   —Republican commercial, 1994 general election campaign

Overall, the outcome of 1992 suggested nothing so much as an Old Democratic win within an established political order, with one big practical and theoretical exception. In practical terms, the fact that Clinton had won meant that split partisan control—formally divided government—would disappear. There would thus be unified partisan control of national government in the first Congress under President Clinton. Moreover, in theoretical terms, an election in which a sitting president is defeated is almost inevitably a referendum on his tenure, not an endorsement of any defined alternative. This was true even with the coming of Franklin Roosevelt in 1932; it could only be more true with the coming of Bill Clinton sixty years later. A New Democrat as president would thus get to put meaning into the 1992 election, and he would have unified partisan control of government with which to do it. And *that* would constitute the true definition of the New Democracy.

In hindsight, the fact that the practical definition of the New Democracy was destined to be hammered out in tandem with the formal definition of an alleged Republican revolution is curious. This fact is also ironic, since it suggests that the two developments were, in some way, inherently connected. But it would be several years before this connection—and the (related) way in which an ongoing political order would constrain both initiatives—could be seen by even the most perceptive analysts. In the meantime, the opening opportunity belonged to the New Democrats, not to any putative Republican revolutionaries. Theirs was the initial chance to shape a program that might appeal to a new social coalition. Theirs was also the immediate chance to set the symbolism that would alert the general public to what a New Democracy could imply.

This is not to deny that, as with the preceding election campaigns, there were established constraints that had to be blended into any New Democratic program. The most fundamental of these was the existing character of the congressional Democratic Party in a period of unified partisan control of Congress. Those in Congress were, of course, overwhelmingly Old Democrats. A majority had been in Congress before there even was a DLC.

A majority of the rest represented the preferences of the active Democratic Party: liberal on economic-welfare issues, and liberal on cultural-national issues as well.

The more evanescent but temporarily intense of these constraints arose from the election itself. Clinton was a minority president; 57 percent of the voting public had opted for someone else. Although his minority status would quickly fade—he was now the president, after all—it undercut any claims for a New Democratic mandate. More to the practical point for any fresh substantive focus, Perot had secured nearly 19 percent of the vote in a campaign focused largely on the federal budget deficit and deficit reduction. Within this, there were seventy-three congressional districts where Perot received more than a quarter of the total, and where successful congressmen might reasonably look on this as the single clearest policy mandate of the election.

Nevertheless, despite the emphasis of the Clinton campaign and the size of the Perot vote, the first act of the Clinton administration came not on economics but on culture. In his first official action, the president issued an executive order restoring the ability to conduct medical research on human fetal tissue—an obscure act for all but a narrow band of issue specialists. The opening symbolism of the new administration for the general public was set by another cultural proposal: to remove the ban on active homosexuals in the military. Argument over lifting this ban would dominate the first two weeks of the new administration and erupt intermittently for months thereafter, generating conflict and headlines out of all proportion to any numerical impact. Along the way, major congressional figures who were also self-conscious New Democrats, especially Sam Nunn of Georgia, chairman of the Senate Foreign Relations Committee, were evidently embarrassed (Towell 1993a, 1993b).

In contrast, two major policy initiatives with great potential impact, the real legislative agenda of the early Clinton presidency, were also launched shortly thereafter, and each again represented at least the temporary triumph of the established Democracy. The first of these initiatives derived from a fiscal choice, between economic stimulus (Old Democratic) and deficit reduction (New Democratic). The second derived from a social welfare choice, between health care (Old) and welfare reform (New).

Between the first pair, the economic stimulus package won out and was announced immediately. Between the second, the health care package won out and was sent to a commission under the direction of none other than the first lady. The first of these choices was justified on the grounds of campaign thematics plus electoral demand. The second was justified on the grounds that it was nearly impossible to do two large and complex policy proposals during one Congress, and health care represented the greater electoral mandate. It was also much easier to develop support for health care than for welfare reform out of the existing Democratic Party.

This second choice was to become a long, slow political agony for most of the main players. The first, by contrast, ran into immediate trouble. Although the economy appeared to have turned the corner, the fiscal deficit, augmented by recession, was continuing to grow. As a result, congressional supporters for the choice of economic stimulus over deficit reduction proved to be in short supply. Republicans had never been invited to participate in the development of either program: the Democratic congressional leadership wanted to make these packages the obvious product of unified party control, and the new president had never known the need to consult a Republican minority. Yet a substantial minority of *Democrats* insisted on giving priority to deficit reduction, with economic stimulus (if any) to follow. As a result, a significant package for deficit reduction would emerge by summer, and a significant package for economic stimulus would never really emerge at all. As a final result, the middle-class tax cut—another rhetorical staple of the election campaign, and one that also might have been taken to represent electoral demand—was sent quietly away (Mills 1992; Clinton's Bold Gamble 1993; Clinton Budget 1993; Angst of Victory 1993).

In any case, the new administration had, in passing, set out its policy stance for all to see: sharply liberal on cultural-national issues, and clearly liberal on economic-welfare issues too. By late summer, administration strategists had themselves come to focus on this perceived stance—their initial self-portrait—and had begun to try to turn and retailor it, shifting back strongly toward the New Democratic agenda. Yet at this point, the main vehicle for that shift, the North American Free Trade Agreement (NAFTA), brought difficulties of its own. NAFTA was a quintessential New Democratic program; of that there was no doubt. But ironically, the president was destined to be successful on it in ways that did not ultimately clarify the New Democratic message but further alienated him from his own congressional party.

Despite being a classic New Democratic program, NAFTA might have been ducked by the new administration had it not already acquired substantial diplomatic momentum by the time Clinton took office. Foreign trade—

with its free-trade versus protectionism cleavage—had long been an issue that crosscut the two parties. Nevertheless, the New Deal had brought free trade into the national policy consensus, and the free-trade wing of each party had remained dominant into the 1970s.

By the 1990s, each party still possessed two wings on the issue. But now, the Republicans were clearly the party of free trade, and the Democrats were just as clearly the party of protectionism—to the point where most of the House leadership worked actively against the president on his own bill. In perhaps his finest leadership and lobbying effort, Clinton managed, in spite of it all, to take much of the remaining southern Democracy into a unified Republican camp and defeat a solid majority of his own party nationwide (Cloud 1992, 1993a; NAFTA Crucible 1993).

This was the great New Democratic triumph of the first Clinton Congress. Moreover, it was a cultural-national triumph of exactly the sort that the New American Choice Resolutions had promised. Yet its symbolic role came largely as a corrective to what had preceded it on cultural-national conflicts in the Clinton administration, and it set the administration squarely against the largest organized interest in its coalition, namely, organized labor. Moreover, its gains here were destined to be neutralized in the longer run by the fate of the Omnibus Crime Bill a year later.

At the same time, a New Democratic triumph on NAFTA meant that Old Democrats, both in Congress and in the country, had not gotten the fiscal stimulus program they desired; instead, they got a program they detested: NAFTA. Finally, and even more to the partisan point, by the time Congress reconvened in the new year, there was a third clear programmatic alternative emerging—no symbolic confusion on this one—through which *Republicans* hoped, and some expected, to brush aside the New Democracy and attract the true majority coalition of the future.

This program would be a formal party product, from the Republican National Committee in coordination with the National Republican Congressional Committee. It would be aimed directly and self-consciously at the midterm election of 1994, and it would intend to provide a comprehensive and consistent alternative to the Clinton program. To that end, it would be strongly conservative on both economics and culture. But its real purpose, as much as anything else, was to suggest that the Republicans were a coherent and prepared alternative to the fumbling Democratic incumbents.

The document embodying all these approaches came to be called the "Contract with America," and even though few members of the American public ever knew what was being contracted, all Republican candidates for the House and some of those for the Senate were at least exposed to it. A total of 367 actually signed it (Gillespie and Schellas 1994; Barbour 1996). Surely most of these, too, thought of the contract as a device for symbolizing their seriousness of purpose and readiness to govern. But for their incipient leader, Newt Gingrich of Georgia, the House minority whip, it represented substantially more. The "Contract with America" represented the ascendance of Gingrich and his allies within the congressional Republican Party, and he would actually get the chance to pursue its implementation. If Bill Clinton was the "poster boy" for the New Democracy, Newt Gingrich was the counterpart for any Republican revolution. As such, the story of postwar politics might as easily have been hung on Gingrich's career as on Clinton's.

In programmatic terms, Gingrich was a founding member of the Conservative Opportunity Society, a counterpart to the Democratic Leadership Council as a key formative influence on new Republican policy thinking. In coalitional terms, he was a central actor in the rise of a southern Republican Party, which ended the "solid South" of the old order. He was also a committed devotee of technological developments, including the use of public television to put out a sharpened House Republican message—quintessential tactics for the new politics. Finally, he had the audacity to aspire to the House Speakership, at a time when neither the Democrats nor his own party would have seen this option as either practical or attractive.

In opposition to any Clinton legacy, then, the Republican Party in 1994 carefully tested a set of propositions for majority attraction or interest-group mobilization, and these came out as the "Contract with America." Their roots in the Conservative Opportunity Society meant that this was, first and foremost, a sharpened message on economics, on the generalized virtues of capitalism and free enterprise. To that end, there were clear economic-welfare planks: a balanced budget amendment and line-item veto, tax cuts for families, fairness for senior citizens, rollback of government regulation, and creation of jobs. Yet there were also clear cultural-national planks: stopping violent criminals, strengthening families and protecting our kids, strong national defense, and congressional term limits. And there were, of course, planks joining the two: welfare reform and commonsense legal reforms. None would have been mistaken for anything other than the consistent conservative approach. Together, they contrasted completely with the early Clinton program.

It was, however, two other policy conflicts, real legislative conflicts with concrete policy outcomes, that set the substantive context for the 1994 election and helped forge the choice for its voters: health care and criminal justice. Each would be disastrously unhappy for congressional Democrats, albeit in nearly opposite ways. But even for voters who missed one or the other of these policy outcomes, they would also, together, establish a "competence context." This was not a result that an incumbent congressman desired, and the situation was only made worse by a large and ongoing scandal involving congressional paychecks and the congressional bank, a scandal that almost inevitably focused on the majority party.

The Clinton administration hardly turned this contextual agenda over to the Republicans without a fight: the administration could read the same polls that encouraged the drafters of the "Contract with America." In response, by the summer of 1994, it had begun a serious correction aimed at bringing New Democratic themes back to the fore. Health care was in deep and obvious trouble, but administration strategists continued to seek compromises aimed at delivering at least some new health care benefits to the general public. That covered the economic-welfare dimension, and if these were Old Democratic benefits, they seemed sure to prove popular. Moreover, the other issue at the center of institutional politicking was quintessentially New Democratic. Indeed, the Omnibus Crime Bill was tailored to reflect the New Democracy, overall and line by line. That covered the cultural-national dimension, and its intended thematics looked unproblematic. But this time, it was the politics of implementing them that would go badly awry (Rubin 1994a, 1994b; Idelson 1994, 1995; Masci 1994).

Analysts would generate whole volumes (and many of them) on the fate of the Clinton health care project. Those most sympathetic would assign this fate to a gross imbalance in fund-raising and lobbying, and gross imbalance there certainly was. Those less sympathetic would focus on Democratic ineptness: a program that could not have been passed, in its time, even in countries more inherently sympathetic than the United States, developed in a manner that built the coalition against it rather than the coalition for it. But here, the point is merely that the president gambled on securing some outcome with which to go to the American public, rather than on using the issue to attack the Republican Party. In the end, he was left with neither a policy nor an issue.

All this might still have come together to produce a different electoral context, or at least a neutralized context in partisan terms, had the Omnibus

Crime Bill played out as administration strategists intended. Crime had been a leading issue with the general public throughout 1994—it topped the *New York Times* poll more often than any other—and both parties hoped to benefit from a focus on criminal justice. If much of the particular substance of the president's approach was classic New Democracy, polls suggested (and had already been used to test) that its main provisions had general public support. Yet in the process of bringing it up and putting it at the center of his legislative program, Clinton, rather than harvesting any latent popularity, was to be whipsawed on the issue instead.

Conservative Republicans attacked parts of the bill as too apologetic, too concerned with criminals rather than their victims. Liberal Democrats attacked parts of it as too punitive, as stigmatizing their very constituencies. And moderate Republicans initially refused to come to the aid of a proposal on which they had not been consulted. By the time a bill succeeded, with moderates wooed back on board and liberals "bought" through new divisible benefits, any impression of presidential leadership had been dissipated. And the stock Republican portrait of another Democratic bill—culturally liberal and full of pork—had been successfully painted.

The verdict in the tally that really mattered, in the general election six weeks later, was devastating. In the Senate, Republicans gained and Democrats lost a net of 8 seats, swinging the balance from 56–44 Democratic to 52–48 Republican, before Richard Shelby, Democratic senator from Alabama, switched parties to make it 53–47. In the House, Republicans gained (and Democrats lost) a net of 53 seats, swinging the balance from 258–176 Democratic to 229–205 Republican (Shafer 1998a; Hames 1995). The details beneath these summary numbers were even more disastrous.

To constitute their net gain of eight in the Senate, the Republicans lost no previously held seats and picked off eight previously Democratic ones. To constitute their net gain of fifty-three in the House, all 165 Republican incumbents were reelected, and the party picked up thirteen of seventeen open seats and another fifty-one from Democratic incumbents. All the usual subpatterns were still present in these details. That is, open seats were more likely to shift than were those with incumbents; among incumbents, freshmen were more likely to lose than were seniors; among seniors, those in districts carried by the other party for president in 1992 were more likely to lose than were those in same-party districts. Yet for 1994, these constituted only a modest firewall against a raging Republican conflagration.

The Era of Divided Government Redux

We're back.
—Legend on a Republican T-shirt issued after the 1994 election,
    showing an elephant lumbering up the steps of the Capitol

The composite result was decisive. Recapturing the Senate would have been pleasant enough, of course. But now the House had been recaptured too, for the first time since 1952—or really for the first time without a successful Republican president at the head of the ticket since 1946, the year of Bill Clinton's birth. However, the same rule would apply to Speaker Newt Gingrich and his Republican Congress in 1995 and 1996 as had applied to President Clinton and his Democratic administration in 1993 and 1994. That is, the Republican revolution, to date, was largely a repudiation of what the New Democracy had turned out to be. Only now could it achieve its actual policy meaning, along with its appropriate social coalition, through the policy leadership that followed. Yet here, at least, there was a distinctive difference.

The New Democrats had possessed their "New American Choice Resolutions," and their unofficial leader, DLC chairman Bill Clinton, had been duly elected. But the results of the 1992 election blew them otherwise off course, and the character of the Old Democracy went a long way toward keeping them there. Similarly, a huge new cohort of successful Republicans had its "Contract with America," and their unofficial leader, Speaker Newt Gingrich of the newly Republican House of Representatives, had also come to power, or at least to office. Yet the results of the 1994 election had no immediate—or rather, immediately disturbing—implications for pursuit of the "Contract." Moreover, that huge influx of new "Contract"-signing members joined a Republican residuum whose members had never had to rally themselves behind any alternative program of their own. The result was that the "Contract with America" did indeed become the agenda for the 104th Congress.

At first, this fact drew analytic comment out of sheer wonder that a national policy agenda could be driven from the House of Representatives. Yet for six months, through the summer of 1995, the "Contract" became the single simplest summary of the agenda for national politics. By some measures, its subsequent success was also phenomenal. Each of the fifteen major bills from the "Contract" package achieved a floor vote in the House within the promised 100 days. All but the proposed constitutional amendment establishing term limits for Congress actually passed, and that exception would have required a two-thirds majority.

Admittedly, the Senate was more dilatory. Fewer Republican senatorial candidates had signed on initially, fewer Republican victors were new to the Senate, and many senators came from states where large areas had voted against House candidates aligned with the "Contract." The president was an even more mixed respondent. He was, for example, happy to sign the line-item veto for the budget, willing to go along with the bar on unfunded mandates, but opposed to many aspects of product liability reform and to tort reform in general.

On the one hand, then, the final concrete product of this agenda, signed into law and implemented, remained much less than Republican revolutionaries had dared to hope. On the other, in terms of seizing and altering the agenda for conflict in American politics, their initial triumph remained overwhelming, to the point where Clinton had to remind a press conference that "the Constitution gives me relevance, the power of our ideas gives me relevance. . . . The president is relevant here." Republican congresspeople and senators were entitled to go home for the summer recess and look forward to completing their revolution in 1996, adding a Republican presidency to their control of Congress and restoring unified government to their side of the partisan aisle (House GOP 1994; Cassata 1995; Ceaser and Busch 1997, 42).

And then, after the 1995 summer recess, it all went strikingly wrong. In fact, it all went strikingly wrong within a few weeks over Christmas and New Year's of 1995–1996. The turnaround began when congressional Republicans returned to Washington and took on a committed effort to solve, not just ameliorate, the problem of the deficit. This meant that there had to be real and substantial spending cuts, which meant that major welfare entitlement programs, especially Medicaid, Medicare, and Social Security, had to be sharply restricted in their projected growth and, ideally, trimmed. To this end, Republicans were willing to draw up a federal budget that would accomplish those goals. And they were willing to shut down the federal government temporarily, rather than pass a continuing resolution, if the president would not sign this or some acceptable compromise version.

The first shutdown came in November 1995, the second came in December–January, and the line from there to the November 1996 election ran relentlessly. The Republicans had taken a clear gamble: that these initiatives would bring them major economic-welfare credit for "fixing" the deficit, along with major competence credit for actually getting a huge job done. The Democrats, in response—and here, the president *was* the highly relevant figure—described those actions as menacing some social insurance programs directly and menacing them all indirectly through payment delays during the shutdown, simultaneously "proving" the irresponsibility of the protagonists. Perhaps those who desired to complete the Republican revolution could have survived this gamble going wrong once, but they could not survive it a second time, and the presidential preference lines tell the story (Shafer 1997, figs. 1, 2).

Throughout 1995, the early presidential preference line ("If the election were held today, for whom would you vote?") matched President Clinton with the Republican front-runner, Senate Majority Leader Bob Dole of Kansas. Although Clinton was universally known and Dole largely unknown in spite of a long, high-profile life in politics, Dole actually tracked Clinton closely across this period, occasionally surpassing him. Clinton then took the lead during the key period of the second governmental shutdown in late 1995 and early 1996, and the lines diverged sharply thereafter. They would never be close again. The Republicans had once more been successfully painted, as they had throughout the New Deal era and into the era of divided government, as stiff conservatives on economics and social welfare. In truth, however, they themselves had successfully pushed that dimension—and hence that perception—to prominence.

The White House still needed to do two major things by way of a response. It needed to keep the economic-welfare dimension in the face of potential voters, and it needed to protect the president's flank on the cultural-national alternative, the one that had done his party so much damage in 1994. The latter was largely accomplished through a return to New Democratic rhetoric and themes. This included small things, such as endorsement of putting the nation's schoolchildren in uniforms. It also included large ones, such as the much-ballyhooed announcement in the president's State of the Union Address that "the era of big government is over." But it had one major legislative element as well. In the spring of 1996, Clinton signed the National Welfare Reform Act, thereby returning to the other priority of his first Congress, the road not taken when he had opted for health care. The resulting bill gave more power back to the states, reduced overall spending to a greater extent, and was far tougher in personal eligibility and time limits than any plan he might have signed during that first Congress, thanks to the aggressive drive of the new Republican majority. But sign it—and claim it—he did (Katz 1996a, 1996b).

The Democratic election campaign then did everything it could to keep economic-welfare concerns at the center of public discussion. In this, the president enjoyed some ironic advantages. Because Clinton had seemed so much at risk of not being reelected during the period in 1995 when Democratic challengers would have had to come forward, none did. As a result, he could spend the entire spring and summer, while the Republicans contested their nomination, doing generic advertising and then specifically attacking Republican front-runner Dole. Worse, Dole, as a comparative moderate, had to emphasize his conservatism on the way to the nomination, and that was what the Democratic attack ads were emphasizing too. In a final irony, whereas Clinton had been the unpopular national leader of 1994, targeted by Republicans as their key demon, it was Gingrich who assumed that mantle for 1996, targeted by Democrats in an amazing manner. Both the generic ads and the pointed attacks on emerging nominee Dole hammered away at "the Dole-Gingrich budget" and "the Dole-Gingrich Republicans," though the actual Republican ticket would be, of course, Dole-Kemp.

In any case, the 1996 presidential outcome was remarkably parallel to—nearly a replay of—the 1992 outcome. The two-party vote in 1992, Clinton over Bush, had been 54 to 46 percent. The two-party vote in 1996, Clinton over Dole, was 55 to 45 percent. The electoral vote in 1992, Clinton over Bush, had been 370 to 168. The electoral vote in 1996, Clinton over Dole, was 379 to 159 (Abramson, Aldrich, and Rohde 1998; Pomper et al. 1997; Nelson et al. 1997; Ceaser and Busch 1997). Yet two other things were strikingly different this time, one of them insistently evident and the second easy to miss.

The insistent fact was that the Republicans had retained control of Congress after their success of 1994, the first time they had done this since 1926–1928. They did, however, lose a net of nine seats in the House, thereby surrendering the conventional gains for a winning president but, crucially, not surrendering enough seats to lose the Speakership. And they actually gained two seats in the Senate while Clinton was being solidly reelected. The fact that no one emphasized at the time but that everyone would soon have cause to notice was that, unlike the situation in either 1992 or 1994, both these partisan successes—Democrats in the presidency and Republicans in

Congress—came without any alleged program for creating a new partisan majority, much less a new partisan era.

The unified Democratic control of national government that followed the elections of 1992 had swept away the surface pattern of divided government that had essentially characterized the previous quarter century: Republicans controlling the presidency, Democrats controlling Congress. It had then been replaced by the opposite model, perhaps temporarily, in 1994: Democrats controlling the presidency, Republicans controlling Congress. But the argument that this might be only a transition to unified Republican control of government, or even to a Republican revolution, had now been dealt a serious blow, by confirmation of the opposite pattern of divided government from that which had preceded the arrival of the New Democrats in the White House.

More to the practical point, this time, neither party came (back) into office with a new program allegedly aimed at creating a new partisanship. There were no "New, Revised American Choice Resolutions." There was no "Contract with America, Part Two." There was only a campaign in which Democrats attacked Republicans on economic-welfare issues, especially protection of major (and existing) social insurance programs, and in which Republicans attacked Democrats on cultural-national issues, especially "character" and its links to drug use, sexual immorality, and, above all, personal dishonesty. Neither of these campaigns provided any basis for major programmatic initiatives, and in fact, there would be none.

That left the 1998 election to introduce any major remaining twists to the partisan legacy of the Clinton presidency. Yet what was inherent in electoral positioning for 1998 was just a shifting restatement of familiar themes. So what resulted, perhaps inevitably, was just a fresh embodiment of an ongoing political order. As 1998 opened, the White House announced that this would be the year the president rescued Social Security by putting it on a financially stable basis for an enduring period and expanded health care by shifting the definitions that governed existing programs: classic economic-welfare initiatives. Republicans countered that this would be the year *they* reformed the Internal Revenue Service in particular and then moved on to systematic tax reform in general: classic Republican ripostes on that same economic-welfare dimension.

By spring, these putative initiatives had been displaced by partisan skirmishing over regulation of the burgeoning health maintenance organization (HMO) sector, with Republicans consciously trying not to cede a major social welfare concern, and over regulation of smoking, especially teenage smoking, one of the main cultural issues on which Democrats already had the majority position. By summer, these too were receding from the national agenda, displaced by partisan conflict over the first fiscal *surplus* in more than a generation. Each side traced that surplus to its first election—of a Democratic president in 1992, of a Republican Congress in 1994—and each circled back to argue for its archetypal response: Democrats using the surplus to reinvest in Social Security, Republicans returning the surplus to its "owners" as tax cuts.

By fall, finally, all the foregoing had been displaced by White House scandal and an impending impeachment, another cultural issue that was never a Democratic asset but brought intrinsic risks to its Republican handlers as well. With many policy questions raised but none resolved, and with a tricky moral and procedural issue on the front burner, the party combatants needed to somehow give the appearance of nonpartisanship. CNN called the election "hard to read" (CNN 1998; Election 1998; Greenblatt 1998).

Yet in the end, it was less obscure than indecisive, less the embodiment than the postponement of any new partisan patterns. The first two elections of the Clinton presidency, in 1992 and 1994, were characterized by partisan upheaval and two sharply divergent visions of the partisan future. The second two elections, in 1996 and 1998, were characterized by a remarkable stasis. Or rather, what was inherent in the outcome of 1998 was that same mix of surface fluidity amid stable underlying contours that had characterized the era of divided government since its beginning.

In the immediate aftermath, commentators rushed to award victory to the Democrats. Part of this perception, despite inconsequential shifts in the actual vote, was the result of accidental collusion between the two political parties. Republicans had hoped for a large win and expected a moderate one; Democrats had feared a moderate loss but hoped for a small one. When the result was no change in the Senate and a Democratic *gain* in the House, that result confounded both expectations. Moreover, in the face of several scholarly benchmarks that had found their way into popular analysis, any gain at all was effectively magnified. These benchmarks included an alleged "six-year itch," in which the party of the president suffered substantial losses at its second midterm, along with the more reliable "surge and decline," in which that party always lost seats in the midterm election in comparison to the preceding presidential election. (Labeling of the "six-year itch" is often credited to Kevin Phillips [1998], though he explicitly turned to other analytic yardsticks for interpretations in advance of the 1998 elections. The notion of "surge and decline" is rooted in an article of the same name by Angus Campbell [1960].)

Objectively, precious little happened. In the Senate, Democrats picked up three seats previously held by Republicans, and Republicans picked up three seats previously held by Democrats. The outcome, of course, was a net of zero. In the House, Republicans lost and Democrats gained a net of five seats, an outcome tied for the second-lowest change in postwar midterms. It occasioned no shift in overall partisan control. Yet the main points for a partisan legacy from the Clinton presidency lay effectively elsewhere. From one side, this aggregate outcome meant that any Republican revolution had certainly stalled. From the other side, its underpinnings represented, if anything, the resurgence of the Old Democracy.

For the Republicans, control of Congress was ultimately maintained. This meant that divided government—split partisan control—was ultimately maintained as well. Although it had been sixty years since an out-party lost seats at the midterm, such a loss in 1998 was conditioned by a specific context, one in which that party had picked up fifty-three seats at the previous midterm and surrendered only nine in the presidential election that followed. Moreover, these two putative exceptions were otherwise strikingly dissimilar. The previous exception (in 1934) was a major aftershock of the New Deal era, which had completed its arrival only two years before. Its current counterpart (in 1998) was a minor adjustment to the era of divided government, born thirty years previously.

For the Democrats, their triumph, though real enough to cause House Republicans to shuffle their leadership, was actually elsewhere. So was its message. Widely expected to lose seats by means of a sharp drop in voter turnout—the usual midterm fall, compounded by an unproductive legislative session and the emergent White House scandal—the party saw neither this exaggerated decline nor its associated loss. Yet here, for a Clinton legacy, the point was that the interest groups that mobilized to support a last-minute blitz by President and Mrs. Clinton, along with the constituencies they targeted—namely, organized labor and racial minorities—were themselves mainstays of the Old Democracy. If they appeared to deserve real credit for stemming what even late polls suggested would be the expected fall, their success really harked back to the partisan world *pre-Clinton*.

Partisan Continuity and Partisan Legacies

*Evidently the processes of political change proceed under the handicap of
considerable friction. Pre-existing party attachments may have a durability that
contributes to the lag. Men generally have a resistance to the salesmen of a new
order whose tasks of indoctrination are not the work of the day. A generation or so
may be required for one outlook to replace another.*
   —V. O. Key, Jr. (1959)

In the end, the partisan situation was effectively unchanged, leaving little
room for a Clinton legacy. Judged by its programmatic offerings or its social
coalitions, the year 1998 could have been the year 1988 or even 1968. At
bottom, the era of divided government merely continued. This was not to
deny that the Clinton presidency had been characterized—littered, really—
with specific partisan events of high individual drama. It had begun with
the defeat of an incumbent Republican president, the archetypal product of
an existing order, by means of a self-consciously new kind of Democrat,
atop the first real unified government in a generation. But that auspicious
beginning had been swept away within one Congress.

It was succeeded by an even more dramatic partisan event: the first
Republican capture of Congress for two generations. If any surprised analysts could have missed the fact, its products went on to bill themselves as
revolutionary. Yet this tide too crested within one Congress. Already by
1996, high partisan drama had folded back into an ongoing political order.
The *labels* had changed within this order. Now, a Democrat controlled the
presidency, while Republicans controlled Congress. But the underlying pattern, split partisan control of national government, obviously continued.

More important, the main elements underpinning its continuation were
not superficial, not just labels at all. The new politics, established in 1968,
continued because its basic substantive and structural underpinnings continued, undisturbed in their essence. The Democratic Party continued to be
the party perceived as best able to handle economic and welfare issues, and
these hardly went away in the shift from an old order to a new politics. The
Republican Party continued to be the party perceived as best able to handle
cultural and national issues, and these actually achieved a substantially
greater priority in the new politics than they had under the old order. The
general public, finally, found itself sitting to the right of the active Demo-

CHAPTER FOUR

We Are All Southern Democrats Now

The structure of American politics, the main factors that shaped politicking in the United States, became more complicated during the postwar years. And the same can be said for the issue context, the substance, of that politics. Nevertheless, structure and substance must be knit back together, into one comprehensible whole, if the changing dynamic of American politics is to be understood. A quick sketch of the contours of two postwar eras, the late New Deal era and the era of divided government, is essential to this effort. But the immersion of those contours in major modern policy conflicts is even more important to understanding the evolution of this dynamic. For our purposes, this means immersion in the budget fiasco of 1990, the battle for endorsement of the Gulf War, the deficit reduction fiasco of 1993, and the struggle over adoption of the North American Free Trade Agreement (NAFTA).

One strategy for such an effort is to begin with the social coalitions that characterized American politics across this period. From one side, these coalitions both shaped and were shaped by the central substantive concerns of their time. Different social groups preferred different outcomes on particular issues, so it was not possible to mobilize the same coalitions across all issues, much less to fasten all new issues on the same old coalitions. From the other side, these coalitions both were gathered by and energized the political parties, those key intermediaries of American politics that linked public wishes to governmental institutions. Again, some coalitions were more easily accommodated by one party, some by the other, just as one party or the other was more or less inherently stressed by various coalitional alternatives.

The Late New Deal Era

With one major exception, the two social coalitions characterizing American politics when the postwar period began were built along lines of social class (Sundquist 1973, chaps. 10–12; Ladd with Hadley 1975, chaps. 1–2). There was a blue-collar coalition, which found its institutional home in the national Democratic Party and comprised working-class Americans generally, the poor, plus a few other religious and ethnic minorities. And there was a white-collar coalition, which found its institutional home in the national Republican Party and comprised middle-class Americans generally, along with northern and western farmers. The New Deal—the coming of the welfare state—had been responsible for changing an old politics in which these coalitions were primarily sectional and cultural into a new politics in which social class was their main organizing principle. Then, Democratic management of the pursuit of World War II kept these coalitions locked in place for the duration of the war.

The political parties on which these coalitions settled—as much through tactical opportunity and mutual discovery as through grand strategy—were actually at different places on what would become a common organizational continuum. The Democrats retained a number of the older big-city machines and managed to extend their operating procedures to the state level in some states, though much of the rest of the party had already given way to volunteer activist branches. The policy successes of the New Deal, especially its social insurance programs, actually further undermined old-fashioned party machinery, but the popularity of these programs was such that popular identification with the Democratic Party remained strong. Indeed, as other (and more Republican) identifiers passed out of society, the Democratic share of the general public continued to expand. Because the Democratic Party was still "where the action was," ambitious new-comers to politics continued to flow disproportionately into it as well.

The Republicans, by contrast, had not just been forced back into their core geographic areas by the policy successes of the New Deal and the newly enlarged Democratic coalition. They were forced back, within these areas, on established party officeholders, so that the formal structure of the official party was simultaneously more consequential than that of the Democrats and more skeletal, that is, in possession of fewer regular party workers. Those Republican officials who had remained in place, often through the depression and World War II, were still principally motivated by opposition to the New Deal. A successful standard-bearer like Dwight Eisenhower could temporarily finesse this; a disastrous standard-bearer like Barry Goldwater would exaggerate it instead.

The greatest exception to all the above, an exception that would prove pivotal at any number of points across the postwar years, was the American South. The New Deal did add social welfare issues to southern politics; indeed, the main social insurance programs of the New Deal were overwhelmingly popular there. But this remained an overlay. The New Deal did not bring class-based coalitions to this region, and it remained monolithically Democratic, as it had been since the American Civil War. In such a world, the old courthouse rings of the rural South continued to hold great organizational sway. Moreover, the presence of a total class structure in one party gave the resulting southern Democrats a much more moderate cast than their northern or western counterparts. Thus, they would have been a reliably dissident wing of the national Democratic Party even if it had not been for the existence of explicit—legal—racial segregation, which was also an organizing principle of the southern Democracy.

Together, these social coalitions, along with their issue preferences and organizational principles, gave a distinctive pattern to partisan politicking, most easily seen through its electoral incarnation. This pattern would unravel slowly across the postwar years (Campbell et al. 1960, 1966). Politics thus remained centered on social welfare issues, on attempts to ensure a full-employment economy and to add the "missing pieces" of the New Deal, the ones that had been enunciated but not implemented in the 1930s. It was not that such policies necessarily carried the day, year in and year out. It was just that conflict over their *substance* was a reliable electoral benefit to the national Democratic Party. The Republicans did, however, benefit from a modest but consistent perception that they were better at handling foreign affairs. The Democrats never consciously conceded this issue realm during these years, so there was no great policy difference between the parties. Yet when foreign policy managed to displace social welfare at the center of public concern, especially when this was coupled with the corruption scandals that seemed endemic to long-running partisan dominance, the Republicans could disrupt established Democratic control.

All this was powerfully buttressed by the place of the great interest groups, of corporate business and, especially, organized labor. While the New Deal was being implemented, labor was becoming the great organized interest supporting the national Democratic Party. The immediate postwar years were then the high point of its aggregate numbers, its geographic reach, and its economic resources. Indeed, labor organization often went so far as to substitute for the declining machinery of the official Democratic Party. The organizational counterpart to this within the Republican Party was not really corporate business but small business, and a hostility to both social welfare programs and the taxes necessary to fund them remained substantively central to small-business sectors of the party. Nevertheless, corporate Republicans, through the provision of "blue-ribbon" candidates and of financial support, played an important indirect role. Moreover, they were the organizational mainstay of any efforts to reach an accommodation with the substance of the New Deal.

Accordingly, when the corporate wing of the Republican Party found itself a presidential candidate who was self-evidently able to capitalize on foreign policy as an issue, as Eisenhower was, the coming of a Republican presidency also implied the coming of unified Republican control of national government. Corporate Republicans and their sympathizers, however, were not a main influence on Republican congressmen across the nation—their hearts belonged to the small-business wing—so that even under Eisenhower, a return to the politics of "rolling back the New Deal" quickly swept the Republican majority back out of Congress. More commonly, in any case, it was organized labor plus the regular Democratic Party that resolved their differences around a unifying candidate, most often through the aid of social welfare issues. And that candidate and his party then appeared to be the "natural" owners of government.

The Era of Divided Government

That arrangement—that interaction of substantive issues, social coalitions, and party structures—attenuated gradually as the postwar years passed. Yet despite its gradualist character, the end of this arrangement is easy to date. The election of 1964 was still a classic incarnation of the late New Deal order; the election of 1968 inaugurated what we have come to know as the era of divided government. Somewhere between these two elections, then, a set of cumulative structural changes and cumulative issue shifts produced a new political order. Its hallmark, uninterpretable at the time but diagnostic after the fact, was a partisan pattern: Republicans capture the presidency, without even threatening to capture Congress. But a new and much more complex set of social coalitions was really the heart of this change, once again linking—affecting and affected by—the substance of political issues from one side and the structure of political parties from the other (Ladd and Hadley 1973; Shafer and Claggett 1995).

Some things did not change. Social welfare issues continued to divide the parties in familiar ways, and they continued to divide them strongly. The public continued to support the main social insurance programs of Franklin Roosevelt's New Deal (unemployment insurance, Social Security), and that public went on to integrate new programs from Lyndon Johnson's Great Society (Head Start, Medicare) into this ongoing liberal consensus. Moreover, these economic and social welfare concerns continued to be the basis for party identification within the general public, so that economic and welfare liberals were Democrats, and economic and welfare conservatives were Republicans—and the Democratic Party remained the majority party in public affections.

What was different, then, was an increased polarization on issues of foreign affairs, additionally stressing the two party coalitions and cumulatively benefiting the Republicans overall. What was also different—even more different—was the arrival of a whole array of previously unpoliticized "cultural" issues dealing with the social character of American life: crime and punishment, educational policy, the public role of religion, child-rearing practices, abortion, public protest. All these gave life to a general concern that had previously seemed consensual and had largely been kept outside of politics.

In the case of foreign affairs, increased polarization, in the wake of the Vietnam War and as the Democratic Party pulled back from containment and anticommunism, emphasized tensions that had always been incipiently present in the two great social coalitions. Here, the liberal coalition on social welfare was not the same as—it was effectively unrelated to—the liberal (accommodationist) coalition on foreign affairs, just as the conservative coalition on social welfare was unrelated—effectively at right angles—to the conservative (nationalist) coalition on foreign affairs. As a result, when foreign affairs was the issue of concern, many welfare liberals, normally Democratic in their preferences, should have preferred (and did prefer) the *anti*welfare party, the Republicans.

This situation, noteworthy as it was, remained modest by comparison to the situation on the newly politicized cultural issues. Once again, the two policy coalitions in this issue realm, the liberal and the conservative coalitions, were strikingly different from the two counterpart coalitions on social welfare. Members of the liberal (progressive) coalition on these issues were as likely to be conservative as liberal on social welfare or economics generally. Conversely, members of the conservative (traditionalist) coalition on issues involving cultural values were as likely to be liberal as conservative on issues of social welfare or economics. The issue substance of American politics became, accordingly, much more complex.

This complexity did not appear to result principally from a polarization on the part of the general public, precipitating a new and crosscutting issue universe to challenge the political parties. Rather, it was structural changes within the political parties that generated a polarized and crosscutting set of *policy options* for the general public (Wilson 1963, 1973, chap. 6; Ware 1985). The Republican Party had actually moved earlier to adopt a modern party structure whereby the formal machinery was run by shifting networks of independent issue activists, motivated by intense but particular substantive concerns. Yet the Democratic Party too had come a long way down that road by the time of the 1968 elections. Initial attempts to see that the Democratic disasters of 1968 were not repeated then effectively dispossessed the residual incumbents of a formal hierarchy of party offices, incumbents who were also the final link to the preferences and principles of the late New Deal era.

In their place, again, came the independent issue activists, and it was this development that completed (and institutionalized) the new arrangement. Democratic activists were no longer much moved by the main issues that had created overall Democratic majorities in the public at large—namely, social welfare and especially social insurance issues. Instead, they were moved secondarily by foreign affairs and principally by cultural values. This, however, did not produce a new—and simple—polarization of American politics, one reflecting a sharply but simply altered social alignment, because it was not mirrored directly on the Republican side. There were new cultural and international activists in the Republican Party too, and they were uniformly conservative. But the old main motivation for internal Republican politics, of cutting taxes even if it meant cutting programs, remained the dominant theme for most Republican Party workers—remaining perfectly comfortable for the new cultural conservatives as well.

All this went a long way toward explaining electoral outcomes in the new political era (Shafer 1996, chap. 2). At least Republican presidents with Democratic Congresses were a logical product of a politics with conservative majorities on cultural values and foreign affairs and liberal majorities on social welfare and economics generally. The presidency could never escape these underlying issue cross-pressures, being nationally elected, and that fact alone vastly improved Republican prospects in the office. But the presidency was also an obvious policy focus for foreign affairs, as well as for cultural values, thanks to its great symbolic potential.

By contrast, Democratic majorities in the public at large could continue, thanks to a continuing social welfare liberalism. When there was unified partisan control of government, then, it was much more likely to be in Democratic hands. Yet even when there was not, a continuing social welfare liberalism could easily be registered in the main local agents of American politics, in its senators and especially in its congressmen. Moreover, most congressional districts were sufficiently homogeneous in social terms that cross-pressures from foreign affairs or cultural values did not reliably intrude and could be much less stressfully addressed when they did. Democratic Congresses, even in the absence of a Democratic president, remained the norm.

Once more, the American South required special attention within this overall matrix. On the one hand, and at long last, the South underwent tremendous economic development during the postwar years, bringing class politics (among other things) to the one region where this had been suppressed for a hundred years. Liberal Democrats—real, genuine, "northern" Democrats—appeared in its industrialized areas. Simultaneously, a real Republican Party—"national" Republicanism—appeared as well, aimed at winning and governing and not just at managing federal patronage. On the other hand, all this occurred while the rest of the nation was shifting from the late New Deal era to the era of divided government. Moreover, this shift would be particularly intense within the American South.

This was true in general terms, given that the South was reliably nationalist in foreign affairs and reliably and deeply traditionalist in cultural values. It was also true in specific and pointed terms, because in the South, the practices of legal segregation—practices reaching into every aspect of life—had to be forcibly dismantled. The challenge of national shifts in the partisan politics of these issues was intensified by continuing southern support for social insurance programs. And it was compounded, of course, by that long-running Democratic predominance, now being shattered and reorganized by economic development. As a result, whereas the rest of the nation was undergoing the kind of major political change that occurs perhaps once every half century, the South was undergoing two such changes at the same time.

The larger result, nationwide, was a partisan world in which Republican presidents facing Democratic Congresses became commonplace. It was a world where unified Democratic control of government was the most common partisan option. It was a world where discontent with a Democratic president could now reasonably be expressed by split partisan control in the other direction: a Democratic president facing a Republican Congress. And it was a world where the remaining option, unified Republican control, was surely back on the table. Nevertheless, these were not the crucial—the defining—characteristics of a new order. They were instead just manifestations of those defining characteristics, of which there were three: (1) stable and crosscutting policy preferences within the general public on the main issues of their time; confronted with (2) stable policy offerings from the two major parties, neither of which matched the overall national preferences; worked out through (3) shifting social coalitions at the grass roots, evolving into shifting party coalitions within national government.

Budgetary Politics in 1990

The same contours—for social coalitions, their issue substance, and the associated party structure—may seem more difficult to isolate for institutional (as opposed to electoral) politicking. Institutions add their own specific twists to the political process, and individual pieces of legislation reflect underlying influences in ways specific to their particular substance. Moreover, the mechanics of legislating normally involves *compromises* across several institutions and even across several issues. Nevertheless, ongoing social coalitions do not disappear. Nor do continuing public majorities in general issue areas. Nor, finally, do the ways in which one or the other—or both—political parties institutionalize social coalitions and issue positions.

Moreover, there is a category of political conflicts, almost always major, that is especially good at stripping away the surface twists and turns of institutional politicking to reveal the ongoing contours of a political order. These are the handful of major issues in any period that become central to politics not because they are chosen by major actors—not by presidents, senators, or congressmen, nor by the governing or opposition party—but because they are forced in by the environment. They are thus policy priorities of a substantial sort, demanding attention from most major actors. Yet they are, by definition, not initiated by the tactical choices of any of the main players. They therefore ought to be particularly good at eliciting grander and deeper influences, influences to which these political tacticians must adapt but that they have been unable to shape in the first instance.

There were, in fact, two such issues (and crises) in the George Bush Sr. presidency, in the time between the end of one election campaign and the beginning of another: the budget conflict of 1990, and the Gulf War. Each was, albeit in different ways, very much "forced in" by the world outside of ongoing policy conflict. In addition, each reinforces half the lessons of an electoral analysis of the era of divided government. Together, then, they make the same composite points in an institutional context. Between them, the one that history is likely to forget, the budget fiasco of 1990, would actually prove to be the more accurate harbinger of the electoral conflicts of 1992.

Before that, however, the election of 1988 had been an archetypal contest for the era of divided government in almost the opposite sense (Elshtain 1989; Ladd 1989). That is, the environment had imposed no obvious issue priorities on the campaign, and the two parties had been free to offer orthodox versions of their standard themes. Not surprisingly, the Republicans focused on foreign affairs and cultural values, while the Democrats countered with social welfare and economic benefit. This was probably enough to produce a stereotypical outcome—a Republican president facing a solidly Democratic Congress—especially given that the Republicans hit very hard on cultural values and benefited from generally good economic conditions, while the Democrats came late to their main social welfare themes and blurred their usual message on group identifications. In any case, the outcome was truly stereotypical: a solid Republican win for Bush as president, with an actual gain by the Democrats of one Senate and three House seats in Congress.

The policy story of the first year of the resulting Bush administration was not characterized by major issues arguably forced in by the environment outside of national government. But at the end of the first financial quarter of 1990, Bush got the bad, private word from his economic policy advisers: the economy was slowing, and there was no longer any hope for growing out of the budget deficit. That was bad enough, but a growing deficit in a slowing economy also suggested that the budget-cutting provisions of the Gramm-Rudman-Hollings Act would automatically kick in

later that year, inflicting true financial chaos on the government. Nevertheless, in an era of split partisan control, even edging away from his promise of
"no new taxes" proved fraught with difficulties for the president (Elving
1990; Rasky 1990; Rosenbaum 1990; Hayer 1990a, 1990b, 1990c). Inevitably, there was no active benefit in cutting programs or in raising taxes, much
less in doing both. But with each party in control of one branch of national
government, each needed to get the other to take the necessary (and un-
pleasant) actions first, so as not to risk paying all the costs and perhaps
ending up with no product anyway.

In late April, then, Bush had his budget director, Richard Darman, call
for White House–congressional talks on a new budget agreement. Bush
himself remained quiet, however, and congressional leaders effectively ignored the offer. Two weeks later, in mid-May, Bush personally weighed in
and called for a White House–congressional summit, with no preconditions. The result—resonant for students of social coalitions, along with their
issue substance and party linkages, but strangely anomalous to most other
analysts—was not shock among the president's personal supporters nor
shock among members of the opposition party. Rather, the shock came
within his own party in Congress.

For presidential Republicans, the logic was inescapable. In order to
continue to control the presidency within the current political order, they
needed to be sure that a presidential campaign did not center on economic
concerns and social welfare matters. Yet a sharp economic downturn was
apparently on the way, absent a substantial policy impact, and this meant an
automatic emphasis on exactly these matters. Bush was fully prepared to
move away from the "no new taxes" pledge, if it guaranteed an escape.

For congressional Democrats, the logic was equally attractive. In order
to avoid automatic cuts to those programs that, after all, sustained their
majority in Congress in the era of divided government, but especially because they might actually shift expenditures from defense to social programs and thus secure clear policy gains, they needed to seize this particular
(and probably transient) opportunity. To that end, the Democratic congressional leadership was fully prepared to join President Bush.

For congressional Republicans, however, the logic was radically different. Neither economic moderation nor social welfare protection had
anything to offer them; what they needed to present on this dimension was
the promise of holding the line on taxes. Naturally, then, they were out-
raged. One hundred Republican congressmen, speaking for an even larger

collection of Republican congressional candidates, signed a letter scolding the president and asserting that any tax increase was "unacceptable."

The dilemma—the box—within which House Republicans in particular found themselves deserves emphasis. Being ideologically committed to the minority side of the energizing issue for party politics in their institution, they had long since resigned themselves, strategically, to making incremental additions (and avoiding incremental losses) to an institutionalized minority. Within that context, any White House deal offered only the latter—further incremental losses—and they responded accordingly. Despite this response, White House negotiators, sometimes including the president himself; Democratic congressional leaders from both houses; and the Republican congressional leadership began an ongoing series of discussions on some grand compromise to control the deficit.

These talks continued throughout the summer, without the elusive deal. While they were grinding on, Iraq invaded Kuwait. For the budget summit, this invasion, by making defense cuts more difficult and by threatening the economy further, suggested that only the actual arrival of a Gramm-Rudman "sequester," by then estimated at a cut of more than $100 billion, would force a deal. In anticipation of precisely that, the negotiators withdrew to Andrews Air Force Base in mid-September and actually produced a package, one that was in fact a major victory for the Republican White House. It sustained defense expenditures; it increased Medicare fees; and it raised only nuisance taxes, along with the gasoline tax.

Remarkably, despite a comprehensive leadership deal, the measure failed in the House (where new revenue measures must originate), and it failed ignominiously: 179 to 254. Perhaps more remarkably, only the dissident faction of the majority party, the southern Democrats, supported it, by a vote of 45 to 38. Still more remarkably, it was House Republicans who pulled the plug on the entire deal, in the ultimate tribute to their commitment to the minority position on economic welfare, but in a response fully consistent with a continuing and institutionalized political order. They voted no, 71 to 105. In return, northern Democrats, who had never liked anything about the proposed package, joined House Republicans to kill the whole thing.

And at that point, congressional Democratic leaders, with impending Gramm-Rudman cuts looming as an aid to their efforts, seized control of the process. The president fell back to a reactive position, and Senate leaders sought to broker a deal, one that might be sold to more liberal colleagues in the House and to a more conservative president. If there had to be some package to contain the deficit (and shore up a Republican president), and if House Republicans would not cooperate, then congressional Democrats—especially Senate Democrats—were effectively entitled to write the relevant legislation.

This they did. They shifted cuts from domestic welfare to defense, they rejected a cut in the capital gains tax, and they finished by increasing income taxation in the upper brackets. Indeed, to the extent that they moderated their economic-welfare preferences, it was to accommodate other Senate Democrats, not congressional Republicans or even the president—who was left hanging, day by day, waiting to sign whatever they could construct. A successful ultimate vote necessarily reflected a national Democratic coalition on economics and social welfare, with maximum influence for that piece of the coalition, the southern Democrats, most needed to put this together. Accordingly, the final vote of 228 to 200 in the House was led by the southern Democrats, 61 to 20; followed by the northern Democrats, 120 to 54; and opposed by the Republicans, 47 to 126.

The Gulf War

Congress actually managed to adjourn from these negotiations with only days remaining in the fall congressional election campaign. And with only days remaining, polls showed the Republicans, already weak in Congress, facing a disaster—Congress being "about" social welfare and economic benefit, and the Republican Party having just highlighted itself as the party on the wrong side of these fundamental concerns. In a response fully reflecting the contours of the current political order, then, George Bush hit the campaign trail to talk about the Gulf and about American values and their place in the world, where Republicans (not Democrats) had their established advantage (Duncan 1990; Alson 1990; for a summary of partisan standing on foreign affairs during the postwar years, see Polsby and Wildavsky 1991, 232–35).

In the immediate sense, this effort was a failure. An already weak party managed to lose another Senate seat and eight more House seats, meaning that even a Bush landslide in 1992 was unlikely to provide the Republicans with a recapture of either the House or the Senate. If this failure held no hint of a larger shift in the existing order, it was because congressional Democrats were about to return every favor that Bush and his congressional partisans had given them over the preceding months. In so doing, they were also about to complete the institutional picture of a political order at work. What congressional Democrats were about to do was to seize on the Gulf conflict, to sketch *themselves* as the party out of step with the American public, and to rescue (at least temporarily) the personal popularity of George Bush. In the process, they were to exemplify—and energize—the great alternative pattern of social coalitions in modern American politics, and the great alternative pattern of partisan alliances that followed from it.

Iraq had seized Kuwait on August 2. By August 8, President Bush had introduced a major American troop presence, his "line in the sand." The usual rally in public opinion followed, sufficient to stifle partisan conflict for a number of weeks. But by mid-September, as the prospects of immediate combat receded, the partisan honeymoon began to ebb as well (Apple 1990; Gordon 1990; Deciding on War 1991; Rosenthal 1991; Cook 1991). At first, Democratic congressional sniping at the Republican president came from both directions. On September 17, the House Foreign Affairs Committee actually began the attack from the right, though hearings effectively organized around the question, Who lost Kuwait? And on September 18, the Foreign Operations Subcommittee of the House Appropriations Committee began the attack from the left, refusing an arms deal for Saudi Arabia and refusing to forgive Egypt's military debt.

Thereafter, however, and for the next four months, there was constant sniping, but all from the same general position, from the left—the accommodationist—side of the issue. Seen one way, this merely reasserted "politics as usual" in the stereotypical and clichéd sense. But seen another way, what it really did was to reassert the normal politics of an established arrangement of coalitions, issues, and parties. Part of this, in turn, was a straightforward reflection of the dominant views of party elites. Thus, Democratic elites were always unhappy with the notion of the use of force, a view expressed throughout this period in a demand for extended economic sanctions. But part of this reassertion was also entangled, as it must be in an era of split partisan control, with issues of institutional prerogative. How far *could* the president go, this Republican president, without seeking authorization from Congress, a Democratic Congress?

In the background of this question, by extension, was always the War Powers Act, which purported to limit the endangerment of American troops without congressional authorization but remained untested—nearly unacknowledged—by any American president. Within this environment, tactical politicking would move back and forth. On November 8, the president massively increased the number of American troops in the Middle East. On November 20, congressional Democrats sued in federal district court to affirm that the president could not use these troops without congressional authorization. On November 29, the United Nations authorized the use of force to remove Iraq from Kuwait. On December 4, the House Democratic Caucus voted 177 to 37 that the president could not support this initiative without congressional approval.

The end of the Christmas recess, and the coming of the January 15 deadline in the UN resolution, finally forced the issue. Rather than face a basic constitutional conflict, but unwilling to invoke the War Powers Act, the White House asked for congressional authorization of the use of force, an authorization granted under the constitutional provision (Article I, Section 8) giving Congress the power "to declare war." The ensuing debate was surprisingly powerful, venting what were, on one level, deeply felt and personal instincts about warfare and the national interest. Yet on a different level, this debate, like the vote to follow, merely registered—objectified, if you will—the current version of party alliances associated with continuing public majorities on major substantive concerns.

The result, most concretely, was a decision to go to war. Yet for students of the accompanying political order, two other things were also effectively accomplished. First, congressional Democrats had put their party on the record, in both houses, as being opposed to the use of force in the Gulf, a position consistent with internal elite preferences for at least the preceding quarter century. But second, congressional Democrats, again in both houses, had provided the necessary votes for an authorization of the use of force, thereby reflecting not elite but underlying mass sentiment. The crucial House vote, where stronger party lines had been expected to make the outcome most unclear, was 250 to 183, with Republicans voting 164 to 3, southern Democrats 53 to 32, and northern Democrats 33 to 147—roughly the same numbers as the vote on deficit reduction, but with different parties (and party factions) attached to them.

Seen one way, a nearly unbroken phalanx of Republicans had been joined by a sizable minority of Democratic defectors to adopt this declaration. Analyzed another way, an ongoing nationalist majority among the American public in foreign affairs had been registered in what was becoming the orthodox way, with a coalition of Republicans and southern Democrats defeating the northern Democratic Party. Presumably, either view guaranteed that the Democrats would acquire full blame if the war went well, no credit if it actually went badly. War did come, on February 23, and it ended, spectacularly, on February 27. In response, Republican President George Bush moved from the low point of his presidential popularity, in the aftermath of the 1990 budget fiasco, to the high point of his—or perhaps any—presidential popularity, all within the space of four explosive months.

In the narrow chronology of these two major conflicts, as well as in the texture of their day-to-day politicking, the practical separation of the two issues may be their most distinctive feature. After a short period when potential Gulf expenditures threatened to dictate budget arrangements, budgetary politics unfolded in apparent disregard of developments in the Middle East. In the same way, in the aftermath of striking victories (and defeats) in budgetary maneuvering, neither Democratic nor Republican strategists showed any inclination to retailor their positions on the Gulf War in order to either build on budgetary successes or use the Gulf to make budgetary politics teach a different public lesson. On the surface, then, this practical separation was surprising.

Yet on a deeper level, it would be more surprising if two such major crises actually managed not to reflect the larger order in which they played out, one that presumably linked them through its dominant characteristics. In fact, of course, this was not the case. A different way to address the paradox of apparent independence for two such major, simultaneous issues—eliminating the paradox by making them fully interdependent and consistent at a deeper level—is to note that each precisely reflected its piece of an overarching order and that the two pieces together reflected that order as a totality. Indeed, these two issues, together, contributed almost a checklist of key structural elements to the contemporary order—of social coalitions, substantive issues, and party alliances.

In this, their politics certainly suggested a continuing nationalist and traditionalist majority in foreign affairs and cultural values, represented first by a sense that American principles had been violated in the Gulf, and then by solid support for the American military presence there. At the same time, this focused period of crisis politics suggested a continuing liberal and activist majority on social welfare and service provision, represented by a consistent concern for protecting basic social programs and, subsequently, by a desire to tilt taxation in the progressive direction.

Conversely, their politics also suggested a continuing—and discordant—menu of policy choices imposed on these social majorities by the political parties. The main party actors remained determined to have a Republican Party program that was conservative across both domains and a Democratic Party program that was liberal across both. In so doing, they effectively insisted that party alliances, within Congress and extending to the presidency, be altered—though this was the farthest thing from their intent—so as to reconcile all these social and substantive tensions.

Inevitably, the result was two very different winning partisan coalitions. Within these, southern Democrats were liberal on social welfare and conservative on foreign affairs. As a result, only southern Democrats should have expected to be on the majority side of both conflicts, and only southern Democrats were. Northern Democrats, by contrast, were liberal on social welfare but also liberal on foreign affairs. They should have contributed the bulk of the winners on deficit reduction and the bulk of the losers on the Gulf War, and again they did. Republicans, finally, were conservative in the two realms, entitling them to lose badly on the deficit and win decisively on the Gulf.

A different way to summarize the same situation, a way that introduces a good deal more asperity, would be to say that elite actors from each party had actually forced the conflict in exactly the issue domain where they logically should have expected to lose. Thus it was congressional Republicans, the group that most needed help on distributional (economic) matters, who created the conflict that rebounded so powerfully to their disadvantage on the budget. And it was congressional Democrats, the group that most needed help on valuational (cultural) matters, who created the conflict on foreign intervention that rebounded so swiftly to their disadvantage on the Gulf.

Deficit Reduction in 1993

With the Gulf rather than the deficit still uppermost in their minds, many analysts (along with many party leaders) assumed that, the congressional elections of 1990 notwithstanding, President Bush could rely on easy reelection. This was not an unreasonable view on its own grounds—the Gulf was closer than the deficit to the vote—but it missed the real place of both issues, not as particular influences on voting behavior but as general indicators of underlying (and ongoing) public preferences.

It was not that people would be asked to choose retrospectively between one or the other. It was not even that either would play a direct role in the 1992 campaign, though the Gulf would clearly have the larger role in that regard. It was rather that the deficit and the Gulf were reasonable incarnations—obvious surface expressions—of a set of underlying and continuing preferences among the American public. Accordingly, if foreign affairs were the dominant theme of 1992, Bush would surely be back. If fiscal priorities were the dominant theme instead, the budget fiasco of 1990 would be a far better guide to the underlying situation, as it indeed proved to be (Pomper et al. 1993, chap. 5; Abramson, Aldrich, and Rohde 1994, chaps. 6–7).

Governmental response to a serious recession—the one, ironically, that Bush had tried to mitigate—became the main issue of the 1992 campaign, the one forced in by the larger policy environment. Thanks partly to fallout from this same recession, but also to deliberate efforts by the Clinton campaign, health care—one of the great social insurance programs—became the main secondary policy concern. Within that context, the Gulf War, for all its unequivocal success, simply receded in prospective consequence. And the Clinton presidency was a logical product.

To add irony, however, the first environmentally imposed policy conflict of the incoming Clinton administration would fall in the same realm as the first policy crisis of the outgoing Bush administration, namely, the continuing fiscal deficit and its appropriate resolution. This outcome gained surface drama from the degree to which Clinton had consistently repudiated deficit reduction as a governmental priority. As an aspirant for the Democratic nomination, he had made economic growth and "good jobs" the centerpiece of his campaign. With the nomination secured, Clinton had moved these priorities into the Democratic platform, hammering them again in his acceptance speech. And in the fall campaign, he had been monotonous—brutal—in giving them a final affirmation, boiled privately to the aphorism "the economy, stupid." Not surprisingly, when the result was victory at the polls, Clinton announced his intention to begin with an economic-stimulus package.

Three factors would quickly undo this year-long affirmation (Mills 1992; Clinton's Bold Gamble 1993; Clinton Budget 1993; Angst of Victory 1993). In the background was a change in the state of the economy, which had begun growing vigorously during the fourth quarter of 1992, albeit too late to rescue George Bush. In the foreground was the electoral showing of independent Ross Perot, amassing an impressive 19 percent of the vote through an assault on "politics as usual," as exemplified by the refusal of the two main parties to tackle the deficit. And in the middle, where these two influences met operationally, was Congress.

Within it, southern Democrats were the group with perennial deficit concerns; they had actually been the faction most supportive of Bush's efforts to address the deficit. But there was now a second group with deficit concerns, in the form of a large cohort of freshman Democrats from the North. Many had run in a policy environment shaped as much by Perot as by Clinton, and many had campaigned on a promise to "do something" about this problem. All could read the November outcome—Clinton 43 percent, Bush 37 percent, and Perot 19 percent—as evidence that their own reelections might turn on progress (at least) on the deficit issue.

What might have been an immediate collision between the president and his own party on Capitol Hill was avoided by the sheer technical requirements of a program that promised job creation, investment incentives, deficit reduction, and middle-class tax cuts. By February 20, when a comprehensive package was unveiled, the new president had recognized the difficult congressional environment, evidenced by the linking of economic stimulus to deficit reduction and the elimination of the promised tax cuts.

Within a week, priorities had perforce changed further. Congressional leaders discovered that they lacked the votes to pass a stimulus package in advance of some bill indicating serious concern with the deficit. So the president agreed to tackle the budget resolution first, thereby institutionalizing his targets for spending cuts and tax *increases*. Even then, further items of deficit reduction had to be added to the resolution before the more hesitant among Democrats on the House and Senate Budget Committees would close ranks behind it. But the necessary items were found, and straight party votes then brought the resolution out of both committees, through both houses, and on to the president for signature by the end of March.

A resolution was not actual deficit reduction, of course. That would have to come later, with the reconciliation bills. Nor, it quickly developed, was a resolution sufficient to save the stimulus package. The House of Representatives had long offered the purest partisanship on economic-welfare matters, and it produced another party-line vote, sending the stimulus package to the Senate. The Senate Democratic leadership, however, began without even a majority for the stimulus plan, until it added even more spending cuts to firm up the southern Democrats. This majority then ran into a Republican filibuster, in part a response to the deliberately partisan strategy followed by the Democrats to date. And the effort to lift this filibuster through a coalition with moderate Republicans next ran—fatally—into the reforms from 1990.

As part of the 1990 fiscal resolution, Congress had decreed that any new spending had to be offset by cuts in the same general realm, unless the president cited a national economic emergency. If Clinton were to comply with this legislation under normal conditions, there would be precious little net economic stimulus. If he were to try to escape it, he would have to get moderate Republicans not only to join his policy coalition but also to affirm that the nation required an "emergency special." In the event, this was asking too much, and the economic-stimulus plan died quietly during the Easter recess.

Having set out with deficit reduction as secondary to economic stimulus, the Clinton administration was left with deficit reduction as its sole possibility for an economic initiative. The main contours of policy conflict within this realm were identical to those that had surfaced in 1990: the balance between spending cuts and tax increases; among cuts, the balance between entitlements and defense; and among taxes, the balance between progressivity and proportionality. Under the Constitution, the Clinton program had to visit the House first, but House politics was additionally complicated in 1993 by a fear among House Democrats that they would again be asked to rally to painful compromises proposed by the president, only to see him deal these away in negotiations with the Senate.

In the House, Chairman Dan Rostenkowski (D-Ill.) of the House Ways and Means Committee nevertheless continued the previous partisan strategy of drafting compromises within the Democratic membership and then driving them through the full committee. The result was a classic northern Democratic package: favoring taxes over cuts, protecting entitlements rather than defense, preferring income taxes over levies on purchases. By the end of May, under extreme partisan pressure and still in fear of a Senate deal, the full House passed this measure by the narrowest of margins, 219 to 213, with all 175 Republicans voting no.

The centerpiece of the Clinton proposal, however, a comprehensive tax on the heat content of all fuels—known as the BTU tax—was already dying in the Senate while Rostenkowski was salvaging it in the House. Southern Democrats from energy-producing states defected first, cracking the Democratic majority while opening a huge revenue hole. These individuals then joined with moderate Republicans to propose a cap on entitlements, restoring the majority and reducing the hole. This caused House Democrats, spearheaded this time by the Congressional Black Caucus, to withdraw their support, signaling the failure of this compromise in the House.

In a response remarkably parallel to the endgame in 1990, the president withdrew from direct involvement and allowed the Senate Democratic leadership to see if it could write a bill. Their proposal rebalanced Rostenkowski's main elements minus the BTU tax, for which an increase in the tax on gasoline and other transport fuels was substituted. That plan passed the Senate by the narrowest of margins, 50 to 49, depending on the tie-breaking vote of Vice President Al Gore. Because there was still no reason to believe that this version would satisfy the House, the entire package came down to protracted negotiations in a conference committee during the month of August.

What emerged was a shift of Medicare caps, away from recipients and onto providers; further sharp cuts in defense spending; sharply higher income taxes in the upper brackets; and a nickel increase on the gasoline tax. The compromise passed the House by 218 to 216, with the Republicans again voting 0 to 175. It passed the Senate by a vote of 51 to 50, with Republicans voting 0 to 44 and Vice President Gore again casting the decisive vote. The fate of all this remained every bit as shaky as previous compromises; votes were every bit as close, and their party-line character was every bit as prominent.

This bill was quickly signed by the president. The obvious result in its time was a measure that would define the fiscal policy of the Clinton administration, at least for the life of the 103rd Congress. In that sense, and especially given its pure surface partisanship, it was a distinctly Clintonian document. But the result was also a remarkable set of parallels, in process and in outcome, with none other than the Bush administration of 1990. Moreover, those parallels go a long way toward exposing a continuing structure of American politics across these same years. Neither president began with any love for deficit reduction. George Bush addressed the issue in order to ameliorate an economic downturn coinciding with what would be his bid for reelection. Bill Clinton addressed the issue in order to advance the economic-stimulus program that had been his main electoral theme— when the sharp recession feared by Bush nevertheless occurred.

When forced to address the deficit, the two presidents began from roughly opposite positions, as befitted a Republican versus a Democratic incumbent on an economic issue. Bush sought a focus on cuts versus taxes, on entitlements versus defense among the cuts, and on proportionality versus progressivity among the taxes. Clinton sought roughly the reverse. But at that point, they encountered a powerfully parallel political environment, leading inevitably toward parallel results. Differences in the subsequent trajectory of politicking thus largely reflected different starting points for the two presidents; ultimate outcomes were still impressively similar, after all that.

Both presidents encountered entrenched and substantial Democratic majorities in the House and the Senate, majorities built on these very issues. But in truth, those Democratic majorities merely embodied continuing majorities in American public opinion in support of social welfare benefits and of solidly progressive taxation. Both presidents thus had to build congressional majorities from the same combination of northern and southern Democrats, a fact that was masked by the difference between Bush's evident conflict with this potential majority and Clinton's conscious intention to make it his own. This outcome was buttressed, ultimately, by the obvious minority status of Republican policy preferences in this realm, and not just of congressional Republicans as a group—along with the intensity by which congressional Republicans held to these (minority) preferences.

When the result was remarkably similar in its policy content, this was variously surprising, ironic, or familiar, depending on whether the surface trajectory or the underlying structure was the main analytic focus. *Congressional Quarterly Weekly Report,* whose own prior commentary had moved from surprise through irony, came to rest at the appropriate (familiar) point:

> If the 1993 budget deal looks a lot like the 1990 deal, it is not by accident. Both were brokered by Democratic Congresses that had few options when they sought ways to balance the budget.
>
> Both packages contain sharply higher taxes on the wealthy, a nickel or less per gallon increase in the gasoline tax, deep cutbacks to Medicare providers but few or no new burdens on Medicare beneficiaries, sharp cuts in defense spending, and, amid all the deficit reduction, some social spending—chiefly an increase in the earned-income tax credit (EITC) for the working poor.
>
> Both packages also are initially identical in size. (Hayer 1993)

The North American Free Trade Agreement

NAFTA, destined to propel a second crisis vote onto the agenda of the Clinton administration within three months of the vote on deficit reduction, began life at the center of a web of trade-policy calculations in the Bush administration. In its substance, the proposal merely called for the addition of Mexico to a previous free-trade pact negotiated with Canada under President Ronald Reagan, thereby creating the "North American Free Trade Area." In its politics, however, NAFTA would attest once more to the continuity of a social coalition in a major policy area and of a set of partisan alignments embodying it, from the Bush through the Clinton administrations—albeit a very different set from that associated with deficit reduction.

Four aspects of American trade policy came together to generate NAFTA. The most general was a perception that the U.S.-Canada pact had been a thorough success. The most specific was a request from the president of Mexico, Carlos Salinas de Gortari, that his country be added to the resulting free-trade zone. A third was the apparent progress of trade liberalization within the European Union, targeted on the symbolic date of "1992." And the fourth was the much more troubled progress of a revised and expanded general agreement on tariffs and trade (GATT), the worldwide free-trade regime. Philosophically, President George Bush had always been in sympathy with free trade. NAFTA, accordingly, could be a means to advance this philosophy, a potential goad to GATT negotiators, and a partial protection against the worst case, in which GATT failed but European economic integration proceeded.

The proposal had already encountered significant congressional opposition under Bush, surfacing the main concerns that would dog it thereafter. In the spring of 1991, Bush sought extension of the so-called fast-track provision, permitting a single up or down vote on the product of international trade negotiations. Opponents worried not so much about GATT as about possible job losses and environmental damage from a pact with Mexico. But these opponents were unable to separate fast-track authorization by geographic realm, and they were unwilling to be branded as all-purpose protectionists. In effect, what they did in the spring of 1991 was to suggest the further, deeper conflict that was likely when an actual agreement finally appeared (Cloud 1992, 1993a, 1993b; NAFTA Crucible 1993).

Bill Clinton, as an aspirant for the Democratic nomination, began his campaign with evident free-trade preferences, too. As a southern Democrat, Clinton came out of the traditionally trade-oriented wing of his party. Moreover, as a candidate for the presidential nomination, Clinton's strategy was to present himself as a New Democrat, supporting economic growth generally, along with the introduction of new technologies and a reduction in governmental regulation. As a successful nominee, he also inherited major partisan interest groups, not just the major environmental groups but also organized labor, interests that had opposed the idea of NAFTA from the start.

His short-term strategy was to temporize, while allowing congressional Democrats to harass President Bush on the issue and otherwise emphasizing his economic-stimulus and health insurance programs. The conclusion of negotiations on the actual pact in mid-August, however, made this policy "straddle" increasingly difficult. From one side, congressional Democrats now called on Clinton to promise to reopen negotiations. From the other, candidate Bush taunted him for taking no position, for abandoning earlier views, and for bowing to organized labor. Accordingly, after two months of silence on the matter, Clinton announced at the beginning of October that he favored the pact. He tempered this support with a promise to do more to protect working conditions and the environment, as well as to provide more funds for adjustment benefits, but he asserted that these things could be accomplished without reopening formal negotiations.

A confrontation with the issue was otherwise destined to wait for some time, while the new Clinton administration moved to other matters—especially economic stimulus and deficit reduction. In the meantime, in March, special trade representative Mickey Kantor turned to negotiating new "supplemental agreements" with Canada and Mexico over issues of labor law and environmental regulation. Negotiations over these supplemental agreements would continue into August, and serious politicking over implementation of NAFTA would not really occur until after the summer congressional recess. This timing had the advantage of not conflating deficit politics, where the president was seeking a pure party-line vote in Congress, with trade politics, where he might have to rely on the congressional Republican Party.

By then, however, a final round of trade politics was to be additionally, institutionally complicated. On June 30, the U.S. Federal District Court for Washington, D.C., delivered an opinion that NAFTA required a full review of environmental impacts, potentially a six-month task in its own right. As a result, the crucial round of politicking over passage of NAFTA would occur after the summer recess, in three separate but related theaters: (1) in the courts, where the administration sought to overturn the district court ruling; (2) in the "court of public opinion," where the administration would battle with its old nemesis Ross Perot in order to create some public groundswell for NAFTA, or at least to provide "cover" for pro-NAFTA congressmen; and (3) in Congress, where the maneuvering involved bicameral procedural gambits, programmatic compromises to expand the supportive coalition, and individual deals—often on extraneous matters—toward the same end.

In mid-August, Kantor announced that supplemental accords had indeed been completed with Mexico and Canada, institutionalizing concern for workers' rights and the environment. In mid-September, however, with Congress back in session, the Democratic Party leadership began to crumble. David Bonior (D-Mich.), majority whip in the House, came out formally against the pact. The White House responded by creating a special extramural lobbying team that included William Daley, a Chicago lawyer with good labor ties, and Bill Frenzel, former Republican minority whip.

Despite their efforts, in late September, Richard Gephardt (D-Mo.), majority leader in the House and longtime spokesman for efforts to restructure NAFTA, came out against it as well. Given these divisions, Thomas Foley, the Speaker of the House, was effectively neutralized. The administration regained some ground in a difficult fight when the U.S. Court of Appeals for the District of Columbia ruled on September 24 that an environmental impact statement was not necessary for NAFTA, moving the crucial debate back into more overtly public theaters.

The opposition in the public debate had already come to center on Ross Perot, who was running nationally televised advertisements and conducting a national speaking tour in conjunction with his new book *Save Your Job, Save Our Country: Why NAFTA Must Be Stopped—Now!* In response, the White House added Lee Iacocca, former chairman of Chrysler Corporation, to make counteradvertisements debunking the alleged loss of jobs through free trade. The ultimate pitched battle in this part of the contest, however, was not to come until early November, just before the crucial vote in Congress, when Vice President Gore faced Perot in a televised debate on the national talk show *Larry King Live.* The press awarded the vice president a clear victory, and polls suggested a surge in public support for NAFTA (Perot with Choate 1993; Duncan 1993).

Well before then, the crucial horse-trading in Congress had gone about as far as it could. The White House considered instituting a variety of maneuvers to bring NAFTA up in the more sympathetic Senate first—Robert Dole, Republican minority leader, was agreeable—but eventually concluded that doing so would cause more ultimate damage than benefit in the House. The administration settled for an arrangement whereby relevant congressional committees would hold "mock markups," thereby delaying the date on which the bill would be officially introduced and the fast-track provisions activated—a deal that actually suited both sides.

On substance, the White House offered adjustments for particular industries: a change in the manner of calculating sugar imports and a mechanism to track orange juice prices. It offered adjustments to particular social groups: public works loans to districts represented by Hispanic congressmen and an extended review (and subsequent expansion) of job retraining programs for newly unemployed workers. And it dealt with individual congressmen on even more particularistic grounds—although some in this group were already predisposed to support the bill and were merely prospecting for additional "sweeteners." Even then, in the week before the final and decisive vote in the House, signals on its fate remained markedly mixed. In that week, three House committees reported the bill, which could no longer be amended: Ways and Means sent it to the floor with a favorable recommendation, Energy and Commerce sent it to the floor without a recommendation, and Banking and Currency sent it to the floor with an unfavorable recommendation.

The result was a narrow but solid victory in the House, 234 to 200, presaging a more substantial win in the Senate, 61 to 38. Given the intensity of the politicking beforehand, this immediate outcome became the story of the moment, though many analysts had already concluded that symbolism had far outrun substance for this particular program. In hindsight, however, most of the outcome's noteworthy aspects sprang from its role as one more incarnation of an underlying (and continuing) policy coalition, of a social coalition in a major policy realm demanding—and getting—an altered party alliance. In fact, there was little difference in the outcome on NAFTA and the outcome on the Gulf War two and a half years earlier. The rhetoric of the debate would never have suggested such a parallel, centering, as it did, on jobs and their fate. And indeed, NAFTA engaged focused economic interests in some states, sufficient to pull them from their cultural-national moorings. South Carolina Republicans thus joined national Democrats in voting no; Washington Democrats joined national Republicans (and the president) in voting yes.

Nevertheless, overall, the issue did not become an economic-welfare concern but remained, in effect, a cultural-national matter. As a result, in the end, NAFTA came to resemble not deficit reduction but the Gulf. In each case, the ultimate majority had been registered through a complex but straightforward and reliable partisan coalition: an overwhelming majority of Republicans had joined with a solid majority of southern Democrats to defeat an overwhelming majority of northern Democrats. The battle over NAFTA called into question, as never before in the postwar years, the reliability of public support for the concept of free trade. But in 1993, the party alliances that had long grouped this issue with foreign affairs remained sufficiently resilient to keep it lodged—firmly—there.

The fillip on this—one that was familiar in American politics but nearly unprecedented elsewhere—was the relationship of the party of the president to the congressional outcome. A Democratic president had managed to win by carrying an overwhelming majority of the opposition party and a solid majority of the perennially dissident faction of his own, while losing a majority of his party as a whole and an overwhelming majority of the dominant tendency within it. Yet the parallel outcome in 1991, on the Gulf War during the Bush presidency, was no less remarkable. There, a president from the minority party—in the nation, but especially in Congress—had been opposed by a majority of the majority party and a heavy majority of its dominant tendency, yet had managed to win in the same essential way.

A different way to summarize the situation for all of the above—the budget fiasco of 1990, the decision to go to war in the Gulf, the budget redux in 1993, and the passage of NAFTA in what might be a last hurrah—is to say that all of them together reflected the ongoing contours of modern American politics. In other words, consistent across them was an underlying set of social coalitions, congealed around a continuing set of substantive concerns, as mobilized (but also strongly shaped) by a continuing party system. There continued to be crosscutting majorities on the basic underlying issues of social welfare and cultural values. But these were crosscutting, in essence, because the political parties did not (or perhaps could not?) offer a policy program that would realign the underlying social coalitions.

There was, in all this, nothing inherently crosscutting about the substance of these issues themselves, and thus no automatic need for the cross-cutting majorities that their underlying social coalitions embodied. Hostility to tax increases did not logically impel the use of force in the Gulf; an emphasis on deficit reduction did not logically impel a trade agreement with Mexico. Moreover, there were major sections of the *mass* Democratic Party, along with major sections of the *mass* Republican Party, that actually did put these issues together in each of the four logically possible combinations.

Nevertheless, what also existed, in terms that were practical and not hypothetical, were two ongoing policy menus: liberal welfare policies and progressive cultural policies from the national Democratic Party, along with conservative welfare policies and traditionalist cultural policies from the national Republican Party—in the face of a set of public preferences that did not coincide with either. The necessary result was some pattern of *differing* party alliances, reshuffling the various factions so as to realize long-standing public majorities, but perhaps also institutionalizing the outcome even as those majorities had begun to move.

And this brings the analysis back—at last—to the key dissident group at every stage of this process, and thus to the title of the chapter itself. Throughout, there was one party faction actually embodying these larger national preferences, a faction moderately supportive of social welfare but concerned about paying its bills, a faction reliably supportive of international activism but concerned about ensuring success, a faction deeply traditionalistic on cultural values in a world where economic development was putting inevitable stresses on them. By definition, then, this faction was crucial to constructing the differentiated party alliances that were perhaps the most striking aspect of politics in this period.

This faction was, of course, the southern Democrats, and their fate mirrors—in reverse—the entire rest of the account. When the issue tensions of what became the era of divided government were at their least intense, in the immediate postwar years, the southern Democrats were at their full complement. In 1946, the year of the first postwar congressional election, there were 105 congressional seats in the Old South, breaking down into 103 Democrats and 2 Republicans, along with 22 Senate seats, yielding 22 Democrats and 0 Republicans. A half century later, heading into the 1996 presidential election, there were 125 congressional seats in this former Confederacy, breaking down into 61 Democrats and 64 Republicans, along with the same 22 Senate seats, now yielding 9 Democrats and 13 Republicans.

Even this understates the scope of the change. Among these formalistic, modern southern Democrats were a number of individuals who were, in fact and self-consciously, orthodox "northern Democrats" instead. It would bias the argument too much to take them out of these numbers based on their policy preferences; a certain heterogeneity always marked the southern Democrats, almost by definition. But if the same numbers are calculated minus black Democrats from the South—congressmen who normally, by ideology and intention, repudiate the "southern Democratic" tag—the situation becomes more self-evidently extreme. After removing these 16 black Democrats, there was a total population of 109 congressional seats for which the partisan balance was 45 Democrats and 64 Republicans. Said differently, the 103 formalistically "southern Democrats" in 1946 had become 45 by 1994—and 3 of them would switch their party allegiance during 1995.

There is a further surface irony in all this, of course. A national politics coming to center on the fundamental issue combination that had originally made the southern Democrats deviant—namely, cautiously liberal on social welfare but cautiously conservative on cultural values—was coinciding with the demise of the southern Democrats as a party faction. Yet this should probably not be treated as irony at all, for if the rest of the nation now finds itself in the same position that southern voters once did—preferring cautious liberals on social welfare, cautious conservatives on cultural values—there is no real basis for such a faction to exist. In short, we are all southern Democrats now.

CHAPTER FIVE

The Changing Structure of American Politics

There are two grand and general interpretations of the state of American politics loose on the American political landscape at the midpoint of the Reagan presidency. One says that an old era, characterized by forty years of Democratic Party dominance, is passing away and that a new Republican era is rapidly being born. The other says that while the old Democratic era is clearly in disarray, no comparable partisan replacement has yet emerged, and perhaps none ever will. Both positions, by now, include an elaborated set of supporting contentions. Both include a body of evidence alleged to affirm their essential correctness. Both have acquired an almost ritual character in exposition.

These arguments, essentially about the current nature of party loyalties in the general public, are so ubiquitous that they cannot readily be ignored in any attempt to address the current structure of American politics. It is not so often recognized, however, that this argument over changing party loyalties in the general public is merely a smaller analog to a much larger discussion about the changing shape of American politics in its totality. And here, political scientists concerned with the "big picture" in American politics are in general agreement that the summary description that was common wisdom for several decades is no longer adequate.

They are also in general disagreement over the appropriate description of current American politics, as well as over whether the current period is in fact the shape of the future or only a transition to some new but more historically familiar shape. What is general and analogous, then, is a perception of an American political system that once had an easily describable order with comparatively predictable outcomes that has clearly changed, without producing some new, easily described, and reasonably predictable order and thus without producing any consensus on the effective structure of current American politics.

111

Fortunately, some initial attention to the popular argument about the changing shape of the American electoral world provides a concrete way to move into the larger discussion about the changing structure of American politics more generally. Fortunately as well, the major elements of this larger theoretical discussion then feed back into—and begin to recast—the popular debate. In fact, it may now be possible to isolate some major and consistent features of the new American political era. Or at least it is clear where one must look to have any chance of isolating these central elements.

One must look, first, at the intermediary organizations of American society, those entities that link individual citizens to the institutions of government. And one must look, second, at those formal institutions of government themselves, since they are, after all, the entities most proximate to the political choices that ultimately emerge. Before turning to that investigation, however, it may be appropriate to survey the conclusions at its end, for a look at the changing structure of American politics—through mass electoral behavior, intermediary organizations, and the formal institutions of government—will ultimately suggest a politics with an increasing range of possible outcomes, a more rapid succession of varying outcomes, less predictability from administration to administration or even from year to year, and, paradoxically, an apparent permanence to this overall picture of changeability, transience, and flux.

The Popular Debate

The central proposition of the current public argument about change in American electoral politics asserts, at bottom, that the election of Ronald Reagan in 1980, as consolidated by his massive reelection in 1984, marks a major reconstitution of the outlines of American politics. This is partly a partisan political argument and partly a journalistic argument, though it has attracted the attention of professional political scientists who have tried to constrain it by confronting it with "hard data." In any case, there are actually three measured versions of this summary argument that can be differentiated.

The first says that this period was indeed a "realignment," one of those eras when a vast number of American citizens change their partisan allegiance for a long time to come. The second says that whether or not this was a realignment, it *was* a period when a vast number of Americans changed their preferences about the activities of government in economic policy, in foreign policy, and in social policy. And a third simply says that whether or not any of this was true—whether this was a real realignment or a major change in public preferences—this period produced public policies that will shape the behavior of subsequent governments for at least another generation.

Substantial and unavoidable pieces of evidence to support this interpretation are present at nearly every level of analysis. Moreover, the core of this evidence is directly and explicitly partisan. Thus, a conservative Republican candidate, a category that we had been told since 1936 was simply unelectable in the United States—the so-called minority candidate within a minority party—was not only elected president in 1980 but also massively reelected in 1984. Beyond that, this same minority Republican Party, with a collection of candidates even more extreme (and hence presumably unelectable), managed simultaneously to capture the U.S. Senate, another feat that had been considered effectively impossible.

Some of the further evidence for this alleged major change in American electoral politics is more indirectly and implicitly partisan—and hence presumably more fundamental, being farther below the surface of politics and thus potentially more powerful and long lasting. The change in party (and ideology) of the president and Senate was, for example, in part the product of the mobilization of new groups, which were likely to be around for some time thereafter. The religious evangelicals were the biggest and best known of these, but there were others, ranging all the way from the Eagle Forum to the National Pro-Life Coalition to the Committee on the Present Danger.

This change in the party and ideology of the president and Senate was also associated with the confirmed arrival of a new style of political action, perhaps even the long-awaited "new politics." This was based on new issues: on culture, for example, rather than on economics. It was based on new forms of organization as well: on a combination of advertising at the top of campaigns and of special interests with new technologies at the grass roots, rather than on the old, reliable, increasingly enfeebled political parties. Finally, beneath all this, there was some consistent evidence of an absolutely elemental nature in explicitly *nonpartisan*—indeed, only implicitly political—realms. One thinks here of the reassertion of the value of traditional marriage, to be followed by a traditional family; of the reassertion of traditional patriotism; or even of the turning away from low fashion toward high fashion, from "dressing down" to "dressing up."

Yet, when other evidence is added to these pieces, and when this collection of evidence is addressed for its implications, what emerges is not a new version of the old order—a conservative rather than a liberal version, a picture of Republican rather than Democratic dominance. What emerges instead is a shift from an older *type* of order to a new one with a fundamentally different structure and fundamentally different characteristics. This is apparent even in the directly and explicitly partisan realm. Indeed, even the Reagan elections are ambiguous *structural* portents. In 1980, the voters appeared to choose primarily on the grounds of potential for leadership, between a discredited incumbent and a strong but risky alternative. And in 1984, those voters returned to office a personally popular incumbent president with a country at peace and an economy on the upswing.

It would be foolish to assert that this did not expand the range of possibilities in American politics. The election and reelection of Ronald Reagan confirmed that there is no longer a simple formula for ensuring Democratic presidents, and that alone makes the Republican candidate reliably stronger. Moreover, the election and reelection of Ronald Reagan underlined the *variability* in outcomes now clearly possible in presidential electioneering. Now, within one generation, it has been possible to nominate and elect presidents ranging all the way from liberal Democrats to conservative Republicans.

But it would be equally foolish to regard the Reagan elections as the new, reliable shape of the future rather than merely as confirmation that stable electoral coalitions have broken down—even disappeared—in American politics. Indeed, while the Republicans also managed to recapture the Senate, a fact that was central to the strength of the Reagan presidency, the Republican *Party* simultaneously failed to make any serious inroads in the House of Representatives, which remained reliably Democratic. And at lower levels, in state and local races, there was even less evidence of any Republican resurgence.

If these are the appropriate conclusions from the direct and explicit partisan record, they are echoed precisely by those more indirect and implicit partisan indicators alleged to be associated with the new political era. For example, the new groups that were part and parcel of the Reagan elections, those intense single-interest organizations that seem likely to be with us for some time, also seem likely to contribute more to an increased fluidity than to any new stability. Seen one way, these new Republican groups simply mirror, and balance, Democratic counterparts that have been active for a long time, from the National Education Association through the National Organization for Women to the Nuclear Weapons Freeze Committee. And seen another way, all these new groups really contribute primarily to the volatility and flux *within their own parties*. They possess neither the societal reach nor the temporal constancy of the official party organizations they have increasingly displaced.

Or consider the appearance of the alleged new politics, with its apparent new issues and its apparent new forms of campaign organization. That is, consider the ability to ride new and intense social issues, not just the old, established economic issues; or the ability to mount campaigns through advertising and then to back them with special interests rather than to use political parties. These too seem to be more the means to expand the realm of political possibilities and to displace one possibility with another quickly, rather than to enshrine one particular political alignment.

Even the apparent new nonpartisan conservatism in lifestyle, community preference, and national pride gives very mixed signals when analyzed this way. A Democratic Party that offends these values should, logically and inevitably, expect to lose and thus help create a new Republican dominance. But a Democratic Party that makes its peace with these values should hardly feel the need for much further concern. Such values, after all, were far stronger in the days when the general public deserted the Republican for the Democratic Party, massively and extendedly, some fifty years ago.

Again, it would be foolish to claim that this new world does not offer improved prospects for the Republican Party and increased difficulties for the Democrats. But it would be equally foolish to fail to note that this is precisely because old and continuing alignments have broken up, without being replaced by stable new ones. And it would be additionally foolish to read this breakup as the product of anything other than the varied and shifting array of coalitions—and outcomes—now possible in American national politics.

Changing Intermediary Organizations

Why is this expanded—even kaleidoscopic—array of outcomes now possible? Why are stable and extended coalitions no longer a feature of American politics? What has changed to produce this new political world?

The answer, perhaps inevitably, has to do with the changing structure of American politics in a much larger sense, with the changing way in which political choices are shaped in the United States. And here, the problem is not in finding changes sufficiently large and sufficiently numerous to suggest the emergence of a new political era. In fact, there are elements of change in such profusion in the formal institutions of government and in the intermediary organizations around them that the problem is knowing where to begin.

Before beginning the elements of such a survey, however, it is worth noting a set of ultimate collective implications. A survey of major contributions to a changing American politics suggests, almost in passing, that the developments central to the popular debate about the changing shape of American electoral politics are only a small part of this larger structure. Indeed, a survey of major contributions to overall change suggests that the apparent shifts in public attitudes and behavior, which figure so prominently in the popular debate, are as much *products* as causes of the new political order. Although the public does change its political mind, that same public also responds differently to a different political environment, without necessarily changing its mind at all. Finally, a larger survey of this new political environment suggests that a new structure and the attitudes associated with it should not end up only reinforcing each other. They should operate, at bottom, to make the new political era a continuing rather than a transitional phenomenon.

What can be said, then, about this changing political structure? About the changing way in which political choices are shaped in the United States? About that changing "big picture" in American politics? Perhaps the best place to begin is well outside the formal institutions of government, with those intermediary organizations that take some sample of citizens' wishes and propel this toward governmental institutions. The most commonly recognized among these intermediary organizations, of course, are political parties. But the most numerically common are those nonparty intermediaries—call them interest groups, pressure groups, or whatever—that are built around a different kind of focused concern.

There is a general belief (or at least a general suspicion) among professional political scientists that this nonparty universe of politically relevant groups has changed substantially since the early 1950s. Back then, local community intermediaries—ethnic and racial associations, neighborhood and school groups, religious and fraternal organizations—were most central to the lives of individual citizens. They were also most central to the operation of political parties and thus fed into, and constrained, American party politics. Now, local community intermediaries have decayed, withdrawn, or been pushed out of politics. In their place, the key intermediary organizations are professionalized, issue or cause oriented, and deliberately created to affect public policy, often with a national focus, and often with a white-collar base.

This general belief may overstate the decline of local community intermediaries in their traditional social roles. Communities that are similar to those of the early 1950s tend to have a similar array of relevant local community organizations. But the general belief probably does not overstate the evolving situation with regard to the realm of national politics. The verifiable elements of change in the universe of intermediary organizations reliably contribute to a very different sort of national political structure.

For example, the ease of creating and then sustaining fully national organizations focused on a specific issue or cause has surely increased in this general period. A more affluent society can more easily create and sustain such organizations, apart from any other considerations. But a more technologically advanced society also provides more means of communicating quickly with members nationwide and of focusing their energies on national government. Even if the number of organized groups in society is, in principle, impossible to calculate, it would be difficult to find any professional observer who does not believe that the number with offices (and staff) in the national capital has increased dramatically in the period in question.

Other elements of social change in the United States during this period, such as a sharply rising level of education and the growth of an increasingly white-collar economy, probably further magnify these trends. The more educated and better off are more likely to take their political cues from issue- or cause-related organizations than from local community groups, just as they are more likely to take their political cues from the media of information, specialized or general, than from political parties.

In any case, the formal rules of politics have clearly changed in ways that benefit these newer intermediary organizations, ordinarily and reliably at the expense of their older community counterparts. Thus, even nominations to public office are now matters of public primary election rather than official party anointment. As a result, local party leaders cannot easily recognize local community groups, and issue-oriented organizations can use their more professional staff and more focused membership attachments to affect these nominations directly.

What results from all this is a world of more varied but more narrow organized intermediaries, which can reasonably hope for a more immediate and direct impact on political outcomes. Such a world necessarily decreases the prospects for stable and continuing governing coalitions, as it facilitates diverse and rapidly changing coalitions on specific issues of the moment. And such a world, in turn, is one where not just coalitions but also policies succeed each other in more rapid and less predictable fashion.

In most variants of democratic theory, political parties then constrain, filter, and meld the demands of these interest groups as those demands move into the formal institutions of government. As the universe of interest groups is changing, parties integrate the new groups into larger and continuing coalitions. If those groups are both new and resistant to integration, parties shift into active competition with them, shaping their behavior (and fate) in the process. In the United States during this period, however, changes in the two major parties as great as or greater than the changes in nonparty intermediary groups were actually exaggerating, rather than constraining and channeling, structural shifts at this intermediary level.

Some of this change in political parties was due to explicit decisions— reforms—about the intended structure of American politics, though intention was rarely synonymous with effect. The best-known example was reform of the process of presidential selection, from a mixed system dominated by party officials to an essentially plebiscitary system dominated by presidential primaries. The main criticisms of this reform are also well known: flash candidacies, idiosyncratic sequencing effects, pivotal roles for evanescent issues, public selections based largely on ignorance.

What is less commonly noted, however, is that this reform was really just the final step in a set of institutional changes that had been under way since at least the turn of the twentieth century. This was the movement for direct public selection of party nominees to public office through primary elections. The presidential reforms merely completed this movement. What this meant, however, was that there was no longer any formal need—at any level of American politics—for any given nominee to be tied to any predecessor in office, nor to any other contemporary nominee of the same party. Hence there was no need to be tied to any continuing party program nor, within some broad limits, to any continuing party constituency.

Had political parties as organizations been getting stronger during this period, they might still have accomplished informally what they could no longer do automatically and by right. That is, major extended party organizations could have built coalitions, endorsed nominees, delivered voters, and then coordinated a government. Instead, American parties were in a late stage of a century-long decline in these respects, too. The jobs, contracts, and favors that had permitted the construction of extended and hierarchical party organizations in many areas during earlier eras had been largely taken out of party politics, and old-fashioned party organizations had disappeared in response.

In turn, with the selection of public officials taken out of the hands of party officeholders, and with parties as organizations in precipitous decline, the nature of those who were active in politics—who did the work of politicking—changed too. These were the individuals who mounted campaigns for nomination to public office; they were the individuals who monitored, and pressured, those who were ultimately elected. Not surprisingly, these tasks were now undertaken by actors from the new universe of interest groups, who were more concerned with the multiple but narrow causes and issues that had brought them into action in the first place. Old-fashioned party officials, more concerned with holding a coalition together and pursuing an established coalitional program, were increasingly shunted aside, to the point where party offices themselves were increasingly held, though less continuously even then, by individuals whose principal ties were to other interest groups.

This change in institutional arrangements and in intermediary elites then contributed powerfully to a third major shift in the central public issues of American politics. With no organization and no continuing set of individuals to insist that politics remain focused on the central concerns of the preceding era, the arena of major political issues expanded sharply and produced a new world of major, shifting, crosscutting concerns. Before, the major issue in American politics had been economic welfare, and it had cut society rather neatly by social class. There had been a foreign policy consensus on simple anticommunism and a social policy consensus on traditional cultural norms.

From the mid-1960s on, the foreign policy consensus disappeared, and the resulting divisions did not parallel those on economic welfare. Beginning in the late 1960s, social policy—the character of American domestic life—became a matter of contention too, with crime, race, public order, education, religion, community life, and so forth now on the public political agenda. And positions on these issues did not parallel those on economic welfare either.

Changing Governmental Institutions

Inevitably, this new intermediary structure of politics fed into, and began to change the operation of, the formal institutions of national government. Different patterns of demands and different possibilities for coalition building inevitably made these institutions work differently as well. But that was only part of the story. These institutions were also changing internally, in ways that altered their receptivity to external demands and their potential for constructing coalitions around them, thereby contributing additional incentives for pushing policy demands at government and additional variety to the coalitions that could potentially be built around such demands.

With regard to the American presidency, much of what needs to be noted has already been covered in analyzing the current popular debate over electoral alignments and the state of the national party system. The expanded variety of possible candidates for nomination and even election, and the way this contributes to breaking down stable coalitions, follows directly from all that. Let it simply be noted, in institutional terms, that what has evolved as the process of presidential selection is in fact a shifting sequence of individual state contests featuring low voter turnout and extremely low public information, where the previous state outcome can sharply—and often idiosyncratically—alter the distribution of resources for the next contest in the chain. Early outcomes in small and unrepresentative states can be crucial. Freak interactions among a stray sample of candidates in an unpredictably key state can be crucial too.

What results, of course, is a further decline in the likelihood of nominees who are central partisan figures, representing party programs and party constituencies built up over time. Moreover, these tendencies are further exaggerated by the possibilities—indeed, the practical necessities—of the effective conduct of the institution of the presidency, once a successful nominee is installed in office. Here, Ronald Reagan is a good example of the path to be followed by an effective modern president. His real strength as a leader, and the ultimate power of the American presidency in the modern era, was his ability to go around the other institutions of government, and even around the Republican Party within them, and attempt to mobilize key elements of the general public on what he viewed as the major issue, so that *they* pressed these other institutions in his preferred direction.

The situation in Congress is less well publicized, but it also partakes, heavily and increasingly, of this evolving political character, of this expanded range of possibilities and this declining chance to construct stable and continuing political coalitions. Throughout the postwar period, the tendency of senators and congressmen to build thoroughly independent and personal campaigns has been increasing, and for a set of very good— and I hope now familiar—reasons: the near-total spread of primary elections for nomination, the long-term decline of political parties as electoral organizations, the shift to a politics based on independent activists with their own narrow and personal policy concerns, the rise of additional media and of advertising alternatives to help sketch out a personalized identity for the candidate. Not surprisingly, when all this is put together, it produces candidates who may acquire a party label but who do not acquire any serious ties to an organized political party and thus to one another as they arrive in Congress.

This development, in turn, is largely the cause, but also a further effect, of reinforcing changes inside the institution of Congress. Candidates arrive with localized, even personalized concerns, and they have largely reworked the internal rules of Congress so that they do not have to subordinate these to larger, more fixed, continuing coalitions there. Indeed, if they should arrive without these localized and personalized concerns, the environment they find within the institution encourages them to develop such concerns, so as to prosper both within and without. There are many who argue that these changes have not increased the ability of Congress as an institution to make public policy. Regardless, they have clearly increased the ability of individual members to work on what concerns them personally and to secure personal attention for doing so.

For example, and perhaps most obviously, these members have shifted internal committee resources so as to benefit the individual congressman or senator. Even committee chairs are no longer assured an automatic hold on their posts, unless they satisfy a wide array of committee members; staff and other committee resources are no longer assigned solely by—much less solely to—these once-autocratic chairmen. Given this change in committee (and subcommittee) operation, and especially given the changed attitudes of members that go along with it, it is not surprising that the norm of deference to committees on the House and Senate floors has declined as well. The floor itself is now a much more open and flexible theater for politics in its own right. Proposals from committees can be extensively amended there. Unrelated matters can much more easily be appended to satisfy individual members or currents of the moment within the chamber.

It is probably least common to think of the Supreme Court in these terms, yet nowhere in American politics are these trends more true than at the Court, and nowhere are they presented in as clear and pure a fashion. The expanded range of possible alternatives, the shifting nature of internal coalitions, the strains that outcomes within the institution reliably place on incipiently stable coalitions: these are almost the hallmarks of the modern Supreme Court. In fact, many (perhaps most) of the major issues in contemporary American politics have been handled—and often created—within the Court. Civil rights and race, civil liberties and crime, the powers of other governmental institutions, education, religion, community life: these have all become central preoccupations of the Court and of many other Americans.

Yet if these issues are considered not for their immediate substance but for their contribution to and impact on the larger structure of American politics, they yield perhaps the most exaggerated examples of its contemporary evolution. Most fundamentally, of course, these issues have meant that the Supreme Court has become yet another major, independent theater for the pursuit of politics and policy. The Court does not act merely as a regulator or respondent to politics elsewhere. Increasingly, it is the "court of first resort" in American politics, displacing Congress and even the presidency. The fact that the Court has been willing to play this role has added to the variety of possible outcomes in American politics and to the variety of available routes to reach those outcomes. At the same time, it has inevitably added to the complexity of the struggle within and among the major institutions of American government.

Nevertheless, these are not the only effects of an activated Court in American politics, large though these effects are. The ultimate contribution of the Supreme Court to the structure of politics in the modern era probably comes from the strains that its role and its decisions impose on any large and continuing coalitions in politics beyond the bounds of the Court. Indeed, if one examines those key realms of Court action since the 1950s, one discovers that almost all its decisions have had the effect, though surely not the intent, of pitting elements within the two major-party coalitions against each other.

In the early 1950s, before the Court began to expand the scope and fluidity of American politics, politics featured two large, comparatively stable coalitions. There was a blue-collar, working-class coalition aligned with the national Democratic Party, and there was a white-collar, middle-class coalition aligned with the national Republican Party. Yet in the interim, almost every major Court decision has contributed to conflict *within* these coalitions, pitting internal elements against each other, rather than to conflict *between* these coalitions, which would have contributed to their coherence and permanence instead. For example, civil liberties and crime decisions have pitted the truly disadvantaged against their blue-collar neighbors, not blue collar against white collar. Decisions on religion and religious display have pitted the most traditional Democrats not against Republicans but against the least traditional elements of the Democratic coalition.

The Changing Structure of American Politics

How can one summarize this new structure of American politics—in interest groups, political parties, the presidency, Congress, and the Court? Perhaps it can be done by saying that far more items can now be brought into politics, and far more varied coalitions-of-the-moment can be built around these items, sometimes with almost incredible speed. But also, surely, it must be said that it is simultaneously much harder to build stable coalitions, and hence continuing policy programs, and that the coalitions and policies that are constructed are subject to rapid disassembly, lending an augmented air of unpredictability to American national politics.

This must not be overstated; it is not the case that "anything goes." There is an implicit policy base that a broad majority of Americans support and that cannot be substantially altered. Indeed, the Reagan administration itself occasionally provides direct testimony to this, for example, with the effects of even speculating about making Social Security "voluntary." Even then, it is remarkable what can be done in practice: switching the Republican Party to Keynesian economics via supply-side doctrine, while switching the Democratic Party to the defense of a balanced budget, for example. It is equally amazing what can, in principle, be contemplated: one can restructure even Social Security in a major way, and sharply alter defense policy as well.

Having said that, however, it must be noted that this new world of American politics appears to be effectively permanent. The environment is becoming more conducive to the emergence of new cause- and issue-related interest groups, with their reliance on increasing education and expanding technology. At the same time, the prospect for the reemergence of political parties as extended and hierarchical organizations is becoming more remote, as the final prerogatives and last tangible resources are taken away from party officials. And let us note parenthetically that high-technology substitutes for old-fashioned party organization—computerized mailing lists and such—cannot undertake coalition building, program development, and governmental coordination.

Within governmental institutions, the presidency appears to be stabilized in its current form, through the increasing independence of presidential selection and the increasing emphasis on personal communication. Congress will still feature independent campaigns for office and individual entrepreneurship once candidates get there, regardless of additional tinkering with its internal rules. And the Court is unlikely to change its structural contributions, except to exaggerate them further. Thus, although the Burger Court was more conservative than the Warren Court on standard ideological measures, it was not more inclined toward a conservatism that would pull it back out of politics, and it was even less coherent internally.

This brings the entire analysis back to individual voters and to the opening popular debate about a new Republican era. Almost all these larger structural changes, these changes in the "big picture" in current American politics, suggest the same conclusion as an analysis of the smaller popular debate—namely, that the old Democratic order is effectively over, but a new Republican counterpart is not only not here but is in fact unlikely to arrive.

The specific attitudes of individual voters—their opinions, preferences, intentions, even party identifications—will fluctuate continually with developments in all these governmental and quasi-governmental institutions and in the larger world outside them. Thus opinion polls will continue to reveal a public that is now more conservative, now again more liberal; now more Republican, once again more Democratic. This seems only a reasonable response to a changed political environment, especially to one with an expanded policy agenda, less stable political coalitions, and exaggerated personal cross-pressures. These fluctuations, then, when they are added to larger changes in intermediary organizations and in the institutions of government, must be seen not as hints of some emerging new stage of political development but as confirmation of the stage that is already there, and as reasons—restraints—to expect it to continue.

There are admittedly developments that might produce a very different order in American politics, or even some new version of the previous order. And although we cannot in principle paint the details of these developments, we can know the general categories into which they fall. Most obvious is some profound national crisis in economics, foreign affairs, perhaps even climatology or epidemiology. At some remove is further institutional reform, perhaps with the goal of restoring larger coalitions, perhaps only with that unintended effect. And at the other extreme is the prospect of individual leadership in the service of some larger and continuing program.

Yet these developments, while possible, are not only hard to predict; they are also unlikely to contribute a new order. Either they are uncommon, such as, perhaps blessedly, national crises, or they are of decreasing effect as the new era progresses, such as more limited institutional reform. Or they may be just inherently constrained in leaving permanent effects, as in the case of individual leadership skills. Once again, what remains is every reason to believe that the new order is not only new but here to stay.

It might be argued, in an afterword, that whether or not this is true in practice, it is not particularly satisfying to the intellect. In this view, saying that a political system has an expanded array of possible outcomes, expanded possibilities for rotation among them, and less predictability as a result is less precise than saying that the key division is this, the major alternatives are these, and the likely outcome is that. Yet for students of American politics, this same situation—a new order with variety, possibility, and chance—is also surely the promise of continued, even increasing, fascination.

Part II

Our Time in Perspective

CHAPTER SIX

The Circulation of Elites, 1946–1996

The governing elite is always in a state of slow and continuous transformation. It flows on like a river, never being today what it was yesterday. From time to time, sudden and violent disturbances occur. There is a flood—the river overflows its banks. Afterwards, the new governing elite again resumes its slow transformation. The flood has subsided; the river is again flowing normally in its wonted bed.
—Pareto (1980, 809)

The coming to partisan politics of new social groups, flagged by the arrival of new group leaders, is not a phenomenon easily missed by even the casual observer. And indeed, a steady stream of such leaders and their groups has characterized American politics across the postwar period. From organized labor and "Modern Republicans" to "New Politics Democrats" and evangelical Protestants, to take only the leading examples from opposite ends of the postwar era, each has met certain common criteria. Thus each began with the emergence of an arguably new social base. Each generated the critical further element, an aspiring institutional leadership. That leadership then managed the transition to an explicitly partisan home. And in the process, invariably, it bid to shape the policy agenda of its time.

Yet social scientists have found study of this phenomenon to be a treacherous realm. What distinguishes an elite? What makes it new? What makes such elites, if they can be demarcated, effectively partisan? How do they become so? To what extent does this matter to the conduct of politics? To the resulting public policy? In a socially egalitarian and politically democratic society, the term itself carries excess baggage, an unattractive—even mocking—overlay. Is not the very presence of "political elites" evidence of incomplete democratic development? In application, most neutral definitions manage to shuck this baggage only by converting the notion into a

129

category so formalistic as to empty it of most behavioral implications. The analytic question gets reduced to the social background of those who occupy, say, the presidency, the Senate, or the U.S. Supreme Court.

These problems did not always seem inherent. When the self-conscious social sciences were themselves arriving in the late nineteenth and early twentieth centuries, elite analysis appeared to hold the prospect of being both analytically sensible and substantively rich. Few social analysts of the time would have instinctively shied away from the concept. Nevertheless, its most central application surely came in the work of Italian sociologist Vilfredo Pareto, especially in his framework for studying the *circulation* of elites—the "heterogeneousness of society and circulation among its various elements" (1980, 791), to use his language. One secondary advantage of using partisan elites as a route into American politics, then, is to reclaim some of the argument offered by Pareto nearly a century ago.

There are two more immediate and practical advantages to beginning with Pareto. One is the opportunity to excise, from the start, any normative overlay in the basic concept. Social groups require group elites as part of their definition, as a condition of their movement from category to group. In turn, this fundamental connection should invigorate the resulting analysis, making it descriptively richer and analytically more dynamic, by imposing a search for the link between emerging social groups and emergent leadership behavior, as well as a search for the factors that produce it and the outcomes that follow from its production. In the beginning, in any case, five decades before there was a postwar world, the notion of an elite was essentially structural in character.

> So let us make a class of the people who have the highest indices of their branch of activity, and to that class give the name of *elite*. It is obvious that the line that separates the elite from the rest of the population is not, and cannot be, precise, no more than is the line that separates youth from maturity. This, however, does not detract from the usefulness of considering this division of things.
>
> For the particular investigation with which we are engaged, a study of the social equilibrium, it will help if we further divide that class into two classes: a *governing elite,* comprising individuals who directly or indirectly play some part in government, and a non-governing elite, comprising the rest. . . . In moving from one group to another, an individual brings with him certain inclinations, sentiments, attitudes

that he has acquired in the group from which he comes, and that circumstance cannot be ignored. To this mixing, in the particular case in which only two groups, the elite and the non-elite, are envisaged, the term "circulation of elites" has been applied. (Pareto 1980, 792–96)

Such circulations, evidently, were to contain three integral elements. There was a social group, with rising consciousness of itself, increasing consequence to society, and potentially increasing consequence to politics. There was a leadership component, not necessarily arising in its entirety from within the broader social group but effectively able to speak in its name. Needless to say, this component would play the crucial role in operationalizing the arrival of the larger group in politics. And there were values (and hence preferences) distinctive to this group, values that were at least passed along by, and often initially embodied within, its emergent elite. These became the policy wishes that would characterize the contribution of the new elite to political debate.

Pareto was confident that this process was reliably central to politics, regardless of institutional arrangements and regardless of societal composition. The specifics would vary—that was part of the power of the framework—but the generic process would inevitably recur. A further consequence of this formulation, apart from its analytic neutrality and structural differentiation, was that it did not insist that the relevant elite be located in any one specific place. Hence an emergent *partisan* elite could be located within an organized group, putting pressure on a political party. It could surface within the aggregate of those who did the actual work of the party, even coming to constitute "the party" itself. Or it could be found increasingly among the incumbents of public offices secured by that party. A newly relevant social category, newly influential spokesmen for it, and distinguishing values and preferences were the essence of the quest. Beyond that, Pareto would have been the first to argue that the utility of this framework had to reside in the specifics of its application, in a particular nation during a particular historical period.

> Such considerations serve to explain, along with the theoretical difficulties, how the solutions that are usually found for the general problem have so little, and sometimes no, bearing on realities. Solutions of particular problems come closer to the mark because, situated as they are in specific times and places, they present fewer theoretical difficulties; and

because practical empiricism implicitly takes account of many circumstances that theory, until it has been carried to a high state of perfection,
cannot explicitly appraise. (Pareto 1980, 902)

Organized Labor

When, in a country, classes that for any reason have long remained separate
mingle or, in more general terms, when a class-circulation that has been sluggish
suddenly acquires an intensity at all considerable, almost always observable is an
appreciable increase in intellectual, economic, and political prosperity in the
country in question. And that is why periods of transition from oligarchic to more
or less democratic regimes are often periods of prosperity.

If the prosperity in question were due to different systems of government, the
prosperity should continue as long as the new regime endured. But that is not the
case. The fluorescence lasts for a certain length of time and then comes a decline.
—Pareto (1980, 1057–58)

Few observers, no matter how casual, could have failed to notice the emergence—really the explosion to prominence—of the first great partisan elite
in postwar American politics. Its social group was organized labor, and the
elite was its recognized formal leadership. The policies championed included not just worker organization and collective bargaining but also, in a
secondary but major way, the general social welfare programs that would
support and supplement the gains of organized workers in their lives outside the workplace. Moreover, in all this, the new labor elite was itself
inescapably central. In one sense, it was, of course, produced by the conversion of an industrial working class into an organized labor movement. Yet it
was also the group that *managed* that conversion (Taft 1964; Zieger 1986;
Derber and Young 1957; Forbath 1991; Bernstein 1969).

And here, as in all the major postwar cases, the details of this management mattered. This new labor elite was also the body of specialized actors
who were determined, this time, to have not just an active role in both
electoral and institutional politicking but a specific partisan linkage as well,
in opposition to the dominant theory guiding the labor movement in the
United States to that time. Having effectuated this partisan link, the new
labor elite went on to establish the machinery to make it concrete and
ongoing, and then to pursue labor interests through that machinery. By

extension, it was this new labor leadership, most centrally, that translated those interests and determined that the agenda for this machinery would be sharply expanded, beyond bread-and-butter union issues.

Nevertheless, in a more pronounced fashion than with any of the other main elite infusions of the postwar period, the emergence of both this social group and its organizational leadership was rooted in formal, national legislation. It could, in fact, be traced directly to changes in the law. The existence of an industrial working class certainly predated legal reform. It had become a national presence by the late nineteenth century; arguably, it had been present in specific sectors and locales before the Civil War. Likewise, there had been previous up-ticks in the translation from industrial working class to organized labor movement, gathered most centrally in the American Federation of Labor (AFL). Union membership had surged at the turn of the twentieth century. Organized industrial conflict—strike activity—had surged at the end of World War I.

Yet the scale of growth in the immediate postwar years was sufficient to suggest a qualitative change. Again, there was a chain of important events that helped convert a social class into a labor movement in the years immediately following World War II: the onset of the Great Depression; the coming of the New Deal; widespread, genuine, and explicit class conflict; reconstitution of the national Democratic coalition; bifurcation in the labor movement itself, producing the Congress of Industrial Organizations (CIO) but ultimately reinvigorating the AFL. All these things contributed to the rise of this first and most inescapable of the postwar partisan elites. In none of the counterpart cases, however—Modern Republicans, New Politics Democrats, or evangelical Protestants—was the simple role of law so central, both in creating the group basis for a new elite and in institutionalizing that elite itself.

The key precursor to this was the National Industrial Recovery Act of 1933, whose Section 7(a) attempted to create an employee right to organize and bargain collectively and did create a National Labor Relations Board (NLRB) to oversee implementation of that right. When the full act was struck down by the Supreme Court in *Schechter Poultry Corporation v. United States* (295 U.S. 495, 1935), supporters responded with the National Labor Relations Act (NLRA) of 1935. The NLRA attempted not just to reestablish the right to organize and bargain collectively but also to guarantee the integrity of union selection, and it established a second NLRB with substantially expanded powers, charged explicitly with preventing unfair management behavior. By the narrowest of margins, five to four, the Supreme Court, in *National Labor Relations Board v. Jones & Laughlin Steel* (301 U.S. 1, 1937), sustained this act.

There were other pieces of New Deal legislation with direct relevance to organized labor, including the Fair Labor Standards Act of 1938. There were other purposes even to the NLRA of 1935: directly partisan goals, such as embedding American working people in the Democratic coalition; more systemic goals, such as regularizing labor-management relations; and even broader aspirations, such as underpinning an economy built on mass consumerism and consumption. And there were partially autonomous contributions to the growth and institutionalization of American labor from, most notably, the new CIO. But it was the NLRA that institutionalized all of these, along with the record keeping that would chart their progress. Michael Barone captures the mix of social forces and legal buttresses that produced a major player in partisan politics:

> They knew they faced steep odds. The Wagner Act [NLRA] might be ruled unconstitutional . . . the companies might prevail, as they had in the 1920s. But at least some of these unionists must have been encouraged by the hope, which turned out to be fulfilled, that they were creating a new institution which would become a part of the fabric of American life and would play a major role in the economy and politics of their country. (Barone 1990, 100)

And for the next thirty years, that progress was to be as prominent as it was remarkable. Figure 1 shows the growth of union membership, both in raw numbers and as a share of the total labor force. Membership growth on this scale could hardly fail to produce the sense of an explosive new social presence, especially since it was concentrated in those economic sectors, especially manufacturing, that came to embody the great postwar economic boom—and because it represented an immediate (and again inescapable) change in power relations within those sectors. Yet at this point, the leadership of organized labor, as militant and as newly numerous as it obviously was, was still not evidently a political elite, much less a partisan one. A social base had become an organized group, and this group was rapidly generating a professionalized leadership. But the latter had not yet moved decisively into politics, partisan or not.

Ironically, it would be another national law—deleterious, not beneficial—that led directly to this second conversion. The Labor-Management Relations Act of 1947, known more commonly as the Taft-Hartley Act after

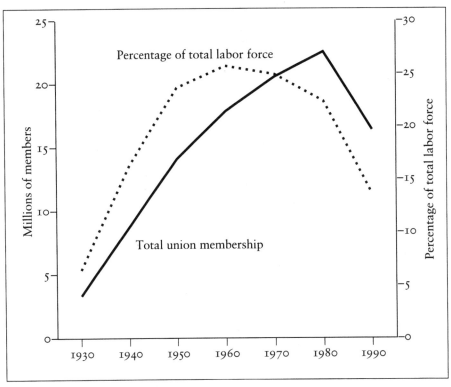

FIGURE I

UNION MEMBERSHIP ACROSS THE POSTWAR YEARS

SOURCES: *Historical Statistics of the United States, Colonial Times to 1970* (Washington, D.C.: Department of Commerce, 1975); *Statistical Abstract of the United States* (Washington, D.C.: Department of Commerce, various years).

its (Republican) sponsors in the Senate and House, respectively, represented the first serious counterattack by those unhappy with the growing role of organized labor. To that end, it added a (longer) list of unfair labor practices to the roster of unfair management practices the NLRA had created, while complicating the process of union certification and slowing use of the ultimate weapon of a certified union, the strike. But what it produced, in Paretian terms, was the final link in this causal chain: the conversion of an organized group into a political elite, while reminding this elite that the exercise of its power had an almost inevitable partisan dimension.

The seeds of Taft-Hartley had been sown during the rise to social power by organized labor. The continuing militancy of some labor leaders during the Second World War—John L. Lewis of the United Mine Workers, a founding figure in the CIO, stood out—had already produced some restraining legislation. But the overall growth of labor unions in American society had been an increasing worry not just to corporate business, its "natural" opponent, but also to the mainstream Republicans who represented areas where small (not corporate) business was still dominant. It was actually the latter who would remain most impressed by the threat from organized labor, as the section on Modern Republicans will suggest.

In any case, these seeds flowered in the early postwar years, characterized, as Figure 2 indicates, by unprecedented strike activity. There

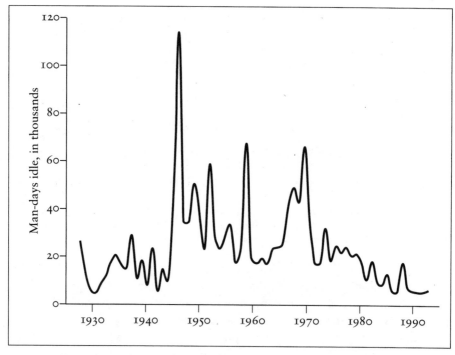

FIGURE 2
WORK STOPPAGES

SOURCE: *Statistical Abstract of the United States* (Washington, D.C.: Department of Commerce, various years).

were other great bulges in such activity during the twentieth century—immediately after World War I, for example. But the year 1946 set the historical record—most strikes, most days lost to strikes—that remains unchallenged a half century later. And on this, the figure sharply understates the situation: the record set in 1946 is all the more remarkable because the workforce generating it was less than half the size of its modern counterpart. Said differently, in 1994, there was a man-day lost to strikes for every twenty-six American workers; in 1946, there was a man-day lost for every *one-half* worker. That was labor strife on an imposing level. It led directly to the Labor-Management Relations Act of 1947. It led indirectly but ineluctably to a newly partisan strategy for the new labor elite.

Previous up-ticks in labor organization had been characterized by a doctrine of explicit nonpartisanship, growing partly out of a tradition of syndicalism in the American labor movement, partly out of a sense that labor interests were best served by possessing partisan alternatives, and partly from the apparent unattractiveness of both major political parties. Samuel Gompers, the dominant figure in AFL history to that point, had argued forcefully that "labor must learn to use parties to advance our principles, and not allow political parties to manipulate us for their own achievement." The constitution of the AFL thus averred that "party politics, whether they be Democratic, Republican, Socialistic, Populistic, Prohibitionist, or any other, shall have no place in the conventions of the American Federation of Labor" (Vale 1971, 34; more generally, see Reed 1966).

In response to restrictive governmental legislation during World War II, the CIO had formed a Political Action Committee, the CIO-PAC. One other immediate response to the passage of Taft-Hartley, then, was the creation by the AFL of the Labor League for Political Education (LLPE), a deliberate counterpart to the CIO-PAC. Moreover, the national AFL convention that created the LLPE called on each of its constituent units to create further counterpart organizations for attending to political matters and urged them to replicate these at every level of the organization in time for the 1948 election.

From there, the partisan die was probably cast. However much the LLPE leadership might flirt with the old AFL maxims, the implicitly partisan facts about the distribution of labor strength argued otherwise, and these had just been powerfully and painfully emphasized by the election of 1946. As Figure 3 demonstrates, the geographic distribution of labor gains was hardly uniform. Nearly a quarter of all working-age Americans were now

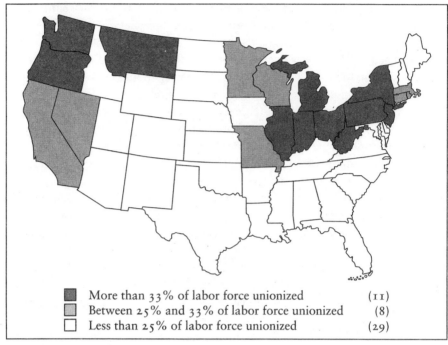

More than 33% of labor force unionized   (11)
Between 25% and 33% of labor force unionized   (8)
Less than 25% of labor force unionized   (29)

FIGURE 3

GEOGRAPHIC DISTRIBUTION OF UNION MEMBERSHIP, 1953

SOURCES: Leo Troy, *Distribution of Union Membership among the States, 1939 and 1953*, Occasional Paper no. 56 (New York: National Bureau of Economic Research, 1975), 18–19; *Statistical Abstract of the United States* (Washington, D.C.: Department of Commerce, 1954).

unionized, but there were areas, such as the Middle Atlantic states, the industrial Midwest, and the far Northwest, where this figure was more than a third; likewise, there were regions, especially the South but also the agricultural Midwest, where the figure for unionization was derisory. Yet if these were merely facts of institutional economic life, they were also key facts of political life—and implicitly partisan facts at that.

The election of 1946 would make them explicit. What happened in 1946, at one level, was a huge resurgence—observers at the time could not know how temporary it was—of the national Republican Party. But this meant not just that the putative party of owners rather than workers controlled both houses of Congress. It also meant that the largest surviving contingent of the national Democratic Party was in the South, where Republican competition was nugatory, and where labor was scantily organized. Table 1 shows the fate of those northern and western Democrats, whose constituents were the bulk of organized labor, for the elections of 1944, 1946, and 1948, with the 1946 election being the one crucial to the fortunes of the Taft-Hartley Act.

The line from there to the status of major *partisan* elite, indisputably the major Democratic elite of the ensuing generation, was short and direct. That line ran through the merger of the two great federations, the AFL and the CIO, in 1955. But by then, all the major means of operating in politics, along with the fact that these would be exercised reliably in conjunction with the Democratic Party, were effectively established. Creation of the AFL-CIO only institutionalized them in the formal framework for the dominant voice of the dominant partisan Democratic elite (Millis and Brown 1950; Lee 1966; Vale 1971; Wilson 1979; Goulden 1972; Bok and Dunlop 1970; Price 1980; Kochan, Katz, and McKersie 1986; Berger 1960).

The original schism that produced two labor federations during the 1930s had been rooted in different approaches to organizing the industrial workforce. The AFL had long proceeded by organizing workers within

TABLE I

PARTISAN IMPACTS OF THE 1946 ELECTION

A. The House

	Democrat	Southern Democrat	Republican	Nonsouthern
1948	160	103	171	1
1946	85	103	246	1
1944	140	103	190	2

B. The Senate

	Democrat	Southern Democrat	Republican	Nonsouthern
1948	32	22	42	0
1946	23	22	51	0
1944	35	22	38	1

SOURCE: *Guide to U.S. Elections* (Washington, D.C.: CQ Press, 1975), 447–880.

trades and across industries. The unions that became the CIO argued that faster progress would come from organizing workers within industries and across trades. By 1955, the CIO unions, the apparent winners of the early argument on the numbers, had been established and stabilized but had reached an apparent plateau in their growth. By 1955, the AFL unions had resumed growing, so that they were by far the larger of the two great families of organized labor. The generation of leaders responsible for the initial split had likewise passed from the scene.

If future Taft-Hartleys were to be avoided, then, in an environment where the easier economic sectors had already been unionized, labor had to marshal every resource. In such an environment, unification made sense to most major players. By the time of unification, the AFL had also delivered its first presidential endorsement, of Democrat Adlai Stevenson against Republican Dwight Eisenhower in 1952, thereby crossing yet another historical barrier. It had also had its first experience (though 1956 would prove to be much worse in this regard) of having to carry the Democratic campaign in areas where the official party was either enfeebled or sat on its hands in the face of Eisenhower's personal popularity.

A partisan political orientation thus became the logical approach for the new Committee on Political Education (COPE) of the newly merged AFL-CIO, even though it represented a double change: not just away from determined nonpartisanship but also away from a concentration on legislative politics, on lobbying, and toward serious and sustained emphasis on electoral politics, on electioneering, at every stage of the process. Lobbying activity hardly retreated, and organized labor had powerful resources to commit to it. Indeed, these resources were effectively augmented once it had established major electoral connections to many congressmen and senators, who were simultaneously given definition by the content of the lobbying campaign.

COPE thus developed and constantly revised a labor program of public policy and made sure that amenable legislators knew its contents, through direct national communication in Washington, through communication from state and local chapters, and, occasionally, through communication efforts from the mass membership. The result was the single most important lobbying operation within the majority party in American politics. With it came a consistent, ongoing, parallel electoral effort that always involved voter registration drives, targeted initially at union members but expanded subsequently to general geographic areas where members were concentrated. When there was a nominee who was programmatically attractive to organized labor—a Democratic nominee, with the rarest of exceptions—this electoral effort could involve major get-out-the-vote drives as well, complete with modern technology as it evolved. As all this became institutionalized, labor became more comfortable intervening in the primary elections that nominated such candidates, so as to have someone attractive to support in the general election.

As it happened, these developments also transpired at a point where the electoral machinery of the official Democratic Party, which historically would have assumed priority for all these activities, was becoming increasingly enfeebled in large areas of the country. As a result, organized labor would often substitute, in effect, for the official party. To that end, it could even dispatch experienced operatives to help in the practical management of a campaign. And the fact that its funding capacities were never, in the aggregate, equal to those of corporate business did not mean that its funds were not crucial to mounting and sustaining such campaigns. A generation later, this trend would come full circle when governmental workers, once the patronage base for an organized Democratic Party, became unionized themselves, in the main recruiting success for organized labor in that generation. But already by the late 1950s, labor *was* the Democratic campaign in major geographic areas.

The ascendant labor elite that undertook these newly partisan activities was distinctive in other important ways—in its collective structure as well as its policy program—in comparison to labor elites in other countries and other elites in American politics. Seen one way, these distinctions were important to the manner in which an emergent partisan elite could organize itself. Seen another way, they were central to the values—to the *transformation* of values—that this elite brought forcefully into American politics. One aspect of this distinctive character was the fact that American union officials—full-time, fully paid union bureaucrats—were considerably more numerous than those in other nations. A variety of characteristics of the American context, including the decentralization of bargaining, the individualized character of politics, and the expected autonomy of workers in pursuing their own interests, underpinned this difference. In any case, Table 2 suggests how substantial it was.

Needless to say, a numerous body of specialized actors, fully supported by extended formal organizations, was advantaged in pursuing its policy goals. This led directly to the other distinctive characteristic of this cadre in

TABLE 2

UNION OFFICIALS AND UNION MEMBERS

Country	Number of full-time officials	Ratio of officials to members
United States	60,000	1: 300
Denmark	1,000	1: 775
Australia	2,750	1: 900
Sweden	900	1: 1,700
Great Britain	4,000	1: 2,000
Norway	240	1: 2,200

SOURCE: Adapted from Seymour Martin Lipset, "Trade Unions and Social Structure: II," *Industrial Relations* 1 (February 1962): 93. Data are from various years in the late 1950s.

the period of labor ascendancy, one that Pareto himself might have expected. This vastly expanded cadre of labor operatives had grown so fast that it had to emerge, by and large, directly out of the organized occupations themselves, at least in this initial generation. Certainly more than at any subsequent point in the evolution of American labor, this meant that new labor bureaucrats brought the general social views of their members directly into politics. Earlier labor activists had been nurtured by union ideology. Later counterparts would be trained in labor-relations courses. This crucial ascendant generation was neither.

In terms of the values guiding conflict over public policy, this combination of bureaucratic muscle and social background had three main implications. First, these new political operatives—this new partisan elite—still gave its highest priority to issues of worker organizing and collective bargaining. Such an emphasis, backed by all the resources of a newly partisan federation, would prove sufficient to find ways to live with the provisions of the Taft-Hartley Act, as well as defuse subsequent legislative attacks. Conversely, this emphasis, even when backed by all these resources, was never sufficient actually to repeal Taft-Hartley as a framework.

Second, the entire operation also turned to supporting (and potentially expanding) the welfare state, those social welfare programs that benefited working people when they were not at work and were intended to benefit others in similar circumstances. Union membership was to stall by the late 1950s. Nevertheless, this orientation would make organized labor central to another great increment to the welfare state, courtesy of the New Frontier and the Great Society in the early 1960s. And it was to remain central to the rearguard defense of these programs when its own membership was in decline and they were under counterattack. Two great elite initiatives were thus represented by, and came together in, this second policy concentration: the decision to make organized labor a central element of the Democratic coalition, and the decision to use a place in that coalition to widen the focus of labor in politics generally.

Third and finally, the fact that labor would thereafter be crucial in keeping economic and social welfare issues at the center of Democratic Party affairs implied an essential moderation on those alternative social and cultural issues that made their way intermittently into politics. On these, labor was to be, for example, anticommunist in foreign affairs and traditionalist in social values. More important, however, a focus on social welfare from a central place in the Democratic coalition implied a conscious decision to try to sustain the general societal consensus on social and cultural issues and thereby keep such issues out of politics.

Modern Republicans

One might suppose that since the interests of employers and strike-breakers are directly contrary to the interest of the strikers, they would use the opposite derivations. But that is not the case, or if they do, they do it in a very mild, apologetic way. . . . As regards employers of labor, the reason is that many of them are "speculators" who hope to make up for their losses in a strike through government aid and at the expense of consumer or taxpayer. Their quarrels with strikers are quarrels between accomplices over the division of the loot.
　—Pareto (1980, 913)

The other newly ascendant partisan elite of the immediate postwar years was utterly different in structure from organized labor, though it was also—as Pareto might have hypothesized?—curiously symbiotic in its political behavior. It was different in the superficial sense of being based in the institutional nemesis of labor, namely, corporate business. But it was also structurally different, and in a whole host of ways. Most fundamentally, it lacked the membership base that characterized labor. In that sense, it was very close to being an elite without a mass. Likewise, it lacked a defining moment, one crystallizing its move into politics, being instead the product of a historical period and a strategic context. Nevertheless, it was to shape the opening years of postwar politics in important ways in conjunction with organized labor. Indeed, to add to the curiosity of the relationship, it was to share certain major policy preferences with its hypothetical adversary: an internationalism in foreign affairs, for example, and support for civil rights.

The elite in question is perhaps best denominated as the "Modern Republicans," in deference to the first self-conscious attempt by practitioners to classify it. In truth, many others acknowledged its distinctiveness in its own time, attaching their hopes or (more often) fears to its prospective rise. Yet their designations normally derived, in effect, from private political preferences. Democratic opponents referred to this group merely as "corporate Republicans"; intraparty rivals dubbed them "me too Republicans." "Modern Republicans" at least leaves the designation to the group itself, while remaining sufficiently vague as to leave its substantive content to the analyst. Despite all that, this second distinctive postwar elite offered all the classic hallmarks demanded by Pareto.

At bottom, there was a newly ascendant—or at least freshly ascendant— social stratum. Beyond it, there was a body of specialized actors emerging directly from this stratum. This elite (for so it certainly was) held clearly distinguishing values and preferences. As a result, its fortunes had potential policy consequences, and their pursuit was destined to influence American politics well into the 1970s. More than with any other postwar elite, this group would have a differential success with different public offices. More than with any other, the *process* by which the Modern Republicans acquired both a political role and partisan attachments was to remain decentralized and amorphous. Yet allowing those facts to obscure its rise would obscure the second main manifestation of the circulation of elites in postwar American politics.

The roots of this new, incipient partisan elite were actually in an organizational form rather than in a specific organization, much less an overhead agency. That form was the modern business corporation, and if it was not strictly new to American life, it was about to acquire a dominance it had never previously possessed, along with other associated characteristics that were arguably new. The form itself had been born a generation before the American Civil War. It had come to dominate specific sectors of the economy (transportation, communication) in the late nineteenth century. And it had shown every sign of becoming broadly dominant in the first quarter of the twentieth century, before the Great Depression brought corporate growth in general to a halt and tarnished the public standing of corporate elites (Chandler 1977; Jacoby 1991; Freeman 1960; Feldstein 1980; Epstein 1969; Bunzel 1962; Galbraith 1967).

Yet the newly invigorated American economy of the postwar years was destined to return to a focus on the business corporation. Wartime production had actually conferred particular benefits on corporate (rather than small or family) business. The consumer boom of the postwar years was a further contribution to the apparently dominating destiny of the form. So was the coming of a huge standing defense establishment, courtesy of new international defense commitments. And so, especially, was the spread of U.S. corporations into foreign markets, at a time when the other main developed economies were in spectacular disarray and the modern corporation had not so clearly displaced either small business or the family firm elsewhere. A new corporate leadership, a truly "managerial" leadership in every sense of the word, completed the picture.

None of this was hidden from public view at the time, and much was made of the social phenomena associated with the resurgence of corporate America. However, contemporary social analysts could not know how temporally distinctive this evolution was. From one side, the evidently increasing concentration of employment inside the manufacturing sector was real enough, as Figure 4 indicates. Yet even there, the great firms, those with more than 1,000 employees, would peak early as a share of all American workers and then begin to recede; their share of value added would follow. Indeed, from the other side, not only would all such concentration reach a ceiling by the 1960s, but the place of manufacturing in the American economy would already have crested, as shown in Figure 5, so that corporate gigantism was not necessarily the wave of the future.

In its time, nevertheless, that gigantism was impressive. Big government had obviously come with the New Deal and World War II. It did not go away. Big labor had arrived with the Great Depression and the NLRA, and it remained an obvious mountain on the postwar landscape. Big business was a central part of the postwar recovery, and this fact was widely noted within its society (Riesman 1950; Potter 1954; Whyte 1956; Lipset 1963).

The rise of an economic form, of course, was not itself a social base, a political elite, a partisan link, or a programmatic orientation—although growth on this scale of what was also a form of social organization brought incipient possibilities for all of the above. Corporate growth automatically

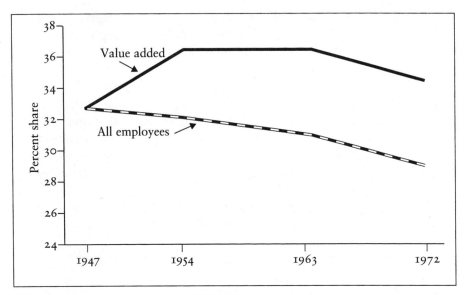

FIGURE 4

GROWTH OF THE POSTWAR CORPORATE WORLD —

EMPLOYMENT AND VALUE ADDED IN FIRMS OF 1,000 AND OVER

SOURCE: *Statistical Abstract of the United States* (Washington, D.C.: Department of Commerce, various years).

implied an increase in "corporate numbers." That category, however, was still too abstract to have much meaning, and indeed, the largest share of corporate employees actually consisted of the people who made up the social base for organized labor. As a result, the social base for what was to become Modern Republicanism was really a burgeoning "middle management" instead.

For a time, this growing social base actually possessed a new and growing *residential location:* the burgeoning suburbs, which were also a critical part of the immediate postwar scene. Suburbanization would ultimately become a defining characteristic of American society, and this period would see the greatest raw explosion of housing starts in American history, almost all of which were intendedly suburban (see Table 3). As a result, it would see the transition of the United States to an archetypically suburban society. Eventually, the status of dominant residential form would lessen the dis-

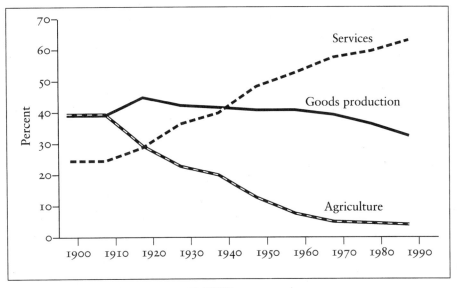

FIGURE 5

GROWTH OF THE POSTWAR CORPORATE WORLD —

EMPLOYMENT DISTRIBUTION BY MAJOR SECTOR

SOURCES: *Historical Statistics of the United States, Colonial Times to 1970* (Washington, D.C.: Department of Commerce, 1975); *Statistical Abstract of the United States* (Washington, D.C.: Department of Commerce, various years).

tinctiveness of the suburbs as a political base, as they came to encompass most of the divisions characterizing American society. But in the immediate postwar years, the suburbs were still disproportionately home to lesser managerial employees of the burgeoning corporations. To the extent that Modern Republicanism had a mass constituency, then, it was increasingly suburban. William Chafe puts the social context around this:

> If the "organization man" came to symbolize the new corporate personality, the suburban housing development came to symbolize the middle-class lifestyle he went home to. . . . In one of the most astounding migrations in history, suburbanites flocked to the new communities that blossomed in ever-widening circles around the nation's metropolitan areas. At the height of the great European migration in the early twentieth century, 1.2 million new citizens came to America in a single

year. During the 1950s, the same number moved to the suburbs every year. . . . During the 1950s, suburbs grew six times faster than cities. Between 1950 and 1960 alone, 18 million people moved to the suburbs.

The move to suburbia represented a miraculous fusion of need and desire. After the war, the number of marriages doubled, and most of the new households had nowhere to go. Over 2 million couples in 1948 were living with relatives. It was against such a backdrop that easy housing loans through VA and FHA combined with a booming economy to make possible a massive program of housing construction. Between 1950 and 1960 more than 13 million homes were built in America—11 million of them in the suburbs. Building contractors wanted cheap land; county governments were happy to welcome them to empty space crying for development. (Chafe 1991, 17; see also Jackson 1985)

The new corporations, so closely associated at first with this suburban constituency, also possessed a higher leadership—a growing corporate elite—by definition. More to the practical point for an inquiry into the rise and fall of partisan elites, the leadership of this newly triumphant corporate form had distinctive values and preferences for incipient transfer into politics. These values differed not just from those of other social groups in contemporary society but also, in important ways, from those of counterpart individuals in an earlier period. Accordingly, these values, along with the geographic distribution of their holders, were more crucial to their place in postwar politics than any institutional device their holders controlled.

To begin with, because these were the key operational elites from corporate management, they were the individuals most likely to encounter the leadership of organized labor across the bargaining table. Not surprisingly, they focused on labor-management relations as a central concern of their economic life and of any related politics. Where they differed from other regular opponents of organized labor, and from their own predecessors in an earlier incarnation, was in an acceptance of labor as part of the normal landscape. There was just no point in denying its existence, its power, or the recurrent need to reach some accommodation with it. The point was instead to be sure that any resulting agreement was mutually beneficial and that the rules governing labor-management negotiations were not tilted in favor of the former.

More abstract thinkers within this newly ascendant managerial stratum actually accepted the virtues of governmental action to maintain consumer

TABLE 3

HOUSING CONSTRUCTION

IN THE TWENTIETH CENTURY

	Total units started (in thousands)	As a percentage of total stock
1990	1,193	1.2
1985	1,742	—
1980	1,292	1.5
1975	1,160	—
1970	1,469	2.2
1965	1,510	—
1960	1,275	2.2
1955	1,646	—
1950	1,952	4.2
1945	326	—
1940	603	1.6
1935	221	—
1930	330	1.0
1925	937	—
1920	247	1.0
1915	433	—
1910	387	1.9
1905	507	—

SOURCES: *Historical Statistics of the United States, Colonial Times to 1970* (Washington, D.C.: Department of Commerce, 1975); *Statistical Abstract of the United States* (Washington, D.C.: Department of Commerce, various years).

demand and full employment. Others, while hardly saluting these values, did their business with government, and did so in a major way now that big government was a feature of the economic marketplace. If they did not want that government to ingest (or even regulate) more sectors of the economy, or to tax away the rewards of business and enterprise, neither did they want it to stop doing business with *them*. Geography then added a key twist to these values, converting them into a much more general political program while providing the incentive structure to pull their holders into partisan politics.

In fact, the new managerial elite was also geographically concentrated in the Northeast, the industrial Midwest, and the West Coast (see Figure 6). As a subset of American regions, however, these areas shared a number of

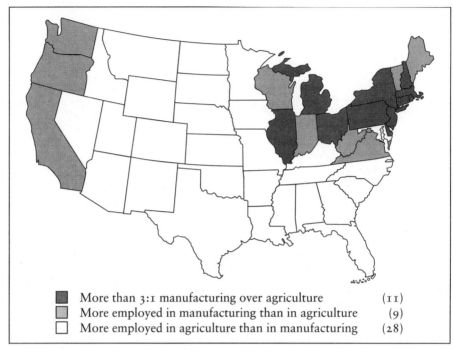

More than 3:1 manufacturing over agriculture   (11)
More employed in manufacturing than in agriculture   (9)
More employed in agriculture than in manufacturing   (28)

FIGURE 6

CORPORATE EMPLOYMENT IN THE STATES, 1950

SOURCE: *Statistical Abstract of the United States* (Washington, D.C.: Department of Commerce, 1952), various tables combined.

other characteristics: they were the place where the general societal consensus on the welfare state was at its most supportive; they were the place where union membership was at its highest—major corporate states were also major labor states; and they were the place where liberal Democrats had *their* best prospects of becoming the dominant partisan tendency. Accordingly, even though this new managerial elite was not necessarily keen on extending social welfare programs, its members were encouraged to accept an overall welfare consensus as contributing the boundaries of public life, within which all subsequent politicking necessarily had to occur.

Those were the contours of a distinctive political outlook. They gained a further practical prospect—this particular elite gained a further prospect in practical politics—from the increased legitimacy of the giant corporations generally in the immediate postwar world. This was never sufficient to carry the Modern Republicans to political dominance, however. Corporate failings remained linked with perceptions of the Great Depression; the public was not even vaguely interested in rolling back the main programs of the New Deal. But the phenomenal growth of the American economy in the immediate postwar years, along with the growth of corporate enterprise in an inextricably entangled fashion, provided substantial background legitimacy.

And that growth and its products were truly phenomenal. Table 4 shows an array of indicators, including that central summary number on well-being—per capita income—and the main capital asset following from it for most people—home ownership. The same point could be made with an aggregate: gross national product was up 250 percent between 1945 and 1960. It could be shown through productivity: it took 310 hours to make a car in 1945, 150 hours in 1960. It could be demonstrated with consumer goods generally: clothes dryers, air conditioners, second cars. It could even be shown in the means for expanding the ability to purchase such goods: short-term consumer credit was up 500 percent from 1946 to 1958. It could be shown in the spread of the device most commonly used by cultural critics to talk about the period—the near blanketing of the nation by television (see Table 4).

What was still missing in this equation was the "draw," some pull from the other side that would bring emergent elites with this distinctive outlook into partisan politics. Yet the background forces for such a draw were already present in other associated aspects of politics in those same states

TABLE 4

THE "CORPORATE BOOM" AT THE PERSONAL LEVEL

	Disposable income ($1,987 per capita)	Home-ownership (%)	Possession of a television set (%)
1990	13,824	64.2	98
1980	11,221	65.5	98
1970	9,875	62.9	95
1960	7,264	61.9	87
1950	6,214	55.0	9
1940	4,787	43.6	0

SOURCE: *Statistical Abstract of the United States* (Washington, D.C.: Department of Commerce, various years).

where a corporate Republicanism was resurgent. Or at least, if there was to be a Republican alternative in those states, its contours were clear enough. In coalitional terms, it needed to constrain labor but accept its legitimacy and not threaten its members. In programmatic terms, it needed to control the costs of social welfare programs while accepting their legitimacy and not threatening the beneficiaries, at least of the major social insurance programs. It needed, in short, to wear the Republican label but be attractive to moderate Democrats (Mayer 1964; Jones 1965; Hess and Broder 1967; Rae 1989; Reichley 1992).

In the abstract, the new corporate elite could offer these assets. As it developed, at least in these particular states, there was usually an existing elite—outside of Modern Republicanism, at first—ready to benefit from this apparent fit between strategic needs and elite assets by introducing its newer counterpart to partisan politics. Or at least there was normally an existing party leadership ready to do the essential operational tasks to convert this new elite first into partisan candidates and then into partisan officeholders. By definition, these states already possessed some established partisan leadership within the regular Republican Party. Given its inherent competitive difficulties, members were often prepared to support a new corporate elite in Republican politics—what would come to be called the Modern Republicans—*if* its members could in fact bring returns.

Accordingly, the fortunes of these implicit Modern Republicans were critically shaped by a combination of geographic location and inherent assets from one side, and the needs and norms of the regular Republican Party from the other. In truth, the natural field of this elite, within partisan politics, remained the Republican Party. This was so by way of ongoing programmatic attachments. The Republicans remained the party of lower spending, lower taxes, and less intervention in private business. It was so by way of contemporary social alignments as well. The Democratic Party, besides being the home of more of those with contrary preferences, was most centrally the home of organized labor, the opposition to corporate management in purely economic terms.

This never led to any overarching political action committee, the counterpart to the AFL-CIO's COPE, that would then register middle-management voters in the suburbs, recruit sympathetic candidates from corporate leadership, and contribute the techniques of campaign organization and campaign finance. Indeed, what was in formal terms the opposite number to the AFL-CIO, the National Association of Manufacturers

(NAM), never undertook systematic electioneering and focused its lobbying activity—which it took very seriously—on scaling back labor gains in labor-management relations and on restraining the welfare state generally. As a result, the new managerial elite, the seedbed of Modern Republicanism, percolated into politics more individually and very much on a person-by-person basis.

Yet in practice, while the "blue-ribbon" assets of this new managerial elite might be welcomed by the existing Republican Party—especially, as it turned out, its fund-raising capabilities—the *values* associated with those assets often were not. This was a further reason why members tended to enter practical politics as individuals, one by one. And it was why they would never possess even associated interest groups, much less an overhead agency. But more to the practical point, this conflict over public values and policy preferences, plus the need to be actively slated by the regular party, explained the peculiar pattern of success (and failure) of the Modern Republicans once they had entered postwar partisan politics.

The Republican Party overall was based in small (not corporate) business, and it was local (not national) business leaders who played an active role in organized party politics across the country. These individuals were decidedly *not* happy with the prospect of "living with" organized labor; they were the force behind the Taft-Hartley counterattack of 1947. They were not really happy with the prospect of accommodating the welfare state either; they regarded themselves as paying its bills, while its beneficiaries were inherently unsympathetic to their needs or values. They were happy—even delighted—to win elections and run government, but if that implied endorsing the products of the New Deal, then the point of it was likely to escape them.

Given this division between an established old and a potential new Republican elite, a clear pattern of success for the Modern Republicans—a clear pattern of conversion from social base to partisan officeholding—followed ineluctably: reliably successful at the presidential level, fluctuatingly successful at the senatorial level, marginally successful at the congressional level. In this, it was not surprising that the new elite showed its greatest gains at the presidential level. Wendell Willkie in 1940, Thomas Dewey in 1944 and 1948, and then Dwight Eisenhower, explicitly and operationally, in 1952 and 1956: these were the presidential candidates of the new managerial elite, and they contributed a generation of presidential dominance within the Republican Party.

These candidates were accepted by the old elite—not necessarily embraced, just accepted—because, as with Dewey most diagnostically, they had shown that they could win in Democratic areas, which the entire country in some sense was. Supporting these candidates was preferable to rallying the established base and losing. But in those areas where the old Republican elite continued to be successful on its own, there was no evident need to search out these new corporate Republicans. And there was good reason, given the difference in values and preferences, not to defer to them if they edged forward.

The home of this attitude, in contraposition to the presidency, was the House of Representatives, where a sizable minority of seats was normally Republican, and where a substantial majority of these was aligned with an established Republican elite. The new managerial elite was welcome—if it really wished, which it usually did not—to undertake those remaining contests with normal Democratic majorities. But this would not add many Modern Republicans to the Republican Party nationwide in the average year. And these offices were, in any case, least attractive to a numerically limited elite whose principal focus was not politics.

In between the presidency and the House, in every sense, was the Senate, and the Republican Party in the Senate thus acquired the clearest divisions along old elite–new elite lines. There were states with reliable Republican majorities here, and they tended to be in the hands of the old (small-business) elite. But there were others with substantial Republican minorities and a chance—but only that—of winning statewide behind a candidate who at least did not alienate Democrats. In these states, even old-line Republicans were willing to try the new managerial alternative. These were the states, unsurprisingly, that produced a leaven of Modern Republicans across the 1950s: Prescott Bush in Connecticut, 1952; Clifford Case in New Jersey, 1954; Jacob Javits in New York, 1956; Kenneth Keating in New York and Hugh Scott, perhaps the true archetype, in Pennsylvania, 1958.

The collective term for this group, "Modern Republicans," owed its currency to the great partisan success of this period, to Dwight Eisenhower and his presidency. The crucial figures in getting Eisenhower to run were in fact from the key "managerial" states: the Northeast, the industrial Midwest, and the West Coast. Likewise, the crucial figures in guaranteeing the funds that would encourage this effort were top managerial leaders from this incipient party elite. Eisenhower was then nominated with the support of those states that most clearly fit this mold, and opposed by those where the older Republican elite was still dominant. When Eisenhower won by drawing Democrats across the partisan line, he became entitled to contribute the summary term for a new and partisan elite. Figure 7 tells this story, a story that would be repeated, if less dramatically, at the state and national levels for the next fifteen years.

The Eisenhower archetype also commented powerfully on the limitations of this emergent Republican elite. Eisenhower explicitly harried corporate business figures about their need to get involved, especially in electoral politics. Yet this was not their natural theater. What they wanted overall was a public policy that did not interfere excessively in business management. Moreover, the limits on the political reach of their underlying

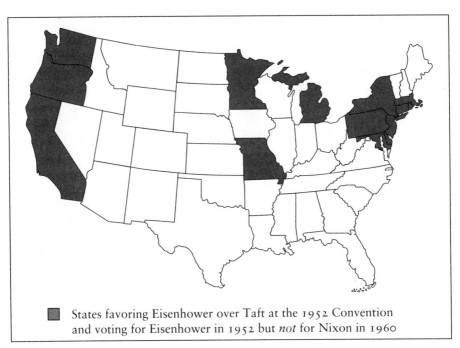

■ States favoring Eisenhower over Taft at the 1952 Convention and voting for Eisenhower in 1952 but *not* for Nixon in 1960

FIGURE 7

HOME BASES FOR MODERN REPUBLICANS

SOURCES: Paul T. David, Malcolm Moos, and Ralph M. Goldman, *Presidential Nominating Politics in 1952* (Baltimore: Johns Hopkins University Press, 1954), vol. 1, *The National Story*, 95–97; and *Presidential Elections since 1789*, 5th ed. (Washington, D.C.: CQ Press, 1991), 205 and 207.

social stratum—their mass base—were always a problem. Explicitly corporate suburbs plus a few "silk-stocking districts" in central cities were never going to be numerically dominant, even within just the Republican Party.

Nevertheless, the extent to which they came to constitute a critical element of the national Republican Party during the 1950s and 1960s was impressive. In battles over international involvement, for example, they would provide a Republican presence behind both pursuing the Cold War and maintaining an active presence in international agencies of cooperation. In the fight over civil rights, perhaps *the* great issue of the late 1950s and early 1960s, they would provide most of the Republicans who joined with northern and western Democrats to support civil rights legislation. Even in the more tangential elements of social welfare, such as disability insurance or health care regulation, they would provide the crucial middle ground that made legislation possible and shaped its specifics, critically at times.

New Politics Democrats

> *Observable, on occasion, is the parallel development of another literature chiefly designed to affect changes in the apportionment of profits between the governing class and its adjutants. . . . The larger the total to be apportioned, the hotter the battle and the more copious the literature it inspires. . . . Not a few "intellectuals" and humanitarians, sincere of faith and poor of spirit, gape in open-mouthed astonishment at such portentous demonstrations, and dream of a world that will some day be ruled by them. . . .*
>
> *Early in the nineteenth century, either because it was richer in Class II residues than now or because it had not yet been taught of experience, the governing class by no means considered such derivations innocuous, and much less to its advantage. It persecuted them, therefore, and tried to control them by law. Gradually in course of time it discovered that they in no way constituted obstacles to ruling-class profits, that sometimes, indeed oftentimes, they were a help. In those days, rich bankers were almost all conservatives. Nowadays, they hobnob with revolutionaries, intellectuals, Socialists, even Anarchists.*
> —Pareto (1980, 1011–12)

The third great elite infusion in postwar American politics, despite being Democratic, actually shared more structural characteristics with the Modern Republicans than with organized labor. Like the Modern Republicans, this third great infusion grew out of a distinctive social base rather than an organized constituency. Like the Modern Republicans, it would always lack a single overhead agency to coordinate its activities, although a variety of issue and cause groups, drawing on the same social base and very much aware of one another, would frequently coordinate common values and positions. Like organized labor, however, its strength as a self-conscious elite would be powerfully augmented by changes in the rules of the game, albeit the formal rules of politics rather than of economics in this case. And to complete the circle, those revised rules would then hasten both the demise of the Modern Republicans and the rise of the final elite group in postwar politics to date, the evangelical Protestants.

This third group was the New Politics Democrats. As with any serious candidate for a Paretian circulation, it sprang from a newly ascendant social stratum; this produced newly emergent, specialized spokesmen who offered distinctive values to give these phenomena policy implications; and there was an ultimate and explicit partisan connection. Moreover, as with all the other serious candidates, this newly emergent elite was not just structurally essential for connecting an ascendant social base with the institutions of government. It was also extremely important in defining—and partially transforming—the policy desires that this elite then pursued through partisan politics. It was arguably ironic that this new insurgent elite was Democratic rather than Republican, given its greater structural affinities with Modern Republicans than with organized labor. It was inescapably ironic that its major direct opponent at the time it came to power was not Modern Republicanism but organized labor instead.

Harbingers of a "new politics" was what elite spokesmen for this group considered themselves, and the Democratic Party would become their institutional—partisan—home. So "New Politics Democrats" became a logical moniker. Once more, there are good reasons for allowing this self-description to stand, in that it avoids alternatives adapted for explicitly tactical purposes but leaves the analyst free to put further defining characteristics into the general label. Within the Democratic Party, Al Barkan, director of the AFL-CIO's COPE, was frequently unprintable in his description of the New Politics Democrats; his definition would certainly not serve. Within the partisan competition, Spiro Agnew, vice presidential candidate on the Republican ticket at the critical moment, fired off some pithy and memorable summary epithets. "New Politics Democrats" at least avoids these (Easterlin 1980; Miller 1994; Shafer 1983a; Matusow 1984; Bell 1973; Integrating the Sixties 1996).

It was a particular slice of the New Politics Democrats—in effect, their "shock troops"—that first brought them to public attention and probably served as their collective catalyst. These were the university-based political activists of the mid-1960s. Heavily influenced by the civil rights revolution of the preceding decade, they borrowed its protest tactics to deal with the central issue of direct concern to them, the Vietnam War and opposition to it. On the one hand, they would prove to be but a fraction, albeit an active one, of the social group they initially represented. On the other hand, the substance of their main issue, involving cultural and national values rather than economics and social welfare, would remain diagnostic. Yet as ever, even here, this "elite within the elite" had a growing social base to underpin it, and this base, in turn, had two key aspects.

One was the baby boom of the immediate postwar years, and Figure 8

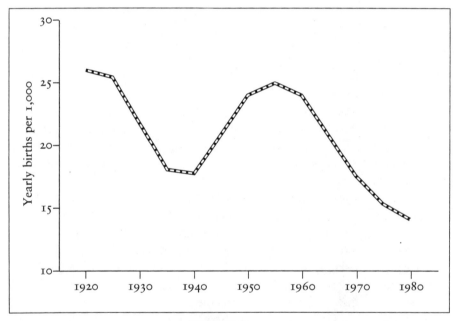

FIGURE 8

A SOCIAL BASE FOR THE VANGUARD
OF THE NEW POLITICS DEMOCRATS —
THE BABY BOOM

SOURCE: Richard A. Easterlin, *Birth and Fortune: The Impact of Numbers on Personal Welfare* (New York: Basic Books, 1980), 8.

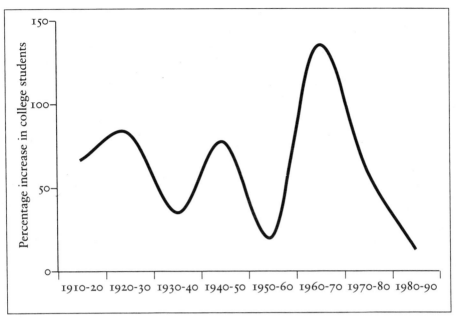

FIGURE 9

A SOCIAL BASE FOR THE VANGUARD

OF THE NEW POLITICS DEMOCRATS —

THE COLLEGE BULGE

SOURCES: *Historical Statistics of the United States, Colonial Times to 1970* (Washington, D.C.: Department of Commerce, 1975); *Statistical Abstract of the United States* (Washington, D.C.: Department of Commerce, various years).

attests to its reality. But this boom occurred within the general context of postwar prosperity, and it was augmented in particular by the burgeoning share of Americans going to college. It was this bulge—in numbers of college students—that was truly distinctive, much more than just the raw (baby boom) numbers beneath it, as Figure 9 affirms. That these individuals had grown up in a world where neither depression nor war had touched them (before Vietnam) and that they had achieved the historically privileged status of a college education (without personal sacrifice, in many cases) were often taken to be key to their values and behavior: political constraints on lifestyle choices seemed merely the residue of a time lag in social thinking. In any case, the 1960s was the decade of their most rapid growth in the entire twentieth century.

This combination of issue substance and social base would have been sufficient to produce extended campus unrest. It was hardly sufficient to produce a major partisan elite, imparting new directions to a national policy agenda. Instead, the larger social base for that elite lay in a striking increase in the share of the Democratic Party comprising higher-status and higher-education individuals. The college-based shock troops came out of this stratum; in some sense, they were both its symbolic incarnation and its real children. But the stratum was much broader, and therefore much longer lasting.

Figure 10 shows the increase in the share of the Democratic Party contributed by those completing a college education across the postwar years, and the change was remarkable. There were two quite different partisan social worlds at the beginning and end of this period. In 1950, college-graduate Democrats were evident rarities, and dissidents to their class. By 1980, they were an obvious and distinctive part of the coalition. Along the way, the share of Democrats with a college education actually rose faster

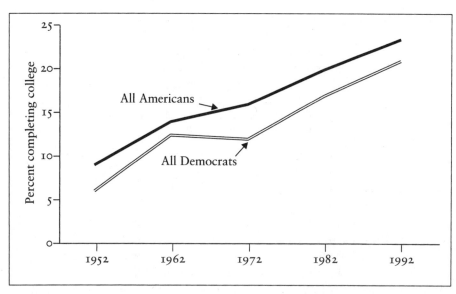

FIGURE 10

THE RISE OF THE COLLEGE-GRADUATE DEMOCRATS

SOURCE: *National Election Study* (Ann Arbor: Interuniversity Consortium for Political and Social Research, various years).

than the share of all Americans with the same. For reasons addressed later, the late 1960s became the historic breakpoint.

Opposition to the Vietnam War united this larger population, albeit more moderately, with the university-based activists. And while Vietnam as an issue would ultimately dissipate, this preference for international accommodation would remain characteristic. A general cultural liberalism united both pieces of the group as well, though again more moderately for the mass base than for those activists who styled themselves as a deliberate "counterculture." The enduring position here was progressive rather than traditional, emphasizing choice rather than constraint and hence rights rather than responsibilities. But the true unifying theme, and the one destined to carry by far the most political weight, concerned the character of politics itself, its proper institutions and the proper behavior within them.

The progressive position on this would prove to be what propelled the New Politics Democrats over time. It would allow their elite to add more international accommodationism and cultural liberalism than the mass base would have demanded; it would simultaneously unite them with an earlier incarnation of the same social tendency and political preference. In their own view, spokesmen dubbed this phenomenon *new* precisely because it would center on a putative new politics, one focused on solving problems rather than dispensing patronage, one addressing issues rather than just rallying loyalties, one dealing with the quality rather than just the quantity of life.

Emphasizing opposition to machine politics, as this view certainly did, its constituents were destined for conflict with the regular party, which in this case came to mean the regular Democratic Party. Emphasizing opposition to organized interests, as it also did, its constituents were destined for conflict with the main organized interest inside the regular Democratic coalition, which by this time was, of course, organized labor. Emphasizing those views, its constituents were destined to be in favor of the reform of political (and especially partisan) institutions, and they reliably were.

As ever with such elite eruptions, these views appeared to follow "naturally" from—they were entirely consistent with, though they did not necessarily exhaust—the social experience of the group from whence they came. Thus members of this group were suburban rather than urban, cosmopolitan rather than local, and white collar rather than blue collar. In turn, they were inclined to get their political information more from the mass media than from established intermediaries, were motivated more by substantive content than by partisan loyalty, and deferred more to voluntary organizations that they chose to join rather than to community organizations provided for them, including the political party.

Such preferences in political style were then joined by distinctive substantive values and policy preferences. This stratum, though more economically liberal than its social counterparts in the Republican Party, was both less liberal and less concerned with economic and social welfare issues than were most other Democrats. Conversely, concerned about the environment, tolerant of social deviance, in favor of personal choice in matters such as divorce and abortion, focused on the social roots of problems such as crime, and hostile to most forms of social control, they were even more liberal on cultural and social issues than the Modern Republicans, whom they otherwise resembled. Needless to say, they were wildly more liberal on these matters than other Democrats, whom they did not resemble.

The preconditions for what was to become this new partisan elite had begun with the postwar economic boom, especially with a few key social changes intimately connected to it. There would be a full generation before these preconditions led to the indisputable arrival of the New Politics Democrats. Nevertheless, the preconditions for their emergence traced directly to the postwar boom. The general characteristics of that boom—rising family income, rising home ownership, the spread of new consumer goods of all sorts—had been crucial to both the appearance and the improved legitimacy of the Modern Republicans as well. But two further elements of this change were crucial to the emergence of the New Politics Democrats as a full-blown partisan elite.

The more general of these was a rapid transformation of the occupational structure of a booming postwar American economy, from a blue-collar base with a substantial component of unskilled labor to a white-collar base with a growing sector of professional occupations instead. Decennial census figures, shown in Figure 11, confirm that the crucial division between a blue-collar and a white-collar majority was reached by 1960, but interim samples suggest, remarkably, that the divide had actually been crossed by 1956. Part and parcel of this occupational (and class) shift were sharply rising educational levels (see Figure 12). This was largely a by-product of the postwar boom, though it also owed a huge amount to direct governmental intervention in the form of the GI Bill, which allowed many returning servicemen to resume an education interrupted by war and

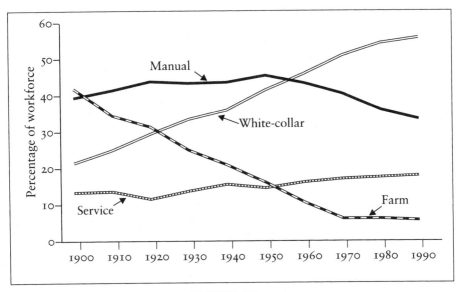

FIGURE 11

THE COMING OF THE WHITE-COLLAR WORLD —
OCCUPATIONAL CHANGE ACROSS THE TWENTIETH CENTURY

SOURCE: *Statistical Abstract of the United States* (Washington, D.C.: Department of Commerce, various years).

allowed many more to get an education that they otherwise would never have secured.

Had this occupational and educational evolution gone hand in hand with the occupational and educational distribution of partisan attachments from the immediate postwar years, its eventual resolution in politics would have been clear. Blue-collar workers were more Democratic, white-collar workers more Republican; less-educated Americans were more Democratic, more-educated Americans more Republican. Ergo, as the share of society that was white collar and more educated increased, so would the share of Republicans in society as a whole. In fact, however—and this was the crucial intermediary fact about the emergence of the New Politics Democrats—this did not occur. The Democratic share of the total population fluctuated randomly for another generation, but there was no doubt that the Democrats remained the majority party. The Republican share,

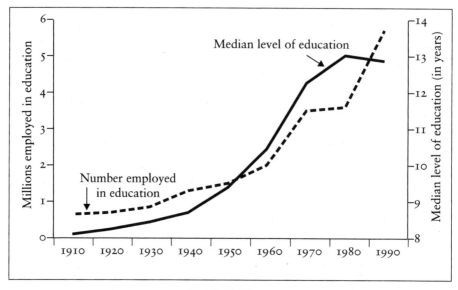

FIGURE 12

THE COMING OF THE WHITE-COLLAR WORLD —

EDUCATIONAL CHANGE ACROSS THE TWENTIETH CENTURY

SOURCES: *Historical Statistics of the United States, Colonial Times to 1970* (Washington, D.C.: Department of Commerce, 1975); *Statistical Abstract of the United States* (Washington, D.C.: Department of Commerce, various years).

despite all those favorable social preconditions, *did not rise*. Table 5 shows the actual trend, measured two ways.

There were many possible explanations for why initial postwar projections about partisanship did not prove accurate. Most of these, however, were ultimately some mix of programmatic appeal and generational effect. For instance, the programs of the New Deal, particularly its social insurance programs—Social Security and unemployment compensation—proved immensely popular. So did immediate postwar extensions such as the GI Bill and the governmental commitment to full employment. The changing internal composition of society, even to this remarkable degree, could not dent that essential popularity. As long as the Democrats were centrally connected with supporting these programs and the Republicans with opposing them, no shift in partisan attachments of any seriousness was in evidence. As Table 6 suggests, for more than a generation after the Second

TABLE 5
TREND OF PARTY IDENTIFICATION
ACROSS THE POSTWAR YEARS
(IN PERCENTAGES)

A. For all those leaning Democratic or Republican

	1952	*1962*	*1972*	*1982*	*1992*
Democrats	57	53	52	55	50
Republicans	35	34	33	32	37
All others	9	12	14	13	13

Democrats = Strong Democrats + Weak Democrats + Independent Democrats; Republicans = Strong Republicans + Weak Republicans + Independent Republicans; All others = Pure Independents.

B. For all those identifying clearly

	1952	*1962*	*1972*	*1982*	*1992*
Democrats	47	46	41	44	36
Republicans	28	28	23	23	25
All others	26	25	35	32	39

Democrats = Strong Democrats + Weak Democrats; Republicans = Strong Republicans + Weak Republicans; All others = Independent Democrats + Independent Republicans + Pure Independents.

SOURCE: *National Election Study* (Ann Arbor: Interuniversity Consortium for Political and Social Research, various years).

World War, most of society still remembered—had experienced—the Great Depression to which these programs had responded. To expect them to shift their partisanship, especially when the Modern Republicans failed to gain overall control of their own party, was almost to expect them to disavow that experience.

So, what was happening in partisan terms was different. Again, if the occupational and educational nature of society was changing but the partisan balance in society as a whole was not, then the occupational and educational composition of identifiers with the two major political parties had to be changing substantially. As it developed, these changes would be especially critical for the Democratic Party, the majority party *and* the party whose previous composition had been most unlike the growth areas of the evolving society. As a result, if an ideological assertion of a new political

TABLE 6

VOTING-AGE AMERICANS WITH CONSCIOUS
ADULT EXPERIENCE OF THE GREAT DEPRESSION
AND WORLD WAR II
(IN PERCENTAGES)

	1952	*1962*	*1972*	*1982*	*1992*
Cohorts born 1927 or later	8	28	55	68	82
Cohorts born 1926 or earlier	92	72	45	32	18

SOURCE: *National Election Study* (Ann Arbor: Interuniversity Consortium for Political and Social Research, various years).

style (reformed, clean, open, participatory) was one side of the equation creating New Politics Democrats, a social base—the more highly educated middle and upper-middle classes among Democratic identifiers—was the other side of that equation.

Once again, as with the Modern Republicans, there had arguably been an earlier incarnation of the same tendency in American politics (Mowry 1958; O'Neill 1975; Link and McCormick 1983). The Progressive movement at the turn of the twentieth century had been nothing if not focused ideologically on reforming political institutions, while being based socially in a newly assertive, educated middle class with a serious leaven of the independent professions. At that time, however, the dominant party, the party of government, had been the Republican Party; the Democratic Party had been little more, in national terms, than an amalgam of disparate interests seeking policy gains. In such an environment, the Progressive tendency was perhaps inevitably the reform faction within Republicanism. Seventy years later, the dominant party was the Democratic Party. It had acquired both a national policy program and a national coalition, courtesy of the New Deal. And this time, the successor tendency surfaced, again perhaps inevitably, as the reform faction of the Democratic Party instead.

There was nevertheless a specific politics that brought this development into being, one catalyzing the New Politics tendency, and catalyzing it with a Democratic attachment. This politics gained consequence from the fact that the partisan outcome of this process was incipiently predisposed but hardly preordained. Indeed, organized labor, the dominant interest group in the

Democratic coalition, did not share the priorities of what became the New Politics Democrats, while the Modern Republicans arguably did. Moreover, many of the most active members of what was to become the New Politics elite were consciously *antipartisan,* opposed on the record as much to the existing Democratic Party as to the existing Republican Party.

Events, however, would underline a partisan necessity and make it clear to the activists that this partisanship was Democratic. The flash point for anti-Vietnam activity proved to be the McCarthy nominating campaign of 1968, an insurgent campaign within the Democratic Party. The Republican alternative was effectively foreclosed by the return of Richard Nixon as its nominee. The frustration of the McCarthy campaign—its active defeat by the regular party, coupled with organized labor—only widened the potential "new politics" base for what became the McGovern nominating campaign of 1972. Its success was then half the story of the institutionalization of the New Politics elite inside the Democratic Party.

Again, the activist fringe of this elite was often explicitly hostile to both parties, even coming out of families in which both parents were Modern Republicans. But the realization of its antiwar wishes was fought out within the Democratic Party, and that proved crucial. So, perhaps even more, did the fact that when Jimmy Carter captured both the Democratic nomination and the presidency in 1976, initially raising high anxieties for New Politics Democrats, Carter then ran a classic administration of New Politics elites: accommodationist in foreign affairs, tolerant of lifestyle choices in cultural matters, unconcerned with social welfare policy. By that point, a significant share of those active in Democratic Party politics had come to be New Politics Democrats. (Pieces of this story are everywhere, but especially helpful are Glad 1980; White 1982; Polsby 1983; Kirkpatrick 1976; Miller and Jennings 1986; Shafer and Claggett 1995.)

They were helped immeasurably in their rise to prominence by a continuing reform movement emphasizing precisely the assets—education, disposable income, control of working schedules—that New Politics Democrats possessed. But in truth, while reform continued to be central to the New Politics ideology, and while New Politics Democrats would drive it further in institutional terms, they were not directly responsible for the reforms that initially benefited them. A conscious reform drive around the turn of the century whose implications had been gradually working their way through society as time passed—the Progressive movement, once again—had in fact both opened the internal processes of party politics to those participants who might turn out in any given forum and, especially, weakened the ongoing organization of the regular party in opposition to them.

The point, then, is merely that by the 1960s, the organized Democratic Party had become an increasingly feeble shell, capable of being captured by a newly energized elite that was more effectively adapted to an increasingly participatory politics. In this, the New Politics Democrats did little more than finish off a century-long evolution. Alan Ware summarizes the situation accurately:

> There can be little doubt that what happened to the Democratic parties in America between the early 1960s and the late 1970s was truly extraordinary. . . . Why did this transformation occur? In doing this, it is perhaps most useful if we attempt to classify the numerous factors which seem to have contributed to party collapse. . . .
>
> The first category is the most obvious; it includes the development of new technologies which could be employed in political campaigning, and the resources which helped incumbents, especially legislators, to divorce themselves from the nominating and electoral activists of their party's organization. The second category includes several different factors which would have affected the parties, irrespective of the state of campaign technology or of political controversies in the 1960s. There were demographic changes in the cities . . . there were declining resources available for attracting professional activists into the parties . . . there was the declining strength and commitment of the Democrats' labor union allies. The third category includes a number of forces which seem to have been the direct product of the convulsions of the 1960s— intra-party divisions and increased party disloyalty; issue extremism; the opportunity for "exit" to non-party political activity; and the institutional reforms which emanated from the conflicts. (Ware 1985, 241–42; see also Mayhew 1986)

By the early 1970s, the New Politics Democrats had driven their preferred formal arrangements to the presidential level as well. When these institutional reforms were combined with the natural growth of their social base, an augmented role in the national Democratic Party followed more or less automatically. In a primary electorate, where turnout might be 30 percent or less, and where it was highly tied to educational background, they could bulk very large indeed. In lesser forums such as party caucuses, where turnout could easily be 2 or 3 percent, they were often a genuine majority. In internal party affairs, then, there were increasing areas where they could expect to overwhelm the "old" party—and be the new.

This process still required new and congruent issues to sustain the involvement of the New Politics Democrats. These were, however, present in abundance. The Vietnam War might inevitably fade, but the women's movement and feminism would fit comfortably into the same coalition. Environmentalism might lose some of its energizing role, but homosexual rights would arrive to provide another substitute. In parallel fashion, a number of interest groups, of issue and cause organizations, would succeed each other in tandem with these issues and provide a diagnostic operational element for the New Politics Democratic elite. Indeed, these groups were singularly successful in defining what it meant to be a "progressive Democrat," in a fashion that the Modern Republicans, for example, had never even approximated. In so doing, they contributed a distinctive but highly effective dynamic to the operation of the third great postwar partisan elite.

Evangelical Protestants

It has often been noted that there were times when religious sentiments seemed to lose ground, others when they seemed to gain strength, and that such undulations corresponded to social movements of very considerable scope. The uniformity might be more exactly described by saying that in the higher stratum of society, Class II residues gradually lose strength, until now and again they are reinforced by ties upswelling from the lower stratum. . . .

An instance in our day would be the United States of America, where this upward thrust of members of the lower classes strong in Class II residues is very intense; and in that country one witnesses the rise of no end of strange and wholly unscientific religions . . . that are utterly at war with any sort of scientific thinking, and a mass of hypocritical laws for the enforcement of morality that are replicas of laws of the European Middle Ages.

—Pareto (1980, 801–3)

The fourth and last great elite infusion in postwar American politics shared some characteristics with each of its three major predecessors. It was probably closest in structure to organized labor, in that it had not just a fully crystallized organizational framework to complement its underlying social base but also a single overhead agency to (attempt to) coordinate its many other explicit organizations. Yet it was also distinguished in substance by its conscious opposition to *all* these other elites. It was born, most directly, in a hostility to the values of New Politics Democrats. It was mobilized around many of the same values, but from the opposite direction. Yet the greatest direct opprobrium from its leaders was still reserved, albeit intermittently, for the handful of descendants of the Modern Republicans. They were the partisan apostates who muddied the message and thwarted its transmission. And from a group perspective, finally—a mass, an elite, or a policy perspective—if organized labor did not receive the same pyrotechnic treatment, that was because labor remained, forever and in principle, beyond the pale. (For example, Thomas [1996] notes, "Big labor's agenda includes far more than the minimum wage and other work-related issues—and it often goes against pro-family goals.")

The group in question, seedbed of this fourth and last great elite infusion, was evangelical Protestants. And it would contribute, from the late 1970s onward, what became known as the "New Christian Right." Yet this particular incarnation was only the latest resurgence of what had been a major contributor to the circulation of elites across all of American history. From the beginning of American politics—from before the beginning, really—there had been surges of evangelical Protestants into secular politics, as Table 7 suggests. And in every case, there had been a clear change in the agenda of political conflict as a result (Goen 1988; Marini 1982; Cross 1950; Carwardine 1983; Levine 1975; Ahlstrom 1972; McLoughlin 1959; Noll 1990).

TABLE 7
PROTESTANT SURGES ACROSS AMERICAN HISTORY

	Designation	Substantive thrust	Dominant issues
1730–1760	First Great Awakening	Religious autonomy	Christianizing and independence
1800–1830	Second Great Awakening	Social leveling	Evangelism and abolition
1890–1920	The Great Divide	Political populism	Temperance and creationism
1970–	New Christian Right	Moral rejuvenation	Family values and abortion

The First Great Awakening, and the first great evangelical Protestant surge, had come in the 1730s to 1760s and had contributed, powerfully if indirectly, to the Revolutionary War. There could hardly be a more critical contribution to the agenda for policy conflict. The Second Great Awakening, roughly 1800 to 1830, had represented a second major Protestant upsurge in church membership and in involvement with politics, and this had contributed, again indirectly but powerfully, to the Civil War. Both these awakenings, however, occurred in a world where evangelical Protestantism began as the reform movement within Protestantism generally and ended by being effectively synonymous with it, renewing the elite structure of mainstream Protestantism as it progressed.

The two subsequent evangelical surges preceding the modern incarnation were different. In the first, evangelicals continued to see themselves as fighting morally degenerative forces, which in the 1890s meant fighting the big interests and the socially privileged. On just those grounds, evangelicals threw in their lot with the Populists. William Jennings Bryan became their symbolic champion, but this time, they were defeated. They managed a dramatic afterword in the first decades of the twentieth century, when they were a crucial influence in securing Prohibition via the Eighteenth Amendment to the U.S. Constitution. But policy success again crashed in ignominious defeat in the 1920s when they fought an unsuccessful rearguard campaign—Bryan was again the symbolic champion—against the teaching of (Darwinian) evolution.

The Protestant evangelical movement appeared politically spent at that point, and subsequent events would sweep politics in very different directions for several generations. Yet it is important to understand the divisions that occurred within Protestantism at the turn of the twentieth century, because one side of these divisions would generate the New Christian Right. Most of the underlying forces contributing to a split were consequences of the massive industrialization of the late nineteenth and early twentieth centuries. Nevertheless, part of the resulting split was explicitly ecclesiastical, and part was social. Together, the two parts would contribute a new and different Protestant stream, submerged for nearly fifty years and then bursting forth in a major elite effervescence in the late twentieth century.

In doctrinal terms, the difference could be summarized as one of modernizers versus fundamentalists. What would become the modernist strand of contemporary Protestantism came to emphasize the adaptation of scripture to a newly scientific world, the place of formal liturgy in religious practice, and the application of sacred organization to secular betterment. In social terms, this proved a much more congenial approach to the urban and then suburban, the middle-class and then upper-middle-class, and the more highly educated sectors of Protestantism. By contrast, what would become the fundamentalist strand of contemporary Protestantism continued to emphasize the inerrancy of the Bible, the role of Christ in direct personal salvation, and the necessity of applying moral—Christian—principles to individual life. In social terms, this remained a more congenial approach for the rural, the lower-middle and working classes, and the less educated among Protestant identifiers.

Fundamentalism was probably also an approach inherently more suited, in its theology, in its organizational form, and in its social base, to maintaining *distance* between religion and politics. But dramatic defeats over the teaching of evolution in the 1920s certainly gave it a push in that direction, and depression, war, and the postwar economic boom then intervened for all Protestants—mainline and evangelical, liturgical and pietistic, modern and fundamental—providing other focuses for their energies and their politics. This half century of apparent quiescence, on top of a general sense of the fundamentalists as a disadvantaged minority in intellectual and social decline, surely exaggerated the impact of evangelical Protestant elites when they returned to American politics in the late 1970s, and it clearly exaggerated the press response to their return.

Three main factors would ultimately reverse the evangelical withdrawal from politics. The first was an underlying pattern of religious growth, accompanied by a set of social changes that were very unlike those suggested by historical caricatures. The second factor, and the key for a Paretian analysis, was the generation of a new elite with different social advantages, an elite consciously intending to capitalize on growth and change. And the third was a set of particular events that served as the catalyst, interacting with broader changes to elicit and encourage a strong and active partisan connection between evangelical Protestants and modern American politics, in the guise of the modern Republican Party.

At the social base for American politics, the long period of political quiescence among the evangelical Protestants was actually characterized by a number of undercurrents important to their eventual reemergence. The prewar years were in truth a period of Catholic growth in the United States, as a massive immigrant influx from southern and eastern Europe fed through society. The immediate postwar years were a period of growth for

TABLE **8**

DENOMINATIONAL TRENDS IN POSTWAR AMERICA

(IN PERCENTAGES)

A. Membership trends across the great "families"
of American religion

	1952	1962	1972	1982	1992
Protestant	72	74	69	65	58
Catholic	22	20	24	22	24
Jewish	3	3	2	2	2
Other/none	3	3	5	11	16

B. Membership trends by denominational affiliation

	1952	1962	1972	1982	1992
Mainline Protestant	n.a.	45	37	32	24
Evangelical Protestant	n.a.	29	32	33	34
Catholic	22	20	24	22	24
Jewish	3	3	2	2	2
Other	n.a.	2	1	2	2
None	n.a.	1	4	9	14

SOURCE: *National Election Study* (Ann Arbor: Interuniversity Consortium for Political and Social Research, various years).

the modernist Protestant denominations, often known as "mainline Protestantism," with new suburbs generating new churches and new churches generating new members (see Table 8A). By the early 1960s, however, the major trend in denominational affiliations was still within Protestantism, but *away* from the mainline and toward the evangelical (see Table 8B). The fact that the share of the population that acknowledged no religious tradition was also growing surely magnified the consequences of these trends.

In any case, a number of factors appeared to be involved in this huge shift within Protestantism, the one trend that was destined to underpin a new partisan elite. Evangelical Protestant supporters argued (and mainline Protestant opponents feared) that the apparent change in vitality that this shift suggested was in fact a reflection of changing theological attractiveness between denominations with moral certainties, and hence answers to questions, and those without. More to the statistical point were three other developments (Kelley 1972; Greeley 1989; Marsden 1980; Hunter 1983; Wald 1992; Reichley 1985; Religion in America 1985; Reed 1995).

First, there was a rising net gain for the evangelicals from familiar patterns of religious shuffling. Upwardly mobile Americans had long been more likely to move from evangelical to mainline denominations, whereas the more devout had been more likely to move from mainline to evangelical. But the net of this balance from the 1960s swung increasingly in an evangelical direction. Second, the mainline Protestant denominations were especially likely to lose their younger members, at least during the young-adult years—a tendency much more effectively countered among evangelicals. Third, the populations that identified with evangelical denominations were growing more indigenously—they were having more children—than those that identified with the mainline.

There was more. In a development very much like the one that produced the New Politics Democrats, a major social trend that benefited the evangelical Protestants across the postwar years did *not* produce its normal countervailing tendency, at least within the first generation of partisan elites. The economic growth that benefited especially the American South but secondarily the Rocky Mountain states as the postwar years passed—the regions that had long been most congenial to evangelical Protestantism—did not cause a shift to mainline Protestantism within those regions as they prospered. Figure 13 shows the distribution of evangelical Protestants by state in the modern United States. Such a distribution was, on its face, a picture of where evangelical elites might expect to do best (and worst) when—if—they reentered American politics. Yet in principle, all this could have produced any number of different results, from extended quiescence to expanded political liberalism. What gave it both political relevance and partisan definition, then, was a set of associated *elite* changes, and these were aggressively conservative. Once more, two among them were particularly important.

The first was a movement in the late 1960s and early 1970s among conservative political strategists of no apparent religious conviction to search out new or emergent constituencies that might serve as a counterweight to the New Politics Democrats but might really serve to create a new Republican (and thereby conservative) majority. These individuals had practical experience in politics, and they had the desire to see evangelical Protestants play a newly active (and conservative) role in it. They just lacked the means to make that happen.

The means were the province of the second change: a new generation of

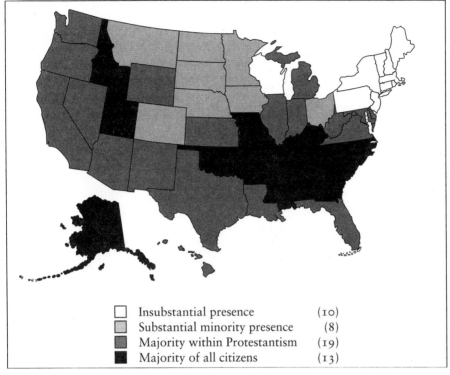

□	Insubstantial presence	(10)
▨	Substantial minority presence	(8)
▧	Majority within Protestantism	(19)
■	Majority of all citizens	(13)

FIGURE 13

EVANGELICAL PROTESTANTS AS A SHARE
OF TOTAL STATE POPULATION

SOURCE: Martin B. Bradley et al., *Churches and Church Membership in the United States, 1990* (Atlanta: Glenmary Research Center, 1992), 12–36.

evangelical Protestant ministers. They were thus the key insurgent elites in the entire movement—key, at least, to its place in postwar politics. After the great split in American Protestantism, and quite apart from postwar economic trends, the evangelical denominations had needed to create their own seminaries, consciously responding to their own theological and organizational needs. By the 1970s, these seminaries were producing a generation of trained ministers who were very much a part of the social base of the new, postwar evangelical Protestantism but also very much aware of the intellectual currents, opposed to many of them, that were sweeping society.

They were also different from their nominal predecessors in possessing an expanded resource base. If the areas of evangelical strength had benefited disproportionately from economic growth while not losing their upwardly mobile members, then the old income and education gaps between them and the rest of American society should have been closing, and in fact they were. As a result, the new generation of evangelical Protestant ministers was itself increasingly suburban rather than rural, with middle- rather than working-class constituencies. Moreover, these ministers were attuned to contemporary technology, especially television, where they were arguably the first generation of American religious leaders to make full and aggressive use of the medium.

They were repelled not just by a variety of trends in American society but also by the different interpretations of them—verging on explicit endorsement—from the New Politics Democrats. Morality in public life was a unifying theme in all the evangelical Protestant surges, from the Great Awakening of the 1730s to the New Christian Right of the 1970s. In earlier incarnations, this had implied religious freedom, social leveling, abolitionism, and temperance. Their modern relevance, however, rested on the fact that they all followed from an emphasis on personal salvation and a subsequently godly life on earth, the signature characteristics of evangelical Protestantism. Established churches, inherited titles, slavery, and drunkenness had been obvious barriers to these in an earlier day. Such wellsprings had not shifted by the late 1960s, but the institutionalized affronts to them in the view of this new evangelical elite—the barriers to personal salvation and a godly life in our time—had changed dramatically.

Among these, the single greatest symbolic affront was probably the Supreme Court decisions removing prayer from the public schools in the early 1960s: *Engel v. Vitale* (370 U.S. 421, 1962), along with *Abington School District v. Schempp* and *Murray v. Curlett* (374 U.S. 203, 1963). A policy so comprehensive and an assault so explicit reached into the lives of most mass identifiers within evangelical Protestantism. By its very universality and its frontal character, it laid a groundwork that degenerative social trends could never achieve. In the demonology of governmental assaults on moral fundamentals, however, the school prayer cases were joined by a stream of other Court decisions, the most consequential of which was surely *Roe v. Wade* (410 U.S. 113, 1973) and its abortion progeny. By legitimizing abortion nationwide, the decision not only sharply increased a previously proscribed activity. It also augmented the *appearance* of an increase, as previously private (and often illegal) abortions came into the legal public record (see Table 9A).

TABLE 9
SOCIAL TRENDS RELATED TO "FAMILY VALUES"
IN THE POSTWAR UNITED STATES

A. The litmus test

	Number of legal abortions			Number of legal abortions
1990	1,429,577		1979	1,251,921
1989	1,396,658		1978	1,157,776
1988	1,371,285		1977	1,079,430
1987	1,353,671		1976	988,287
1986	1,326,112		1975	854,853
1985	1,328,570		1974	763,476
1984	1,333,521		1973	615,831
1983	1,268,987		1972	586,750
1982	1,303,980		1971	485,816
1981	1,300,760		1970	193,491
1980	1,297,606			

B. The degenerative trends

	1. Divorce		*2. Illegitimacy*		*3. Crime*	
	Raw number (1,000s)	Rate per 1,000	Raw number (1,000s)	Rate per 1,000	Raw number (1,000s)	Rate per 1,000
1990	1,175	4.7	1,225	43.8	12,430	66.5
1980	1,189	5.2	666	29.4	11,110	66.5
1970	708	3.5	339	26.4	5,208	34.9
1960	393	2.2	224	21.6	1,096	8.8
1950	385	2.6	142	14.1	737	7.6
1940	256	2.0	90	7.1	662	8.9

SOURCES: Abortion data from U.S. Center for Disease Control and Prevention, *Morbidity and Mortality Weekly Report,* vol. 46 (no. SS-4, 8 August 1997):49. Divorce, illegitimacy, and crime data from *Historical Statistics of the United States, Colonial Times to 1970* (Washington, D.C.: Department of Commerce, 1975), and *Statistical Abstract of the United States* (Washington, D.C.: Department of Commerce, various years). Divorce rate is calculated per total population; illegitimate birthrate is calculated per total number of unmarried women; crime rate is per total population.

Nevertheless, abortion remained only the most dramatic touchstone—the symbolic litmus—for a set of larger trends in American society, trends that dwarfed the impact of any (and perhaps all) Supreme Court decisions (see Table 9B). Here, the perceived breakdown of the American family was the diagnostic element. And the fate of the family, along with an emphasis on family protection and family values, would become the great rallying cry through which evangelical elites mobilized their mass constituency in politics. At one end of the causal chain, the rising tide of divorce was the definitional indicator. Rising illegitimacy was an even more pernicious product of the decline of the family. And at the end of that causal chain was rising crime.

The new generation of evangelical ministers did not need secular conservative strategists to call these trends to their attention, to frame them negatively, or to suggest that traditional solutions were the right ones. What such strategists could do was help the evangelical ministers form local, regional, and then national linkages—networks—to pursue a reintroduction of traditional values into public life. Along the way, they could also help them add techniques such as direct-mail fund-raising to their arsenal to supplement their personal (and televised) theological appeals. Christopher Soper catches the absolute centrality of this new Protestant elite in responding:

> Interpreting the Bible to condemn a social practice is a necessary condition for evangelical activism, but it is not a sufficient condition. Human society is full of "sins" which evangelical Christians deplore, but not all of them serve as conduits for political mobilization. Moral issues are not necessarily political ones. . . .
>
> Evangelical leaders have an important role to play in helping to form groups. Leaders need to convince evangelicals that a social practice is sinful and that the consequences of that particular sin are grave enough to demand their political involvement. Leaders in the early temperance movement in America and Britain had the intractable problem of convincing sceptical evangelicals that there was a biblical warrant and a political necessity for temperance societies. . . . Temperance did not become a political passion until evangelicals were convinced that drinking threatened their religious goals of the conversion of the sinner and the reformation of his social world. . . .
>
> This does not mean that any issue, given the right set of leaders, has an equal capacity to mobilize evangelicals. Evangelical theology, with its stress on personal faith and practice, leads believers to be more concerned with political issues which can be interpreted in terms of an individual's lifestyle, behavior, and morality than those issues which are corporate in nature. (Soper 1994, 55–56)

The result was a plethora of politically relevant organizations, all built essentially around the conservative position on cultural values. The one among them that would bring such organizations to national prominence (and national media attention) was the Moral Majority, a nationwide network of fundamentalist Protestant ministers. It was joined by Christian Voice, the ideological monitoring arm of the movement; the Religious Roundtable, a coordinating body reaching out to other denominations that shared conservative theologies; and the National Christian Action Coalition, a policy development arm. These were joined by such family-oriented organizations as Concerned Women of America and Focus on the Family, which proved to have greater staying power than the first influx of more narrowly political bodies.

Given that such organizations were built on conservative social and cultural principles and that they were partly a response to the (liberal) social and cultural preferences of the New Politics Democrats, it might appear in hindsight that they were destined to follow an obvious partisan trajectory into the Republican Party. Yet their social base among rank-and-file evangelicals also preferred some policy options to which the Democratic Party was arguably more responsive. Moreover, specific, potentially catalytic partisan events at first argued for a much more conditional outcome.

The initial contact for most nonevangelical Americans with evangelical Protestantism in politics was actually the election of Democrat Jimmy Carter in 1976, with his evident and easy public references to evangelical themes. Carter, however, proved a total disappointment to the newly formed network of evangelical Protestant ministers. In operation, on social and cultural grounds, he ran an administration built around New Politics Democrats. There were no governmental initiatives to restore the place of prayer; abortion rights were safeguarded and extended. Accordingly, it was only when Republican Ronald Reagan made deliberate overtures to the Protestant evangelical leadership in 1980 and succeeded Carter as president, and when Reagan spent the next eight years articulating Moral Majority themes, that the partisan die was effectively cast.

None of this came without growing pains for a population that had disdained politics for half a century, with a mass base still lagging the national average in personal resources and with an elite still riven by important doctrinal differences. The Moral Majority, in fact, did not survive the Reagan years. George Bush, who did, was a quintessential mainline Protestant, leading some analysts to pronounce the demise of the New Christian Right. However provocative, this pronouncement was also premature, for the Moral Majority was in turn succeeded by the Christian Coalition, playing the same role for the 1990s but with a broader numerical base, a more professionalized staff, and a more comprehensive political armory—both in practical techniques and in policy proposals.

Founded in 1989 by the Reverend Marion "Pat" Robertson, a Pentecostal minister, but under the daily direction of Ralph Reed, an established Republican operative, the Christian Coalition would bring the organizational voice of the evangelical Protestant elite to a new high. Like the AFL-CIO, the other postwar coordinating body that it most resembled in structural terms, the Christian Coalition would engage actively in both electioneering and lobbying. In operation, the organization was a curious amalgam. It claimed 1,200 chapters nationwide, with a membership of 1.7 million and a mailing list of 30 million. It had an annual budget of $20 million, and it distributed 33 million voter guides in 1994.

Much of this material, however, actually went out through 60,000 churches, and the links among its pastors remained the key to operational effectiveness. The key to motivating them, in turn, remained some familiar cultural concerns, such as opposition to abortion, along with some new additions, such as opposition to the "endorsement" of homosexuality. Its annual "Road to Victory" conferences, every September, were the national focus for the electioneering effort, rallying activists for a voter registration drive, then an issue awareness drive, and then a get-out-the-vote drive in their areas.

In any case, if the network had appeared defunct by the late 1980s, it seemed to be at maximum influence by 1994, when Republicans recaptured control of Congress for the first time in forty years, with the active support of the Christian Coalition. By that point, the group was a significant faction within the state Republican Parties of at least three-fifths of the states and the dominant faction within a third, though the identity of such parties inevitably shifted with changes in their state and local leadership. Figure 14 suggests that this strength was related to the underlying strength of evangelical Protestantism but that the localized vitality of the Christian Coalition owed something to its own organizational initiatives (or lack thereof) as well.

The 1994 victory, in any case, gave increased emphasis to the national lobbying effort. The Christian Coalition had already been publishing a congressional rating system, scoring all congressmen and senators on a number of votes central to coalition preferences and then publicizing these scores in constituencies. The 1994 result allowed them to bring some of these together in a "Contract with the American Family" (1995), which

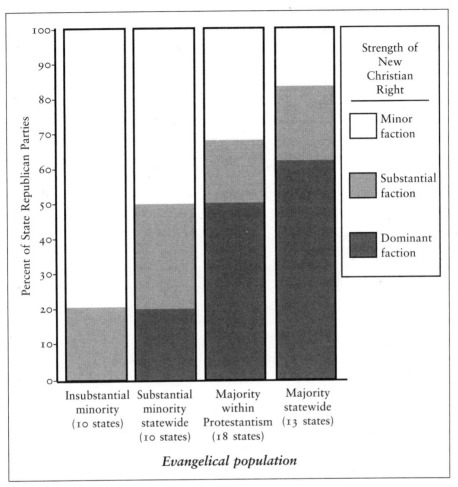

FIGURE 14

EVANGELICAL PROTESTANTS, THE NEW CHRISTIAN RIGHT,
AND REPUBLICAN PARTIES IN THE STATES

SOURCES: See figure 3.10; and "Who's Got the Power? Levels of Christian Right Strength in the State Republican Party Organizations," *Campaigns & Elections*, September 1994, 22.

suggested both the thrust and the range of relevant proposals. The result was also the single largest organized interest within the national Republican Party.

It was not, however, an interest that fit without stress. Many wealthier, more educated, more suburban, more corporate Republicans were also mainline Protestants, even seculars, and they were often liberal rather than conservative on social and cultural issues. The addition of evangelical Protestants to the national Republican coalition thus could not be accomplished without diminishing their proportionate presence and their policy preferences. In related fashion, the extraction of evangelical Protestants from the Democratic Party was not stress-free or successful in any linear fashion. On economic rather than cultural grounds, many evangelicals still "belonged" to the Democrats, being less well-off and having more need for basic social welfare programs. They were still a crucial audience for appeals to defect from the Democratic Party, and such appeals were often successful, but evangelical Democrats did not reliably become Republicans as a result.

The evangelical Protestant elite, however, no longer experienced these tensions. Or rather, it resolved them by emphasizing moral conservatism—social and cultural conservatism—and by giving priority to it. Their organizations reliably followed suit, and this in turn produced an institutionalized resolution. Yet in doing so, they were very much trading off one set of values within their larger constituency for another—cultural conservatism over economic moderation—to create a uniformly conservative presence. In this, they were the mirror image of the New Politics elite: trading off the economic moderation of their larger constituency for its cultural liberalism, and hence creating a uniformly liberal presence. In doing so, both were underlining the importance of elite eruptions, and elite circulations, in American politics.

Change

In fact, there are many cases in which conclusions drawn from residues of group-persistence (or, in other words, by "intuition") come much closer to realities than conclusions that are drawn from the combination instinct and go to make up the derivations of that pseudo-science which, in social matters, continues to be mistaken for experimental science. And, again in many cases, these latter derivations seem so harmful that the society which is not eager to decline or perish must necessarily reject them.

But not less deleterious are the consequences of an exclusive predominance of Class II residues, not only in the physical arts and sciences, where their harmfulness is obvious, but in social matters as well, where it is perfectly apparent that but for the combination instinct and the use of experimental thinking, there could be no progress. So there is no stopping, either, at the extreme where Class II residues predominate; and a new oscillation sets in heading back toward the first extreme where Class I residues predominated.

And so the pendulum continues swinging back and forth from one extreme to the other, indefinitely.

—Pareto (1980, 1026)

The rise and fall of partisan elites across postwar American politics did not coincide neatly with the passing of either decades or generations. Nevertheless, there were two obvious arrivals at the beginning of this period, in the immediate postwar years. These were organized labor and the Modern Republicans. And there were two obvious incarnations on the political landscape at the end of this period, at the beginning of the post–Cold War era. These were the New Politics Democrats and the evangelical Protestants. If all four seemed superficially unrelated to one another and to the key elites that had preceded them, all were at least united not just in embodying the overall notion of a circulation of elites but in offering all the signature characteristics for such a circulation. As it turned out, they were additionally united, in pairwise comparisons, by the way the forces feeding into one social group also fed into another, or even by the way the behavior of one partisan elite served partially to reshape the forces that would ultimately result in the appearance of a successor.

For example, the mass base from which organized labor had emerged was a social stratum of long standing, the industrial working class. Indeed, this was not even expanded during the (depression) years when it began to generate a newly consequential, incipiently partisan elite. What *was* new was a vastly expanded organizational embodiment, tracing to the NLRA of 1935 and culminating in the creation of the AFL-CIO (and COPE) in 1955. With it came, in remarkably short order, a newly professionalized elite—an extensive labor bureaucracy—that seized upon the rise of unionized labor and converted it not just into an explicitly political operation but, this time, into a key component of the national Democratic coalition. In doing so, this newly ascendant elite both broadened the policy focus of labor in American politics, to social welfare issues and not just labor-management concerns, and guaranteed that this focus would remain central to Democratic Party appeals for another generation.

By contrast, although the social stratum that produced the Modern Republicans was not new either—it had arrived in the late nineteenth century and spread in the early twentieth—it was strikingly expanded in the late 1940s and early 1950s. In turn, this expansion brought substantive values and policy preferences that distinguished this stratum from earlier incarnations, as well as from organized labor on one side and regular Republicans on the other. Yet unlike labor, it never produced any formal embodiment, much less an overhead agency. Rather, it percolated into politics on an individual basis, by virtue of distinctive values and by means of official party deference. Perhaps surprisingly, such an amorphous structure was not obviously a bar to influence. The nature of presidential Republicanism and occasionally the operation of the presidency itself, the character of the Senate as a legislative institution, the lines of conflict within the Republican Party in the House, and the potential for building moderate cross-party coalitions in American politics generally—all these followed crucially from the presence of the Modern Republicans on the political landscape.

The New Politics Democrats were different yet again. Like the Modern Republicans, they issued from a vastly expanded social stratum, the nontraditional but rapidly growing stratum of white-collar—college-graduate—Democratic Party identifiers. Like the Modern Republicans more than organized labor, these New Politics Democrats would never have an overhead agency of any sort. However, a shifting array of issue and cause groups would prove remarkably and continually successful at pumping substance into what it meant to be a New Politics Democrat: antiwar, pro-feminist, pro-environment, pro-abortion, anti–social control, pro-homosexual rights. Unlike the Modern Republicans, and much more like organized labor as a result, these New Politics Democrats were able to attempt self-consciously to take over the Democratic Party, without the need for some overhead coordinating agency. In the process, they kept what were essentially *cultural* concerns at the center of American politics.

The last major, concentrated elite input to postwar American politics, the last great surge of postwar elites to date, actually sprang from the group that was least new to American politics among those on this list. Indeed, although evangelical Protestantism was clearly growing again, it was not enjoying a resurgence that was particularly noteworthy in historical terms. Like the Modern Republicans, the evangelical Protestant elite—the New

Christian Right—experienced its resurgence under different conditions and with an altered programmatic core. Otherwise, however, its social base was already much more clearly formed and focused. As with unionized labor, it was the *organized* flow into politics that was important, and it was the resulting issue organizations, along with their overhead agencies—the Moral Majority and then the Christian Coalition—that were the real base for a new partisan elite. Like organized labor, it too became the largest single organized presence within its chosen party, the Republican rather than the Democratic Party. But despite these structural similarities, it was the substance propounded by the New Politics Democrats that served as the catalyst to draw the evangelicals back into politics: that same cluster of essentially cultural issues, the proper operative values for daily social life.

Political change is certainly evident in such a summary—change in the structural characteristics of new partisan elites and change in the policy preferences they brought with them into politics. Yet the extent of this change is still understated by a simple compare-and-contrast approach to the four key elites. In fact, the fortunes of each pair of postwar elites did not just feed off each other: Modern Republicans in response to the rise of organized labor, evangelical Protestants in response to the rise of New Politics Democrats. Rather, the rise—and then the fortunes—of the first pair were also intimately related to the rise (and fortunes) of the second. And in this change lies more than just a difference in identity among four elite contenders. In it lies much of the central change in American politics during the postwar years.

For example, those forces that created an incipient base for the New Politics Democrats, on which they eventually capitalized under the impetus of specific events, were actually forces that were remaking organized labor at the same time. Analyses of the fortunes of union labor often focus on the declining share of the workforce that a more white collar and more highly educated economy would leave in its hands. But here, it is more important to note that these were the *same* forces that would eventuate in the appearance of the New Politics Democrats. Moreover, and even more to the point, they were changing organized labor in ways that, if anything, would integrate it into the New Politics coalition.

Table 10 suggests, forcefully, that whereas "old labor" was blue collar and private sector, "new labor" was increasingly white collar and public sector instead. The identity of the winners in this comparison tells that story: the National Education Association over the United Auto Workers. So

TABLE 10

THE LARGEST LABOR UNIONS — 1952 AND 1993
(MEMBERSHIP IN THOUSANDS)

1952		1993	
1. United Automobile, Aircraft and Agricultural Implement Workers Union	1,185	1. National Education Association	2,000
2. United Steelworkers Union	1,100	2. International Brotherhood of Teamsters	1,700
3. International Brotherhood of Teamsters	1,000	3. American Federation of State, County and Municipal Employees	1,300
4. United Brotherhood of Carpenters and Joiners	750	4. United Food and Commercial Workers International Union	1,300
5. International Association of Machinists	699	5. Service Employees International Union	1,000
6. United Mine Workers of America	600	6. United Automobile, Aerospace and Agricultural Implement Workers of America	862
7. International Brotherhood of Electrical Workers	500	7. International Brotherhood of Electrical Workers	845
8. Hotel and Restaurant Employees' International Alliance	402	8. American Federation of Teachers	830
9. International Ladies' Garment Workers' Union	390	9. Communications Workers of America	600
10. International Hod Carriers, Building and Common Laborers Union	386	10. International Association of Machinists and Aerospace Workers	550
		United Steelworkers of America	550

SOURCE: *The Public Perspective: A Roper Center Review of Public Opinion and Polling* 5 (July/August 1994): 9.

does the identity of those unions that appear only on the modern list: not just the National Education Association but also the American Federation of Teachers and the American Federation of State, County, and Municipal Employees. So, for that matter, does the identity of those from the old list that do not appear on the new: the United Brotherhood of Carpenters and Joiners, the United Mine Workers, and the International Ladies' Garment Workers' Union. By 1990—a remarkable statistic—only 10.8 percent of private-sector employees were unionized, but 38.7 percent of public-sector employees were.

One result was that organized labor was becoming more like the New Politics Democrats structurally. A second result was that it was becoming more like them substantively as well. New growth areas for organized labor arrived at a point in time when the New Politics Democrats were emerging to elite prominence, so that getting along with the active Democratic Party meant adjusting to New Politics priorities. Moreover, new labor operatives were coming up through the same social milieu—even the same educational structure—as New Politics Democrats and thus were being exposed to the same substantive concerns. At bottom, finally, blue-collar and private-sector unions appeared to be led naturally toward social welfare issues, toward programs that would support the ordinary economic well-being of their members. Similarly, white-collar and public-sector unions appeared to be led naturally toward quality-of-life concerns, in part because the public sector could grow only if these concerns were advanced, in part because blue-collar, private-sector unions had helped ensure their basic economic security. In any case, these were in fact the *same* concerns motivating New Politics Democrats generally.

A different version of the same phenomenon affected the Modern Republicans. But ironically for the postwar elite that had always operated most informally, it was formal changes that proved most consequential and most deleterious—not that informal changes were inconsequential. At the point when the social base for the Modern Republicans was newly ascendant and notably emergent, in an explosion of middle management and the managerial suburbs, Modern Republicans were the main alternative thrust to the regular party. By the time the great corporations were not so obviously the story of American economic life, and the suburbs were instead the story of social life for everyone, the main alternative to the regular party within Republicanism was the evangelical Protestants—and the remnants of Modern Republicanism were part of the regular party.

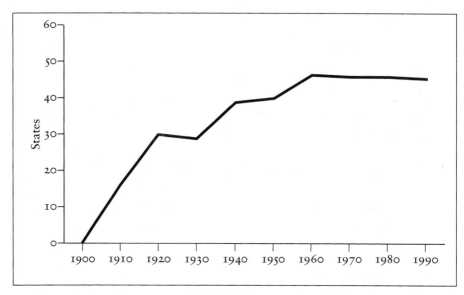

FIGURE 15
PROCEDURAL REFORM AND THE SPREAD
OF PARTICIPATORY INSTITUTIONS FOR PARTY BUSINESS —
GUBERNATORIAL NOMINATIONS VIA PRIMARY ELECTIONS:
THE REPUBLICANS

SOURCE: *The Book of the States* (Lexington, Ky.: Council of State Governments, various years).

Yet central to all this was also a procedural change. The Modern Republicans had always been dependent on deference from the official party structure, as well as on their success at the presidential level within it. As Figure 15 shows, the formal means for ensuring this deference, and thus for allowing party leaders to pick Modern Republicans as candidates even when they lacked a sufficient mass base to claim nominations on their own, had been eroding at the state level for many years. After 1968—at the impetus, ironically, of the New Politics Democrats—this ability disappeared at the presidential level as well, and with remarkable speed (see Figure 16). A tolerance for social welfare programs and an active dislike of cultural conservatism, by an elite that had always lacked the mass base of small-business Republicanism and now lacked the base of the New Christian Right as well, was not a formula for success under these (nondeferential) arrangements.

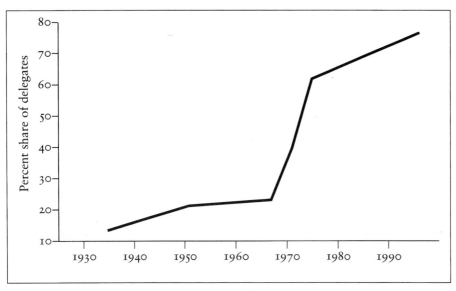

FIGURE 16

PROCEDURAL REFORM AND THE SPREAD
OF PARTICIPATORY INSTITUTIONS FOR PARTY BUSINESS —
PRESIDENTIAL NOMINATIONS VIA CANDIDATE PRIMARY:
THE REPUBLICANS

SOURCES: Byron E. Shafer, *Bifurcated Politics: Evolution and Reform in the National Party Convention* (Cambridge, Mass.: Harvard University Press, 1988), 90; *Congressional Quarterly Weekly Report* 1996, various issues.

Conversely, policy impacts from such changes (impressive as these changes were) were not guaranteed by the details of the change itself, which is to say that major changes in the social structure of key partisan elites across a major period of time are not the same as major impacts on the *outcomes* of public policy. It would be hard to argue that a world in which organized labor and Modern Republicans contributed the great elite infusions to the effort to shape policy conflict would handle any given issue in the same way as a world in which New Politics Democrats and evangelical Protestants contributed the major new partisan elites. But can the question of impact be taken further than that?

Surely it can also be taken to the difference in the overall agenda for political conflict and to elite contributions to the content of that agenda.

Here, the difference remains striking. A large tranche of immediate postwar partisan conflict was over labor-management issues themselves, and a huge tranche involved the social welfare issues that seemed integral to a politics formed along labor-management lines. The rise of a comprehensive labor elite was obviously central to keeping these issues at the center of American politics, and although the Modern Republicans might be argued to have defined themselves partly in response to organized labor, their presence in politics actually further reinforced a concentration on these concerns.

By contrast, these issues were not central to the New Politics Democrats, born, as they were, out of antiwar, civil rights, environmentalist, and feminist concerns. New Politics elites were certainly not hostile to social welfare programs, but these programs were not a priority, especially in comparison to the cultural issues that remained central to their concerns. The evangelical Protestants then mirrored this from the other side. Like New Politics Democrats, evangelical Protestant elites attempted to add economic issues—lower taxes, a balanced budget—to their cultural and (especially) religious agenda. But again, priority was clearly on the latter, especially for the mass base and, in truth, most especially for the elites whenever they were in their sharpest conflict with New Politics Democrats.

So, there was a sharply different agenda in national politics at the beginning as opposed to the end of the postwar period, and the preferences of ascendant elites were a crucial aspect of agenda change. Inevitably, of course, many other issues were forced into politics by changes in the larger environment, changes that were not controlled by partisan elites of any stripe: North Korea invaded South Korea; widespread rioting broke out in American cities; OPEC induced an "oil shock" to the economy; AIDS surfaced as a major menace to public health. These were not the preferred policy focus for any of these elites, and they were certainly not the products of their individual agendas. Yet even here, the four key elites could be expected to approach each of these concerns in a different and distinctive manner, so that their presence powerfully affected how such definitionally extraneous political issues were addressed.

Still, there are caveats. First and foremost, an agenda is not legislation. Indeed, organized labor elites in the 1950s or evangelical Protestant elites in the 1990s would have emphasized how limited and frustrating their policy successes actually were (Hosansky 1996). Setting an agenda for conflict is a task that an emergent elite has a fair chance of accomplishing. Seeing it converted into law involves that elite in negotiations—and contests—with all the other elite claimants, ascendant or receding, and the outcome is not nearly so obvious.

This leads to a second caveat: key insurgent elites are not the elite universe, not by a long shot. Other elites are always propelling (or sustaining) other items on the agenda, and they are prevailing (or retreating) on all such items in ways that affect their ultimate legislative fate. The particular interpretation of the circulation of elites used here, for example, leads away from two other, obvious, and hugely influential sets of specialized partisan actors—the southern Democrats and the regular Republicans. Or rather, what it really does is treat them as an established context rather than an operational focus. Likewise, the particular periodization used here leads away from a lesser but still important partisan infusion falling between these two pairs during the postwar years, that of black Democrats.

This is not the place to tell these other stories, although elements of the first two have surfaced in constructing the ones that had to be told. Nevertheless, the success of organized labor and the Modern Republicans, both in imposing an agenda and in securing policy details, was heavily influenced by the behavior of the southern Democrats and the regular Republicans, just as the success of the New Politics Democrats and the evangelical Protestants was heavily influenced by details of the *evolution* of the southern Democrats and regular Republicans by the time the former became major forces on the political scene. Still, with these caveats entered, the share of the story of postwar American politics captured by this particular focus on the circulation of elites remains impressive.

These are substantive findings of real consequence. Yet an analytic focus on these elites provides a further discipline. From one side, their social base, leadership component, and distinctive values require specific attention. From the other side, the roots and products of these elements require specific attention as well. The first demands a cross-sectional focus; the second demands a longitudinal focus instead. By the same token, application of this analytic focus to these specific elites at least touches on the main postwar alternatives, both for alternative partisan elites and for alternative policy preferences. If such a focus does not present these alternatives in the same detail, there must be some backdrop and some foreground to any analysis.

Under a focus that offers *this* backdrop and *this* foreground, the differences in the partisan character of postwar politics remain striking. Its structure is as different as organized labor, Modern Republicans, New Politics

Democrats, and evangelical Protestants. Its substance is as different as social welfare, labor relations, alternative lifestyles, and traditional values. Pareto, perhaps inevitably, would have found such differences to be important, to be inherent, and to be constantly undergoing change.

> In the economic system, the non-logical element is relegated entirely to tastes and disregarded, since tastes are taken as data of fact. One might wonder whether the same thing might not be done for the social system, whether we might not relegate the non-logical element to the residues, then take the residues as data of fact and proceed to examine the logical conduct that originates in the residues. That would yield a science similar to pure, or even to applied, economics. But unfortunately, the similarity ceases when we come to the question of correspondences with reality.
>
> The hypotheses that, in satisfying their tastes human beings perform economic actions which may on the whole be considered logical is not too far removed from realities, and the inferences from those hypotheses yield a general form of the economic phenomenon in which divergences from reality are few and not very great, save in certain cases (most important among them the matter of savings). Far removed from realities, instead, is the hypothesis that human beings draw logical inferences from residues and then proceed to act accordingly. In activity based on residues human beings use derivations more frequently than strictly logical reasonings, and therefore to try to predict their conduct by considering their manner of reasoning would be to lose all contact with the real. (Pareto 1980, 831)

CHAPTER SEVEN

Reform in the American Experience

"Reform" has been a recurrent theme across American political history. As a theme, it has seen periods of ascendancy, when the banner of reform has been at the center of practical politics. It has seen periods of neglect as well, when other concerns have effectively displaced it. Yet even in these latter periods of indifference, when reform programs and reform partisans have seemed inconsequential on the national stage, elements of what might be called a "reform mentality" have still characterized American policy making. When reform has instead been at the center of the national agenda, its banner has served as the unifying device for an ideology, a social movement, an operational program, and, ultimately, an influence on the practical content of national politics.

Accordingly, this chapter attempts to break down the notion of reform into those same elements—reform as ideology, reform as social movement, reform as operational program, and reform as practical influence. These constitute the first four sections of the chapter. A fifth and final section surveys the current agenda of reform proposals, asking where the domestic reform impulse seems likely to go. Needless to say, such an approach requires an inevitably broad and abstracted argument, supplemented with some pointed and precise examples. Yet the potential pieces of that argument, as pieces, have already acquired substantial empirical attention. Their reassembly, then, becomes an exercise in empirical theory with substantive annotation for this most central element in the American experience.

Reform as Ideology

Reform has always been one of the main strands in American thinking about public institutions, public policy, and public life. By the same token, calls for reform have reliably been produced by the growing recognition of almost any public problem (Huntington 1981; Schlesinger 1986). In the evident reform eras in American political history, this combined impulse has been at the center of public debate about political institutions, and these eras are thus the most dramatic indication of the power of reform as an integrating goal, as practical political ideology. But reform as an abstract and overarching doctrine—as an approach that involves the conscious restructuring of current arrangements to a different and better recurring set of outcomes—has in fact been present in American approaches to public policy in most eras, where it has exercised less dramatic but equally compelling influence. Indeed, reform in this particular (ideological) sense, a search for improvements in the framework for action without an attempt to determine the outcomes within that framework, has spread well beyond the realm of government to surface in realms such as news gathering and reporting, for example.

There have been two great and generally recognized "reform eras" in American political history, eras when the abstract banner of a self-conscious effort at institutional reform could be most easily observed. One of these was a period in the late nineteenth and early twentieth centuries, when the great struggles of American public life were over attempts to democratize the making of public policy and, secondarily, to guarantee fairness of procedure in economic life as well. The institutional hallmark of this era was the primary election for making nominations to public office, but it was accompanied by such additional political devices as the initiative and referendum, as well as by efforts at trust-busting in the more explicitly economic realm, at breaking up the large business and financial conglomerates. The second of these reform eras was much more recent, through the 1960s and 1970s, a period that centered even more on attempts to democratize the making of public policy. The products of this era actually reached into most institutions of government, seeking a more general openness to public influence. Yet these products were focused most fundamentally on the intermediary institutions closest to government—namely, political parties and interest groups—while they again included an economic component, featuring new regulatory agencies and expanded governmental regulations. (Many are gathered in Crotty 1977; see also Wilson 1980.)

It will be necessary to return to these eras both to isolate the social dynamics of reform as a movement and to look in more detail at the particular policies that follow from this movement and its mentality. But it is necessary to note beforehand that reform as an overarching doctrine, as an abstract approach to shaping institutional behavior, has been a much more general (if less dramatic and self-conscious) contribution to the content of public policy in the United States. That is, the notion of changing the rules of the game while deliberately refraining from prescribing its outcome is a powerful if implicit guiding principle through many more eras than those commonly identified with the sweeping reform of governmental institutions, precisely because this notion underlies many specific public policies in many historical eras.

This more general application of the notion of reform can be discerned in the substance of particular policies across time. In the historically most common approach to public policy on housing, for example, the question is usually not How should the government build what it regards as desirable? but rather How can the government foster and extract desirable housing outcomes? In a different but complementary fashion, the power of reform as abstract ideology can be seen in the recurring desire to be associated publicly with the purported "reform position." This emerges clearly in historical and contemporary arguments by both sides in battles over the regulation of labor-management relations, for example, where the debate is ordinarily over what needs to be reformed in order to guarantee a fair contest. Not surprisingly, then, many major issues in contemporary American politics, ranging all the way from weapons procurement through welfare provision, partake heavily and continually of reform ideology, to the point of being couched as a debate, in these particular cases, over "purchasing reform" and "welfare reform" (Headey 1978; Kochan 1980; Rowner 1988; Towell 1988; Hobson 1987).

Even that, however, does not exhaust the reach of reform as ideology. As a strand in American thinking about the organization of public life, the reform approach has been extended to many nongovernmental institutions, and especially to their relationship with the political process. This is most evident in the regulation of organized interests, the interest groups that are best able to attempt to influence public policy making. A fear that the interests are subverting the fair play of politics has surfaced continually across American history (Madison 1961; Steffens 1904; Green, Fallows, and Zwick 1972). So has an attempt to reform the situation, by requiring disclosure and publicity or by placing actual limitations on behavior. Sometimes, this has meant regulating the interactions of those interests with government, such as requiring that they register as lobbyists and record any financial contributions. Occasionally, this has meant regulating their own internal structure and procedures, such as with rules specifying who can (and cannot) be solicited for political donations or rules specifying the organizational form that any politically active committee must take.

Yet the same basic impulse, albeit manifested somewhat differently, can be detected even further afield, in reform efforts within and around institutions that are neither governmental in formal terms nor explicitly in the business of influencing government. The development of American news media provides a case in point, through deliberate reforms of their internal practices of reporting and deliberate reforms of their external links to government. Internally, the struggle to move from a deliberately partisan to an aspiringly nonpartisan press is a classic example of trying to realize the doctrine of evenhandedness of framework rather than to ensure the delivery of specific and guaranteed results. Externally, the drive to secure press access and protect press comment, pursued by means ranging from legislation requiring freedom of information in government to court decisions narrowing the grounds for charges of libel, is an attempt to see that the public has a full range of materials from which to make up its own mind (Mott 1962; Epstein 1973; Ranney 1983).

The pervasiveness of this grand and general ideology of reform leads to the possibility—indeed, the suspicion—that American politics can be understood not as a conflict between the left and right of the orthodox ideological spectrum but as a conflict between the program (and promise) of reform versus a defense of "politics as usual." At its extreme, this is the view that reform is a substitute for ideology in the United States. One need not go nearly that far, however, to agree that reform has been a major strand in American thinking about public life—a continuing strand throughout all eras, and the dominant one in some (Schlesinger 1950). A doctrine this large and persistent, in turn, can hardly have existed in thin air. Its very scope suggests that it was attached to (or certainly suggests the need to search for) continuing features of American social and political structure that can explain the persistence of this ideology in all periods and its insistent rise in some.

Reform as Social Movement

The obvious starting point for an explanation of why the ideology of reform would be particularly attractive in American society is the array of elements normally used for an explanation of what makes the American experience itself distinctive. This ordinarily begins with the very process of creating a nation that was, exceptionally, "new"—begun at a clear point in time and separated from any existing (largely feudal) social order. Such explanations ordinarily continue with the twin themes of immigration and the frontier, a geographically vast nation settled through external immigration and internal migration. Such explanations often take note of the inherent individualism and intuitive reliance on voluntarism associated with a pattern of development based on these twin themes. These elements are often summarized, finally, through their contribution to a dominant American culture: individualist but populist, formally democratic but informally emphasizing the role of society, not government. Succeeding incarnations of this culture, of course, are what give modern social, economic, and even technological conditions their connections with a particular—a distant but continuing—American past (Lipset 1963, 1991).

Different students of American society have assigned different weights to these factors. Some have added further elements, and some have asserted that all these elements, together, are not as powerfully distinctive as earlier writers were prone to suggest. Looked at under the particular lens of reform, however, the key fact in this framework for thinking about the evolution of American society is not its inclusiveness or even its distinctiveness. Rather, the key fact is the way these particular elements seem ideally suited to a continuing concern with restoring the fairness of the basic rules of the political game while avoiding fixed and determinative policy resolutions, a veritable definition of the reform approach. Indeed, it is not difficult to see this concern embodied concretely in the U.S. Constitution itself, the document that institutionalized a new and independent nation. The Constitution is inherently a reform document in the sense that it took the colonists' perceptions of the workings of British government and of their own prior Articles of Confederation and "corrected" these in light of their experiences. But it is also a reform document in the sense of attempting to guarantee effective government while safeguarding individual differences and preventing artificially imposed and sustained (and thereby tyrannical) outcomes (Roche 1961; Eidelberg 1968).

It is even more commonplace to note the close association a hundred years later between the evolving character of American society and the first great self-conscious round of political reforms. The growth of highly organized political parties to manage (and benefit from) the waves of new immigrants in the late nineteenth century, known pejoratively as "machines," was the direct spur to reforms aimed at cleaning up politics. But the massive presence of these same immigrants, with attendant barriers of culture, language, and, at bottom, stages of assimilation, was also critical to the *character* of those reforms. This vast immigrant presence, along with these additional barriers to any simple social integration, almost guaranteed that a reform response to problems of political corruption would take the form of trying to ensure "fair play for all" and attempting to contain the (obviously corrupting) role of the organized interests, rather than the form of programs aimed at redistributing concrete benefits to newly arrived, not yet American, incipiently "corrupt" groups (Hammack 1982; Merton 1957; Gosnell, 1937).

Perhaps surprisingly, what all this has produced, another century later, is a society in which the reform impulse still seems integral and natural. The frontier is largely gone; immigration, though remaining substantial by comparison to most other developed nations, is no longer diagnostic. Yet a political culture based on individualism and populism, one aspiring to "equality of opportunity" rather than "equality of condition," certainly persists. So does what is probably its inseparable obverse: a continuing concern that the major, existing, organized interests will dominate government in such a culture, along with continuing reforms aimed at guaranteeing that they do not (McClosky and Zaller 1984; Verba and Orren 1985; Lowi 1971, 1981). Said differently, this political culture has in fact asserted itself in the peculiar social and economic conditions of the late twentieth century, just as it asserted itself in earlier eras with conditions peculiar to their time too. And once again, a reform movement and specific institutional reforms have been integral to this.

In fact, these continuing cultural roots of reform are probably further reinforced by some factors specific to the late twentieth century. Informally, for example, they have probably been reinforced by a sense of growing diversity in individual lifestyles, a sense of increasingly varied realities in the way people live. When this is superimposed on regional and ethnic or racial differences, it contributes to the sense that *everyone* is in the minority—and that fair play in the political arena, rather than some given outcome, must be the goal. Formally, these impulses are also reinforced by such things as a series of contemporary Supreme Court decisions enshrining individual rights and liberties. In areas as diverse as religious display, personal health, criminal procedure, and sexual behavior, these are rights and liberties not just *for* the individual but also *against* majoritarian preference and *against* governmental policies (Yankelovich 1984; Pritchett 1984; O'Brien 1986).

All that can serve as an explanation for why reform as a grand (and often vague) ideology—as a general approach to public life—could secure a central place in an evolving American society. It cannot, however, serve as an explanation for why reform has come to the fore in certain eras, that is, why certain periods have been dominated by an attempt to *operationalize* the abstract ideology of reform, and why it has just as obviously receded in others. This requires a much more specific rooting of the reform ideology in particular political constituencies, along with changes in the situations of those constituencies that are at least plausible as explanations for the surge or decline of reform movements. Unfortunately, attempts to locate reform in this more pointed and social sense have produced a welter of alternatives, neither sufficiently consistent to provide a dominant explanation nor sufficiently inconsistent to allow definitive comparisons.

Thus reform has been argued to be the program of those on the way up, of rising social groups that see their political influence fail to keep pace with their improving material standards and turn to reform as a way to align the two. Yet reform has also been argued to be the program of those on the way down, of declining social groups that see their former perquisites and status eroding and turn to reform as a way to attack malefactors and restore a "proper" condition to themselves. Reform has even been argued to be the program of those with *inconsistent* social standing, of those whose occupational status, wealth, education, and community position do not cohere and who are likely to turn to reform in order to facilitate a (positive) integration (Buenker 1969; Mowry 1949; Thelen 1969). The real world, unfortunately, has been unkind to all these hypotheses, providing support for one in one place, support for another somewhere else, along with an apparent mix of these perspectives in most places.

What is much easier to elaborate, however, is the social location of a specific reform movement once it becomes associated with explicit party politics. Reformers, in fact, are normally the challenging faction, just as reform is reliably their challenging doctrine, *within the dominant party* in American politics. There are also tantalizing connections among such reform factions across time, and these will reappear at various places later. But the key point is the apparently ineluctable rise of their adherents as a major challenging faction to the dominant coalition within the dominant party in every era. This has meant, of course, that the main reform faction in the two great reform eras in the last hundred years has been located in a different political party each time. But while that fact may serve to mask the larger continuity, it also dramatically underlines the essential similarity of reformers—and reform.

During the first great self-conscious reform era in American politics, in the late nineteenth and early twentieth centuries, the self-conscious reformers were one of two major factions within the dominant political party of the time, the Republican Party (Hofstadter 1955; Mowry 1951, 1958; DeWitt 1915). William McKinley, president from 1897 to 1901, was perhaps the great symbol of the "regulars," the antireformers, who were the dominant faction during much of this period. Their main support among the organized interests was from big (corporate) business; their main promise was effectively "politics as usual," leading to economic betterment for all. Theodore Roosevelt, president from 1901 to 1909, best symbolized their internal opposition, the reformers, recognized historically by the designation "progressives." Their social base was a much more amorphous, growing middle class, and especially the independent professionals within it: attorneys, teachers, doctors, and ministers. Their promise was reform, especially in the political realm with things such as the primary election, but extending to the economic realm with things such as regulation of business combinations and trusts.

A half century later, in the 1960s and 1970s, it was the dominant Democratic Party that produced the recognizable reform faction (Shafer 1983a; Kearns 1976; Schlesinger 1975). In this era, Lyndon Johnson, president from 1963 to 1969, would symbolize the regulars. Their main support among the organized interests was from big (organized) labor; their clear preference was again for "politics as usual," leading to social equality and economic betterment for the disadvantaged. The very splits that occurred within the party under Johnson were one of the main reasons why reformers never acquired an actual president to symbolize their faction this time. Yet they otherwise showed the same rough historical continuities, in being based most generally in middle-class areas of the party and in acquiring the more specific support of organized interests based there as well— environmentalists, feminists, and antiwar protesters. More consequentially, they also acquired a stream of procedural reforms in the traditional mold, emphasizing process over policy. Some of these are addressed in the next section; others appear in the final section, on the current reform agenda. But here, it is worth noting especially that these reforms included changes in the process of presidential selection itself, so that there was far less likelihood that the regular faction could *ever* fully recapture the presidency.

Reform as Operational Program

What was most striking about the rise of the reformers in both cases was the apparent—and apparently ineluctable—similarity in the cycle of their appearance. A party previously out of power began to lay claim to majority status. Simultaneously, it began to address the central substantive concerns that had helped bring it to power. As it consolidated its majority position in national politics, and as it implemented the most consensual part of its program, it consolidated a dominant coalition centered on the official party organization but augmented by certain key organized interests. This very consolidation then led some of those who were inside the dominant party coalition but outside its dominant internal groups to become concerned with the content of public policy and the tone of national politics. When they turned to procedural reform as the obvious way to break up the existing internal coalition and ensure control by the general public, a new reform era was effectively born (Burnham 1970; Sundquist 1973).

There appeared to be additional similarities in the social base of these reform movements, such as the overrepresentation of highly educated, independent professionals, suggesting that such individuals inevitably look to the governing party for the actions they desire while finding themselves (perhaps also inherently?) underrepresented in the official party organization and in its principal allies among the organized interests. Indeed, there were further suggestive parallels in the inclusion in the reform movement of certain public issues peculiarly attractive to these individuals, in particular, environmentalism and feminism. Nevertheless, what was ultimately most striking in these parallels was their doctrinal similarity, the essential similarity in programmatic thrust between the two grand reform factions separated not just by differences in partisan allegiance but also by more than half a century of history.

It was this doctrine, of course, that gave reform its practical meaning. Beyond that, it was this doctrine that gave reform its impact—sometimes anticipated, sometimes not—on American politics and American society around it. Structural and procedural democratization was always the hallmark of these programs, their central value and their overarching institutional thrust. At bottom, the effort was nothing less than to make the mechanics of politics and government embody the essence of democracy itself (Banfield and Wilson 1963, chap. 11; 1964; 1971). In both eras, the principal means for accomplishing these ends was an assault, a structurally and procedurally democratizing assault, on the political party, the principal organizational means for connecting individual citizens with the institutions of government. In both eras, this assault on the parties was visualized as, and combined with, a secondary assault on the major organized interests of the time—a secondary assault on big business at the turn of the twentieth century, and on big business plus big labor in the second half of that century. In the first great round of institutional reform, this went on to a halting effort to restructure and democratize economic life as well. In the second great round, it was limited to an effort to regulate economic life instead, though this was probably a more extensive and practically effective effort.

At the most basic level, in any case, an openness to public access and some ultimate mechanism for the direct vote of the relevant public always constituted the procedural core of reform. This was taken to be the best way to get an incontrovertible expression of the popular will, of course. But it was simultaneously seen as the best way to "get around" the (usually contrary) influence of the organized interests. Accordingly, the principal target of reform was the political party, especially the dominant party. Parties, after all, were justified abstractly as the means of creating public control of government. More to the practical point, they controlled, evidently and concretely, the choice the public ultimately received (Commission on Party Structure and Delegate Selection 1970; Saloma and Sontag 1973). Yet the reform impulse was also reliably fueled by a belief that other major organized interests—business corporations, farm associations, labor unions, or all of the preceding—were further distorting and defeating the popular will by way of political parties. Accordingly, this impulse sometimes went further and tried to affect these organized interests directly, or at least to affect their role in politics through disclosure, registration, reconstitution, or even prohibition.

The first great era of deliberate structural reform, from approximately 1890 to 1915, established all these central themes, while producing their main institutional embodiments as well. Any number of new and creative twists on the basic thrust of opening up politics to direct citizen participation, and on the basic device of a direct vote by the relevant general public, achieved some success in this period. These included the initiative, whereby members of the public could put a policy question directly on the ballot; the referendum, whereby certain types of policies had to go on the ballot and be endorsed by the public before enactment; and the recall, in which that same public, when discontented with the performance of a duly elected official, could force that official to stand for reelection before the end of his formal term (Magleby 1984; Kaplan 1988). Yet both the symbolic emblem for this first great reform impulse and its true procedural embodiment, which became one of the diagnostic innovations in the entire history of American politics and government, was the institutional device of the primary election.

A primary election, of course, is a formal public ballot arranged by the government and conducted in a neutral manner to select the nominees of the parties for the offices to be contested in the subsequent general election (Key 1956; Merriam and Overacker 1928). The political party, as an organization of party officials, can normally still make an endorsement among the potential nominees for a given office and can even work on behalf of its choice, though some states go so far as to prohibit both activities. Yet anyone who can collect enough signatures can ordinarily run for nomination, and this is the crucial fact. As a result, the winner of the primary election, not the endorsee of the official party, becomes the party's candidate for the general election. Thus "the party's candidate" can be (and intermittently is) someone who has defeated the person endorsed by the official party organization.

There were additional reform efforts associated with the primary that were destined not to receive serious consideration until the second great round of reform politics half a century later. Efforts to limit and control campaign financing were among these, and although they received much discussion and a few modest legislative nods in the early twentieth century, they did not receive serious attention until the 1970s—and still have not reached their full extension (Overacker 1932, 1946). They were, however, an obvious incarnation of a major secondary goal of the various devices for direct election—namely, circumventing, constraining, or eliminating the influence of major organized interests outside the political party, which especially meant organized business corporations in the 1890s. In fact, the first great reform era was roughly bracketed by the two major instances when the reform impulse reached all the way over into an effort to democratize economic life. These were the Sherman Antitrust Act of 1890 and the Clayton Antitrust Act of 1915, both aimed at breaking up giant holding companies and allowing individual enterprise coupled with public control—structural and procedural democratization, if you will—in the economic marketplace (Letwin 1955, 1966; Thorelli 1954).

The second great reform era, the 1960s and 1970s, did not produce institutional reforms of comparable depth or innovation. In part, this was a tribute to the reach and success of the first great round of political reform. The primary election had appeared in response to an era of genuinely strong parties in American history. Yet the primary then helped undermine the strength of parties as organizations, so that those that came under attack in the second great reform wave were not nearly as organizationally impressive as those that had gone before. Nevertheless, this second period probably offered more total innovations (and successes) than its historic predecessor, and it certainly pushed the reform impulse into additional areas, including not just campaign financing but also the actual operation of major governmental institutions. If this second reform era was not as fundamental or as novel in its proposals, it was more diverse in its focus and even broader in its impacts (Shafer 1983b; Crotty 1977).

Once again, structural and procedural democratization were the hallmarks—and rallying cries—of the reform movement. Indeed, as if to emphasize continuity with an earlier generation, a crucial part of this second set of political reforms was the extension of the primary election to its last great target, to nominations for president of the United States, though with an implied assault on big labor, not big business, this time. In our time, the reform impulse reached beyond the direct mechanics of nomination by trying to affect—to regulate and to democratize—the financing of campaigns for nomination to public office. And in our time, the reform impulse reached beyond campaigns for selection to public office, even in their totality, by trying to affect the operation of governmental institutions after the general election. This included, most extendedly, the U.S. Congress, but it even included the federal bureaucracy, reaching out to affect the entire executive branch.

Because these reforms are products of our own time and because they have been analyzed and debated so extensively, their practical career is generally familiar. The growth of presidential primaries to the point where they now dominate the process of presidential nomination in both political parties is a major change from the period before 1968, when this was decidedly not the case. Campaign finance reform, the crucial aspiring supplement to this revolution in nominating politics, has had a more mixed fate, becoming an important part of the framework for presidential selection but having much less impact below the presidential level. Inside the larger institutionalized executive branch, a collection of so-called sunshine laws, attempting to guarantee free access to information about governmental activity, has become a major element in journalistic and scholarly inquiry into the politics of governance, while their so-called sunset counterparts have attempted to force executive agencies to justify their continuation (or go out of existence) periodically (Ceaser 1982; Alexander 1984; Relyea 1975; West 1985).

In the same way, reforms inside Congress have aimed at more open access and greater ultimate majority control. This has meant more equitable distribution not just of committee and subcommittee leadership posts, the crucial means by which members of Congress influence policy, but also of the staffs and budgets that automatically go with them, along with changes in the effective rules of activity for decision making on the floors of the full Senate and House chambers, partially transforming the operation of both bodies. There has been no direct counterpart to the Sherman and Clayton Acts in this second great wave of structural reforms, and thus no direct and frontal attempt to reshape the economy while restructuring politics. Yet the flood of new political reforms was accompanied by more numerous and wide-ranging and, ultimately, more successful *regulatory* initiatives for the major economic actors in realms as diverse as consumer protection, waste disposal, occupational health and safety, and environmental protection, and these have surely achieved a much greater direct impact than the Sherman and Clayton Acts ever did (Rieselbach 1977; Rudder 1978; Wilson 1980).

Reform as Practical Impact

The question of the character and reach of structural and procedural reforms—from two great reform eras or, indeed, from a wide-ranging set of proposals on the current political agenda—has never been coterminous with the question of their practical impact on politics and government. Indeed, serious students of reform have rarely failed to note that its practical impact is not a simple and automatic extension of the general ideology of reform, nor of the wishes of the more specific constituency for reform, nor even of the precise operational program of reform as implemented (Pye 1962; Black 1966; Huntington 1968). Some of this recurrent slippage, between the aspirations of reformers and the character of politics after reform, is due to normal confusion in the politics of implementation. Supporters feel compelled to promise more than they can possibly deliver; opponents likewise blame all problems thereafter on the implementation of reform. Beyond that, the *coalition* of supporters (or opponents) normally contains quite varied impressions of the justification for, or the impact of, reform.

Any attempt to restructure politics and government in a deliberate fashion, however, appears to produce a second major and inevitable set of arguments about the impact of reform, over and above those growing out of reform politics itself. These involve the extent to which reforms have produced intended or unintended impacts, and the balance between the two. Both sorts of impacts are real consequences of reform, whether they were preimagined or not. It is worth beginning with the distinction between intended and unintended consequences precisely because it helps illuminate not just the way reforms succeed or fail on their own terms but also the way they ultimately have a practical impact on politics or not, quite apart from intentions (Merton 1936; Boudon 1982).

At the outset, it is worth noting perhaps the most ironic potential impact of reform politics: it is possible for reform initiatives to fail—to be kept from consideration or to be formally rejected—yet have substantial practical effects, even effects in the intended direction. For example, in the period after 1968, the national Democratic Party engaged in a thorough and self-conscious internal process of reform that resulted in sweeping changes in the way delegates to national party conventions were selected and presidential candidates themselves were nominated. At the same time, the national Republican Party decided, just as deliberately and consciously, not to have an extended internal reform process and not to engage in sweeping procedural reforms. Yet within only one election, the unreformed Republican process of presidential nomination had changed to look almost identical to the thoroughly reformed Democratic process (Shafer 1988, chap. 2). Part of this similar outcome was the result of simple coercion, when Democratically controlled state legislatures imposed the same reform on both parties. But part of it resulted from the fact that the same social forces that were pushing state and national Democratic Parties toward reform were falling on many state Republican Parties too—these were, after all, the same states. When state Democrats then produced (and trumpeted) reform arrangements, state Republicans, not to be outdone, simply followed suit.

The disjunction between intentions and effects, at least in reforms of any scope, is more commonly encountered in the other direction. That is, the reform is successfully implemented, and implementation inherently fulfills *some* of the goals of its proponents. The reform just as clearly does not fulfill other goals, while it evidently produces further practical effects expected by neither proponents nor opponents. In recent years, the most numerous examples of this pattern have come in the area of campaign finance reform, and one of these is discussed in more detail later. One of the most striking examples of this phenomenon, however—of successful implementation that inherently secures some reform goals but simultaneously produces outcomes that surprise the reformers—came from the same reform process inside the national Democratic Party that produced the Republican anomaly noted earlier.

That process, begun after the disastrous Democratic convention and campaign of 1968, resulted in sweeping proposals for reform of the process of delegate selection and presidential nomination. Although these proposals reached into nearly every area of party business, their drafters were explicit in their belief—and indeed their desire—that these reforms should not increase the number of state presidential primaries. When they were ultimately implemented, however, they not only produced a sharp increase in the number of primaries; those primaries, when added together, produced one of the greatest shifts in the mechanics of presidential selection in all of American history (Commission on Party Structure and Delegate Selection 1970; Ranney 1975). Before reform, the process of presidential selection was actually dominated by state conventions of the official party leadership. After reform, the process was overwhelmingly dominated by state presidential primary elections, in which these same party officials had very little role.

Obviously, there was a veritable chain of miscalculations on the way to this result. Bulking large among them, however, was the principal misconception of the original drafters of reform: that the outlines of the process would remain roughly the same. Initially, state party leaders, faced with a booklet of reform demands reaching into nearly every facet of party business, looked for a way to deal with these reform proposals that would both guarantee compliance, so that they could not be accused of subverting democratization, and ensure that reform did not disrupt their other party business, the part unrelated to presidential politics. The simple solution, occurring independently and automatically to many of them, was to switch to a presidential primary. When these "simple solutions" were aggregated across the country as a whole, however, they produced not just the multi-plication of presidential primaries, which was itself neither expected nor desired by proponents. They also produced nothing less than the largest composite change in the mechanics of presidential selection since 1832 (Shafer 1983a, pt. 2).

The realm of campaign finance has, in recent times, produced an even larger array of unintended consequences, one of which is particularly useful in elaborating the pattern. This particular impact, in which deliberate for-mal change appeared to produce almost the opposite of its desired practical effect, stemmed from campaign finance regulations for all national offices. In an effort to contain the narrowly monetary influence of larger organized interests, which in this case meant primarily large business corporations, reformers created extensive regulations that forced those corporations to reorganize the process by which they contributed money to political candi-dates, thereby not just channeling their financial activity but actually *in-creasing* their collective contributions (Epstein 1979a, 1979b; Alexander 1984). It is not that these reforms failed to operate; they were fully imple-mented and largely successful on form. It is not that they failed to achieve powerful impacts; the ubiquity of the notorious political action committees (PACs) traces almost entirely to this reform. It is not even that their impact was uniformly contrary; campaign financing did become much more rule bound and much more open to public scrutiny. It is just that the effect of these PACs was almost entirely opposite to the aspirations of the reformers.

These examples, especially when taken together, are also useful for sug-gesting why structural and procedural reforms are so often associated with additional, unexpected, anomalous consequences. The most general way to summarize this answer is to say that formal changes, however grand their scope, are still only part of the explanation, even for their own ultimate operation. The way they interact with the society around them constitutes the full explanation, and although formal changes can influence the opera-tion of other social forces, those forces can just as easily (and usually more so) influence their operation in turn. (Waltz [1979] deploys an elegant variant of the same theme in the international arena.) But a more pointed and applied version of this interpretation, one that is also inherent in these examples, is to say that the way in which reforms actually operate in prac-tice is determined by the response of *organized intermediaries* to the en-vironment created by them. Party officials, organized interest groups, or even, on occasion, diffuse social categories (racial, ethnic, religious, cultural, or regional)—these are the intermediaries whose response will determine the practical impact of reform at its full extension.

It is clear that in each of the examples presented here, the response of organized intermediaries was central to the real impact of reforms. In the case of reform within the Republican Party, the need of local party officials not to look "unprincipled" by comparison to their Democratic counterparts produced real impacts without any reform regulations. In the case of the major change in the system for selecting delegates and nominating presidential candidates, the "natural" response of local Democratic Party officials to a cumbersome set of national party regulations led directly to a huge shift toward the presidential primary. And in the case of campaign finance reforms and the rise of PACs, the search by corporate officials for ways to maintain their influence in politics while complying with new regulations led them to revitalize an old organizational form, the PAC, which has now spread to most other organized interest groups as well (Shafer 1983b; Fenno 1986).

An element of pessimism often accompanies the recognition of these developments, and hence the acknowledgment of the central role that organized intermediaries play in creating the real impact of reform. Indeed, such analyses often appear to emphasize not just unintended but perverse consequences. Yet there appears to be no inherent intellectual need for pessimism. An analyst who knows that the response of major organized intermediaries is likely to be crucial can at least focus analytic attention there—an immediate gain in estimating the impact of reform (Ford 1898; Huntington 1988). Indeed, in each of the cases noted above, there *were* analysts who took this route and arrived at the proper result. That is, there were people who argued that successful Democratic Party reform would sweep the Republican Party along in its wake; there were people who argued that, the intentions of the reformers notwithstanding, the imposition of detailed new codes for delegate selection would drive state parties to the presidential primary; and there were observers who argued that all campaign finance reforms could reasonably hope to do was force political money onto the public record and make its use more available to public scrutiny, and that this alone would be a substantial improvement.

All that, no matter how it is approached analytically, is a far cry from arguing that the main products of the two great eras of American political reform did not shape—did not reshape—American politics in major ways. If some of this was major and unintended, much of it was intended, and real impacts were still real impacts, regardless of intent. Indeed, many of these are not just "influences" on American politics; they are integral to it and are often cited as essential elements distinguishing that politics (Shafer 1989; 1991, chap. 8). Surely the best example of this, the one best demonstrating the potential impact of reform and best summarizing the mix of intended and unintended consequences, is nomination to public office by way of primary elections. Nomination through the primary is still peculiar to American politics. Yet its implications reach into, and color, nearly every aspect of that politics. And this is actually more true today than it was when this reform was initially implemented.

The drive for nomination via primary election was a reform move of the late nineteenth and early twentieth centuries, justified specifically as a device for breaking the hold of party machines on democratic politics and returning responsiveness to the people. Yet after fierce initial battles for implementation in the states and cities, many reformers found themselves disappointed. Existing party organizations, which had fought the primary as a reform proposal, faced the fact that they had to live under this new procedural arrangement, and in many areas, they managed to do precisely that. An existing organization, skilled political leaders, and a mass clientele dependent on them all combined to make the primary look much less effective in practice than in theory.

Yet as time passed, society would change sharply, and the influence of the primary would only grow (Key 1964; Ranney and Kendall 1956, chap. 12). As the government moved to provide basic social welfare programs, for example, citizens were less directly dependent on political parties. As the public as a whole became more educated, it was increasingly disinclined to work through party officials and more inclined to participate on its own. As mass media of information evolved, people acquired the means to make their own decisions. And at every step, the primary was available as the basic framework for that politics, to allow these changes to have political impact. As a result, the weakness of political party organizations in our time; the tendency (and ability) of candidates to run for office on the basis of whatever concerns are most useful in their localities; and the decentralized, coalitional, and constantly shifting character of a composite American politics ultimately owed a major debt to the implementation of one particular reform, the primary election.

Reform in the American Future

Reform has reshaped American politics and government, and if this has often occurred in ways that no single actor intended, it has also occurred in ways that most careful analysts anywhere can understand. At the same time, however, this particular agenda for reform has derived from (and been successful because of) certain characteristics of the larger American experience that clearly are not part of the experience of many other nations. This fact makes the projection of lesser elements from the American case a problematic enterprise; at the very least, intelligent extrapolation to non-American contexts requires substantial local detail before it can reasonably be undertaken. Yet what of the American case—which is to say, the future of the American case—on its own terms? Such a dominant political and procedural thread, especially given its integral connection to other main features of the American experience, ought not disappear. Indeed, it ought not just resurface but demonstrate continuing characteristics: as ideology, as social movement, as operational program, and ultimately as practical impact.

What, then, is on the reform agenda in the United States in our time? Which reforms are already enmeshed in daily American politics? And which others are likely to come to the fore if we should move into a third great reform era? Precisely because major reform proposals must still find their way through the existing process of politics before being implemented, it is often possible to see an emerging agenda of reforms before they become an operational part of that politics. Some reforms are created instantaneously, it is true, and many acquire unforeseen twists by responding to a peculiar (and unforeseen) situation. But most exist in draft form well before either the crisis or the grand reform era that takes them effectively off the drafting board and converts them into practical operating arrangements (Polsby 1984).

As a consequence, it should be possible to close an overview of reform in the American experience by asking what proposals are already on that metaphorical agenda for the future of American government and politics. In this case, that possibility is more than amply realized; only the most self-consciously crabbed sort of impressionistic sample can avoid becoming mired in a veritable "grocery list" of reforms already receiving extended attention. An attempt to suggest the breadth and depth of such a list must, accordingly, suffice. Yet even such a sampling supports a number of closing thoughts about the centrality—the continued centrality—of the process of reform in American life.

Congress alone offers an impressive array of reforms widely bruited and awaiting serious decision. From the outside, the major focus is reform of the mechanics of nomination and election. Nomination by primary has, of course, long since come to categorize all congressional elections (with a few contingent exceptions). But regulation of the financing of congressional nominating and electing campaigns has lagged behind such regulation on the presidential level, and public financing of either phase of those campaigns has not arrived at all. As a result, the struggle for campaign finance reform—an active and extended struggle, as this is written—is surely the major one waiting to affect selection to Congress (Fenno 1973, 1978, 1982).

Once inside this institution, there are a number of reform proposals that would affect the operation of both chambers. Many of these involve the budgetary process and fiscal policy making, including such things as moving to a two-year budget cycle and streamlining the appropriations process. Others involve proposals that are specific to the peculiarities of each chamber, such as proposals to reduce requirements for shutting off debate or to jettison nongermane amendments in the Senate, and proposals altering leadership powers and prerogatives—a cyclic perennial—in the House. In any case, such a necessarily vague and truncated roster of reforms for only one institution, however impressive these reforms may be in their own right, serves only as an introduction (Granat 1984; Cohodas 1984).

The same approach could in fact be taken with most other institutions of American national government, with roughly the same result (President's Commission for a National Agenda for the Eighties 1980; Pious 1981). For example, there are proposed elaborations of the so-called sunshine and sunset regulations affecting the federal executive branch, just as there are reform proposals that would affect the operations of the Supreme Court, especially involving control of its own workload and, conversely, access by petitioners to the Court. If these additional notations indicate the potential *breadth* of current reform proposals, the potential *depth* of impact by reforms already on the American political agenda can perhaps best be conveyed by focusing on two other possibilities. One of these is well on its way to implementation; the other is slower in arriving but equally inevitable. Together, the two cover the entire span of political life, from top to bottom, from the individual citizen to the president of the United States.

At the very bottom, at the level of mass public participation, the reform that is clearly awaiting its moment is universal and automatic voter registration. Indeed, as this is written, major variants are already receiving extended congressional debate. [Since this piece was originally written, universal and automatic voter registration has been substantially achieved. Crucial background to its impact can be found in Kelley, Ayres, and Bowen 1967; Rosenstone and Wolfinger 1978; and Wolfinger and Rosenstone 1980.] At the very top, by contrast, in an effort to shape the highest office in the land, the reform that awaits is the culmination of a 200-year trend toward the national presidential primary. The national primary is not so obviously on the active political agenda, but it awaits only one or another of a growing list of plausible related crises before its moment too arrives (Ranney 1981; Shafer 1988, afterword).

Proponents claim the greatest possible impact for each of these prospective arrangements. And if there is reason to argue with any one (or all) of their claims, these particular reforms do bulk very large, in formal terms, in comparison to most others on the currently visible list. It is tempting, accordingly, to try to apply the lessons of earlier reform efforts about arguments, constituencies, procedures, and, especially, impacts. Done systematically, however, that would take another paper. Indeed, these two reforms alone, not to mention all the others, would presumably interact in their operation, making the analysis even more difficult. Not only would a presidential contest by means of a national primary presumably differ in major ways from a contest run under contemporary arrangements; a presidential contest run via a national primary with the current electorate might well differ from one run via a national primary with an electorate created by universal, automatic voter enrollment.

This is not the place to go on with that particular analysis. Yet the larger roster of contemporary reform proposals, in which this is only a particularly consequential example, implicitly returns to the central theme of this paper and to the central place of the phenomenon of reform in the American experience. The very size of this necessarily partial list, its breadth and depth, affirms that reform—as ideology, as social movement, and as operational program—remains alive and well in American politics as it enters the twenty-first century. Beyond that, the potential impact of these reforms, individually and together, argues for the importance of analysis *in the present*, before pressures of the moment make detachment more difficult. Finally, whether analysts get this right or not, such a list also suggests the continued, inescapable, major impact of deliberate reform in shaping—in reshaping—American public life.

CHAPTER EIGHT

From Social Welfare to Cultural Values
in Anglo-America

On Thursday, July, 5, 1945, the British electorate appeared to draw a line under the prewar political world. This electorate turned the wartime government, led by the Conservative Party, out of office. Moreover, it dismissed the Conservatives in favor of a party that still harbored doubts about its proper governing role, namely, British Labour. The scale of this reversal was additionally unprecedented. Previously, Labour had formed only minority, short-lived governments; its last such venture, in 1929, had seen the party take power just in time to acquire responsibility for the Great Depression. The Tories had thus returned to effective leadership in 1931, and Tory electoral and governmental dominance was still the context for the 1945 election. Now, however, Labour returned with not just an absolute but an enormous majority in Parliament: it gained more seats than the Tories were left holding. And it did this over a party that had arguably weathered the Great Depression and saved the nation in World War II (McCallum and Readman 1947; Addison 1994).

On Tuesday, November 5, 1946, the American electorate produced an only slightly less portentous outcome. This electorate threw out the stewards of both economic recovery and military victory, the Democratic Party of Franklin Roosevelt, of the New Deal, and of D day. Moreover, it did so by means of a party that had largely not come to terms with interim political developments, namely, the Republicans. Like British Labour, the American Republicans had secured their last collective victory just in time to take office in 1929. Like the British Tories, the American Democrats would reverse this outcome in 1931, taking control of both houses of Congress.

Special thanks to my coauthor Marc D. Stears for allowing this piece to appear here.

They would add the presidency two years later and would not cede the majority in any of these three great national institutions until 1946, when the Republicans reseized control of both houses of Congress with an agenda no less aggressive than, albeit opposite to, that of Labour. Few doubted that the presidency, in the hands of a weak and accidental Democratic caretaker, would follow shortly (Strahan 1998; Hartmann 1971).

Comparative political history is an enterprise calculated to tempt fate, and this particular comparison—grand, portentous, and false—is as good an example as any of the pitfalls that await. Nevertheless, the comparison contributes three major analytic reminders. One involves *sequence* and *context*. A half century later, we know that these two elections were not analogous, because we know that they fell in a different sequence of political (even partisan) developments in the two nations and that they offered a different reflection of the context for politics and government in their time. This may be a knowledge available largely by hindsight, but it is no less central to a historical reading because of that.

A second fundamental reminder involves *structure* and *substance*. Perhaps the key reason we can quickly dismiss these two elections as analogous is that we know that the substance of their politics—its policy core and even its ideological center—was about to be changed in one nation, reaffirmed in the other. As a result, we know that treating partisanship and partisan balance as joint key indicators of political structure at the time is an obvious mistake.

The third basic point subsumes the other two. Said one way, these two elections fit very differently within the larger eras in which they resided and within the larger orders to which they contributed. Said another way, any sensible comparison needs to counterpoise *era* and *order* in one nation with *era* and *order* in the other, not any one partisan outcome with any other, however close in "current political time" (as opposed to "real political time") they might be (Skowronek 1993, 49–52).

So, before integrating the postwar political history of two great nations into one short comparison, we need to convert these three analytic points into a comparative framework. That framework, alas, must carry a heavy load. There are infinite comparisons available for this general period: deference versus populism, tea versus coffee, the Beatles versus Elvis, football versus "football." It is the framework within which any such comparisons are placed that must ultimately provide the analytic purchase. To that end, the comparison of postwar politics in Britain and America offered here is organized through the notions of political eras and political orders, where a political era is an extended period in which policy conflict revolves around the same underlying concerns and where a political order is a complex of social structures that shape this conflict in an extended fashion.

Within these notions, the terrain of the traditional political historian and the terrain of the conventional political scientist combine to create a political landscape. The terrain of the historian—the area in which the historical guild has its greatest value-added—has always involved notions of sequence and context. The point about sequence here is that roughly similar developments in different nations can have similar roots and consequences, or not, depending on the point at which they arrive, especially in relation to other arrivals. And the point about context is that any given development will inevitably work differently, in and of itself, depending on what else is operative in national politics at the time of its arrival.

The terrain of the political scientist, by contrast, has its greatest value-added in a focus on the interaction of substance and structure. For a cross-national examination of change in postwar politics, then, substance means issue content, including grand rhetorical themes and crude concrete promises, but always with at least implications for public policy. And structure encompasses those major and ongoing influences that shape the conflict over substance, just as substantive content makes varying structures more or less potentially influential.

It will become clear in this particular case that issue substance can be usefully divided into two grand clusters: economic and social welfare issues (distributional concerns) versus cultural and national issues (behavioral concerns). And it will become clear that there are three general locations into which structural influences can be usefully parsed: the social base for politics, the intermediary organizations of politics, and the innards of governmental institutions themselves. But these latter points can be allowed to arise naturally and in passing from the argument that follows. (A collaborative attempt to work cross-nationally within this framework is Shafer 1996.)

The New Deal Era

The political era in which the American election of 1946 fell had been in existence, incipiently, since the great stock market crash of 1929. It had been in existence, formally, since the arrival of the Roosevelt administration in

Washington in 1933. And it had been in existence, practically, since that administration got to work propounding the mix of public policies that came to be recognized as the New Deal (Mitchell 1947; Schlesinger 1959; Leuchtenberg 1963). The great and dominating substantive concern of this era was social welfare and economics, as befitted a political era called into being by economic catastrophe. The great and continuing secondary substantive concern was foreign affairs, again befitting an order forced within a painfully few years to confront the catastrophe of total war.

Before the election of 1946, the policy content of the dominant economic-welfare dimension included all the hallmark programs of the New Deal: unemployment compensation, social security, industrial recovery, farm price supports, labor-management regulation, rural electrification, and so on. The policy content of the same dimension after 1946 would include full employment plus the "missing pieces" of the original New Deal agenda: health care, housing assistance, poverty amelioration, and, last but not least, civil rights. The policy content of foreign affairs was even more easily summarized: pursuit of World War II before the 1946 election, through a huge buildup of defense manpower and industry, and pursuit of the Cold War thereafter, with its mixture of international alliances, military support, and conventional foreign aid (Thomas 1986; Hamby 1973; Sundquist 1968).

The political order that largely fell into place around these New Deal programs, but that always required institutionalization by political elites and was increasingly fostered by them, began at the social base for American politics. By 1946, two great social coalitions underpinned this order, built principally on social class but with important ethnic and regional twists. One was a blue-collar coalition, aligned with the national Democratic Party, that featured working-class Americans generally, plus key ethnic minorities (especially Jews and blacks), the poor, and the entire (the "solid") South. The other was a white-collar coalition, aligned with the national Republican Party, that featured middle-class Americans generally, plus farmers outside the South (Sundquist 1973, chaps. 10–12; Ladd with Hadley 1975, pt. 1; Burner 1968).

The key intermediary organizations for politics remained political parties. By 1946, however, these were not just organized around the New Deal policy core—Democrats supportive, Republicans still opposed. They had also become parties different in kind. The Democrats were an amalgam of urban machines in the North, courthouse rings in the South, and volunteer activist branches scattered throughout the country. New Deal programs had actually helped extend the effective life of the organized (the "regular") Democratic Party within this mix. The Republicans, having fallen early on hard partisan times, had moved earlier to become the kind of activist-based political party that both parties would become in the second postwar era, relying on ideology and issues to motivate party workers. Although they retained some rural rings of their own in the North, New Deal programs had essentially wiped out the Republican machines present in the pre-depression years (Ware 1985; Mayer 1964; Mayhew 1986).

These parties were then additionally buttressed by organized interests of a highly partisan sort. Labor-management tensions mobilized both sides of the major interest-group divide, and labor-management issues and politicking were central to the economic and social welfare concerns of the era. There were notable ironies to this division. On the one hand, industrial recovery as fostered by the Democrats, and then a wartime boom, restored profitability to corporate business. On the other, corporate gigantism was especially good at producing numerical gains for organized labor. But regardless, labor became an increasingly important operational adjunct to the Democratic Party, in legislative and then in electoral politics, to the point where it actually substituted for the party in more and more places. By contrast, although corporate management provided some funding and the occasional "blue-ribbon" candidate for the Republicans, it was really small business—the Chamber of Commerce, not the National Association of Manufacturers—that carried the supportive load for the Republican Party among interest groups (Zieger 1986; Wilson 1979; Vogel 1989; Rae 1989).

The product in government then had a partisan character that was at once very familiar and sharply different. In the familiar tendency, the majority party still provided the basic framework for policy coalitions. In the change, Democrats were now that majority party, and Democrats tended to control both main elective branches of national government as a result. Indeed, from 1932 through 1968, the unity and vitality of the Democratic coalition were often the central story of electoral and institutional politics. After 1946, however, Republicans could potentially break this hold, especially when they had an attractive presidential candidate, and especially when foreign affairs rather than social welfare was the dominant substantive issue. Dwight Eisenhower was to embody both, and the Republicans were entitled to achieve unified partisan control of national government when he did.

The result was a characteristic dynamic to political conflict, but one shaped additionally and crucially by the structure of American national government. At bottom, the party on the Left, the Democratic Party, was widely perceived as being more in tune with public preferences on social welfare issues. The party on the Right, especially once Eisenhower had ended the Korean War and cemented his Republicans into the Cold War consensus, was widely perceived as being more in tune with public preferences on foreign policy issues. And the public gave a much higher priority to social welfare than to foreign affairs (Campbell et al. 1960, chaps. 2, 16). The strategic advice following from such a context might seem straightforward—Democrats to emphasize social welfare; Republicans to accommodate social welfare and emphasize foreign affairs. Yet this advice ran directly into a governmental structure that made it particularly difficult for the Republicans to follow through.

Because the president and Congress were separately elected, there had to be, in effect, *four* institutional parties within the American two-party system: a presidential and a congressional Democratic and Republican Party. And here, it was the response of the minority Republicans that proved crucial (Eidelberg 1968, chaps. 4, 5, 9; Binkley 1937; Jones 1965). In a presidential contest, all those state Republican Parties that found themselves in either competitive or Democratic states (at that time, states representing the majority of Americans) needed an economic moderate as their nominee. In congressional contests, in contrast, many seats were already reliably Republican, so there was no need for social welfare accommodation, while many of the rest were reliably Democratic, so accommodation (or not) was irrelevant.

The clearest Republican success story of this era, the Eisenhower interlude, was especially good at showing the full dynamic at work. Eisenhower himself accepted the strategic imperatives of his environment, featuring foreign policy issues but emphasizing that he was a "modern Republican," at home with the welfare state. This was sufficient not just to earn him the presidency but also to draw a Republican congressional majority into office with him. But his fellow officeholders, those same congressional Republicans, had not begun to make their peace with the New Deal.

Accordingly, the public threw them out at its first opportunity, in the midterm election of 1954, and even Eisenhower could not drag them back in with him a second time, when he was reelected by a landslide in 1956 (Ambrose 1990; Campbell 1960; Thomson and Shattuck 1960). To make

the composite picture more stark—and Republican problems more severe—
an institutional structure that helped hobble a Republican response to the
New Deal program and its order presented no counterpart difficulties for
the majority Democrats. For them, differing presidential and congressional
parties, both dominant, could comfortably go their separate ways under the
Democratic label.

The Social Democratic Era

By contrast, a new era in British politics arrived considerably later but even
more comprehensively. And it arrived, effectively, at a stroke. The events of
July 5, 1945—the British election—mattered tremendously, for reasons of
both substance and structure. In this, the policy response of the resulting
Labour government was extremely important. But so were several major
shifts in explicitly political structures. Those events mattered for reasons of
sequence and context as well. The timing of the depression, the war, and,
especially, the election itself delayed any major reconstruction of social
welfare policy and made such reconstruction look—but also surely be—
larger when it came. Certain key events during this interim provided a
crucial further context for subsequent developments.

No one could have missed the fact that the essence of political conflict in
Britain in the immediate postwar years involved economics and social welfare, overwhelmingly. The policy impact of this economic-welfare dimension was broad, deep, and remarkably concentrated in the first postwar
Labour administration. There was nationalization of coal, gas, electricity,
railroads, steel, and road haulage. There were social insurance programs,
with a universal unemployment and sickness system, enhanced state pensions, and, at the far end of this continuum, a National Health Service that
represented the most advanced state of socialized medicine in the democratic world. There were powers unprecedented in peacetime to plan, organize, and direct from the center—powers that had not survived the First
World War in Britain and would not survive the Second in the United States
(Cairncross 1985; Francis 1995).

Like the United States, Britain also featured a secondary policy dimension in this first postwar era, involving foreign affairs. Despite a national
exhaustion at the end of the Second World War, Britain accepted the need to
play a major role in the formation of the international institutions of the

Cold War. Yet Britain, unlike the United States, was also plunged imme-diately into the long-running issue of decolonization; Indian independence was to be granted by 1947. In both nations, this secondary dimension to public policy was a modest asset to the party that was not driving the social welfare revolution—namely, the (British) Conservatives and the (Ameri-can) Republicans (Morgan 1984; Gorst 1991).

At the social base for politics in Britain, there were again two great class-based coalitions, uncluttered with the racial and ethnic overlays that charac-terized America. Indeed, even the regional divisions that would add defini-tion to the second postwar order—Conservatives doing consistently better in England, Labour doing better on the Celtic fringe—were not factors of any great consequence. Instead, there was principally a blue-collar Labour-leaning coalition facing a white-collar Tory-leaning coalition, in a society where social class mattered enormously, and where there was an evident and inescapable blue-collar majority (Butler and Stokes 1974, 172–81). Yet the great and often underappreciated fact about the application of these two coalitions to the postwar world was the extent to which the 1945 electorate had changed not so much in its preferences as in its composition since the last Labour victory in 1929.

The change itself was the arrival in British politics of a whole new gener-ation of working-class voters, and their additional consolidation within the Labour Party. Any change across the generations was, of course, magnified in its impact by the calendar. The scheduled wartime election of 1940 had been canceled, so there would be ten years between elections in Britain, time for this particular generational change to gather steam quietly. As a result, one in five electors had been too young to vote in the previous election. Yet this huge new increment was additionally distinctive in important ways (Franklin and Ladner 1995).

Its growth had been facilitated, in effect, by serious suffrage expansion as long ago as 1918. But this growth had then been masked by the Great Depression, with its disastrous impact on a minority Labour government, and by the Second World War. Its distinctiveness was further augmented, in the negative sense, by the collapse of the Liberal Party during the inter-war years; new working-class electors would no longer become Liberals. Those electors were likewise freed of long-standing Tory cross-pressures on governmental competence and national attachment, courtesy of the Labour leadership's participation in the wartime coalition government un-der Churchill (Richards 1945).

It is difficult to overstate the role of this generational shift as the engine for a set of further structural elements shaping its impact. The "Report on Social Insurance and Allied Services" (under Beveridge) and the "White Paper on Full Employment" (under Keynes), developed under the coalition government during the war, suggested a general move toward social welfare programs for all parties in its aftermath. Yet the Conservatives would just as surely have been less enthusiastic in the reach of what they did, more responsive to the argument for the need to rebuild the nation before undertaking too much, and actively averse to some elements of the eventual Labour program (Jeffreys 1991; Brooke 1992). In any case, newly refreshed and refashioned partisan coalitions then met two main political parties whose structural contribution had its own distinctive characteristics.

The British Labour Party was still a party grown directly out of the labor movement, not, as with the Democratic Party in the United States, a party increasingly energized, even salvaged, by a resurgent labor organization. For organized labor in Britain, then, the dominant focus was inevitably worker organizing and collective bargaining, and the main secondary focus was governmental programs for social welfare. As long as these could be delivered within national boundaries—it was important that the postwar Labour government move faster and farther than the United States or the Continent—there was little practical reason to be uncomfortable with a bipartisan foreign policy and even, initially, with the Cold War (How to Win 1950; McCallum and Readman 1947, 49).

For the Tories, the analogous situation was more complex. In Britain, the small-business–big-business divide that characterized the Republican Party in the United States was more a matter of cities or areas where a particular local or regional industry could provide finance and leadership, that is, where there were major businesses critical to a parliamentary constituency. Otherwise, the party still demonstrated a much earlier—not a more modern—organizational form, in which the *social* leadership of an area provided its Tory leadership as well (Harrison 1996). National corporations would have to learn to fight in postwar politics, and they would become mobilized as Tory contributors and supporters as the first postwar era aged. In the immediate postwar years, however, they were actually not central, and this marginality proved to be a curious practical asset.

Part of the impact of the 1945 election on the Tories was direct, unmediated, and available to everyone else as well: the size of the partisan reversal was universally stunning. Active Tories had long entertained a vague but nagging worry about the class divide as it potentially affected British politics, so they, in particular, had no difficulty perceiving the arrival of a new working-class generation after 1945 (McKibbin 1994). But part of the reason the Tories moved more quickly than their Republican counterparts to face both the substantive and the structural reality of a new social democratic era was a product of the structure of the Conservative Party itself—coupling, as it did, programmatic centralization with organizational decentralization.

In the constituencies, the election had been harder on one wing of the party than the other. Losing more severely in London and the English boroughs than in more rural areas, the Conservatives had shed more of the industrial and commercial than of the landed and governmental members of the parliamentary party, more of the free-market than of the social-traditionalist wing overall, and more of those who had already declared a public opposition to social welfare initiatives than of those who privately counseled gradualism and accommodation. The Maxwell-Fyfe reforms instituted while in opposition during the first postwar government then professionalized Conservative Party offices both in the constituencies and at the center, where the job of all these new party operatives was explicitly to take the Tories back into government. At the center, finally, the national Tory leadership went on to try to augment this organizational effort through programs.

Such centralized initiatives stretched from the celebrated reformulation of policy via the Conservative Research Department of R. A. Butler to the little-noticed efforts of Anthony Eden to ensure that "progressive" Conservatives who had lost their seats in 1945 found new constituencies before the "die-hards" (McCallum and Readman 1947, 259; Ramsden 1995, 97; Ross 1955, 346; Charmley 1996, 131). The Conservative Party thus accepted the fact that the national policy consensus had shifted massively, and moved quickly back—it may not have seemed so fast to concerned participants—to compete around the new, moving center. Eden, Butler, and Harold Macmillan were Tory leaders for the social welfare era. What they did was allow the Conservatives to return to government by 1951. What resulted was a remarkably competitive partisan situation, across that moving center of British politics. What this implied, finally, was that social democratic politics would last and last: a bit more public housing here, a retreat from nationalization there, an extension of medical services here, a contraction of central planning there, and so on, into the more troubled 1970s.

In this, there was little to say—little on its own terms, though much to say comparatively—about the contribution of the structure of government. Within the nation, this was already unitary government with little counter-vailing locality, and it would become only more so. Within the central government, this was already executive rather than legislative dominance, and it too would become only more so. This was not yet prime ministerial rather than cabinet government, as it would become in the second postwar order. But the main point about the election that kicked the first postwar order into being is that such a governmental structure would block or transform other pressures only if there was a narrow partisan majority in Parliament, or none. The election of 1945 provided a huge majority instead, and the adaptation of both parties to a new era and order proceeded to eliminate the threat of a recurrent nonmajority until this first postwar order itself began to break up (Hennessy 1986, 36–47; Morgan 1984, 409–62).

The result was a practical dynamic to political conflict in the social democratic era that was significantly different from its American counter-part, having been shaped by the structure of British national government instead. Many things remained familiar. In both nations, one party—the Democrats and Labour—was more closely identified with social welfare issues and economics generally. In both nations, the other party—the Re-publicans and the Conservatives—was more closely identified with foreign policy and national symbols generally (McCallum and Readman 1947, 47). In both, the former concerns dominated the latter in underlying public preference. And in both, the resulting strategic advice was the same, sug-gesting here that Labour emphasize social welfare and the Conservatives accommodate social welfare and emphasize foreign affairs.

Yet in Britain, this analogous advice met governmental institutions that caused it to be taken very differently. There were no four-party institutions, as in America, to demand both parliamentary and executive Labour and Conservative Parties. There was just Labour facing the Conservatives na-tionwide. Accordingly, this was not just the period when the Labour Party became confirmed as one of two constant governing possibilities. It was also the period when any alternations in government had to be defined either by Tory responses to this strategic environment or by Labour errors and mis-fortunes within it. The Tories could still win by capitalizing on "national" issues, provided they could find a way to counter institutionalized Labour advantages on social welfare and economics. And party leaders understood that constraint.

By extension, Labour would lose only if it forfeited its hold on the main underlying public preference. There proved, however, to be two grand and easy ways to do so. One was to move farther left than the national center on social welfare. Although sitting Labour governments usually recognized this risk, internal conflict over social welfare within the party as a whole (internecine warfare, really) damaged its governing attractions with some regularity (Shaw 1988; Ellison 1996). The other way to lose was to mismanage the economy—or to appear to mismanage it, or to hold public responsibility for it at the wrong point in the business cycle—and both parties would acquire bitter experience with this during the first postwar order. Put back together, in any case, this strategic mix added up to a remarkably balanced partisan era, balanced essentially around social democratic concerns.

The Era of Divided Government

The New Deal party system did not break apart dramatically in the late 1960s. In some sense, it arguably staggers on, providing an increasingly tangential partisan framework to the American politics even of our day. The New Deal *era,* however, came to an end in 1968. Moreover, most of the substantive and structural contours of its replacement were actually registered by 1968. Few observers at the time failed to notice extensive differences in the 1968 election, differences, that is, from the dominant patterns of the New Deal order. Race riots, campus unrest, Vietnam protest, political assassinations, the implosion of the national Democratic Party in convention— all these led to the narrow election of Richard Nixon as president, while the Democratic Party retained solid—overwhelming—control of both houses of Congress (White 1969; Chester, Hodgson, and Page 1969).

Yet within that context, it was still reasonable to believe that the American political sequence might feature a Nixon interregnum, as it had earlier featured an Eisenhower interregnum, followed by restoration of unified Democratic control of national government. Reasonable, but wrong. It would, in the nature of politics, require the passage of time for new relationships to be consolidated, and these would necessarily acquire their operational impact in the detailed politics of particular events. But the constituent elements of a new era and order were all incipiently present after the 1968 election. And Jimmy Carter, Ronald Reagan, Bill Clinton, and even

Newt Gingrich—to take a superficially unlikely set of descendants—were all the progeny of Richard Nixon, midwife, not of Franklin Roosevelt, grandfather.

There are many ways to distinguish the substantive core of the new era, and the refusal of most analysts to seek a different kind of successor framework has encouraged the proliferation of these. But at bottom, the old era had featured partisan division and political conflict around concerns for the (re)distribution of material goods, around economics and social welfare. The new era added—indeed, often featured—partisan division and political conflict around concerns for the character of national life, around the behavior operationalizing a national culture. The first set of concerns was essentially distributional, involving the proper share of divisible goods allocated to various sectors of society. The second set was essentially valuational, involving the proper behavioral norms within which social life should proceed (Lipset and Rokkan, 1967; Inglehart 1977).

The older economic-welfare concerns hardly went away, and their continuing presence remained central to the substantive character of the new era. But they were joined by new cultural-national concerns on a secondary, equal, or superior footing, depending on the context of the day. In that sense, the key substantive characteristic of the successor era in both nations was the vigorous presence of two great (and crosscutting) dimensions to political conflict. Yet what was equally remarkable was how often previously distributional concerns were themselves recast as valuational issues in the new era (compare Marshall 1950 with Commission on Social Justice 1994, 306–73, and compare Hamby 1973 with Katz 1996a, 1996b; see also Harris 1977, 419–51).

One has only to revisit the two great postwar debates about welfare, about public policy toward those regularly outside the normal workplace, to see a striking difference in approach to what is literally the same program, 1946 versus 1996. In both nations in the first round of this debate, the central issue was the proper material entitlements of the poorest part of society. In both nations in the second round, the central issue was instead the incentive structures being created, and hence the sort of citizens being produced.

Nevertheless, when it first arrived, the substantive breakup of the old era in the United States was easier to recognize in foreign affairs, where the Cold War consensus disintegrated. The Vietnam War gave this division its initial edge, but a panoply of security issues, from arms control through defense budgets, would be available to keep the division alive. More to the point, Vietnam *protest* was a key route into the rest of the valuational dimension, within which foreign affairs was only one large but supporting element (Holsti and Rosenau 1984; Ladd and Hadley 1973; Jensen 1981). Vietnam protesters themselves often underlined this link by insisting that they were part of a "counterculture," and this was as good an introduction as any to the larger valuational division, which eventually included the public role of religion, community prerogatives, patriotism and national integration, educational orientations, public deportment, and even the proper attitude toward human life, especially at its beginning and end (Davies 1996; Scammon and Wattenberg 1970; Matusow 1984).

This newly invigorated dimension of conflict received additional impetus in the United States, in a manner that would have no direct counterpart in Britain, from the actions of the Supreme Court. Beginning in the 1960s, the Court addressed a string of essentially cultural conflicts, elevating their public importance as it did so. The Warren Court, at the end of an era in which economic regulation dominated the Court's agenda and the beginning of an era characterized by civil liberties instead, reliably offered the progressive position on these cultural issues—often in clear contraposition to public preferences. These issues included busing, school prayer, abortion, capital punishment, criminal justice, homosexual rights, and so on (Pacelle 1991; O'Brien 1986). Yet even when the Burger and the Rehnquist justices were appointed to "rein the Court back in," this became more a matter of policy direction than of issue emphasis. The Court became more ideologically conservative, but it did not stop being a further institutional engine for cultural issues in American politics.

The abstract fundamentals for understanding the structure of politics at the social base for an era characterized by such dual concerns—that is, the social coalitions to go with a substantive division between social welfare and cultural values—had long been incipiently familiar. Or at least it had long been understood that economic liberals, those most concerned with the welfare essence of the New Deal program, were often social conservatives, emphasizing family, neighborhood, community, and country and, within them, emphasizing norms over choices, obligations over entitlements, responsibilities over rights. Similarly, it had long been known that economic conservatives, especially the highly educated, occupationally prestigious, and financially well-off among them, were often cultural liberals (Adorno et al. 1950; Lipset 1960; Shafer and Claggett 1995).

What changed, then, was only the arrival—some would say the reap-pearance (Kleppner 1979; Jensen 1971; Carwardine 1983)—of a second great dimension, the cultural dimension, to equal prominence in national politics. The underlying social relationships between these divisions had always held, at least across the postwar years for which we have data. But the presence of a traditionalist cultural majority had always been intuitively accepted by party operatives and candidates for public office, understood to be so overwhelming as to make this dimension the "third rail" of American politics. Events of the late 1960s made this no longer so self-evidently the case. At a minimum, a huge postwar generation had grown up without the need to consider economic security. For them, there was mainly the long postwar boom, backed up by the social insurance programs of the New Deal whenever it hesitated. In that light, cultural traditionalism and orthodox social controls could seem principally the residue of a time lag in social thinking.

Changes in the structure of political parties, largely occurring for other reasons, then institutionalized these divisions. Both American political parties now shared the dominant structural characteristics of the immediate postwar Republicans. That is, both were now effectively networks of issue-oriented political activists, not individuals for whom partisan solidarity displaced ideology, much less individuals for whom patronage or pecuniary concerns explained their willingness to do the work of the party.

The New Deal program had sustained the organized Democratic Party for another generation after its inception, actually funneling some fresh resources through party channels. Yet the institutionalization of these bene-fits was principally through formal governmental machinery even then. Beyond that, continuing civil service reform was joined by the gradual unionization of government, taking far more resources out of the hands of either party than the government had given back. The gradual passing of a New Deal generation of partisans—no subsequent generation could achieve the same programmatic fervor—was then topped off by institutional reform of presidential selection, the last holdout against reform generally. And the old structure of the political parties was gone (Ware 1985, conclusion).

In its place were networks of individual activists whose support was now essential to mounting campaigns and gaining public office. In turn, they were also the key to institutionalizing a partisan connection between the economic-welfare and cultural-national dimensions. These activists con-tinued comfortably with the old social welfare basis of the party system.

Accordingly, Republican activists remained very conservative and Democratic activists very liberal on these matters. They merely added the new cultural bases, in a way that they found to be ideologically consistent. The result was Republican activists who were traditionalistic in social matters and nationalistic in foreign affairs, and Democratic activists who were progressive in social matters and accommodationist in foreign affairs.

Had these increasingly consequential activists not been naturally inclined to this particular combination of positions, they might well have been driven to it anyway by the nature of the new (ideological and issue-oriented) organized interests that joined one or the other party coalition. For the Democrats, these included environmentalists, peace groups, feminists, and homosexuals. For the Republicans, they included antiabortionists, gun owners, tax reformers, and religious fundamentalists. But in truth, there was no need for pressure from these groups to secure these two opposing partisan programs. Party activists were now the natural products of membership in precisely these organizations (Schlozman and Tierney 1985; Walker 1991; Shafer 1983a).

There was, of course, not just a heightened interparty conflict inherent in this tension, between consistent liberals and consistent conservatives. There was a further intraparty conflict, an elite-mass conflict as well, between activists and their own rank and file. This latter was at its most intense between economically conservative but culturally liberal Republicans and their leaders, and between economically liberal but culturally conservative Democrats and theirs. Yet the institutions of American government provided a simple resolution for these tensions—note that they did not have to change their formal arrangements to do so—and it was this resolution that provided not just the context for public policy making in our time but the name for that time itself (Jacobson 1990; Cox and Kernell 1991; Mayhew 1991).

At bottom, there were now two opposing majorities simultaneously present in the general public, more liberal than the active Republican Party on economics and social welfare, more conservative than the active Democratic Party on cultural values and nationalism. The obvious solution in the United States was simply to colonize one elective branch of national government with one majority and one elective branch with the other. Split partisan control was what this solution contributed practically. "Divided government" was what it came to be called, and the era of divided government had been born.

In the particular sequence in which this order initially arose—led off by Vietnam, race, and countercultural protest—the opening resolution was a Republican presidency stapled onto a Democratic Congress. This was the most common partisan product of the new era. Yet the larger point is that unified partisan control of national government was now the deviant outcome, requiring strategic disasters, that is, dramatically unhappy events or major strategic miscalculations. This happened in 1976, when circumstance allowed Jimmy Carter to be simultaneously the economic liberal and the social conservative in the aftermath of Watergate. But such a resolution could not last: Carter was not interested in economic liberalism, and a Democratic administration was not going to be culturally conservative. Unified government was thus swept away (Glad 1980, secs. 3–6; Jones 1988, chaps. 4–8).

Other issue sequences were easily capable of other partisan results, however, in a structural order with these enduring characteristics. Unified government threatened to return in 1992, when circumstance allowed Bill Clinton to appear as an economic liberal and a social conservative, thanks to a serious economic recession plus skillful advertising for an essentially unknown candidate. But within two years, it was clear that this was an inaccurate perception, and a different substantive sequence now dictated that the Republicans seize control of Congress, restoring split partisan control in the other direction. Divided government, the natural product of this era and its order, merely resurfaced with a Democratic president facing a Republican Congress—having already given the era its name.

The Thatcherite Era

In its time, there was no reason to compare the election of Margaret Thatcher as prime minister with the election of Richard Nixon as president: different calendar dates, different surface issues, different personal styles, even a different partisan patterning to the outcome (Butler and Kavanagh 1979). Moreover, Thatcher quickly became half of a different, frequent journalistic comparison with Ronald Reagan, elected president of the United States in 1980. Neither dates nor issues nor even personal beliefs were violated in that comparison. Yet this was one more example of the dangers inherent in the comparative enterprise. This was true even in the journalistic mode, where

Reagan was often described as "big brother" to Thatcher's "little sister." In terms of their ultimate impact on domestic policy, Thatcher was probably "big sister" to Reagan's "little brother."

The comparison was, however, desperately misleading at a deeper level because, like the juxtaposition of 1945 and 1946 in British and American elections, it fell at the wrong point in a sequence marked by a new versus an established political order. In this sequence, and much more than with Nixon, Thatcher was instantly distinguishable from the political leaders preceding her. Even among Tories she was distinguishable, not just from Butler, Eden, and Macmillan but also from Alec Douglas-Home and Edward Heath, her immediate Tory predecessors, who would prove to have more to do with Clement Attlee than with Thatcher. Like Nixon, nevertheless, she was to mark the beginning of a new era in British politics, rather than a new twist on the old. In the ultimate tribute to this role, her first Labour successor, Tony Blair, would have more to do with Thatcher than with his own Labour predecessors, Harold Wilson and James Callaghan.

As with the situation greeting Nixon, all the elements of a new political era and order were inherent in the 1979 Thatcher victory, though again, it would require the passage of time to consolidate these elements and hence make them recognizable. And again, what these elements represented, above all else, was the coming of cultural and national concerns in British politics—or perhaps their resurgence—to an equal and frequently a superior position with regard to the old economic and social welfare concerns (Collini 1985; Harrison 1994). Indeed, when social welfare issues began to be consciously addressed, the cultural-national overlay sounded very much like the rhetorical overlay to the welfare debate in the postwar era. (Compare the lead positions in our time with the contemporary justification for expanded social welfare programs in MacDonald 1908 versus the established criticisms of those schemes in Bosanquet 1896.)

By comparison with the United States, this arrival would yield not just a roughly analogous matrix of central issues but even (and perhaps inevitably) a similar interaction between substance and structure, in the form of a pattern of crosscutting policy preferences within the general public. Nevertheless, the specifics of these new issues also mattered. In Britain, part of this change was embodied in the appearance of cultural-national issues either underemphasized or entirely missing from the previous era, valuational issues destined to be of continuing concern thereafter: nationalist discontent in Scotland and Wales, actual sectarian strife in Northern Ireland, an apparent general heightening of tensions in national dealings with the wider world. Yet in Britain, this issue transformation went further still.

Indeed, even conflict over the proper role of trade unions in national life, a conflict central to producing the Thatcher government and one destined to take up a lot of its time, came to acquire this basically cultural character. A massive expansion in the scale of industrial unrest—the first national miners strike of the postwar years in 1973, leading by steps but inexorably to the "winter of discontent" in 1978–1979—was quintessential economic conflict to the immediate participants. But for much of the public, under the equally relentless and more effective articulation of the new prime minister, what would surely have been cast as labor-management conflict in the social democratic era became instead conflict over democracy and governance in Thatcherite times. (This helps to explain, in passing, how public support for union power could fall while public support for management power did not rise. For the trend line on business and union power—public perceptions and public support—see Crewe, Day, and Fox 1991, table 8.1, 251.)

As in the United States, this arrival did not necessarily imply the diminution of economic-welfare conflict. Rather, what it implied was the potential for simultaneous policy conflict on two major (and countervailing) dimensions. In order to see such conflict arrive and unfold in a second country, however, it was necessary to look in a somewhat different place. Similar policy conflicts might coincide with similar (and similarly crosscutting) social coalitions. Yet the coming of a Thatcherite era necessitated a new (or at least a reshuffled) mix of structural supports, and these were different not just from an earlier version in Britain but also from their counterpart in the United States.

In particular, politics in Britain remained more a mediated than a direct conflict, more a matter for parties and pressure groups than for individual entrepreneurs, and this meant that it had to be observed more within those key intermediaries and less within the general public, at least at the inception of the shift. The structural preconditions for this new era in Britain had been assembling within these political parties for some years before the 1979 election. At the extreme, it might be argued that the Labour side of these preconditions had been assembling since the time the Tories returned to government in 1951. By that time, Labour already possessed a deep and enduring internal split on economic issues, between those who wanted to consolidate and institutionalize on its right, and those who wanted to push on and further redistribute on its left.

Critically, in terms of the subsequent political order, the main way to hold the party together in the face of this split would be to concentrate on a progressive response to cultural and national issues, where party activists, at least, could be united (compare Bevin 1961 with Crosland 1956; see also Crick 1964; Freeden 1997, 471–72). This was not necessarily the preferred emphasis of major Labour politicians. Indeed, unlike their Democratic counterparts in the United States, many actively begrudged the shift. Yet the interaction of substance and structure led them, ineluctably and unerringly, to the cultural-national cluster. Not surprisingly, then, when Harold Wilson brought Labour back into government in 1964, this evolving orientation was put centrally on display.

Wilson was elected on the promise of some vague and general "modernization" of British public life. But in economic and social welfare matters, his major modernizing responses would run up against a brutally uncooperative economy. The illuminating detail involved Wilson's earlier resignation from the cabinet over the imposition of National Health Service charges in 1951, his cancellation of those charges upon his return as prime minister in 1964, and his reimposition of related charges in 1968, in the face of that deteriorating economy. Wilson's short-lived "National Plan," however, along with his Department of Economic Affairs, which increased governmental direction of the economy in a major way, was really just a much larger embodiment of that same trajectory.

As a result, when these major initiatives collapsed, Wilson's lasting policy impact was destined to come through modernization of a different sort, on cultural matters, by way of a series of private member's bills assisted by the government: the Murder Act, abolishing capital punishment; the Sexual Offenses Act, legalizing homosexuality; the Abortion Act, legitimizing abortion and taking it into the National Health Service; and the Divorce Reform Act, sharply liberalizing procedures (Wilson 1964; Stewart 1977; Ponting 1990). Such projects would have been deeply controversial under the first Labour majority government. Now, they could bring unity to a fractious active party, giving it something to be *for* under difficult economic circumstances.

Moreover, there were structural shifts internal to the Labour Party to reinforce this gradual but ineluctable up-weighting of the cultural left. In the United States, this up-weighting came by means of the gradual rise to partisan centrality of independent issue activists who were directly responsive to the new cultural and national issues. They were helped on their way, especially in the Democratic Party, by rising levels of education generally, coupled with participatory procedural reforms. In Britain—and this perception, both in its parallels and in its distinctiveness, is a typical further benefit of comparative analysis—the same ultimate outcome had to be accomplished instead through organized labor.

It was accomplished, and the changing relationship of the trade union movement to the Labour Party became one of the spectacular reversals of British political history. Put starkly, this transformation saw the unions move from being stalwarts of the party right on social welfare and foreign affairs in the first two decades of the postwar years to being key advocates of the party left on both social welfare and the rising cultural-national concerns in the next two decades. A radical decentralization in union decision making contributed to this transformation, along with the rise of a generation not forged in depression and war, plus further procedural democratization within decentralized bargaining units.

Substantively, the break was best symbolized, as in the United States, by the change in preferences on foreign policy, from support for a strong defense to advocacy of unilateral disarmament. Structurally, what these changes did was to allow for the quick integration of pressure groups focused on cultural values and foreign affairs into the union movement. It was no coincidence, in such an environment, that the unilateral disarmament motion submitted to the Labour Party Conference of 1980 by the printers' union SOGAT was jointly drafted by the Campaign for Nuclear Disarmament and the Bertrand Russell Foundation (Undy et al. 1981, 91–126, 262–313; Shaw 1988; Pelling 1987; Taylor 1991; Pimlott 1991).

A parallel development occurred, much more implicitly, within the Conservative Party over the same period. The Tories demonstrated little explicit intraparty conflict for much of the first postwar era over their moderate response to economic and social welfare issues or, for that matter, to cultural and national concerns. There was a Tory right on decolonization and then on immigration, and there were even groupings, like the one that followed Enoch Powell, that connected these views to a bolder economic conservatism. From the 1950s to the mid-1970s, however, their fortunes had been severely circumscribed. During all that time, the party was dominated at the parliamentary level by an established elite, the Tory "grandees," who joined an enduring social welfare commitment, within an inescapable fiscal straitjacket, to a generalized distaste for populist politicking. That combination proved sufficient to proscribe serious internal party conflict (Green 1988; Kavanagh 1997).

In the aftermath of the Thatcher leadership victory in 1975, major Tory policy developments, as gathered in "The Right Approach" and "The Right Approach to the Economy," suggested an incipient new programmatic combination of refreshed economic conservatism with stiff cultural conservatism. These policy developments were accompanied by the rise of think tanks and cause groups within the Tory Party, along with issue-motivated individuals to energize their causes. Yet there remained substantial room for argument over whether any such incipient program would be implemented in government. It was thought that Thatcher might well prove more pragmatic as leader, and that collective responsibility would further temper her ideological impulses (Young 1991, 107–8; Wickham-Jones 1997; Elst 1975; Moran 1979; Wintour and Rogers 1979).

In the event, of course, she proved committed. Moreover, her party as a whole proved newly responsive. And here, apparently endless labor strife, resurging to remarkable proportions—army vehicles covering for fire engines was a dramatic symbol of the time, though the miners strike of 1984–1985 provided the critical reinforcement—produced a mirror image of the situation within the Labour Party. Being united in opposition to contemporary economic developments, the Tories were willing to paper over their divisions on cultural policy and try populist conservatism (Adeney and Lloyd 1986; Bloomfield, Boanas, and Samuel 1986).

This resolution was further aided by social change within the parliamentary Conservative Party. Members from the traditional sectors and those from constituencies north of Birmingham, who had once counseled compromise with social democracy, were in decline. Those most directly damaged by rampant labor unrest—namely, corporate and commercial members, plus those from the south of England—were on the rise (Beer 1982, 169–80; Adonis 1996). Finally, the expected institutional constraint failed to materialize: cabinet responsibility proved over the years to have given way, at least when shoved, to prime ministerial governance.

As a result, the program was generally attempted, and a new era followed. The cluster of concerns at the substantive core of this new era showed some similarities to and some differences from the counterpart cluster in the United States. The overarching theme was roughly the same: a multifaceted concern with the behavioral norms appropriate to national life. So were some of the specifics. In Britain as in the United States, crime was an increasing worry, and immigration was an increasingly politicized issue. The British Nationality Act of 1981 and the Police and Criminal Evidence Act of 1984 were early and central legislative responses to these concerns. Yet many other embodiments were conditioned by essential differences of culture and circumstance.

Much more than in the United States, for example—always a more populist and mass culture—the decline of deference and of norms of social restraint in daily life was a central concern in Britain (Beer 1982, pt. 3; Pimlott 1996, 397–417). In the same way, even more than in the United States, where it was hardly absent, a reinvigoration of personal responsibilities to go with governmental entitlements was a central connecting issue in Britain. Thatcher, in her pronouncements (and even in her persona), underlined the importance of individual responsibility at every turn. Labour was at least willing to expand programs going very much in the other direction, and a vocal minority within the party was willing to denigrate the value itself. Indeed, the Tory leadership sometimes sounded as if the whole of national economic policy, too, could be recast in essentially cultural terms. "This is not a fight about national solvency," Thatcher insisted, "it is a fight about the very foundations of the social order." In such a fight, the enemy was "decline." The goal was "making Britain *great* again" (Verbatim Report 1976, 140; Tomlinson 1996).

Conversely, and again as in the United States, this did not mean the end of an older social welfare consensus. The public had gradually backed away from further nationalization; the fact that the Labour Party Conference would not do so did it no good. Yet this public never backed away from the social welfare hallmarks of the initial postwar Labour government: unemployment and sickness insurance, expanded pensions, full-employment policy (Crewe and Searing 1988, 288–89). Had Margaret Thatcher promoted herself as a vehicle for privatizing the National Health Service and cutting child benefits rather than for making Britain great again, there might have been a Tory electoral victory in 1979; the decline in industrial relations was that disastrous. But a new political era would have been about as likely as a new era in the United States in 1932 had Roosevelt eschewed the New Deal, stopped further spending, and cut taxes sharply.

All this was testimony to the impact of roughly similar issue divisions in Britain and America, coupled with roughly similar social coalitions. Yet similar elements still encountered institutions of government that made them work very differently as a governing dynamic. In Britain, there was never any possibility of an American-style solution, that is, of split partisan control of government—Conservative prime ministers coupled with a Labour House of Commons, or vice versa. Whether they wanted to or not, British voters had to create unified partisan control. As a result, what these voters went on to create was unified Tory government for a long period, followed eventually by unified Labour government—"New" Labour government, to go with (and cement) the new political era.

A more direct result was that the Tories received the opportunity to pursue a consistently conservative program on cultural-national concerns and economic-welfare matters. Major economic privatizations, of gas, water, electricity, and the railroads, were one product. Key populist initiatives on crime, on public order generally, and especially on the rapid expansion of home ownership in Britain—once more, an economic policy with valuational intentions—were another product. Some ultimately disastrous combined applications, such as the poll tax, were a third (Gamble 1994; Butler, Adonis, and Travers 1994).

In all this, there was an incipient division at the elite level clearly parallel to that in the United States. On one side was a party of the Left that was liberal on both economics and culture. On the other side was a party of the Right that was now conservative on both. This underlying shift was not self-evident in the original Thatcher election, where the public was arguably voting against a distressing state of affairs rather than for a new program. But thereafter, Thatcher was able to operationalize the conservative position on both major dimensions within the Tory Party. The Labour Party then cooperated additionally, by moving left on both dimensions in response (Shaw 1994, 1–28; Kogan and Kogan 1982).

As a result, it was the Thatcher reelection that had to be diagnostic of any new order, as indeed it was. Support for (and victory in) the Falklands War, which maximized partisan advantage on the cultural-national dimension, was coupled with a recovering economy, which minimized partisan disadvantage on the economic-welfare dimension. This was the classic combination for Tory (or, for that matter, Republican) victory in the modern era, and it was cashed out by the Tories with a vengeance in 1983. The result should have made it much easier to affirm that a new era had arrived in British politics.

Nevertheless, it would require the two elections after Thatcher was gone to confirm its arrival definitively, by showcasing its insistent contours under different personalities *and even different parties.* Thus, while Labour was still insufficiently reconfigured on the cultural-national dimension—while it was still well left of national values—John Major could be elected as the Tory successor to Thatcher, even though the economy was in recession. Yet when Major's own efforts to capitalize on this agenda foundered on internal party division plus scandal, a counterpart opportunity was opened for Labour. Once Tony Blair had reconfigured the public presentation of Labour on cultural-national matters—welfare-to-work, tough-on-crime, Christian identifications to the fore—then the Conservatives could be defeated even in the midst of an economic boom (Denver 1998; Butler and Kavanagh 1992, 1997; Norris 1998).

Political Change

Britain and America faced a remarkably similar political context in the immediate postwar years, shaped first in both cases by the Great Depression and then by World War II. Nothing to follow would have anywhere near the focused common stimulus to substantive policy making or to the formation of domestic social coalitions. Seen one way, depression and war combined to form an exceptionally powerful demand on the policy process in each nation individually. Seen the other way, that combination was perhaps unique in all their histories in the scale of its joint impact. Seen either way, the experience of depression and war contributed a common context while simultaneously giving both these societies a greater sense of national unity: more sense that common members deserved collective benefits, less embarrassment in claiming these benefits by those who had just suffered two grand and sequential disasters.

Even then, differences in the simple sequencing of these developments had a separable impact on the eras and orders that resulted. In the United States, the depression arrived earlier and the war later. Moreover, it is important to remember that the timing of the latter was to some degree a "policy choice" for the United States; it was hardly that for Britain. The result was that the first "postwar" order in American politics was actually constructed *prewar,* well before U.S. entry into World War II. The counterpart era in Britain, by contrast, beginning fifteen years later and focused even more centrally on economic and welfare concerns, began within sixty days of VE day. In such a context, the later arrival of Britain in the policy realm of social welfare probably by itself contributed to a stronger response, implying, as it did, more extended suffering, more protracted demands, more comprehensive preplanning, and even a desire by British planners to surpass the New Deal from the start.

Depression and war, as common substantive stimuli, also interacted differently with the social structures of the two nations. The marked social heterogeneity of the United States, for example, which so often explained why policy majorities were difficult to construct, was substantially overcome by this shared experience. Perhaps the diagnostic product in this regard, for seeing both the socially unifying effect of the war and its policy integration with the focus of the depression, was the so-called GI Bill, a major piece of policy intervention that (among other things) sharply broadened access to higher education (Bennett 1996; Goulden 1976, 55–60; Ravitch 1983, 14ff.; McKibbin 1998, 257–59). Seen from the perspective of prewar access, this was very much redistributive legislation. Seen in hindsight, the vast expansion of higher education in the postwar United States received crucial impetus from the GI Bill.

Seen from Britain, in contrast, this was largely "Tory social welfare," which is to say that Labour saw little relevance in higher education for its social coalition. In all the initiatives of the first postwar Labour government, it remained content with the (Tory) Butler Act of 1944, and Labour would largely continue in this vein. Although funding opportunities were expanded in the late 1940s, it would be left to Tory governments of the 1950s to introduce the new universities to Britain. Said differently, although the class coalitions characteristic of American politics in the immediate postwar years may have been as sharp as they had ever been, they were nowhere near as sharp as their counterparts in Britain. Different policy deductions followed from that fact alone.

In Britain, the "common'" experiences of depression and war were still filtered powerfully by the class divide. It was not that the combination of these two huge events did not heighten feelings of national unity; no one can read the story of wartime British life without palpably feeling that effect. It was just that social welfare differences along class lines remained alive and acute throughout the war, and the war's blocking effect on addressing these concerns may actually have heightened economic resentments. Indeed, even the operational experience of war itself, that is, of service in the British military—on one level, a formalistic and interchangeable bureaucracy—differed sharply along class lines. Social divisions between the officer corps and the enlisted ranks paralleled class divisions in the larger society much more than in the United States, where the divisions were not as sharp to begin with and where a vast military establishment had to be created more or less out of whole cloth (Calder 1969, 1992; Blum 1976; Stouffer et al. 1949).

Still, the main issue emphasis of an overall policy response and the main outline of its programmatic substance were clearly related in both countries, as befitted a response to such common stimuli for policy making. Or at least, both nations turned to economics and, especially, social welfare as the substantive core of their first postwar era. In that sense, war variously delayed and intensified the impact of depression, but that was all. Said differently, neither nation was diverted from a social welfare focus as the central substantive core of an extended political era, even by alternative stimuli as intense as world war and then cold war. However, the overall policy contours of the response—in which the United States moved first, while Britain moved farther when its turn came—retained some notable differences, thanks to different structural influences in the associated political orders.

Among these latter, two stand out: the difference in heterogeneity or homogeneity in the social base for politics, and the difference in division or unification in the governmental institutions for policy making. Moreover, for these particular nations, these two grand factors interacted in a highly reinforcing way. Put roughly but accurately, the more socially heterogeneous and governmentally dispersed nation, the United States, moved first but went less far. The more socially homogeneous and governmentally unified nation, Britain, moved later and went farther. And sequence and context were not sufficient to explain those facts, without further attention to substance and structure.

The more socially heterogeneous society—divided internally by race, ethnicity, religion, region, economic base, historical evolution, and even contemporary "lifestyle"—simply possessed more bases for generating policy demands. In the case of the United States, it also had more "response points" within its governmental institutions to register those demands, though nothing required social heterogeneity and institutional fragmentation to go together in any other nation. Yet in the United States, they did, and as a result, in the face of diverse but generalized demands for action, the government bundled these together and acted early. By the same token, that government faced more demands for other change and further adjustment, while offering more points for attempting to slow or reverse previous initiatives. It should not be a surprise that it went less far.

The opposite could be said for Britain. It had fewer bases for demanding action, but this social homogeneity had a paradoxical effect. Normally, it encouraged a kind of policy inertia—fine-tuning rather than experimentation—once a previously acceptable package had been implemented. Yet when it was characterized by a general (and naturally more uniform) demand for governmental action, that demand automatically acquired additional force. In the same way, Britain had fewer institutional "receptors" for picking up such demands and for bundling them into jerry-built programs. Yet this governmental concentration showed the same paradoxical impact: societal trends were less likely to register, but government was more able to act comprehensively when they did.

The same analysis can be carried a step further. As the postwar orders aged, the United States would have a second major round of social welfare initiatives, in the form of Lyndon Johnson's Great Society. Johnson would complete major pieces of the New Deal agenda, and many of these pieces—Medicare, Medicaid, Head Start—would join the policy consensus in American society. Britain, by contrast, having already moved farther and more coherently, but with fewer bases for further demands and fewer governmental receptors for them, would offer only a much weaker echo, despite the initial efforts of Harold Wilson when Labour returned to government at about the same time (Davies 1996; Stewart 1977).

The successor eras in both these nations, the Thatcherite era and the era of divided government, were similar in major respects. They were arguably similar in their grand substance, in the arrival of a second major cluster of policy issues to contend with and crosscut the older cluster of economics and social welfare. This arrival was, of course, the cultural and national cluster, ranging from foreign affairs through schooling and family life to behavior in the street, but centered on matters of national integration, on proper values for a collective social life. These successor eras were likewise similar in some of the crucial structural elements that determined how this new issue cluster would work in their two societies.

In particular, roughly parallel social cleavages in the mass base for politics went hand in hand with roughly parallel elite evolutions within key intermediary organizations. At the mass level, economic liberalism or conservatism was randomly related to cultural liberalism or conservatism. At the elite level, these preferences were instead tightly bound: economic liberalism with cultural liberalism, economic conservatism with cultural conservatism. The result was not only crosscutting policy majorities within the mass public—*parallel* crosscutting majorities in these two nations—leaning left of the partisan center on economics, right of the partisan center on culture. The result was also parallel policy tensions between partisan activists and their own putative rank and file, as the two political levels put these two grand dimensions together differently.

From there, the temptation to posit similar grand dynamics to the creation of these two successor eras, similar engines driving the shift from one set of parallel eras to another, is difficult to resist—difficult but essential. A serious comparative framework abruptly confronts this temptation with two major problems. At a minimum, there were no grand and obvious counterparts to depression and war in the joint shift to a second postwar era, hence no obviously parallel context. Worse still, for eras established only twenty to thirty years ago, depending on which nation is used as the benchmark, the two new eras managed to arrive more than ten years apart, hence there were evident difficulties in sequencing as well. Although the passage of time might make this latter difference look less disturbing, the comparative specifics leading up to this joint change of eras will not look any more analogous ten or twenty years from now.

The closest substantive counterpart to depression or world war, in terms of new policy problems for new eras, was the end of the long postwar boom and the coming of generalized stagflation, punctuated by oil shocks, in the late 1960s and 1970s (Calleo 1982; Keohane and Nye 1977). Yet the "end of the long boom" remains imprecise even as a point in time, and desperately so as a common context for politics. About the only way to make it the driving force for new eras beginning in 1968 in the United States and in 1979 in Britain is to work backward—using those dates as proof that this point is the end of the long boom in each society. The two major oil shocks, by contrast, do possess specific dates. But the problem introduced by specific dates for these two related major events of the 1970s is equally severe: they follow the arrival of the second postwar era in the United States and precede it in Britain.

In turn, the closest structural counterpart to those social forces that underpinned the arrival of a new "moving center" in American politics after 1932 or in British politics after 1945 was a parallel underlying change across the postwar years in the occupational composition of both societies. Most generally, this structural shift involved a change from a blue-collar to a white-collar social base. That change gained elaboration—and potential structural bite—in a sharper decline of the manual working class and a sharper increase of the professional middle class. And it did truly characterize both societies (Heath, Jowell, and Curtice 1985, 35–37; *Statistical Abstract*, various years, sec. 8). Even then, there were national distinctions of some consequence. In the United States, this was a more generalized and aggregate phenomenon, applicable across the broad middle of society. In Britain, where it had gone less far at the first Thatcher election, this development made the better-off members of the working class especially central: able to move beyond narrowly economic concerns—indeed, concerned with the well-being of the general economy—while remaining clearly conservative on cultural and national matters (Crewe 1985, 1987; Shaw 1994, 80).

Yet the critical point is what this roughly similar grand development, even adjusted for national differences, could not explain in *either* country. Such a shift may have eroded support for the most stereotypically "welfarist" aspects of the welfare state, that is, for those programs least aimed at temporary disruptions to economic life and least demanding of their recipients in return for benefits. But the larger point is that overall support for basic social welfare programs did not erode. Many of these had always concerned not just the working class but also substantial portions of the middle class—they were nearly as important in both categories—and they did not lose public support (LeGrand 1982; Crewe, Day, and Fox 1991, 21–37; Miller and Traugott 1989, 173–84).

Worse still, such a shift cannot explain (indeed, it runs opposite to) the coming of cultural conservatism as a serious option in mainstream politics. The growth sectors in this underlying class shift were in fact culturally moderate; it was the shrinking sectors that were culturally conservative. As a result, this class shift does not work very well as a common stimulus. Not only does it begin at different points and progress at different rates in the two societies; it does not appear to drive directly the structure of the second postwar order in either. Or at least, in neither society does this (otherwise huge) shift produce a widespread desire to go back to the world before the social welfare revolution of the preceding era. Nor is it capable, at least on its own, of explaining the rise of a more populist cultural conservatism.

What results from the comparison, instead, is reinforcement for the injunction that grand and similar but *vague* social trends should be expected to have distinguishable impacts, depending, once again, on what else is on the substantive agenda when they arrive, and on what structural factors must in principle shape their impact. In this regard, the United States prefaced the arrival of this period with both the civil rights revolution and the comprehensive Vietnam debacle. Britain simply had no counterparts, and the new era arrived later in Britain, in part as a result (Williams 1987; Gitlin 1993; Patterson 1996, chaps. 20–22). However, as with the change to the first postwar era, in arriving later it also arrived more forcefully when it did come. The policy response even of a Reagan was not as great as that of a Thatcher. But Nixon is the proper contrast, and there, the Nixon-Thatcher policy difference was gigantic.

Finally, at an even higher level of abstraction and framed in a properly comparative mode, some of the main structural influences on the coming of the previous postwar eras in these two nations, the social democratic and the New Deal eras, continued to shape the coming of their successors. Once again, the more socially heterogeneous and more governmentally dispersed nation, the United States, moved earlier and more modestly. Once again, the more socially homogeneous and more governmentally centralized nation, Britain, moved later but more comprehensively—and shows less sign of a counterattack as this is written. Other nations could, of course, mix social homogeneity-heterogeneity and governmental centralization-decentralization in additionally different ways. But for these two nations, the actual mix served as a powerful and continuing influence across all the postwar years.

Conclusion

The bane of comparative history is the lure of an analytic framework based on the notions of "convergence" and "divergence," with an incipient preference for the former. Such a framework imputes a bias to the analysis that is, at the very least, unproved. Along the way, it skirts much of consequence in the actual comparison, as the story of postwar eras and orders in Britain and the United States strongly attests. Similarities and differences are the essence of comparison, by definition. And they are essential to refining—to both extending and restricting—an explanation. But so too are underlying similarities sought in the face of superficial differences, as well as underlying differences that buttress superficial similarities. There is no reason to presume that such discoveries should be parallel across nations or across time.

Within an alternative framework based on the notions of "political eras" and "political orders" instead, roughly parallel eras and orders do indeed emerge in these two nations across the postwar years, propelled additionally by some analogous substantive issues and analogous structural influences. Yet from the start, this framework is essential to the comparison, and the comparison yields a very open-ended product. Without this framework, for example, the obvious temporal analogy is 1945 in Britain and 1946 in the United States; with it, the proper comparison is 1945 and 1932. Without it, the nearly inescapable analogy is 1979 in Britain and 1980 in the United States; with it, the comparison becomes 1979 and 1968. Needless to say, with greater analytic precision, in this case, comes more temporal diversity.

One final summary comparison of eras and orders in these two nations can underline this point about simultaneous similarity and difference in its full complexity. Once again, the comparison can best be approached by focusing on the intermediary organizations, especially political parties, which sat in the center of these orders and were thus responsible for translating policy demands into governmental action, for connecting the social base with political institutions. Our point at the beginning of this chapter was that parties and partisanship are not nearly sufficient to differentiate, much less to drive, the change between political eras and political orders in major societies. The comparison of two such societies over an extended period should by now have reinforced that contention. Yet our point as we approach the end is that it is hard to imagine an era and order in which these parties do not at least reflect—objectify and display concretely—the larger changes around them.

At a minimum, then, it ought to be easiest to observe a new order assembling and a new era being institutionalized through a focus on political parties. Moreover, such a focus gives a fresh and concrete incarnation to one specific change of the greatest potential consequence, one dismissed a few paragraphs ago in another role—and thus the one great "loose end" in all that has gone before. This change is that great shift in social structure on the way to a new era in both nations—namely, the shift to a middle-class and white-collar society. Its status as a loose end arises from the fact that, because it was not *directly* useful in explaining the parallel move into the divided government and Thatcherite eras—indeed, its impact appeared to run in the wrong direction—that move was less fully explained than the change into the New Deal and social democratic eras that preceded them.

Rejoined with political parties, however, this fundamental shift in the social base for politics resumes much of its potential explanatory power.

Seen by way of political parties and the party system, this first grand aspect of the long postwar boom—a real and undeniable shift in the occupational base of society—could have only two possible grand impacts on the key intermediaries for a new political order. Both options follow from the fact that in the first postwar order (in both nations), one of these parties was more evidently the choice of the middle class, the other just as clearly the choice of the working class (Kavanagh 1982; Shaw 1994, 192–99). If the middle class was to grow and the working class to shrink—as they did—one obvious option would be for the working-class party to decline and the middle-class party to grow.

The immediate point here is that in neither of these two nations, during the period leading up to a break, did this occur. In the United States, the Democratic Party declined a bit in terms of mass public identification, but the Republican Party did not rise at all in this regard; in addition, the Democratic hold on national public office, especially Congress, actually continued to expand. In Britain, the Conservatives returned to governing status after the great postwar Labour landslide, but the balance then moved back to a highly competitive situation in terms of government formation. Moreover, the balance of seats in Parliament across this entire period remained remarkably—almost unbelievably—equal, despite the huge social changes going on below.

What had to happen, as a result, was the other main option, in which a growing portion of a growing middle class became increasingly comfortable in the party previously identified with the working class (Kavanagh 1982, 105; Shafer 1998b, 101–14). In both nations, this did indeed happen, though with two critical twists. In the first twist, this shifting pattern of party identification mattered more, by definition, in the party that had previously possessed more working-class attraction—the Democrats and Labour—than it did in the previously more middle-class party—the Republicans and Conservatives. In the second twist, this impact was magnified by a shift in the structure of all these parties toward reliance on issue-oriented activists, who were more likely to be middle class (than working class) in background. In the United States, as ever, this second trend was more direct and unmediated. In Britain, by contrast, more of it came by way of the trade unions.

Together, these trends went a long way toward institutionalizing a new era in both nations. In both, those who became middle-class activists in a previously working-class party were distinctly liberal on economics and distinctly progressive on culture, thereby contributing powerfully both to exacerbating the new splits on cultural and national issues and to creating a set of policy options in which voters had to choose between a uniformly liberal and a uniformly conservative party. A counterfactual echo then occurred in the other major party, previously more middle class, where the absence of those middle-class partisans who were more liberal and who would have been identifiers in an earlier time made this other party, by definition, both more economically and more culturally conservative, thereby reinforcing the same pure-conservative versus pure-liberal menu.

In summary, these two nations sometimes converge, in the central substance of their politics and even in some key structures shaping it, in various temporal sequences or in various policy contexts, just as, at various other points and in other contexts, they diverge. Presumably, they will continue to do so. A more useful summary of the same developments, then, is to say that explicit comparison is especially helpful in teasing out the elements shaping postwar political change in these two nations, and even in imposing some causal relationships on them. This does not tilt the analysis toward convergence or, for that matter, divergence. What it does is isolate shaping influences and causal chains and contribute to an explanation of how these operate—while providing a simultaneous reminder that they do not operate in isolation from other sequences that can make the same factors operate differently or from other factors that are likely to be quite different at the same point in time.

Constraining an argument and confirming partial and contingent influences are major analytic gains. They have the optimistic virtue that they allow analytic progress. They have the pessimistic virtue that they establish limits to its precision. They have nothing logically to do with convergence or divergence, writ large.

Yet in the end, in this particular case, those thoughts are still elaborations on a grand, underlying shift from an era dominated by social welfare issues to an era where these are joined centrally by cultural values issues as well, and thus from an era characterized by class-based coalitions to one where these are crosscut too. As this is written, the Democratic and Labour Parties have finally and obviously adapted and are now competitive within a new era and order. By adapting, they moderate the policy impact of a political era, shifting public policy back toward the metaphorical "moving center." By adapting, they simultaneously, of course, help institutionalize a political order. Having further institutionalized it, they then deny the analyst any easy sense of what might come next—any simple clue to what a third postwar era and order might look like in Britain or in the United States.

CHAPTER NINE

Issue Evolution, Institutional Structure, and Public Preferences in the G-7

The place of the United States in the wider world is a persistent concern of professional observers, not to mention governmental practitioners, in many places within that wider world. Curiously, then, the relationship between American politics and politics elsewhere has received much less attention from students of American or comparative politics. Some of this curious lack has to do with the difficulties of realistic comparison. Nations at radically different stages of economic or democratic development have only a limited potential for much common political experience. Conversely, some of this lack has to do with assertions of American exceptionalism. If the nation can be understood only in terms of itself, the comparative enterprise is inherently limited.

And some of this lack has to do with counterpart dismissals by self-conscious comparativists. If the United States is a reliable outlier, but if it is also by many standards the biggest player, it can only mess up the analysis. One simple way forward, in this curiously undercharted territory, is by using the G-7 nations as a logically connected, intrinsically constrained frame for comparison. One way to attempt this, in turn, is to begin with individual comparisons among these nations, across their eras and orders, adding a nation and extending the analysis as the comparison proceeds. That is the strategy for this penultimate chapter. Such a (partially self-limiting) strategy is only reinforced by the evident diversity in the postwar politics of these nations.

Happily, when this strategy is adopted, partial comparisons, with their insistent similarities and crucial differences, present an implicit, unequivocal, further message. From one side, they affirm the possibility of generalization, and hence the limits on national individuality. From the other side, however, they suggest a requirement of national specification, and thus limits on generalizability. From one side, they hint constantly at general forces: at universal issues, universal structures, and resulting universal dynamics. From the other side, they insist simultaneously that these be embedded in specifically national contexts in order to understand their operation. Along the way, these partial comparisons tease out parallel developments—similar issue sequences, similar structural interactions, and similar patterns of conflict—while *denying* any similarity of outcome.

Thus it proves possible to cut postwar history in each of these nations into political eras, into extended periods in which policy conflicts revolved around the same underlying and continuing concerns. Indeed, it proves possible to further subclassify substantive issues within these eras into clusters, into an economic-welfare and a cultural-national cluster. And it proves possible to isolate accompanying political orders, accompanying combinations of social structures that shape these conflicts in an extended fashion. Moreover, it is possible to gather these key structural influences into another small set of supporting categories: into social bases, intermediary organizations, and governmental institutions.

Yet even when this is done, the crucial explanation of the products in individual nations is still dependent on a set of critical interactions: across issues to create an era, among structures to shape an order, between eras and orders to establish a political dynamic. Common elements, and thus incentives for comparison, are still central to this analysis, but so is an emphasis on the contingent character of any resulting generalizations, on the inherently varying interactions that make these comparisons inevitably— and appropriately—partial.

North America

Simple, direct, concrete comparisons flow easily from the first two countries in this analysis: the United States and Canada. Geographic propinquity is surely involved, but it is not the main explanation. Indeed, geographic propinquity fares badly in producing similarities nearly everywhere in the G-7. Thus, France and Britain are notably short of parallels, while Italy and Japan produce more than any other pair. Instead, in an analysis built self-consciously around eras and orders, the role of World War II in the politics of these nations is what makes opening parallels easy to detect. Said differently, these two nations are distinguished from the other G-7 members by the more limited—not small, just more limited—impact of the Second World War.

What this means is that unlike everywhere else except France, where the counterpart effect was merely delayed, the United States and Canada did not feature the end of World War II as the beginning of a new substantive era in national politics, much less of a new structural order. Rather, in both, the first great political era of the postwar years stretched back before the Second World War, back, in fact, to the domestic political fallout from the arrival of the Great Depression. The political dynamics and policy responses generated by the depression varied substantially between them. Yet both nations began the postwar years in the midst of an extended political era stretching back into the 1930s.

Not surprisingly, the central policy issues in these two earlier parallel eras were much the same: principally some policy response to the hardships of the Great Depression, secondarily some response to the conflagration that was World War II. Both stimuli were sufficiently global and sufficiently strong to command a response from governments of all the developed nations, of course. But the point here is that the war, for all its breadth, depth, and horror, was obviously not strong enough to have a transformative effect on a political era beginning earlier and continuing later in both these countries.

In contrast, the political orders associated with this common era varied significantly between the two. In the United States, the Great Depression encountered a politics still organized around geographic regions at its grass roots, and it elicited a politics built around two broad, class-based, national coalitions instead. The majority coalition was reflected (partly by accidents of incumbency) in what became the blue-collar party, the Democrats, to be opposed by the white-collar party, the Republicans. The Democrats gained such strong and uniform control of the otherwise separate institutions of national government that they could take major steps toward implementing an American "welfare state."

In Canada, by contrast, the old ethnocultural and regional distinctions that dominated social coalitions at the grass roots were not powerfully disturbed by the Great Depression. The depression did sweep the Conservative Party out of government and bring the Liberals in for the duration of this first postwar era, but there was less policy difference between these two parties than between the U.S. Republicans and Democrats. The Conservatives actually began a policy response to the depression via increased provision of social welfare; the Liberals then took this up, consolidated it, and expanded it modestly. Facing a parliamentary system whose governing majorities were exaggerated by first-past-the-post elections, they had comparatively less difficulty doing so than did their Democratic counterparts in the United States.

Similar issue concerns with different structural underpinnings implied similar policy conflicts but a very different political dynamic. The United States, despite the indiscipline of its individual parties, offered a dynamic approximating the classic two-party model, at least in this particular era. One party, the Democrats, found the policy preferences of a majority and became dominant. The other party, the Republicans, continued to resist the program of the dominant party long after its implementation. Moderate Democrats thus normally controlled all the institutions of government. Moderate Republicans were nevertheless capable of doing the same. One result was that the United States took both earlier and stronger action with its incipient welfare state. Another result was that it did not carry it as far as Canada in the course of the postwar years.

The counterpart dynamic in Canada centered on a multiparty system, but of a peculiar sort, with a dominant national party, a much weaker pretender to national opposition, and serious regional opposition parties. In that environment, what drove social welfare policy was actually the programmatic goals—and numerical growth—of one of these splinters. In the immediate postwar years, this was the Cooperative Commonwealth Federation (CCF), the most explicitly socialist of the major Canadian or American parties. In order to maintain national power, the Liberals then co-opted large parts of the CCF program. To stay potentially competitive, and lacking sufficient class crystallization to block such a move, the Conservatives tagged along. In return, the CCF receded. When it did, governmental policy response eased.

In both countries, in any case, the end of this first postwar political era came with the rise of a set of individually specific cultural and national issues to equal prominence with the economic and social welfare issues of the first postwar era. In the nature of such developments, these new issues were accompanied by a change in political structure, partly impelling and partly resulting from this issue shift. Diagnostically, however, the shift could have been confirmed first (and is best introduced) through a change in the place of foreign affairs in domestic politics.

In the first postwar era, foreign affairs had been noteworthy, in both the United States and Canada, for the way that it did *not* change in its domestic role and impact. That is, a transfer of the cross-party consensus on fighting World War II to a cross-party consensus on pursuing the Cold War was effectively accomplished in both nations with lots of surface struggle, especially in the United States, but with no insuperable difficulties. This still represented a break with older eras in the political history of the United States, whereas it merely extended enduring divisions from earlier eras in Canada. The surprising similarity was that a cross-party consensus characterized the two nations on these issues in both wartime and the immediate postwar years.

That consensus came apart first in Canada, where the unraveling was symbolized by policy tensions arising from the Suez crisis of 1956. Yet within the framework of political eras and orders, Suez was really just a concrete if dramatic touchstone for general adjustments to Canadian foreign policy in the face of a changing international realm. These adjustments, in turn, were only indicative of a deeper tension between a British and an American orientation for Canadian foreign policy in the Cold War years. And that tension was still more deeply rooted in ethnic and cultural differences within Canada. As a result, it would ultimately be these latter, more explicitly domestic tensions that would most clearly distinguish this second postwar era in Canadian politics from the first.

What would in fact characterize this era was the coming of cultural as well as national issues to prominence in Canadian politics to join the old commercial and developmental issues, along with those intermittent social welfare concerns. The Conservative government, whose rupture of Liberal dominance most clearly marked the coming of a new era, shifted an old alignment on commercial policy to favor the West over the East. The Liberal government that then regained power introduced a second postwar round of social welfare enhancement. Those issues were, accordingly, hardly absent from Canadian politics. But they were joined by a whole cluster of additional issues, from international alliance behavior through domestic language policy, which involved the explicit form of integration for the nation. It was these essentially cultural and national issues that would give the new era a new cast.

On the surface, partisan politics actually masked this change. The same dominant party, the Liberals, faced the same putative opposition, the Conservatives, again with a set of regional splinters. Indeed, the rise of another major splinter, the New Democratic Party (NDP), which grew out of the CCF, caused the associated political dynamic to look initially much as it had before. This time, the Liberals co-opted the NDP program through a second round of social welfare increases. The Conservatives then followed along, and the NDP, though not so seriously undercut as the CCF had been, merely stabilized for an extended period.

Yet underneath, the new order was noticeably different, and gradually rising cultural and national issues would play into it in a noticeably different way. At the grass roots, the mass public balance between Liberals and Conservatives was closer, so that national governments had much less leeway in addressing ethnocultural concerns. Moreover, the dominant party, the Liberals, had acquired a geographically narrowed focus because ethnocultural attachments—Catholic for the Liberals, Protestant for the Conservatives— were much sharper. Finally, and most crucially, a previously consequential element of Canadian political structure worked in a new way.

That element was the critical place of the province of Quebec, always the single largest influence on electoral outcomes and governmental formation, thanks principally to its sheer size but also to its often distinctive policy preferences. In the old political order, these preferences had involved both commercial and foreign policy. Quebec had joined Ontario in favoring the industrial East over the agricultural and mining West; it had differed over a more self-consciously British orientation toward the outside world. In the new political order, by contrast, Quebec had shifted to a focus on language rights and cultural support, seeking provincial autonomy on these issues and making it very difficult for coherent national coalitions to be put together—which had always been difficult without Quebec, but now was difficult with it.

Foreign affairs was the diagnostic entry point to a new political era in the United States as well, though the break there came later, when the war in Vietnam served as its symbolic focus. As in Canada, economic and social welfare issues hardly went away in this second postwar era. As in Canada, these were, however, joined by a huge array of cultural and national issues, playing across them in consequential ways. In Canada, these issues were probably more pointed and more profound, going ultimately to the basis of national integration itself. In the United States, they were pointed and profound enough, but they moved on to constitute a far broader array of less encompassing concerns, including crime, abortion, public prayer, permissiveness, public protest, sex roles, capital punishment, and so on, all of them involving the character of national life.

These issues surely reflected a variety of background changes in American society: greater affluence, spreading education, technological development, national media. Many were brought into politics and given their specific focus by way of decisions from the U.S. Supreme Court. Two structural points follow from this. In one, a court system became an important structural influence and played an important substantive role, as it would in many of the other G-7 nations. In the other, the new cultural and national issues propelled by the Supreme Court did not so much fragment the general public as simply and forcefully crosscut it. There were now two majorities in politics—an economic-welfare majority and a cultural-national majority—and they were effectively unrelated to each other.

A first-past-the-post electoral system, a decentralized party system, and, crucially, the separation of powers caused this pattern of preferences to create a distinctive political dynamic. In this, nationally, the two parties offered ideologically consistent policies: liberal in both realms for Democrats, conservative in both for Republicans. The two underlying majorities inevitably bounced between—or straddled—these two parties, depending on the offices in conflict and the dominant issues of the day. Split partisan control of government was the outcome that made the new order seem most stereotypically different. Yet the underlying tension, between policies and between majorities, would surface constantly even when one party controlled both major elective institutions of national government.

Over and around these elements of change between two political eras in two nations was a larger and more amorphous structural development, crucial to both. In abstract terms, this was a change in the essential character of political brokerage. Nothing is more integral to the story of postwar politics in these nations than the story of this shift: the movement from a political order in which national public policy was created through bargaining among delegates from local communities and regions, to a political order in which national policy was instead critically shaped by national—essentially plebiscitary—processes.

That is a highly abstract description. More concretely, this change was registered by a shift in the character of the brokers themselves, again in both societies. Indeed, if parliamentary versus presidential governments or two-party versus multiparty systems differentiate these nations, a powerful parallel shift in the social character of their major partisan actors corresponding-ingly unifies them and coincides with the shift from the first to the second postwar political era. In both countries, local brokers, whose job was to bring national rewards home to the community or region and to hammer out some sort of national compromise on other issues, were replaced by actors motivated instead by intense policy concerns, and usually national concerns at that.

This second postwar era continued, essentially unchanged, into the 1990s in the United States. Thus it continued easily through the defeat of President George Bush by Bill Clinton, and thereby through the shift from formalistically divided to formalistically unified national government. It also continued through the further shift to an opposite pattern of partisan division, with a Democratic president but a Republican Congress this time. The nation might mix and match partisan preferences, and then mix and match again. This did not, however, guarantee a change in the associated political order, and as long as it did not, a political era would continue, and the dynamic of American politics would continue to be of a piece.

The situation was not so clear in Canada, where the dominance of cultural issues in Canadian politics by the 1990s raised the insistent pos-sibility of a third great postwar era. By the early 1980s, ethnocultural is-sues had already taken center stage in Canadian politics. Issues of language use and cultural priority, as they defined the appropriate place of French speakers, were the cutting edge of the linguistic issue cluster. Yet in their wake, they produced additional ethnocultural claims for political reorgani-zation and expanded group rights. By extension, as the linguistic issue— ultimately an issue of national integration—moved to the center of politick-ing, the two main parties, each in turn, attempted to solve this central problem by becoming broader, intendedly national coalitions.

Yet in doing so, these parties became simultaneously less coherent, in-gesting the elements that were both necessary to any acceptable solution and consecutively unwilling to accept any of the solutions offered. Accordingly, the Meech Lake Accord went down, the Charlottetown Accord went down, the Liberal Party went down, the Conservative Party went down. And again simultaneously, in the face of two huge but incoherent parties alternating in the attempt to find a solution, splinters on the extremes (splinters that *had* a simple solution) came up: the Parti Quebecois at one end, Reform at the other. Their preferred resolutions promised a new order, almost by defini-tion. Policy compromises, if they could be found, or simple public exhaustion with these issues if compromises could not be found, promised to mark the extension of a second postwar era.

Canada thus becomes the first of the cases (Germany, Italy, and Japan will join it) where precise specification of both temporal cuts and structural influences for the modern era is (and must be) dependent on further developments. The residual tasks of any analytic framework, in the face of such an obviously indeterminate future, are to provide general building blocks leading up to the present, along with key checkpoints for examining the change proceeding from it. In this, a framework involving political eras and the composition of their political orders can still help highlight alternative possibilities and provide some means for thinking concretely about them. Indeed, viewed in this light, the resulting alternatives only enrich the possibilities for comparison across all the G-7 nations in the postwar years.

Anglo-America

Had it not been for the Second World War, the timing of postwar political eras in Britain might well have coincided more closely with that of the United States and Canada. After all, the Great Depression had been an undeniably powerful stimulus to policy making; expansion of the welfare state was an equally plausible policy response. Yet the war did intervene, at three levels of abstraction. Most generally, it focused political attention on national survival. To this end, it demanded a government of national unity, to pursue a defense. That government, most concretely, then postponed the election of 1940, which might otherwise have foreshadowed the sharp change to come in 1945.

Nevertheless, because that election was postponed, it became the one to register the arrival of a new political era. The central concerns of this new era would be the appropriate provision—the appropriate extension and level—of social welfare benefits to ensure against the disruptions, and simple harshness, of the economic marketplace. The largest single structural change underpinning this new era, in turn, was a change in the composition of the mass electorate. An entire new generation of working-class Britons grew up not just with universal suffrage as the norm but with the trade union movement as the organizational context for their participation. It was not that they too had failed to recognize the need to subordinate social welfare desires to the demands of national survival during the war. It was just that there had also been constant reassurances that "things would get better" when the war ended.

The war did end, and the long-delayed response to the depression came in 1945, with the massive election of a new Labour government. Major policy changes followed quickly: nationalization of utilities and strategic industries, social insurance for unemployment and disability, broader and richer pensions, socialized medicine. In no other G-7 nation during the postwar years (with the potential exception of Germany today) was raw expansion of the electorate such a decisive factor in ending one political era and beginning another. As a result, the main direct parallel with the situation in the United States and Canada was that the same basic concerns, economic and social welfare concerns, would dominate the first great postwar era in all three nations.

That is half the inaugural story. The other half of a complete description of the first postwar political order in Britain involves its national embodiment of the two other general factors that were also shaping politics at the time, critically, in Canada and the United States. Said differently, the same key elements, social homogeneity or heterogeneity, along with governmental centralization or decentralization, complete the picture of the political order in postwar Britain and explain the timing and force of policy responses in these three nations: the United States moved first and produced the most restrained welfare state; Canada moved second and produced a larger programmatic response; Britain was third and delivered by far the most thoroughgoing reforms.

In Britain, a homogeneous society was, by its nature, less prone to generate the continual conflicts out of which individual policies might emerge. Class was by far the dominant dimension of social cleavage, unlike in the United States and Canada, or in France and Italy for that matter. Yet when such a society did have a policy demand, and then a party response to that demand, such homogeneity certainly facilitated policy change. When such a society was coupled with truly centralized institutions of government—an executive that dominated both Parliament and the majority party, without even serious alternative layers of government to serve as the home of an ongoing opposition—the government of the day might still resist change, as a reelected Conservative government might well have done. But that government was advantaged in moving forcefully when society (that impressively homogeneous society) appeared to demand it.

The United States was different, even opposite. There, an extremely heterogeneous society—on grounds of race, ethnicity, religion, class, occupation, lifestyle, geography, history, and so on—was coupled with highly fragmented governmental arrangements: not just a real and strong "separation of powers" in its institutions, but a genuinely federal organization to its politics as well. One result was that widespread if varying demands for a response to the Great Depression were generated and registered early; the United States moved first among these three nations. A second result was that once the most consensually acceptable programs had been implemented, brakes on further initiatives, or at least much greater conflicts, also followed.

Canada fell neatly in the middle, as it should when these two great structural influences are the focus. On the one hand, it was closer to the United States than to Britain in terms of social heterogeneity: less heterogeneous than the United States, though with a complicated internal patterning, but indisputably closer to the United States than to Britain. That status betokened a later start than in the United States, an earlier start than in Britain. On the other hand, Canada was closer to Britain than to the United States in terms of governmental centralization: parliamentary institutions buttressed by first-past-the-post elections clearly outweighed, on balance, real federal pressures and a fragmented party system. All this betokened a stronger policy response than in the United States, a clearly weaker one than in Britain.

These same two critical and ongoing elements of the political order in Britain, a homogeneous society with centralized institutions of government, are also useful for emphasizing the way the same basic structural factors can underpin quite different substantive concerns in different periods. Said differently, they emphasize the way the same factors can work very differently under different pressures. Homogeneity and centralization in Britain did not, of course, change between 1944 and 1946. Yet when the depression, the delay in responding to it caused by the Second World War, the growing body of Labour support beneath the wartime effort at national unity, and then the election of 1945 were all imposed on top of these two elements of the political order, a new political era (and order) emerged.

Britain, however, was very much parallel to both Canada and the United States with regard to the major aspect of the new political era that was undisturbed by the end of the Second World War. This was the place of foreign affairs, and especially of conflicts over an orientation to the brave new situation in international security. In Canada and the United States, a shift from pursuit of World War II to pursuit of the Cold War, perhaps surprisingly, brought no serious shift in the domestic political order. In both countries, tensions over foreign affairs would come considerably later and would thus be important in a change to the second major postwar era.

In Britain, more remarkably, the same was true. In spite of the size of the change in public policy associated with the coming of a new Labour government, an underlying orientation to foreign affairs remained intact. A large part of the explanation was elite continuity, as it was, in truth, in the United States and Canada. In Britain, common experience in the pursuit of foreign affairs in the wartime government, for Labour as well as Conservative leaders, was buttressed at a deeper level by a common social background among those who handled foreign affairs. When there was no serious mass opposition to their acceptance of Cold War burdens, the result was even more dramatic in Britain, in that the underlying place of foreign affairs was unaffected by a huge change in the domestic political order.

The dynamic of postwar British politics, however, the way this interaction of eras and orders worked in practice, was noticeably different from the dynamic in the United States or Canada. Moreover, in this difference probably lies the explanation both for how the first postwar political era in Britain managed to last so long in comparative terms and for the specific character of the change in eras when it did arrive. In Canada, a second order had actually arrived by the late 1950s. In the United States, it arrived in the late 1960s instead. In Britain, it did not arrive until the late 1970s. Characteristically, when it did, no one could be in doubt about the date.

Nevertheless, when it did arrive, the new political dynamic would still be easily recognizable in terms of the old. In this dynamic, the crucial element was actually the behavior of the opposition party (or parties). Within a very short time, they too were competing on the same issues and programs that the turning-point election had brought into government. Thus, for the long period from 1945 to 1979, the point was that the Conservatives argued for their version of the welfare state—more appropriately targeted, better managed, cheaper—so that Labour-Conservative competition oscillated around the same basic programs, at roughly the same midpoint. It has taken longer, for reasons addressed later, for Labour to argue for its version of individual opportunity and personal choice after 1979—more widely available, more humane, and no more expensive—but as this is written, it has apparently done so.

In any case, the break that registered in 1979 had all the surface hallmarks of the one that registered in 1945. It had partisan change in the control of government, of course. More consequentially, it prefaced a sharp and extended shift in policy responses as the policy aggregate known as "Thatcherism" came quickly to the fore. But below the surface and more consequentially, it had the counterpart crucial shift in the composition of the social base for British politics. It was the election of 1979 that registered the gradual demise of the manual working-class majority and the gradual rise of a new middle class.

When this shift was added to a continuing absence of other major principles of division in society, and to the continuing presence of a centralized government, the structural preconditions for a revised political order were all at hand. What followed was a revised version of the old political dynamic, in which the opposition either competed on the new issue concerns associated with this new order or lost. Yet the new issue concerns around which these older structural elements recrystallized were remarkably similar to—in effect, the national embodiment of—central concerns that would have been very familiar from the North American context.

In the United States, when the Democratic Party moved off from the Cold War consensus on the containment of communism in the late 1960s, national Republicans received one set of promising (foreign policy) advantages. When a spate of cultural issues arose, more or less independent of either party, these national Republicans received a second set. In Canada, foreign relations played the same role a bit earlier, through general questions about a Canadian orientation to the Cold War world. As in the United States, neither political party had to look very hard for—in truth, neither really wanted to see—a second set of newly contentious issues involving language and ethnocultural rights, which then came to dominate politics despite this partisan aversion.

Counterpart shifts were delayed in Britain by social homogeneity, governmental centralization, and a dominant political dynamic. Yet they could not be delayed indefinitely, and when they did arrive, so did a new political era. Academic and journalistic debate about Thatcherism often focused on the fate of the welfare state, and thus (mistakenly) on the diagnostic policies and politicking of the first postwar era. But in fact, those were not the issue areas that brought the Thatcher government to power nor sustained an era and order after Thatcher was gone. To emphasize the point, public support for the main elements of the British social welfare program never seriously wavered across the new political period.

Foreign policy was, however, one important element of change, focusing as it did on Britain's role in the wider world. One party, the Conservatives, remained unabashed about serving as a pillar of containment in a bipolar division. The other, Labour, renounced this position, to the point of flirting with unilateral disarmament. In truth, the issue stressed both party coalitions. But majority opinion sat principally with the former pole, so it was the Labour coalition that was under pressure. At the time, this fact was masked by more general debates about governing competence. Yet the perceived ability to conduct a foreign policy—a "proper" foreign policy—was inevitably a concrete referent within those debates.

At the same time, cultural and lifestyle issues came to play an even more influential role in this second postwar political era. Questions about the character of ordinary British life—public deportment, personal responsibility, criminal control—not only became more central to political debate; they also became much less consensual across the political parties. To the extent that these touched on social welfare concerns, they involved questions of the kind of citizenry being produced, not the distribution of benefits per se. Had Margaret Thatcher presented her Conservative government as seeking instead to cut child benefits, restructure the National Health Service, and so on, it might never have survived.

In a kind of further parallel to the immediate postwar situation, when this new era finally arrived in Britain, it arrived with considerably more force than it did in the United States or Canada. In many ways, the underlying situation, in terms of public preferences, was really quite similar, even comparing the two extremes of the United States and the United Kingdom. In both, the public obviously approved of existing commitments to the welfare state. In both, however, it clearly preferred traditionalism on cultural values and nationalism in foreign affairs. In the United States, this provided the makings for split partisan control of government. In the United Kingdom, neither the party system nor governmental arrangements could countenance that.

Forces this fundamental—underlying and crosscutting public preferences and thus social majorities—called forth some related echoes, even in Britain. Thus, if the Conservatives had staked out the ideological Right on both dimensions, and if Labour had then staked out the Left on both, there was, in principle, ideological "room" for two other parties. The old Liberals actually offered one of these possibilities—liberal on cultural-national issues and conservative on economic-welfare matters. A new party, the Social

Democrats, then sprang up to offer the other—conservative on cultural-national affairs and liberal on economic-welfare matters—before an amalgamation of Liberals and Social Democrats muddled the distinction.

Neither of those minor parties ultimately threatened to bring a different combination of basic preferences into the new political order. As a result, and more to the practical point in Britain, one public opinion majority or the other—an economic-welfare or a cultural-national majority—was likely to determine the control of national government. However, given the nature of the party system through which this was done, a party awarded control of government by one majority would be able, within some limits, to use that government to pursue its wishes on the other set of issues as well, despite the fact that these might be minority wishes. More concretely, a conservative cultural-national government in Britain did get to implement conservative economic-welfare policies: sweeping privatization of prior nationalizations, imposition of national standards in education, introduction of "internal markets" for governmental services, a per capita tax, and so on.

That the Labour Party left these initiatives effectively unchallenged for a surprising length of time was due, finally, to the national embodiment of another general trend shared with most of the other G-7 nations: the gradual shift to a politics built around partisan activists motivated by issues and ideology, rather than around party loyalists moved by organizational attachments and brokerage concerns. The rise of such "issue activists" was integral to the Labourite withdrawal from the Cold War consensus and to its adoption of the progressive posture (the minority position) on cultural issues generally. By the same token, the increasing presence of these activists—though here, buttressed by representatives of the party's major interest group, the trade unions—was an important part of the explanation for why the party did not quickly reorient to the new era and begin to compete around a new set of concerns.

A different kind of Conservative Party had done this relatively quickly in the immediate postwar years. The rise, in the interim, of nonbrokerage activists—set free from localized connections, motivated primarily by the national issues of their era instead, and making a partially autonomous contribution to their political order as a result—was a key element of difference between the two eras in Britain, as it was in the United States and Canada. By extension, this same change in the nature of political intermediation contributed toward the same overall dynamic in most of the G-7 nations, with countervailing public preferences on economic-welfare versus cultural-national issues, policy options from the political parties that differed from the composite preferences of the general public, and a special polarization on cultural-national concerns thrown in.

Despite all this, the parallels should not be overdrawn. Ultimately, this did not imply the same characteristic political dynamic, nor the same resulting governments of the day, even in just the Anglo-American countries. The societies in which all this was happening, and the institutional arrangements through which it was happening, were still noticeably different—too different for such an all-encompassing parallel. Instead, what resulted in the United States was "divided government"; in Canada, "minority government with majority rule"; in Britain, "artificial amalgamation."

The Allies

The last of the former Allies in the prosecution of World War II among the G-7 nations is France. From the beginning, however, the war figured in a different way in its postwar politics. For the United States and Canada, with a few dramatic exceptions, the war had never been a directly territorial matter, and it neither marked a new postwar era nor even interrupted a prewar order. Britain, by contrast, had been under direct and sustained territorial attack, and this attack effectively postponed the arrival of a new political era until the war formally ended, when that era arrived with a vengeance. France, however, had been occupied, and the fallout from occupation would spill over into postwar politics in a crucial way. This spillover would in fact delay a change of era (and order) that seemed otherwise destined to occur. That delay would be far longer than the war itself had delayed such a shift in Britain, and with even more convulsive consequences for France when it finally came.

A second line is also crossed with the arrival of France in the analysis, a line that makes a comparison with the former Axis powers just as appropriate as a comparison with the former Allies. In the most abstract sense, France would show some similarities to the United States and Canada in the immediate postwar years. These were the three nations, for example, that resumed a prewar political order. But in the specifics of their politics, this is patently the wrong comparison. In the nature of its postwar policy challenges, France looked much more like Germany than like Canada or the United States in the dozen years after the Second World War. And in the character of the politicking that addressed them—the disruptions to society and the instabilities in government—it was surely Italy, much more than Britain, that provided the apparent parallels for analysts at the time.

As a result, France sits, appropriately, between the Anglo-American democracies on the one hand and the former Axis powers on the other. Nevertheless, for a brief period after World War II, it must have seemed that none of this might ultimately prove true. Or at least, there was a serious battle within France over constitutional arrangements for postwar politics, and there was a serious strong-executive option within this battle. Had that option prevailed, a new structural order might have followed from major constitutional change. But many of the proponents of this option were critically handicapped by associations with the wartime occupation and its Vichy regime, while more of the obvious resistance figures were in favor of a return to strong parliamentary arrangements instead. In the immediate run, the latter prevailed.

Unsurprisingly, then, France mirrored the United States and Canada in beginning the postwar years with a political era reaching back well before the Second World War. In this, central policy conflicts continued to revolve around economics and social welfare. That fact was frequently masked by the surface drama of French politics, by the proliferation of regionally based subissues from one side and by constant struggles just to form a national government from the other. Yet underneath all these was a pressing need to rebuild the postwar French economy, and this would generate the defining policies—and policy conflicts—of this first postwar era.

Economic rebuilding, besides being substantively related to the concerns of the prewar political era, slotted comfortably into a structural order reflecting prewar contours. That order had grown out of a heterogeneous but sharply divided and segmented society—in the latter respect, unlike the United States, which was also heterogeneous. These divisions had previously gained expression through a party system reflecting, and ultimately "freezing," their major contours. The main principle of organization within this party system was still economic, along a classic Left-Right axis. But there were additional class-based fillips to this party system, along with a heavy clerical-secular overlay. Regional divisions were additionally important to the actual politicking that played out within the system.

If that had been all there was to the postwar political order—fragmented society, fragmented intermediaries, fragmented constitutional arrangements—the same simple argument that covered the response of the United

States, Canada, and Britain to these same economic-welfare issues would have made a clear prediction about France as well: that it would move early but hesitantly on extension of the welfare state. That this was an insufficient description (and prediction) was due to another major, complicating element of the political order: the continuation from prewar years of a strong central bureaucracy.

Prewar France had possessed a much stronger statist tradition than the United States, Canada, or Britain. The postwar French bureaucracy found itself aided in a general sense by the fragmentation of Parliament, which made this one centralizing actor more influential than it would otherwise have been. At a minimum, that made bureaucratic drafting of comprehensive economic plans much more practically possible. The bureaucracy was also aided, in two senses, by the fact that the largest single party in Parliament was the Communists, who could not come into the government of the day. In the abstract, this limited the kaleidoscopic character of those many short-lived governments. More practically, it gave the bureaucracy some additional leverage with the moderately conservative parties when it was pushing explicit social welfare reforms, on grounds that the more extreme opposition had to be contained and undercut.

The resulting political dynamic was superficially still one of protest and disruption, of governmental instability and policy fragmentation, and these surface manifestations contained the larger part of the truth. Yet they also masked the rest of the dynamic, in which an indirect centralization—though not nearly to the extent permitted by true centralization in Britain—meant that many policy initiatives of this first postwar era in France were centered in the bureaucracy rather than in the elected government. Thus it was the bureaucracy that was most concerned with programs for economic recovery, just as it was the bureaucracy that managed initiatives to extend the French welfare state.

This order came apart dramatically in the late 1950s, and an obviously new era in postwar politics arrived. Decolonization provided the general issue context. Algeria provided its crucial specific embodiment and brought on a crisis seemingly fated, in hindsight, to produce new institutional arrangements. As it emerged, the crisis still strongly reflected the old political order. A fragmented party system inside fragmented governmental arrangements was once again being challenged by the bureaucracy in setting policy—only this time, the critical piece of that bureaucracy was the military. In any case, the crisis, as it was resolved, would produce entirely new constitutional arrangements, albeit a variant of the same arrangements that might have been implemented immediately after World War II.

The new structure of government, *intended* as the bedrock of a new political order, was characterized principally by an executive focus among national institutions, including a separately elected president, and secondarily by a majoritarian electoral system with two-stage (two-ballot) elections. The principal goal of this new structure was to introduce a reliably strong central executive that was, this time, democratically accountable. Its secondary goal was to force politicking into an essentially bilateral context, so that the fragmentation and irresponsibility of the first postwar order would not be repeated. And for the next twenty-five years, remarkable as it may seem, those influences did shape a new political order roughly as intended. Thus the president, even after Charles de Gaulle, acquired the ability to address major national issues, and the party system was reformed into two broad tendencies, a moderate Right and (eventually) a moderate Left.

The combination of these two great events, of the constitutional threat from an Algerian crisis and then the imposition of a serious new constitution, probably overstates the uniformity with which cultural and national issues would dominate this second political era in postwar French politics. Yet the theory under which French administrative arrangements had been conducted (that the colonies *were* France) meant that decolonization had to be a powerful issue of national identity. Afterward, effective implementation of a new structure of national government was likewise inevitably a central focus to politics. Part of the impetus behind the latter, and not for the last time, was also a direct comparison with Germany, involving the perception that the postwar German economic boom was proceeding even better than its French counterpart. Yet ironically, this latter perception would not actually reintroduce economic and welfare issues (and conflicts) into French politics for some time.

Over time, the great cultural-national issues of the day, decolonization plus implementation of the new constitution, were successfully handled. Yet the influence of these new issues was arguably extended by the way the great issue *undermining* substantive continuity in the United States, Canada, and Britain—a growing division over national positioning in the Cold War—was effectively circumscribed in France. The fact that one of the major political parties, the Communists, actually favored switching sides in this conflict served to delegitimize more moderate hesitations and realignments. The further sidelining of this issue reflected additional factors distinctive to the French context. Central to these was the way that de Gaulle himself insisted on a position of individuality for France within the Western alliance, thereby defusing any argument that French national interests were being subverted.

None of this would necessarily have worked out as it did, however, had it not been for two other developments crucial to the new political order. The first of these was broad-scale social change associated with a French version of the postwar economic miracle, the "thirty glorious years," which reduced many divisions in French society and actually altered others. The coming of a truly national economy, along with the growth of middle-class sectors within it, on top of a generalized economic boom, all seemed to blur the sharpness of class lines. The same underlying developments drew the regions, in effect, into a national system. These shifts were joined, finally, by an increasingly secular character to French society and a concomitant decline in the importance of the clerical-anticlerical cleavage.

The second development, equally crucial and more pointed, was the drawing of the Socialists into the new political order, this time as the potential alternative government of the day. In the first postwar order, the Socialists had been frequent (and crucial) governmental partners, though they could not simply be the government. In the second postwar order, despite their initial aversion to its constitutional underpinnings, they could. The culmination of this change was the election of Francois Mitterrand in 1981, through a "Union of the Left." Broad societal changes in the potential electorate for such a party were central to this development. So was more than a decade of focused internal party politicking. Either way, the arrival of a broad-left alternative, and then of an actual alternation in government, confirmed the stability of basic governmental arrangements. The vast middle of French society was thus attached to these arrangements. A dynamic of moderate competition, broad Left versus broad Right, was equally a part of this attachment.

The early years after the arrival of the Socialists in power would actually bridge two eras in postwar politics, in as dramatic a fashion as any in the postwar history of the entire G-7. From one side, this arrival affirmed the stability—the institutionalization—of an encompassing constitutional framework. In that sense, the early years of a new Socialist government helped stabilize and extend an older political era. Yet within only a few years, this arrival would coincide with a clear break in political eras and orders (note that the break did not coincide with an actual election), propelled by a changing issue agenda in society at large but also facilitated, albeit perversely, by the policy aspirations of the Socialists themselves.

Accordingly, if the lesson of the second postwar era in France is the power of basic constitutional arrangements to shape a political order, then the lesson of the third era is the power of new issues and new social coalitions to make those basic constitutional arrangements work differently, and sometimes to modify their very content. The Socialists began with a truly comprehensive program for social change through governmental action, the heart of which was actually in economic and social welfare concerns. Had they succeeded with these, through further nationalization, expanded social insurance, and new labor-management compacts, they might well have heralded a new era most closely resembling immediate postwar Britain in the substance and reach of its policy impact.

They would, however, quickly run afoul of two major forces. One was the long-run economic cycle. Anxieties about the putative end of the thirty glorious years might have been instrumental in bringing the Socialists to power, but the factors associated with that putative end made governmental economic intervention much more difficult. The other main brake on these economic-welfare initiatives was growing economic integration with Europe, especially between Germany and France. Ironically, this was an outcome consciously fostered by French policy in the preceding political era. Yet it was also a powerful restraint on autonomous change in French policy in the succeeding era, when Germany was not inclined to go along.

The result was a transition between two eras in France, a transition that possessed the greatest parallels with, of all nations, the United States. Both nations, by this time, featured not just formal but practical presidential governance, at least in comparison to Britain or Canada. Both also featured, in effect, a two-ballot system of elections. In France, this meant multiparty competition in the first round, followed by a runoff between leading figures from the two general tendencies in the second. In the United States, it meant factional competition in a primary election, followed by two-party competition in a general election—and the two parties were nothing if not "broad tendencies" in the French mode.

When both political systems then encountered major new crosscutting pressures from cultural and national issues, the stage was set for a parallel change of eras. For France, issues of European integration, and all the individual adaptations at home that this would require, were the great national issues of this new era. Issues of domestic social integration, especially those involving crime in general and immigration in particular, from the rest of Europe but especially from former French colonies, were the main cultural incarnations. What resulted from these newly powerful cultural and national concerns was characterized in the United States as an era of divided government. But the more accurate term for France, divided *governance*, might have been more accurate for the United States too.

The old Left-Right division, now moderated, still underlay the party system. Individual issues tapping into this division could still be important to politics in both the United States and France; class attachments in voting could still intermittently rise and not just fall, so the existing parties remained the main vehicle for building social coalitions. However, the new cultural and national issues, now often more central to politics, could not in principle be aligned in these same terms: the majority coalition for economic-welfare issues was not the same as the majority coalition for cultural-national affairs. Split partisan control of national institutions, divided government, was the signature characteristic of the result in both nations. But divided *governance*, in the sense of reliably crosscutting majority coalitions, was its practical essence.

Thus, for both the United States and France, the diagnostic feature inaugurating the new political order was split partisanship in the American mode: Republican presidents with Democratic Congresses in the United States, Socialist presidents with Conservative Chambers of Deputies in France. But what was really present was divided governance in the French sense. Both countries could still easily experience unified partisan control of government, but the underlying cross-alignment of economic-welfare versus cultural-national concerns did not go away. France even provided a *procedural* parallel to the situation in the United States. In this, French presidents and prime ministers began to refine (and distinguish) their powers and responsibilities in the face of reliably divided governance, much as Congress and the president developed their own autonomous supporting bureaucracies in the United States to reflect that same recurrence. In this way, dominant informal arrangements began to reshape the underlying formal structures in both nations.

At this point, the search for parallels should probably stop, for in another key respect, involving the main dynamic to politics within the new political order, France actually resembled Canada more than the United States (and again, much more than Britain). In the new order, the job of injecting these new crosscutting issues into politics was actually played by splinter parties in France, as it was in Canada. In both countries, the established national parties preferred not to handle these countervailing issues, which did not, of course, sit neatly with their underlying social coalitions. Splinter parties then moved to capitalize on these issues, in the process injecting them into politics anyway. At that point, the major national parties had to work out a position on these emergent issues because they were now loose on the landscape. And that position was often roughly consensual between these two national parties (in Canada) or tendencies (in France), precisely because such issues tended to feature a dominant majority preference.

The West

Germany is unique among the G-7 nations in the way the benchmark events for this analysis, the end of World War II and the end of the Cold War, actually shaped the geographic boundaries—the physical definition—of the nation. The relationship between this change and change in the temporal boundaries of postwar eras and orders in German politics is, however, a good deal more complex than such a simple benchmarking might suggest. The focus of Germany's first postwar political era, an inescapable focus, involved the same two central considerations as in Japan, Italy, and, in a more uneven way, France. This focus was the need to create an entire governmental framework, along with the even more pressing need for economic life.

France, of course, consciously decided not to adopt major constitutional change in the immediate postwar years. For Germany (and Italy and Japan), that was never an option: a new governmental framework could look back and reclaim some elements from the past, but it still had to be created afresh. Early on, however, it became clear that this would—and could—be created for only part of the former Germany. The Soviet Union demanded a separate, nondemocratic East Germany in its zone of occupation. It was thus the new West Germany that would become a major member of the G-7 in the course of the Cold War years. Within its confines, the drafting and then the practical implementation of a new constitutional framework were essential. But it would be the economic rebuilding of this (partially new) nation that was the central substantive focus for politics during the first postwar era.

The political order within which this politics played out was characterized by a strong public bureaucracy, one that was allowed to continue from earlier years to address some of the immediate service needs of postwar society. Yet unlike the situation in France or especially Japan, where an established bureaucracy was an even larger element of the first postwar order, the associated elements of the political order in Germany caused this bureaucracy to contribute to a very different overall dynamic. In France, partial bureaucratic autonomy was encouraged by a fragmented party system plus governmental instability, albeit limited simultaneously by these same factors. In Japan, a greater bureaucratic autonomy was encouraged by the fact that a dominant party, though it ultimately emerged, was slow to do so; indeed, it grew initially under the tutelage of the central bureaucracy.

In Germany, by contrast, the main vehicle for connecting a rough national consensus on dominant issues with a strong and continuing bureaucracy, and thus the key intermediary organization of the first postwar order, was the Christian Democratic Party. And it came together very quickly as the lead element in postwar German politics. In fact, the Christian Democratic Party quickly became the main vehicle for implementing the new constitutional framework, the main vehicle for brokering economic arrangements aimed at national revitalization, and the main vehicle for making Germany a critical element in the Western alliance.

The predominance of the Christian Democrats was underpinned by a large remaining rural population and by substantial remaining confessional elements. These were joined, in a loose but effective alliance, by a reemerging business leadership, as they would be joined in Japan and as they were already joined in the United States of the same period. Party predominance was also implicitly underpinned—in reverse—by the residual Marxist heritage and the more militant trade union tradition of the main partisan opposition, the Social Democratic Party, which suffered additionally from the fact that many of its best areas had been hived off to create the new East Germany. All this was additionally reinforced by a generalized revulsion against the (extreme) ideologies of the past.

A comparatively high degree of social homogeneity, along with a middling level of governmental centralization, added the key bracketing characteristics for a politics that would rapidly come to be concentrated on the establishment of nationwide frameworks for negotiating new economic relationships. Moreover, this was to be a politics concentrated additionally and especially on the development of an intricate and encompassing system of direct labor-management relations, including nationwide works councils, annual and formalized attention to working conditions, and so on. Explicit debates over nationalization were not lacking; it was just that these had little programmatic outcome. Indeed, an immediate part of economic rebuilding was a structural liberalization to counteract the extreme integration of the late Nazi era. Likewise, explicit public debates over social insurance were not lacking, but they too came to little in programmatic terms. The Christian Democrats argued (successfully) that extended social welfare programs were too much of a luxury for the period. Instead, economic rebuilding remained the focus, and labor-management relations gave this focus its most direct expression.

The resulting political dynamic featured Christian Democratic dominance at the center of all this, both facilitated and personified for much of the first postwar era by the extended chancellorship of Konrad Adenauer, a predominant figure within a predominant party. Beyond Adenauer, and much more like Italy than like Japan among the former Axis powers, Germany had a substantial incipient corps of aspiring democratic politicians waiting for the resumption of postwar politics. Many of these became the key brokers for the Christian Democrats, brokering policy demands among the Lander, across the economy, and between voters and the bureaucracy, without serious risk of electoral displacement but also without great pressure to do more than revitalize a nation.

Historical hindsight contributes an air of inevitability to this first postwar order. How *could* something other than restarting a shattered economy have been the initial focus of postwar German politics? How could adjustments to frontline status in the Cold War not have been a major secondary focus? Indeed, given the options, how could the Christian Democratic Party not have been the main intermediary vehicle for expressing (and simultaneously shaping) these policy needs? And how could public wishes and a continuing bureaucracy—the latter could have been challenged by the Allies in principle, but maybe not in practice—not have underpinned the role of the Christian Democratic Union?

In that light, it is worth emphasizing the conditionality of even these seeming inevitables. Thus, although restarting the postwar economy was a priority in the United States as well, and even more so in Britain, it produced little change in order or era for the United States and produced a *fundamental* change in era, order, and resulting public policy for Britain. Likewise, the same general policy environment was not associated with the rise of a dominating Christian Democratic Party in postwar France; in Italy, where it was associated with a similar rise, the other elements of the political order did not give that party the same character or the same role to play. The theme, here, is one of *contingent* interactions.

In any case, as with so many other breaks between political eras among the G-7 nations, the break in this first postwar German era was underlined most forcefully by a shift in partisan control of government. But that shift was itself only a reflection—and culmination—of changes in the issue base for politics and in the structural elements that shaped politicking. Among political issues, successful economic regeneration, in the form of a genuine "economic miracle," was widely recognized by the late 1960s. Nevertheless, a short but sharp recession suggested that the boom was not endless and appeared to force economic and social welfare choices. In the same way, successful integration into the Western alliance had produced a sense of strategic security, or, rather, strategic stasis. This was punctuated by occasional stresses and testings in the Cold War, so that a widespread desire to find some way to move beyond this partially successful stasis was equally logical and equally evident.

From the perspective of key political structures, the break was even more insistent, thanks to a partisan change in their midst. An initial "grand coalition" of the Christian Democratic Union and the Social Democratic Party in 1966, itself an unprecedented event in postwar German politics, was followed in 1969 by an actual government based on the Social Democratic Party, with the Christian Democratic Union in opposition. In the immediate sense, this confirmed the arrival of the possibility of partisan alternation in government, and hence of the single greatest test (passed successfully) of the institutionalization of postwar constitutional arrangements. But together with a change in issue themes, it also signaled the likelihood that a new order, with different key supports, had arrived.

The new era began, as the third postwar era was to begin in France, with a simple expansion of policy possibilities—and hence possibilities for conflict—on established issue dimensions. The initial foreign policy consensus of the immediate postwar years, though never as total as in the United States or Britain, began to fray noticeably. But in Germany, the possibility of lessening tensions with the Soviet Union and thus of building bridges to the East was initially much more popular, so that the party urging a move away from the Cold War consensus, the Social Democrats, was not obviously moving into minority territory. In the same way, the initial postwar consensus on economic growth as the main social welfare "safety net" came under stress. Ironically, this consensus was challenged both by recognized success, which suggested the possibility of having more social welfare legislation, and by economic hesitation, which argued the apparent need for the same. Though here—very much like the situation in France and Canada at the beginning of their counterpart eras—the notion of moving toward a more generous welfare state was not obviously a minority preference when it was proposed.

Events would ultimately prove unkind to both possibilities. Developments in eastern Europe, with increasingly harsh Soviet responses, would make possibilities for accommodation and a more "easterly" posture look less promising and become less popular. Developments in the world economy—oil shocks, generalized stagflation—would make major social welfare reforms, after an initial burst of initiatives, much more difficult to offer without high associated costs. Seen the other way around, however, what these changes confirmed was that cultural and national issues had come to contribute an increasing share of the substantive backbone of the new political era, as they had in Canada and the United States, and as they would in France and Britain. For Germany, this did not mean that Social Democrat–led governments, in particular, could not produce liberalizing initiatives in areas such as abortion reform or education policy. They could, and they did. It just meant that the fundamental issue basis of the new era was incipiently different, a fact that would become inescapable as Europeanization, immigration, and then finally unification all appeared on the domestic political agenda.

There was inevitably a new political order associated with all this as well. Growing public divisions around the successor issues to those of the old order were the bedrock of this changed structure, except in the case of implementation of the basic constitutional framework, where a mature national consensus effectively took the issue out of politics. Yet a changing place for the bureaucracy—less the autonomous initiator of policy—was part and parcel of the same shift. The possibility of partisan alternation in government meant that a bureaucracy hewing to one party line risked setting itself up for reform when governments changed, whereas a bureaucracy distancing itself from either party was not going to drive government in a major way. All this only emphasized the centrality of the changed role of the Social Democratic Party to a new order, while focusing attention on the associated changes in the background of that party shift.

Within Germany, the long postwar economic boom had lessened the sharp edges of class lines while it reduced the possibility that an explicitly working-class party would ever again have the numbers to come to power on those terms alone. The successful implementation of a new democratic constitution also meant both that there was a reliable way to power if the Christian Democrats could be beaten electorally and that the Christian Democratic Union would otherwise remain the government indefinitely. This produced a debate within the Social Democratic Party throughout the 1950s over an appropriate party program and over shucking the increasingly unattractive Marxist overlay in the existing one. More consequentially (though not unrelated), it produced a reaching out to sections of the white-collar middle class—teachers and civil servants were two of the earliest targets—that might share some Left-leaning ideological values and might contribute the numbers necessary to move beyond the old blue-collar base.

All these elements have evident parallels with the situation of the Socialists in France. The French Socialists entered government much earlier in the postwar period but took considerably longer to become a government by themselves. Nevertheless, the stages of development on the way to that outcome—economic boom, blurred class lines, internal party debate, outreach to the liberal middle class—were quite similar. They were also related to the situation of the Socialists in Italy, though the parallels had inherent limitations, in that differences in other elements of the political order meant that the Italian Socialists would never become an obvious replacement for the Christian Democrats. The situation differed, just as strongly, from the Canadian and Japanese contexts, where the socialist party was inherently circumscribed, in permanent opposition. It differed from the American context, where there was no socialist party to "tame." And it differed from the situation in Britain, where the Labour Party actually came to power early and thus implemented huge parts of the program common to democratic socialist parties at the time.

In any case, the result in Germany was to confirm a second postwar order. The same result would evolve rapidly into a German incarnation (or at least a clear German echo) of divided governance as a more comprehensive summary notion. Once again, this would feature extended intervals of superficial split partisan control in the institutions of national government. Yet once again, it would be the presence of crosscutting issue preferences rather than this split partisanship that was particularly diagnostic. Moreover, in the German case and unlike that of the United States or France, it was not so much the partisan balance across governmental institutions as the coalitional composition of governments of the day that gave divided governance a distinctive further twist.

The policy-making institutions of German government were less inherently conducive to split partisan control than were those of the United States or France, having no independently elected executive to embody one majority against another. Conversely, they were more conducive than those of Canada or Britain, and indeed, for eighteen of the twenty-six years of the second postwar era to date, the party controlling the lower house, the Bundestag—and hence the chancellorship—did not reliably control the upper house, the Bundesrat. Nevertheless, this was not a central operational feature of the second postwar order. Instead, the larger part of what gave a distinctively German cast to this incarnation of divided governance was the coalitional structure of national governments during this second era. The key to appreciating this, in turn, was a focus on the critical role within these coalitions of the small Free Democratic Party.

In fact, the Social Democratic government at the beginning of this era, as well as the Christian Democratic government that returned to succeed it, were actually *coalitions* with these (same) Free Democrats. More than anything else, it was this coalitional arrangement that gave a national expression to the crosscutting impact of cultural-national issues. Said differently, in Germany, the Social Democrats offered the moderate Left on both economic-welfare and cultural-national issues. The Christian Democrats offered the moderate Right on both. And the Free Democrats leaned left on cultural-national issues, right on economic-welfare concerns. They were thus potential coalition partners for either major party, depending, as it turned out, on which element of crosscutting preferences was most worrisome to the general public at a given time.

In this role, the Free Democrats could—and did—give expression to public preferences for greater liberality on cultural-national policies when they broke with the Christian Democratic Union and joined in coalition with the Social Democratic Party, while providing reassurance that the Social Democrats would not take "dangerous" risks on economic-welfare matters. Then they were the perfect agent when they broke subsequently with the Social Democrats and joined in coalition with the Christian Democratic Union to express public preferences for greater caution on economic and welfare issues, while reassuring the general public that the Christian Democrats would not do "extreme" things on cultural and national concerns.

In the abstract, this still left ideological space for a party offering the alternative combination to that of the Free Democrats—that is, left on economic-welfare issues, right on cultural-national affairs. In practice, this proved to be a problematic space in most G-7 nations during the postwar years. In Britain, for example, it was filled for a short time by the Social Democratic Party, which was then merged away. In the United States, Canada, and France, major parties flirted intermittently with this combination but reliably withdrew. In Germany, the space remained empty, but for nationally peculiar reasons. In one sense, it was the Communists who most obviously offered this combination. Yet the West German Communist Party was marginalized early, and the East German version was profoundly outside any Western pattern of divided governance, at least until unification brought a remnant back into the total system as the Party of Democratic Socialism.

In any case, this order (and its era) lasted well into the 1980s, when the intensification of cultural-national issues, coupled with a major change in the geographic boundaries of the nation itself, raised the possibility of a third postwar political era for Germany. The reintegration of the pieces divided by the Allies at the end of World War II would have raised this possibility in an unavoidably symbolic way. But the process of unification—the implementation of democratic governmental institutions and the extension of free-market economics—generated most of the associated day-to-day issues of politics. Concerns about immigration, nationality, and citizenship were already "in the air" before the reality of unification, and these concerns were almost inevitably associated with the related drive toward Europeanization—again predating unification and again given greater intensity and complexity by it.

It is more difficult to say with certainty, without the benefit of hindsight, what the specific elements of an associated new political order would be, though a different general dynamic may already be perceptible. In this, the old coalitional patterns are less automatic, and the two main parties are less operationally dominant. The role of splinter parties—the Free Democrats, but now also the Greens, perhaps the Party of Democratic Socialism, and potentially even the Republicans—is to raise issues, not unlike the Canadian situation. The role of the two major parties is then to work out a roughly consensual response, not unlike the Canadian and French situations. Such a dynamic may reflect the structures of a third political era for postwar Germany, or it may reflect only the "growing pains" from merging the former East Germany into the second era. All that can safely be said in the mid-1990s is that even the serious possibility of a third postwar German political era underlines the open-endedness of political evolution and political history.

Outliers

No sequence is self-evidently right for introducing the postwar politics of the G-7 nations. Yet Japan and Italy, which complete the sequence here, share one huge formal similarity. They were the last two nations within this collectivity to secure a major benchmark in the institutionalization of democratic politics, namely, the alternation of partisan control within government and thus the ability to relegate the previous governing party (or coalition) to full opposition status. Indeed, these last two G-7 nations also share the fact that this development required more than the entire Cold War period to accomplish, though they then accomplished it within months of each other.

More important for our purposes and for both nations, the attainment of this benchmark appeared to guarantee a new political era and order in a way that even conflict over national identity in Canada or stresses from national unification in Germany did not. For Italy, this possibility of a shift in the postwar pattern of politics had been evidently (if gradually) building, to the point of inviting speculation about its eventual contours. But for Japan, the shift seemed both seismic and unprecedented. Admittedly, hindsight suggests that there was evidence of this same possibility in Japan. Yet incipient portents had surfaced intermittently before, without any subsequent effect, so the wise analyst did not expect any given product. Accordingly, when the change arrived, a short time before its counterpart in Italy, it seemed all the more imposing.

The historical and institutional backdrop to this change, in the form of the first postwar political era in Japan, was best isolated not so much by its underlying issue content as by the structural character of its political order. Japan shared with all the G-7 nations a central focus on restarting the postwar economy in these years. Yet its first postwar era was distinguished among them by the degree of effective concentration on this goal, along with the degree to which other issues, associated elsewhere with this same goal, were effectively squeezed out. It is the character of the underlying political order that best explains this concentration. And it is the centrality—

really the essential dominance—of the central government bureaucracy that is at the core of that concentrated focus on the economic task.

With hindsight, it is hard to imagine a situation more conducive to a political order centered on a national bureaucracy—not on policy preferences, not on societal cleavages, not on political parties—than that of postwar Japan. This was, to begin with, a deeply traditionalistic society without a deeply rooted democratic experience, one where established leaderships were accepted but where policy making by open and public conflict was not. Nevertheless, the situation was much exaggerated by the way the Allies purged most of the available alternative elites—the military leadership, of course, but also the wartime political elite and even, initially, the leaders of major industrial combines—removing them as an option.

There was no obvious "resistance" leadership waiting to fill the void, with the partial exception of antisystem organizations that were not going to be acceptable to the occupying forces. There was no strong party system waiting to be reinvigorated, to organize issue conflicts and discipline the central bureaucracy. And in fact, the electoral system, a distinctive multimember, single-vote arrangement, would militate against the rapid appearance of either, by fostering a highly personalistic politics of social and economic notables.

Some of the existing issues associated with this first postwar political order were not so different from those in the other G-7 nations, especially Germany and Italy. An operational framework for government was necessary; restarting the national economy was all the more so. Even more than in Germany, however, which provided the closest analog, the diagnostic fact about postwar Japanese politics was that these underlying and consensual concerns went no further. That is, they were not joined by further economic and social welfare initiatives on the proper distribution of wealth in society and on the provision of appropriate social welfare services.

The central bureaucracy was not concerned with those matters at the start. Neither were the great industrial combines, which became influential as the postwar economic recovery began to happen. Nor, until its own predominance seemed threatened, was the main political party, the Liberal Democratic Party (LDP), which would come to form the third coordinate element in this triumvirate. That left all these other associated themes, in what was a cluster of economic and welfare issues in Britain, the United States, Canada, and France, to be raised by the most militant trade unions and by arguably antisystem parties.

Such a combination produced a great deal of surface conflict in the immediate postwar years, but it would not produce much actual public policy. Said differently, in the absence of widespread demand for an extended welfare state at the social base for politics, in the absence of an immediately dominant party or even party system institutionalizing economic-welfare conflict, and in the presence of a strong and continuing governmental bureaucracy with a new and at least potentially consensual "mission," the dominance of this bureaucracy was sufficient not just to describe a postwar political order but also to constrict its issue content more than in any of the other G-7 nations.

There was one giant challenge to this bureaucratic dominance, around the ratification of the Security Treaty with the United States in 1960. In this sense, the first major division over an appropriate response to the bipolar world of the Cold War came roughly at the same time as that issue was arising in Canada, and earlier than it arose in the United States, Britain, or Germany. In practice, however, the strength of the issue's associated order—almost a "machine," in the classic American sense—was sufficient to turn this challenge aside. In this, a central bureaucracy fostering economic growth helped rapidly expanding corporate businesses to prosper, which then provided substantial campaign contributions to a gradually strengthening dominant party (the LDP), in order to elect a parliamentary majority that could underpin the continuing policy initiatives of the bureaucracy. The resulting triumph was destined to last for another decade.

But even the strongest political order could not sustain its era indefinitely, in the face of issue evolution and social change. Japan might remain an outlier in the extent to which the component parts of a shift appeared in effectively glacial fashion. Nevertheless, the break between eras, even in Japan, was clear enough when it came. This break arrived in the early 1970s, most specifically with the arrival of the Tanaka government in 1973. This time, it was the issue focus of a new government of the day that really confirmed the arrival of a second postwar era. Again, it was the (evolving) nature of background social factors that was most crucial to this change, and change still achieved expression through a political dynamic that was distinctively Japanese.

From the substantive side, it was noteworthy that there was still no single precipitating issue or crisis, no crystallizing conflict, that led to a new political era. There was general social change, and there was personal incentive to capitalize on (and thus crystallize) it, but that was all. From the structural side, this change was also noteworthy—perhaps more than in any of the other G-7 nations, except Italy—for the degree to which all the key elements of the new order would have been easily recognizable from the old. They were distinguishable; indeed, they were obviously sufficient to generate a new order; but they were also successors to the same small set of elements, critically reshuffled.

In substantive terms, what the Tanaka government did was to bring social welfare issues as they would have been recognized elsewhere—old-age pensions, diverse social services, along with legal protections for both— onto the agenda of government generally. Previously, these had been the province of the opposition, especially the Socialists. What Tanaka really did, then, was to seize on them as a way to halt erosion of support for the LDP, while shifting the focus of these concerns away from labor and labor-management relations and toward care of the elderly and of women with children.

Prosperity appeared to make these changes increasingly possible. Social shifts—urbanization, education, geographic and occupational mobility— appeared to make them increasingly necessary. In structural terms, a rural society had become urban and was on its way to being suburban, with all the changes that this implied in, for example, the ability of the extended family to provide "social welfare." However, the joining of these specific substantive gambits with those grand background forces still occurred by way of a political dynamic that was distinctively Japanese. Said differently, if these background shifts implicitly encouraged conflict over social welfare, actual reform was still produced out of explicit factional conflicts within the increasingly dominant LDP. New issues became, in effect, a way for one or another factional leader to distinguish and then sustain himself, along with his faction.

In this dynamic, what was most obviously changed was the balance between a central bureaucracy and a dominant party. With a limited welfare state and a focus on economic development and foreign trade, the bureaucracy had remained relatively united—and relatively unchanged. What changed around it was the growing dominance of one party, the LDP. The initial tutelage of the bureaucracy, even in this, was symbolized by the key role of bureaucrats-turned-politicians in making it happen. The coming of the Tanaka government could thus symbolize the shift in personal terms as well, since Tanaka was not only not a former bureaucrat but also a self-made businessman with an active distaste for the bureaucracy.

In any case, by the late 1960s, the pattern of one clearly dominant party, facing a set of smaller (fragmented) opposition parties, was established. So was the pattern of relatively stable factional divisions within that party, competing behind the scenes for influence within government. This was hardly sufficient to remove the bureaucracy from a political role. Its major business clientele would not have wanted that, and a dominant party was certainly not averse to using the bureaucracy to pursue policies and politics. It was, however, gradually sufficient to remix the direction of influence. In this second postwar political order, the symbiosis among these three elements shifted such that corporate support for LDP politicians helped them institutionalize their actions and influence the governing coalition, which then used the bureaucracy to reward supporters and attempt to sustain factional fortunes.

Factional conflict within the LDP thus became the central political dynamic. By contrast, the social coalitions sustaining this dynamic remained relatively unchanged. At bottom, the earlier "marriage of iron and rice," a coalition between corporate business and the rural areas, continued into the second political era. It was, however, increasingly and crucially dependent, despite these other social changes, on malapportionment of seats in the Diet, favoring rural areas, and on the peculiar nature of party competition for these seats, where multimember districts encouraged the individual factions of the LDP to pour personal benefits into husbanding favorable districts.

Such a coalition within the LDP (of corporate business and rural residents) was not in itself unusual among the G-7 nations. Roughly similar alliances had characterized the social base for the Republicans in the United States, the Conservatives in Britain, and the Christian Democrats in Germany and Italy in the first postwar era in each of these nations. Yet this had remained a secondary aspect of the structure of postwar politics in the United States and Britain, while France, in keeping with the rest of its political order, had fragmented these social elements as well. Only Canada had offered no serious echoes of such a coalition, actually pitting its rural elements against its corporate sector.

More consequential for all these nations, and more distinguishing for Japan, was the evolution of this implicit alliance. Because rural areas were reliably in decline, the crucial question was whether the party that most directly and practically gave the coalition its expression could successfully substitute a growing middle class for this declining rural sector. In Germany, the transition occurred in apparently seamless fashion. In the United States and Britain, it actually allowed the Republicans and especially the Conservatives to return to power and begin to set the policy agenda. In France, a newly consolidated conservative tendency was also symbiotically successful at this maneuver, as part of a new order congealing around new constitutional arrangements.

That left Canada, where ethnocultural conflict intensified before such a coalition could ever be constructed, along with Italy and Japan, where the old coalitions were largely just rebalanced. In the kind of similarity that would increasingly link two otherwise disparate nations, both Italy and Japan continued to feature the same underlying coalition as a pillar of the second postwar order, albeit with gradually intensifying difficulties. As a result, the breakup of this coalition and the breakup of the old order were probably destined to be intertwined. Seen one way, it was the substitution of a burgeoning middle class for the older rural elements that marked the transition to a third postwar order in these countries. Seen another way, this substitution was in fact essential to breaking up the second order, and its delay (by comparison to other G-7 nations) was why the old order managed to last so long.

Only in Japan was all this tied additionally and so strongly to formal malapportionment. Nevertheless, a politics based on concrete favors for the districts, one largely conducted in an individualized and private manner, had as one by-product a continual if intermittent series of major financial scandals. Their very continuity left analysts unprepared when these escalated to interact with widespread public discontent about the character of politics generally, in a way that signaled an end to this second postwar era. Arriving only in the spring of 1993, the third great postwar era in Japanese politics cannot, in principle, be described in any definitive way. Yet it is already so different as to leave little room for argument about the presence of a break point.

The inescapable structural signal of this break was the end of LDP hegemony and the coming to power of a new, multiparty, anti-LDP coalition. This coalition and its first successor were themselves short-lived, but even the return of the LDP to government did not signal a return to the old order—coming, as it did, in coalition with its longtime postwar opponent, the Japanese Socialists. None of this change contained a safe prediction of the contours of a new political order, but the differences remained clear enough. There were new and serious challengers within the party system;

there were factions of the LDP spinning off into additional parties (and more threatening to do so); there were factions aspiring to lead a reform movement within that (still-largest) party as well.

Perhaps surprisingly, especially in Japan, the issue contents of a third postwar era actually began to clarify earlier, at least in general terms, than did its structural contours. First, issues involving a more effective democracy—issues of democratic responsiveness in Japan—had been implicitly associated with the shift to a second postwar era and had resurfaced with every subsequent scandal along the way. In the third era, however, they produced not just a serious reform drive aimed at political finance and corruption but also serious reform conflict over the electoral system that had been so central to the first and second postwar orders.

Next, issues involving the place of the nation in world politics, and thus the place of foreign affairs in Japanese domestic politics, had been growing during the second era. Then, independent shifts in American policy, from containment through currency, had necessitated growing policy responses. Now, with the Cold War over, a mature and wealthy Japan was under broad international pressure to take a more active role in world affairs in its aftermath, financially but even militarily, and this inevitably raised social and constitutional issues within the nation.

Third—and on the back burner, but hardly likely to go away—were new incarnations of the old economic and social welfare concerns. Many of these were fueled by an apparent desire to shift the nature of domestic life away from the austerity of postwar recovery and toward a more openly consumer-oriented lifestyle. More seemed destined to receive emphasis from the dramatic aging of the Japanese population as a whole: demography seemed likely to become destiny earlier in Japan than in any of the other G-7 nations.

There were in Japan even incipient indications of the issue cross-pressures that characterized most of the other G-7 nations, pitting economic-welfare issues (and associated economic-welfare coalitions) against cultural-national issues (and the associated coalitions there). Thus, for example, in a new era when different governing coalitions were possible, basic social welfare issues featured the Liberal Democrats and the old-line Socialists at opposite ends of the ideological spectrum. Yet basic issues of procedural reform actually united those two parties—the winner and the main opposition from the old order—against most of the others, which could only benefit from deliberate change in the rules of the contest.

There remained one outstanding difference in the character of Japanese politics. All the other G-7 nations, to one degree or another, had moved from a politics of local and regional brokerage to one of national, even plebiscitary, policy combat. Many of the facilitating elements for such a shift were present in Japan as well. But this was the one counterpart trend that had clearly not been automatically registered with the end of ritualized LDP dominance. Or at least, the arrangements that followed in its immediate wake were all characterized—that is, managed—by politicians acting in a very old-fashioned, brokerage mode. Electoral reapportionment combined with financial reform might end this historical continuity too. But they did not automatically and immediately do so in the change from a second to a third postwar era.

The Group of Seven

Italy completes the reintroduction of the entire G-7, along with the partial comparisons produced by reintroducing them one by one. Some of the elements of Italian postwar politics distinguish Italy from any of the other G-7 nations: a Communist Party that remained a serious domestic player throughout all these years, for example, plus a church hierarchy with a partisan role unrivaled in the other six. Some of the elements of Italian postwar politics are likewise common to each of the others: metropolitan change, from rural to urban to suburban, for example, or the rising role of courts in the political process. Yet as a composite, in direct bilateral comparison, Italy began its postwar politics not like the other (former) Axis powers of Germany and Japan but like France.

These two countries were in fact "united" by having deeply divided societies, along lines of cleavage stretching back well before the Second World War: Left-Right, clerical-secular, urban-rural, and regional as well. France possessed a prewar party system reflecting these cleavages, one that could be reflated directly; for Italy, it had been a much longer time since prewar democratic politics. Yet both had serious resistance figures, with a variety of ideologies, to plug immediately into postwar politicking. And both would plug them into governmental structures that were likewise extremely similar at first: electoral arrangements enshrining full-blown proportionality, leading to policy-making arrangements embodying fully realized notions of parliamentary government.

The Italian context added distinctive twists even here. For example, although Italy featured a number of deep and serious social cleavages, there was, at least in the earlier postwar years, a clear social plurality in a self-consciously Catholic constituency. This became, in turn, the bedrock for a single predominant party, the Christian Democratic Party, facing a fragmented opposition—a pattern foreshadowing subsequent similarities to postwar Japan rather than France. Moreover, the dominance of that party was effectively secured, even as its plurality status declined, by the fact that its largest single opponent was the Communist Party.

The structures of this first order—this social base, these intermediaries, and this set of governmental institutions—were, as ever, intimately connected to the issues contributing its associated political era. But for Italy, again like Japan, the story of this first postwar era is much more the influence of structures than the substance of issues. Despite that, there were obvious and central themes to postwar policy conflict, in economic regeneration and democratic institutionalism. And there were obvious public ructions over a posture toward the emerging Cold War, although the practical effect of these latter conflicts would brand what would otherwise become a comparatively national and accommodating Communist Party as an impossible member for any governing coalition.

Yet at that point, the issue content of the first postwar era was essentially completed. There would be further surface disputes over the social welfare programs that were implemented comprehensively in Britain and piecemeal in the United States and Canada, as well as over the economic planning programs that received major attention in Germany, France, and Japan. Yet Italy would feature few major policy initiatives in these realms, so that what resulted was, in effect, a "welfare state by default." The governmental health service of the fascist era was retained, as were institutional devices, including prior nationalization, for coordinating major sectors of the economy. But Christian Democratic policy ran largely in the opposite direction.

The political dynamic to this first postwar era was thus easily described. The numerical dominance of the Christian Democratic Party, which would have made it central to governmental formation in any case, was powerfully reinforced by the second-competitor status of a party that could not enter government, the Communists. This predominance was further reinforced—quickly cemented—through a kind of patronage dominance. A single, preponderant Christian Democratic Party would use the resources of government to buttress its electoral support across the country. In this, it benefited initially from an implicit alliance between rural areas, with their local notables as leaders, and the more diffuse population more directly concerned with economic regeneration, with corporate business as its implicit standard-bearers.

By the 1950s, what emerged was more akin to the Japanese "machine politics" of a somewhat later time than to the French politics of the same period. This Italian version of a "coalition of iron and rice" at the grass roots was reflected in a dominant party in governmental formulation, which could use active public works from one side and conservative economic policies from the other to reward the elements of its coalition, which could then provide reliable votes and cash contributions to sustain party control of government, and so on. What was noticeably lacking from the Japanese or French comparison was the directive role of a central bureaucracy. The Italian version had never been professionalized and autonomous, and it quickly became a kind of grand patronage resource for the Christian Democrats and, ultimately, for a much broader array of parties, a fact that lessened its directional prospects even further.

There had actually been a point—one political moment—when all this might have been different. Or at least, there had been a serious early effort to reform the basic electoral system, destined to be a crucial underpinning to both the first and the second postwar orders in Italy. This point gains historical interest because it was parallel to the change that accompanied the breakup of the first order in France. It gains analytic interest because not just France but also Germany was deliberately forced to address the issue. Germany and Italy had in fact faced very similar stimuli in designing postwar institutional arrangements in this realm. In Italy, an additionally elaborated system of proportional representation was seen as a natural move against the structures of the fascist era, one more effort to ensure that it could not happen again. In Germany, carefully calculated limits to proportional representation were viewed as a way to guard against the failures of the Weimar Republic, which had led to fascism there.

In any case, Alcide De Gasperi, who formed the first eleven postwar governments in Italy, made a serious effort to change the electoral system of the country in a more majoritarian direction. When he failed, the existing system went on to underpin both the first and the second postwar political orders. What this system implied was an ostensibly precise reflection not just of party support but of factional support within parties, and especially within the Christian Democrats. And what that encouraged was a political dynamic focused on incremental, incessant elite bargaining, a dynamic that would be fundamentally interrupted—though perhaps even then not swept away—by the third postwar era.

All this did not imply that the first postwar era was capable of sustaining itself indefinitely, and that era drew more or less naturally to a close. In policy terms, the Christian Democrats could not govern forever on the issue of implementing democracy. Nor could they do so on the virtues of cementing Italy to the Western alliance. Nor, in fact, could they do so with simple economic recovery, though the continued presence of the Communists as a major opposition force helped with all three. Once all these had happened, however, there was only declining sustenance in serving as their guarantor.

Likewise in structural terms, the Christian Democrats might continue to monopolize the formation of national governments, but society itself was changing rapidly around these governments. By the early 1960s, economic growth had already created much more of a modern, industrial, urban, integrated society, especially in the North, with two pointed effects. In one, Italians were demanding more of the welfare-state programs that went with those social arrangements in most (not all) other G-7 nations. In the other, the electoral base of the Christian Democrats was being gradually but ineluctably eroded, along with the rural base of the nation as a whole.

Perhaps more than with any other G-7 nation, there was room for argument about when these general developments produced a distinctively different (second) postwar era, though the argument is only between the obvious initial break point and the point when its evolution had become inescapable. The former was 1963, when the Socialist Party first entered government. The latter was 1974, when minority Christian Democratic governments returned and when Communist entry into government seemed a possibility. Yet in this, the more important fact remains that the choice was largely one of deciding how far issue evolution and structural shift had to go before they signaled the indisputable break. In that sense, both are of a piece.

The entry of the Socialists into government in 1963 was meant to shore up Christian Democratic dominance by adding an urban working-class component to it—ideally making the party more acceptable to such voters but at least keeping a substantial share of them cemented into the government of the day. From the other side, the "price" of adding the Socialists to the coalition was twofold. First, there was a set of policy responses to increasingly insistent social welfare demands in realms such as pension policy and industrial relations. And second, there was expanded access to the patronage resources of national government to institutionalize a Socialist Party presence in power, albeit simultaneously augmenting the demands on these resources and intensifying the bargaining over them.

On the one hand, then, the Italian Socialists actually both moderated and entered the government earlier than their counterparts in Germany or Japan. On the other hand (and here, much more like Japan than like Germany or especially France), they would never enter government as the governing alternative. They entered only as part of a coalition whose dominant member was another party. The continued success of the Italian Communists was also part of this story. They were not dominated electorally by the Socialists, as in Germany, France, or Japan. Indeed, successful administration of major municipalities across Italy actually gave governing credentials (and patronage resources) to the Communists too.

By this time, the earlier postwar analogy with French politics had effectively dissipated. Or rather, France had terminated the comparison with a new political era built around strikingly different constitutional arrangements, giving rise to a political dynamic that was to feature the serious possibility of partisan alternations in the actual control of national government. In the aftermath, politics in Italy came to look not so much like its European counterparts but like politics in Japan. Electoral arrangements encouraging divisible exchange, the continued absence of serious partisan alternatives, a consequent political dynamic featuring unpredictable adaptations and idiosyncratic "safety valves," and an ultimate crash in the 1990s united these two countries, whose citizens seem most unlikely to compare themselves with each other.

The issue contents of this second Italian era were not as different from those in most other G-7 nations as this comparison of political orders might suggest. The initial issue emphases of the new political era on economic-welfare matters were joined quickly by cultural-national concerns, with the latter growing gradually more insistent as this second era aged, a trend not unfamiliar in the other G-7 countries. In this, Italy went on to offer analogs to the cultural issues that would have been widely recognized elsewhere, such as abortion, crime and punishment, and the role of nuclear power. It also offered items more inherently tied to Italian society, such as divorce or the role of religious (that is, Catholic) teaching in the public schools. And it included, of course, basic anticorruption thrusts, which became more insistent as the era aged but actually surfaced relatively early (if ineffectually) within it.

The order associated with this new political era had two central parts that were superficially distinctive but practically connected, even integral. To say the same thing more forcefully: the ability of old-fashioned, brokerage-style Italian politicians to fashion a political dynamic amidst these crosscutting issue pressures and across these very different structural elements is the major explanation for why the resulting order could last a remarkable thirty years. One of its main elements was thus the structure of bargaining at its governmental core. The other was an evolving set of institutionalized "safety valves" to prod those negotiators—and to bypass them when they could not be prodded.

At the center of this order, a still-dominant Christian Democratic Party engaged in increasingly stylized negotiations over governments of the day, shaped by certain major and recurring structural constraints. The deepest of these was self-imposed as the defining aspect of Christian Democracy: a refusal to add either Communists or neofascists explicitly to the government. Within the ideological space that remained, elections served largely as a way to "keep score," though governments actually rose and fell much more rapidly than elections came and went. Old social loyalties were still sufficient to guarantee only lesser movements in the vote in an electoral system that was designed not to amplify small shifts. What such shifts did, instead, was to register comparative adjustments among the increasingly institutionalized factions within the parties, as well as comparative adjustments among those parties.

Because governing coalitions had to be built across the broad middle of economic-welfare issues, excluding the far Left and the far Right, such coalitions were particularly incapacitated by cultural-national issues, which crosscut these other concerns and often left no residual majority. This situation was serious enough even at the beginning of this second postwar era, when the overall decline of the Christian Democrats, the simultaneous rise of their factions, and the inescapability of the Socialists had already imposed severe limits on policy responses to crosscutting issues. Indeed, subsequent efforts at keeping policy focused on economic-welfare matters, especially in the realm of pensions and retirement benefits, would come back to haunt policy makers in the third postwar era. In short order, however, the underlying situation—the presence of strong but crosscutting issue preferences in the general public—would demand additional policy outlets.

Had these not been forthcoming, they might well have consigned this era to the status of an afterword on the first postwar period.

These mechanisms were, however, found. One such mechanism was simple public protest, especially in the late 1960s and early 1970s. Protest demonstrations could force particular issues into the negotiations over cabinet formation, though they were less effective as a device for policy resolution, not least because they made these negotiations more intricate and their coalitions more fragile. A second such mechanism was old-fashioned protest voting. And here, the early moderation of the Italian Communists, making them an indigenously Italian (rather than a sub-Soviet) party, coupled with their continuing exclusion from government, made them the perfect vehicle for protest on cultural issues, where they offered the secular and libertarian side. Especially in the mid-1970s, this helped explain their apparent rise in public support.

A final and more curious response, becoming more and more common as this second order aged, was to turn to another aspect of the formal constitution and use it in a new way, a way dependent on the particular forces loose in national politics at the time. This device was the referendum, a legacy of American influence in the framing of the postwar constitution. It was invigorated and increasingly pressed into service in this second postwar era, especially to address cultural-national issues—the very ones that either split the governing coalition (on clerical-secular lines, for example) or united the governing coalition in opposition to procedural reform, which was then tackled via referendum.

This arrangement, this era and its order, appeared to be living on borrowed time for many of its later years, unlike its Japanese counterpart, which appeared capable of sustaining itself a good deal longer. Both, however, came apart within a year of each other, and in dramatic fashion. In Japan, the superficial crises precipitating the breakup involved scandals leaked by competing politicians and then amplified by the press. In Italy, similar scandals were unearthed by the magistrates instead, in yet another instance of the invigoration and refocusing of an element of the written constitution, which had remained formally the same throughout the postwar years.

A new generation of judges, less knit into the evolving arrangements of the second postwar era, turned first to judicial reforms aimed at combating the influence of the Mafia in Italian politics, where reform had substantial support even among established party politicians. When they refocused these newly energized devices on political corruption more generally, the old order indeed proved to have been living on borrowed time and rapidly unraveled. Nevertheless, underneath the dramatic surface scandals that led most directly to this unraveling was sweeping social change, along with increasingly insistent issues of public policy that could not be effectively addressed by an entrenched "machine."

A society as radically transformed as any (except possibly Japan), Italy was now urban rather than rural; educated rather than ignorant; middle class rather than peasant, baronial, or blue collar; even secular rather than sacred. More to the practical point, members of the growth areas within each aspect of this change were increasingly distressed not just at the character of Italian politics but also at their own exclusion from governmental influence. Simultaneously, the social divisions that had once been buttressed by an organizational network divided along subcultural lines and focused on peculiarly subcultural parties, to help guarantee a nearly automatic vote, were in strong decline as well.

It may be that no system of patronage disbursements would have been sufficient to keep most policy issues out of politics and to hold a national coalition together through brokerage under such changed conditions. In any case, in 1994, in the midst of an apparently unending series of corruption scandals coupled with an internal war with the Mafia—the latter adding insult to injury for members of the most rapidly changing sectors of society—the old order broke apart in spectacular fashion. There was a series of electoral and finance reforms, aimed at ending the contribution of proportionality and of raw cash to the maintenance of the old order; there was the promise of more to come. A remarkable share of national political figures from the recent past ended up either in prison or under indictment for politically related crimes. Indeed, the Christian Democrats and the Socialists, the dominant party and its lead support for thirty years, looked likely to disappear as a consequence.

All this was convincing evidence of the end of an era. It was much less reliable in indicating the structure of a successor. New bodies contested the election of 1994, and new coalitions formed after it. Yet the latter still appeared unreliable as a guide, for example, to the specific intermediaries that might come to structure Italian politics. Indeed, the campaign itself—populist and only loosely brokered, featuring direct appeals to the potential electorate on grounds of embodying general public values—looked increasingly similar to an American or Canadian or even a German, French, or British counterpart, without recasting Italian politics definitively in one or another of those national modes.

CHAPTER TEN

What Is the American Way?
Four Themes in Search of Their Next Incarnation

American exceptionalism, summarized, is the notion that the United States was created differently, developed differently, and thus has to be *understood* differently, essentially on its own terms and within its own context. Exceptionalism has, in truth, joined that handful of concepts that attempt to characterize a society as a whole, and this fact alone surely gives arguments involving the concept—arguments over the essential elements of distinctiveness in Japanese society or French society or that of any other chosen country—a certain intellectual intensity. Yet in the beginning, there was *American* exceptionalism, and because the notion crystallized there first, and especially because the phenomena connected with it offered an apparently inescapable challenge to broad descriptions of societal developments elsewhere, the American version has proved most able to stimulate continuing debate.

As is often the case, the notions underlying a putative American exceptionalism—a sense of critical distinctiveness in political, economic, religious, or cultural life—predated the creation of a summarizing term. Nevertheless, when that term was ultimately created, to assemble and highlight the existing alleged elements of the American difference, its creation appeared only to fuel the argument—from the convinced and the skeptical, the foreign and the domestic, even the admiring and the denigrating—about the precise critical elements of a distinctively American model and about their continuing reality. So, what is the American model? What has happened to this model during, specifically, the last thirty years? What is, finally and in that light, the apparent fate of American exceptionalism?

Populism, Individualism, Democratization, and Market-Making

To cut directly to the chase, four themes appear central to any answer: populism and individualism at the personal level, democratization and market-making at the institutional level. These themes surface across a remarkable array of social sectors. They have surfaced across the full range of national history. As a result, whether or not they sum up to an American exceptionalism, they appear to constitute the American model, and they are thus likely to be integral to the next incarnation of that model, if and when someone stops to inquire about the fate of American exceptionalism another generation down the road.

At the start, then, it seems necessary to set these notions out, very concisely, in the abstract. It then seems even more necessary to plunge them back into specific social realms—into government, of course, but also into economics, religion, culture, education, and public policy. Accordingly, in the abstract, with numerous concrete referents to follow, four definitions must begin the analysis.

On the personal level, *populism* is the doctrine that all members of society should be conceived as social equals, quite apart from any circumstances of birth or achievement. This implies that collective public life, including public activities in the widest sense and not just politics and government, should reflect the social *style*—the operational values—of modal members of society.

Individualism is the doctrine that the single and independent members of that society ought to have a right to construct their personal lives according to their own (single and independent) preferences. This implies a collective social life that is effectively an aggregate of these preferences, or of accommodations among them.

On the institutional level, *democratization* is the notion that major social institutions (again in the widest sense) should be run so as to be directly responsive to the wishes of their (often varied and various) publics. This ordinarily implies structural mechanisms for collective decision making, ranging from open participation to arrangements for majority voting, that aspire to guarantee such responsiveness.

Finally, *market-making* is the notion that organized alternatives—in products and services, of course, but also in occupations, entertainments, and even lifestyles—ought to appear or disappear as there is (or is not) sufficient demand to sustain them. This includes the further presumption that a constant change in the menu of these available alternatives (by way of marketplaces, broadly conceived) is itself a further, desirable goal.

Before looking for the presence of these organizing notions in a variety of social realms, and thus defining them much more effectively in context, it is again worth noting that each of these pairs of concepts is usually treated, in the abstract, as constituting pairs of *opposites*. That is, it is more common to emphasize populism *versus* individualism, democratization *versus* market-making, and thus to portray these abstract descriptions as ends of a continuum, not as simultaneous characteristics. If there is something additionally distinctive about American life in these terms, it is that such frequently antithetical concepts can in practice be made compatible.

The most definitionally straightforward way to search for this compatibility might be to begin with the realms of government and economics, from which the basic names for the four key integrating concepts derive. Conversely, for that very reason, it may be more convincing to use a different realm to inaugurate the survey—for example, the realm of religious life—since neither populism nor individualism, neither democratization nor market-making, are usually associated with it. Moreover, among these four concepts, market-making may provide the best introductory example, precisely because it is so apparently alien to sacred discourse. Yet it is surely convention and inertia that separate even this notion from the religious realm, at least in the United States, since there may be no more extended, no more varied or more deliberately promotional religious marketplace anywhere in the world.

The fundamental variety essential to such a marketplace includes, of course, not just a major presence for the Protestant, Catholic, and Jewish faiths in the large. It extends, especially within the single largest category of these, Protestantism, to a multiplicity of denominations and sects. This variety is then effectively energized, made real, by the fact that these are separable and active, not definitional, categories. The full dynamic of market-making is completed, finally, by multiple and recurring investments of conscious energy, both by the denominations and by their individual churches, in seeking (active) members, that is, to continue the metaphor, in "competing" for membership and support.

This is perhaps most commonly (if a bit superficially) noted in the use of modern communications technology, especially television, which provides everything from broadcasts of mainstream liturgical services through forums for self-conscious televangelists. Yet these more dramatizable manifestations are only, at bottom, further evidence of the general and continuing drive to survive and prosper in the religious marketplace. Here as elsewhere, however, in a general phenomenon to receive more attention below, the presence of extended market-making does not imply the absence of institutionalized democratization. Indeed, the latter is also evidently central, even diagnostic, in the specifically American incarnations of these various churches.

Much of this institutionalized democratization was historically inherent. As the nation developed through immigration and westward migration, through the settling of a huge geographic frontier, churches were established as soon as there were communities large enough to people them. Such churches were inevitably free of much central (administrative or theological) direction. Even more to the point, they had to be responsive to the needs and wishes of their prospective clienteles rather than to any external hierarchy—which was largely nonexistent, in any case. But in fact, these historical patterns continue comfortably into the present, for different but clearly related reasons.

The geographic territory for church expansion, for example, the modern practical counterpart to the frontier, may no longer be the West as a physical region, but it clearly *is* the suburbs as a territorial category. New communities in our time are generally suburban rather than specifically western; new suburbs need new social institutions, including—early on—new churches; new churches need to attract members by providing desired services, that is, by being responsive (once again) to membership wishes. Moreover, while the self-consciously (and physically) new churches are appearing in the suburbs, older church districts are simultaneously acquiring a socially different—and in that sense, also new—clientele, which recapitulates the process again, needing a different set of programs and requiring a different set of concerns.

By the same token, the governmental aspect of these churches makes the theme of continuity even clearer. In the modern world, as in the nineteenth century, territorial expansion, congregational creation, and physical church construction have all been facilitated by the same democratizing mechanism, by the institutionalization of lay boards to manage most church activities. And while the practical reach of this device is most complete in the Protestant sects, with their emphasis on individual churches that form themselves and select their own preachers, its ability to penetrate the American Catholic Church may be its most impressive achievement. Operational rule by the laity, or operational decay if the laity withdraws its support, is now a general, not a Protestant, American characteristic.

Individualism, like market-making, is a notion not commonly encountered in the realm of religious life. Yet it clearly applies, in two distinct fashions. One stems from the variety of religious options that are practically available to individual Americans. Even if most Americans grow up within one denomination, learning its rituals and becoming associated with its dominant clientele, there is a process of choice inherent in that. There is also the minority that actually chooses an entirely different religious tradition, shifting most commonly in our time from high to low Protestant (from the liturgical to the pietist denominations within Protestantism), but accompanied by other eddies as well.

Individualism is even more relevant in a second sense, however—in the sense that in the United States, but surely not in all societies, the choice of a religious identity is a central part of self-definition. "What are you?" is in part answered by "a Lutheran," "a Catholic," or "a Southern Baptist." It may well be that this answer gains consequence where religious identities are themselves diverse. It may be that it gains additional consequence where social roles, ordained or even achieved "places," are ambiguous and fluid. In any case, this answer—Lutheran, Catholic, Baptist, or whatever—is important to establishing individual identity, to giving boundary and definition to the individual American.

Once again, however, that boundary is *not* the site of conflict between the abstractions of individualism and populism, at least when made concrete in the realm of religion. In fact, the populist side of the American religious experience has several distinctive facets that not only reinforce one another but also sit quite comfortably with religious individualism. The most evident and direct of these applies to internal church governance. This infusion of populism within religious life is exemplified in the view that not only church activities but even the identity and character of the living local embodiments of church officialdom (indeed, even their sermons) should accord with the social outlook of the congregation. Such an insistence on "representation," in the sense of sharing modal premises about the world outside, is, of course, populism at its most pointed.

There is a second larger but more amorphous aspect of populism that is intimately associated with the realm of religious life. This second aspect is concerned with guaranteeing that religious values shape a larger national—especially governmental—life. In other words, rather than being concerned with the central place of populist values within American religion, a full-blown populism is concerned with the central place of religion in American public life. This second, complementary aspect is perhaps best captured in the general view that public officials of all sorts ought to *have* a religion and ought to value it. Support for self-consciously religious values, with their content deliberately left undefined, is in fact a central tenet of a distinctively American populism. If religious officials in one's own church ought to reflect congregational values, then public officials in larger national life ought to reflect the centrality of religious values to community life more generally.

It is easy to see the historical roots of this peculiar pattern, this distinctive combination of four main themes. America had a heavy leaven of religious dissenters from the start, who viewed religious life and religious freedom as essential. It then grew through massive immigration and simultaneous migration westward, which added further national religious variety, along with the multiplication of largely autonomous and self-governing local congregations. The extent to which the basic patterns underlying this development *remain* vital and central was dramatically demonstrated, yet again, in early 1989. Formally, the least yielding of the great faiths to all these notions is Catholicism. Neither democratization nor market-making, neither populism nor individualism, are supposed to be relevant to the organization tracing to St. Peter.

Nevertheless, when Pope John Paul II and his main doctrinal lieutenant, Cardinal Joseph Ratzinger, came to America in March 1989 to meet with the American Catholic bishops, it was hard not to hear echoes of an argument first mounted by Jay Lovestone, leader of the American Communist Party, to *his* international counterparts more than sixty years before—an argument about American exceptionalism. If the assertions of the bishops had to be summarized in one notion, it was that although they were indeed dedicated followers of Rome, their superiors had to understand that, given the inherent and extreme differences of American life, the bishops were forced to do things differently in order to accomplish the same (mutually desired) results.

Politics and Economics: Home Grounds

Whereas the realm of religion shows these themes at their most stark, precisely because of their apparent formal irrelevance, the realm of government has been intimately and inherently associated with two of the four, namely, populism and democratization. The very word *populism* owes its existence to an explicitly political movement of the late nineteenth century, though the underlying impulse runs back nearly to the beginnings of a separable American politics and has continued, in easily recognizable form, to the present. In the same way, the explicitly political, general notion of democratization was inherent in the rationale for a separate American republic, though only later did self-conscious efforts at a particular kind of structural reform make that notion part of a recurring political movement, with a recurring and specific procedural agenda. If the realm of religion best attests to the societal reach of these general terms, then the realm of government gives two of them their most pointed definition.

In the case of populism, this definition is still not without confusion or controversy. The various incidents associated with the populist impulse across history—from the original American Revolution, to the more metaphorical Jacksonian "revolution" a half century later, to the formation of an actual Populist Party a half century after that, and all the way up to the "anti-Washington" electoral campaigns of the late twentieth century—each contain elements peculiar to their own time and place. Nevertheless, a minimal definition, from elements found in all these incarnations, would emphasize social equality, the belief that all members of society have the same right to be treated as personal equals. Leaders, accordingly, in any walk of life, should have (and demonstrate) the "common touch," operating on shared premises about appropriate behavior.

At the aggregate level, such social equality implies that collective public life—again, not just in politics but in religion and, as we shall see, in economics or culture as well—should reflect the dominant attitudes and values, the modal social style, of the populace. These propositions, fundamental planks in the platform of Americanism, have ordinarily implied certain further characteristics. They have, for example, produced a politics organized less in terms of Left versus Right and more in terms of "the little man" versus "the interests." This particular (populist) orientation is essential to understanding, in turn, how a mass public can be anti–big business at one point, anti–big labor at another, and anti–big government at yet a third, the wrath of the little man merely shifting as the relevant, offending big interest shifts. Finally, the impulse also has its associated dark side. Social majoritarianism is not necessarily tolerant of deviant views and styles; an insistence on dominant cultural values can easily slide over into nativism or racism.

No less a source than the Constitution itself affirmed the abstract centrality of deliberate structural democratization, in its determination to have representative government and individual rights. Yet the Constitution actually offered as much a "republican" as a "democratic" institutional solution, providing for substantial indirect representation and decision making. Across time, however, in an intermittent but apparently relentless trend, there has been an attempt to open the proceedings of that government to public intervention, most often by attempting to transfer key decisions directly into public hands. As a result, democratization in the American context has come to imply a more specific procedural program involving a central place for citizen participants and, ultimately, some means for decision by majority vote.

Toward this end, the original nonparty system favored by the founding fathers was quickly converted into an internal two-party system and then into external mass parties at a very early point by comparative international standards. What eventually stopped at that point in most other nations, however, continued in the United States with the introduction of the formal primary election into these parties, so that the mass public could choose not just ultimate officeholders but party nominees. Along with this came the more symbolic embodiments of structural democratization: the initiative, the referendum, and the recall. And lest these seem a unique but essentially historical development, two further facts should be noted. One is that most of these democratizing procedures, especially the primary, remain as the institutional framework for *current* American politics. The other is that one of the great rounds of self-conscious democratizing reforms in all of American history actually falls comfortably within our time, within the last thirty years in fact.

The realm of politics, then, has explicitly contributed two of the main themes running through all these essays, or at least the *terms* that are most often used to denote those themes. This does not mean, however, that the other pair of themes in this fourfold interpretation is in any sense absent from the governmental realm. Indeed, a comprehension of American politics and government would be impoverished—would be nearly impossible—without the notions of individualism and market-making or their equivalents. If the definitions of these notions are more commonly derived from economic life, and if they gain perhaps their most striking validation from their utility in understanding American religious life, they nevertheless claim a central place in American politics.

The standard interpretation of individualism in American life (albeit defined more precisely in the economic realm and developed more richly in the cultural realm) crosses easily, with inescapable implications, into politics. Historical settlement through foreign immigration and internal migration, along with the resulting social diversity and emphasis on self-reliance, institutionalized in everything from a free-enterprise economy to a rights-based jurisprudence—these are the preconditions for a politics in which individuals (collected into individual electoral districts) demand that their particular and personal collection of wishes and values be represented in government, rather than some rationalized, even homogenized, national program. Once again, such individualism coexists comfortably with (rather than standing in opposition to) populism. Indeed, it is precisely this combination that underlies the American preference for social equality but not material leveling.

If that could be described as "individualism from below," however, it is met equally by an "individualism from above," in the behavior of the public officials elected by these individual citizens. A federal system with single-member districts, whose members are chosen by plurality vote, surely encourages a decentralized, entrepreneurial, and locally adaptive politics from the elite side as well. The introduction of primary elections into such an arrangement then seals its inherent individualism, from both sides. Individual citizens acquire a means for ensuring that their representatives stand for district interests, not some national party platform; individual candidates acquire a means for securing a party nomination on their own initiative, quite apart from the wishes of any party apparatus. In this way, structural democratization actually increases the variety of options—the market, if you will—available to the general public.

The presence of market-making in a description of American politics hardly seems discordant, since the historical preference in American society for a weak "state" that leaves most activities outside the compass of government has long been accepted as a general characterization. Government has left most potential spheres of policy to the external (economic) marketplace. When government *has* sought a policy-making role, even this has frequently involved a market-making character—seeking not so much to set down a comprehensive bureaucratic program as to manipulate incentives in order to elicit the desired outcome. These tendencies, in particular, have been grist for those who have argued that American politics is driven not so much by classical ideologies as by cycles of "reform."

Yet in a more metaphorical sense, American government and politics themselves can be conceived as a huge marketplace in which a variety of alternatives will always be competing and in which change in the menu of these alternatives, combinations and recombinations, is assumed to be both natural and desirable. This is true even of the fundamental organizing issues of politics. Socioeconomic issues may dominate this marketplace at some times; foreign policy concerns may dominate it at others; social and cultural policy may dominate it at still others. Even then, this mix of central political concerns is still only half the picture. At the same time, different mass constituencies and districts will *always* be mixing these basic concerns in different ways, just as different elite political actors will be seeking personal or group advantage through different coalitions, since all participants are theoretically entitled to pursue their own peculiar, individual, and idio-syncratic visions in this huge, metaphorical, and amorphous (political) marketplace.

If two of the terms for these main connecting threads in the American model (populism and democratization) are originally and intimately asso-ciated with the realm of government, the remaining two (individualism and market-making) are just as commonly and reliably associated with the realm of economics. Indeed, within economics, these two are frequently treated as having a mutual, inherent link: individualism conducing toward a market economy, the market economy conducing toward individualism. But again, economics (like government) provides major roles for their two apparent opposites, so that practical links must evidently be found among *four*, not two, connecting themes. Accordingly, another sketch of the place of these four themes in American economic life, when added to previous sketches from American religious and political life, sets the stage for asking how two pairs of superficially antithetical concepts can coexist comfortably, even symbiotically, within a society—and then for asking why four themes should surface and be sustained in such apparently disparate realms as religion, government, and economics.

Although individualism as a notion clearly encompasses more than its place in the economic realm, that place is central. In most American ap-proaches to thinking about economics, the individual surfaces first as a key productive unit, and then again as an autonomous consumer. Yet the notion is not just stereotypical in economic theorizing; it was also stereotypically connected with actual economic development in the United States. Histori-cally, the United States was the ultimate laissez-faire society, and "rugged individualism" was long asserted to be at the heart of this. The roots of this are painfully familiar. A nation peopled originally by diverse groups, often of dissidents, would grow by internal migration and external immigration, making collectivism a very difficult (and unlikely) personal orientation and reinforcing the decentralized and autonomous economic activity that, in turn, further reinforced individualism.

More critically, this same symbiotic relationship continued over time. The individualism intrinsic to a mercantile and, especially, agricultural economy of the late eighteenth and early nineteenth centuries was thus to become the individualism intrinsic to the emerging industrial economy of the late nineteenth and early twentieth centuries, and ultimately the individualism intrinsic to the increasingly postindustrial economy of the late twentieth and early twenty-first centuries. At each point, the individual as a partially autonomous economic unit was necessarily central to an evolving economy, just as that economy found ways of transferring this individualism into new economic (and social) contexts. The larger economic framework and its main diagnostic elements might change dramatically from era to era, but the individualist impulse continued and was easily recognizable within each.

Markets and market-making may be even more definitionally economic—and stereotypically American. Most concretely, there was first the "American system" of manufacture as the United States began to take off economically, followed by American pioneering of the modern corporate organizational form, the multilayered industrial corporation. Again, these were both cause and effect of the emergence of a true mass market and (especially) mass *marketing,* originally every bit as characteristic of what was then taken to be a quintessentially American phenomenon. Moreover, these are hardly historical relics. They have been taken even further in the last thirty years, producing a sense that one can "market" nearly anything in a self-conscious consumer society—not just goods and services but also entertainment and leisure and even (sub)cultures and lifestyles.

How did this apparent preference for market-making, even as buttressed by a continuing individualism, manage to persist? A nation of dissenters, created through an essentially antistatist revolution, might suffice to explain its origins. But the changes from agricultural to industrial to post-industrial economy were massive, and if market-making and an associated individualism can be discerned within each, that symbiosis only pushes the question one step back. The answer, in fact, appears to lie in marked and continuing *social diversity,* as these factors played across governmental arrangements that were better at responding to particularistic needs than at formulating national policies.

Said differently, a nation distinguished by an allegiance to an ideology of Americanism, and that needed constantly to reaffirm the place of that ideology as a unifying factor, was a nation that was *not* highly unified and integrated in most other realms. Not just ethnic and cultural diversity, constantly reinforced, but geographic diversity, along with extreme diversity in the character of local *economies* and in the level of *economic development,* continued to characterize the nation as a whole. Government might well be open to the demands of the various (and diverse) groups within it— might, indeed, be increasingly open by virtue of increased structural democratization. But that did not mean that those groups were increasingly unified around major public programs to be managed by the government, nor that they were likely to give up more narrowly targeted benefits in order to take a chance on more nationally oriented policies, especially in a governmental system that specialized in bringing in new demands and in constantly renegotiating earlier understandings.

Once more, however (and as oddly here as anywhere), the other main themes of the American model, populism and democratization, surface in the economic realm as well. Thus populism, that oft-alleged opposite to individualism, proves instead to be central to the operation of an evolving mass economy. In the simplest sense, this has to be so. Aggressive mass marketing cannot succeed without a popular desire to acquire the (ever-changing) products of an aspiring consumer society. Yet in a second sense, populism also shapes the *operation* of that society in crucial ways. At bottom, the popular desire for a particular product is, of course, what shapes the drive first to produce it, then to look for cheaper ways to produce it, and then to find ways to produce cheaper but acceptable substitutes.

At the same time, however, individuals left free to design their own lives, though they may insist on having an array of alternatives and on making their own choices among them, are nevertheless very likely to want, at most, some variant of what others have. Part of this is inherent in market choice as well. Even "free" markets do not provide unlimited alternatives, even in the home of the laissez-faire economy. More to the point of populism, however, is that if markets are good at generating a changing range of options, people still tend to demand roughly similar things (or at least, *their version* of those things) as they learn about and experience emerging alternatives. One way to put this is to say that Americans, naturally, want the accoutrements of an "American" lifestyle. Seen from the institutional side, conversely, gauging this economic populism is an important part of being successful in the mass (economic) marketplace.

Finally, democratization, perhaps the least traditional of these notions for classical economics, appears in one guise or another nearly everywhere one looks in the American economic realm, though there may be no other realm where the implications of this fact are so easily misperceived. Once, the corporate form itself might have been offered as evidence of an effective democratization, in the sense that it was a distinct move away from the dominance of economic activity by extended families and social elites and toward responsiveness to an organized "constituency." Yet this development has not gone much further over time, and it has not reached nearly the level of structural democratization characteristic of government and politics, or even of organized religion.

More to the point, then, are aspects of society—essentially democratizing aspects, though none of them are unequivocally beneficial by virtue of that fact—that flow from the thorough *commercialization* of that society, from the injection of *economic criteria* into most aspects of American life. Here, as explicit and formalized economic transactions became part of the management of much of social life (not just employment but also housing, education, leisure, or even geographic mobility), they simultaneously replaced other central (and usually less democratic) criteria for decisions in these realms. Such criteria included birth, manners, and connection; more ambivalently, they also included experience, training, and certification.

On the individual level, vigorous economic growth through commercialization, and the attendant extension of the cash nexus to more and more realms of social life, meant the abolition of the possibility of any consensual sense of "proper place" for individuals. This guaranteed them the ability to mix their resources differently, so as to construct a personal identity more on the basis of their own choice. More ambivalently, again, it implied that anyone who could pay the bill could have the item or experience in question. At the societal level, what this same composite pattern of economic development really implied was the dominance of a broad economic and social middle. It meant a broad range of essentially middle-class opportunities. It implied even broader middle-class *styles* for society as a whole, so that many of those who might not otherwise be categorized as middle class could aspire to have their version of these styles. All this, of course, went a long way toward guaranteeing that developments, economic or otherwise, that did not please this broad middle stratum would not succeed.

The Persistence of Four Grand Cultural Themes

The realms of economics, government, and even religion thus attest to the fact that pairs of major and allegedly antithetical characteristics—populism and individualism on the personal level, democratization and market-making on the institutional level—can indeed coexist comfortably. This is hardly the first time that conditions that are arguably inconsistent in the abstract have been discovered together in concrete application. But these grand characteristics can not only coexist; they can also function as central themes in describing major realms—the *same* major realms—in American society. Given that fact, it would be surprising if such large and apparently tension-filled conjunctions were not diagnostic characteristics of the society in which they actually appear. Nevertheless, when all this is recognized, the question remains: what is the explanation for the concrete coexistence of abstractly antithetical characteristics? How can this be?

The immediate—true but tricky—answer is that an explanation lies (and must lie) within the even more encompassing realm of American culture. In a sense, the appearance of these four grand characteristics in realm after realm of American society goes a long way toward suggesting the essence of that culture. However, an explanation rooted in American culture, so defined, need not be simply definitional. At a minimum, *socialization* into existing values and arrangements that embody a prior coexistence of these four characteristics surely makes their continued (co)existence more likely. Yet this is still not an explanation of how these four themes cohere. That requires some further elaboration of the means for the rise, and then the contemporary reach, of the elements that together constitute this culture, an elaboration buttressed by further concrete examples.

How do populism and individualism, then—to take the first allegedly antithetical pair of cultural themes—coexist with (and even reinforce) each other? A quick review of their evolution in the realm of politics is highly suggestive. The American Revolution itself, the very beginning of a separate United States, combined the desire to affirm a recognizably different form of societal organization, much more self-consciously egalitarian in social terms, with an even more inescapable assertion of the right to be left alone, to do things according to autonomous local standards. By the same token, the first great upheaval in an independent American politics, the Jacksonian revolution of the 1830s, combined these same values in the same way. The Jacksonians were more western, more rural, more agricultural, less wealthy, and more occupationally autonomous than their political opponents. Given this social situation, they were able to assert simultaneously the virtues of the "common man" and the right to manage their individual lives without coordination by some instrument of a single, national will—which in this case meant a national bank.

Both of these early (diagnostic and shaping) experiences showed a heavy strand of antistatism, against the British government in the first case and against the new American government in the second. But if antistatism was a frequent component of political upheavals in the United States, it was not a necessary concomitant. In the late nineteenth century, the period that spawned a self-designated populist movement, the popular complaint was principally against big business instead, against its stifling of individual preferences and individual opportunities. To the extent that this was inter- mittently a complaint against big (that is, national) government as well, that was because government was seen as (illegitimately) in the thrall of busi- ness. Yet government was also viewed, potentially, as a tool for *disciplining* business on behalf of the public. What was not different, then—what was constant and continuing—was the joint impact of individualism and popu- lism as a stimulus for fighting the perceivedly dominant institutions.

Massive waves of immigrants, coming at roughly the same time, only reinforced this synthesis. These new immigrants, coming from different nations and normally coming with different languages and even different cultural premises, inevitably reinforced the individualism of American so- ciety. Being different, they made the natives, too, additionally distinctive; lacking a shared tradition with those natives, they could not be relied on for common, consensual social responses. In addition, their very presence raised, most acutely, the need for—and anxieties about—integrating them into American life so that they would come to share the dominant social values characterizing their new society. Americanization classes through the public schools were one product of this anxiety; intermittent nativist up- surges were a much less attractive variant.

More to this particular point, however, the period around the turn of the twentieth century may well have been critical to the fixing of the link between populism and individualism within American culture. Or at least, this period reaffirmed that an extended and continuing social diversity— an ethnic and subcultural diversity, of course, but also a geographic and regional diversity, an occupational and developmental diversity, and so on— was central to generating and sustaining this particular linkage. A society without this extended diversity might not have produced such a linkage; the United States, however, was just such a society. Moreover, this was also the period when a joint mentality, sustained for over a century by a sequence of congruent but disparate historical events, was converted into an explicit ideology, into an "Americanism" that could thereafter be consciously taught—and consciously learned. Central to that ideology, of course, were both populism and individualism.

All this is evidence of the way these two themes increasingly came to be logically and intimately connected or, rather, evidence of the way they *could* be logically and intimately connected in the United States, though they might be missing or antithetical in other societies. If citizens were to be free to pursue their individual preferences, opportunities, and lifestyles with a minimum of intervention by ostensibly collective institutions, then some way had to be found to permit effective social interaction among those citizens and to guarantee some consensual standards within which they could operate. Populism, as a demand for general observances of modal social styles, could—had to—provide this social lubricant. Seen from the other side, if social pressures rather than institutional coordination were to regulate society, then some reliable way had to be found to guarantee that only those social preferences that were widely shared were actually allowed to constrain personal behavior. An aggressive, resistant individualism could—again, perhaps had to—provide this check.

In any case, by now, the continuing conjunction of populism and individualism has not just roots in, but also consequences for, American culture. For example, this otherwise peculiar conjunction is itself a central explanation for the peculiarly American definition of "equality," implying social but not material leveling. Such a definition is productive of continued misunderstandings with the non-American world. Thus Americans are forever discovering rampant inequality in nations, even self-consciously "social democratic" nations, that accept notions of deference associated with the holding of various positions, either ascribed or achieved. Conversely, non-Americans are forever discovering a United States characterized by rampant inequality in material conditions. Yet a society that blends populism with individualism insists, quite logically, that no person is "better" (intrinsically) than any other, but that each person must be permitted to construct his or her individual life as best (and as advantageously as) he or she can.

An inherent or at least explainable consistency between populism and individualism on the personal level probably makes the linkage between democratization and market-making on the institutional level more plausible and easier to conceive as well. Again, there is nothing automatic about this linkage. But it surfaces in such an array of disparate realms as to suggest its centrality to American culture more generally. And again, given the evident coexistence of democratization and market-making as major institutional themes in the United States, along with the lack of any inherent need for them to coexist, some further general explanation for their linkage in American culture is required. For the sake of consistency, the realm of politics can be tapped once more to help explain why this coexistence can, in some circumstances, be entirely logical and natural. Yet this time, it is worth using instances from *contemporary* political life, to dismiss the possibility that some "historical overhang" is actually the main explanatory force.

Fortunately, the tendency for democratization and market-making to exist side by side and to draw sustenance from each other is nowhere better illustrated than in the politics of our time. In fact, the period from the mid-1960s to the late 1970s was one of the great reform eras in American history—the founding, the Jacksonian era, and the Progressive era at the turn of the twentieth century are the others—when questions of structural democratization were explicitly at the center of politics. Whether the product of this period came to countervail, to coexist with, or actually to expand the reach of market-making in American society can thus become a key test not only of coherence between these two grand institutional themes but also of potential continuation in the modern world. Assuming that this institutional linkage, like the personal one between populism and individualism, passes that test, the details of its passage can be addressed for a more general explanation of this practical compatibility among putatively incompatible concepts.

The modern reform era has certainly been characterized by multiple and extended, structurally democratizing initiatives. Thus it featured such self-conscious institutional adjustments as the extension of primary elections, at long last, to presidential selection, so that individual citizens could not just elect but also nominate their presidents. The modern era featured a thorough reform of congressional procedures as well, changing the rules of operation for that last great bastion of intermediary elites in American politics by dispersing formal positions and resources more broadly and by opening legislative activity, even at the ultimate stage on the House and Senate floors, to a much broader array of participants. Such a list, however, hits only the high points. The modern reform era actually went much further, to freedom-of-information and open-access rules inside the executive bureaucracy, for example, but really to almost any realm one could name.

Yet what it did *not* feature was equally important for this particular argument. All these reforms, despite recasting not just the institutional structure of government but also the practical politics occurring within it, did not produce more governmental programs and thus an expanded role for the central state. As a result, they did not produce a contraction in the use of market-making in pursuit of public preferences, even public policies. In fact, most strikingly, this reform era was directly succeeded by a period when the increase of governmental programs and the expansion of the state bureaucracy, proceeding more or less continually since the Great Depression and the New Deal, came to a halt. Some programs were actually terminated; others were consciously moved out into the commercial marketplace.

In practical terms, then, the coincidence of major efforts at structural democratization with expansion in the scope of market-making reaffirmed the historical link between these two great institutional themes in American life, while bringing that link comfortably into the contemporary world. Moreover, the particular instance once again contains a potential key to explaining why this link can be (and is) inherent in the United States. What happened in the late twentieth century to link democratization and market-making is already clear. The rise of new issues and new political coalitions, the central phenomenon behind all this, was not just a stimulus to structural reform, though it was certainly that. This rise was also an *explanation* of the preference for market-making within these newly democratized institutions.

By itself, the coordinated rise of new issues, and of the new political coalitions associated with them, constituted a perfectly simple and straightforward explanation for the coming of a reform drive. An older set of (in this case, social welfare) issues, mobilizing and supported by an older (class-based) coalition, came to stand in the way of newly significant divisions on cultural policy (abortion, permissiveness, crime) and foreign affairs (nationalism, interventionism, military preparedness) that required very different social coalitions for their pursuit. Structurally democratizing reforms, to restore democratic responsiveness, were the nearly inevitable response—in the late eighteenth, early to middle nineteenth, late nineteenth to early twentieth, and now late twentieth centuries. Old issues and old coalitions clearly were in the way; democratization clearly appealed as the means to circumvent them.

The same new issues and new coalitions that were behind the democratizing drive, however, were also the reason that successful democratization produced the expansion, not the contraction, of market-making. Some of this was direct and intended, as with those issues (ranging from school prayer through economic deregulation) in which a desire to get the national government out of local activity was inherent in the new issue itself. More of it was indirect and unintended, when a welter of crosscutting issues and of shifting coalitions in effect prevented government from imposing any programmatic solution. Increasing social (and hence political) diversity, when focused on an increasingly democratized (and receptive) government, resulted not in governmental growth but either in stalemate or in an active preference for letting a decentralized market actually provide the solution.

Seen in a more historical perspective, the specific example of the late twentieth century was only the latest incarnation of the generic American case. Impressive social diversity, along with a peculiar governmental structure, made democratization and market-making compatible, now as in the past. A society with numerous and diverse groups, holding amorphous and crosscutting value preferences, would naturally acquire a politics featuring numerous and diverse social coalitions around amorphous and crosscutting policy issues. If its governmental structure was then continually reformed, seeking to reflect this diversity rather than to countervail it and produce some sort of programmatic response regardless, the result was likely to be a "natural" compatibility between such democratization and a tendency toward market-making.

The absence of uniform social experiences and of widespread interpersonal bonds in such a society probably made a turn to the market (rather than to government) a logical strategy for pursuing what would elsewhere be "policy" wishes. Individual members of such a society were likely to prefer to be allowed to pursue their own preferences in a societal "marketplace" rather than risk having too many (non)preferences imposed on them by others, through government. When their demands *were* pressed on government, however, especially if its structure was sufficiently democratized to provide some point that would register those demands, three general outcomes were likely. The first was stalemate; the second was a consciously narrow and localized policy response; and the third was some national response, followed shortly by reconsideration in all but the most consensual cases. When that is an accurate description, democratization and market-making should, naturally and logically, be linked.

Applications of the American Model

Populism and individualism, democratization and market-making, can be linked in practice, as they obviously are in American society. They can be linked in theory as well, through historical and contemporary explanations for their conjunction. Accordingly, they can plausibly serve as central—even diagnostic—themes for American society, for an "American model." That being the case, they ought to be reflected in the smaller and more focused operational realms of that society. If these are the dominant themes characterizing the major realms of American society, and if they are united and sustained through a continuing American culture, then they ought to be applied and reflected—further "operationalized"—in additional practical realms of that society.

Prime among these, by virtue of both its importance and its frequently asserted role in reflecting (and sustaining) an American exceptionalism, is education. Education, especially higher education, can potentially play this role not so much because these other realms (politics, economics, religion, culture) are "the shapers" and it is "the shaped." Obviously, once in place, an educational system plays a crucial role in shaping subsequent developments in many other realms. Rather, the educational realm can play this analytic role because it is less global than these others, and its characteristics can thus be specified more concretely, and because it must both reflect and transmit themes from these other realms—if they are indeed as dominant as they appear to be. As a major applied realm, education should thus reflect, operationalize, transmit, and shape the four grand themes of the American model.

Distinctive elements in American higher education are not difficult to locate. The very size of the American effort at higher education remains unique among the developed nations; so does its internal variety. Its organizational structure is distinctive, with lay boards, strong presidents, and a flat faculty hierarchy. Its relationship to students is distinctive, both in what they can demand and in the services it aspires to provide. Its links to the society outside, finally, are distinctive as well, through fund-raising, research, and service provision. Cumulated, these elements only reinforce a sense of distinctiveness. Indeed, this is a realm where the United States remains noticeably different not just from Europe but also from the emerging Asian states.

Conversely, there are incipient signs of efforts at *convergence* among the developed nations. If this is a realm where Europe and Asia join in differing from the United States, it is also one where they appear to be Americanizing, through growth and diversification, through ties to other kinds of postsecondary education, through development of strong administrative leadership, and so forth. All this only suggests, for higher education as for the other realms under investigation, that the key question remains the one "in the middle," the question of whether there are larger clusters of traits that remain distinctive. Are the four major themes embodied within American higher education? Are they, indeed, central to its description—and comprehension? Can it, in turn, further validate them?

Evident incarnations of each of these four major themes are not hard to find in the realm of higher education. Populism, for example, is immediately apparent in the most fundamental American proposition about higher education, the one that gives rise to much of the rest: that such education is a good thing, that as much as possible should be available, and that as *many* as possible should be encouraged to seek it. Populism is also inherent in the major concrete elements of the educational system. It is present in the main educational program itself, in an insistence on a "liberal" or "general" education for all undergraduates, an approach that seeks integration in a diverse educational population but also helps bring as many students as possible into college. Populism is also embodied in the very institutional structure of higher education, as with the generation of so-called community colleges, created to ensure that there is wide access to higher education, in a setting that nevertheless reflects local values.

Not surprisingly, an infusion of populism throughout the realm of higher education does not appear to be at the expense of individualism. Thus, within that huge educational establishment, there is also a huge variety of educational alternatives. Seen from one side, and despite a general commitment to a liberal education, colleges and universities manage to project strikingly diverse identities, differentiating themselves by academic stringency, substantive focus, career orientation, teaching or research emphasis, sacred or secular ties, and so on. Seen from the other side, despite a general quest for a college education, students are encouraged to "shop"— the first of many market-making metaphors—for their individually preferred arrangements, including not just the main educational product but also ancillary services and even recreational opportunities. In this interaction, colleges can maintain high individual autonomy, subject to their ability to get various "constituencies" (a democratizing metaphor) to respond to their offers.

Within American culture, the combination of populism and individualism was responsible for a peculiarly American definition of equality, implying social but not material leveling. That definition, proceeding from that same combination, resurfaces in the realm of higher education. In the case of the leading clientele for colleges and universities—the students—the combination of the popular drive for a college education with individual autonomy in the choice of educational packages means that the widespread social categorization of "college student" can coincide with a situation in which some degrees will ultimately be much more facilitative of material attainments than others, but the market, not the university system, will sort that out. In the case of the faculty, the result is even more stereotypical. Within individual institutions, the hierarchy of positions is quite flat, and most individuals can expect to reach its top rung. At the same time, faculty members are rewarded on the basis of their individual performance, though what this really means is that most will have to move among institutions to achieve material benefits from their formally similar status.

Incarnations of democratization are as easily located. In a summary sense, democratization is inherent in the need—and willingness—to be broadly linked to the larger society. The general means for this, the variety of sources of support for institutions of higher education (tuition, grants and gifts, public and private research support, subventions from several different levels of government), manages to keep these institutions simultaneously responsive to an array of constituencies and yet buffered from the wishes of any one. But the same situation is also recapitulated structurally. The simplest and most direct embodiment of this is the nearly ubiquitous lay board. Even in the public (and more so in the private) institutions, such a board is charged, from one side, with linking the educational institution to its external constituencies. From the other side, a president actually manages the institution if he or she can maintain the support of a majority of the lay board.

Market-making in some sense also lies behind all these characteristics, often quite explicitly. The commercial market actually predated the establishment of institutions of higher education in the United States. What resulted, for the composite sector of higher education, almost asks to be cast in market terms: competition, of course, for students, faculty, and financing, but also diversity of academic product, responsiveness to almost any organized interest that can conceivably pay the bill, institutional autonomy for decisions about placement in the larger market, and a mixed and shifting array of sources of external finance. Yet what resulted *inside* these institutions can perhaps best be portrayed in the same way. An elective system, modular courses, credit accumulation, and transfer based on a transcript really are the American system of higher education. They are the interchangeable parts of a national system that is simultaneously autonomous and localized.

Again, the link between democratization and market-making is as direct and comfortable here as anywhere. The single most distinguishing characteristic of American higher education, its massive size, is crucially underpinned by this particular link. The size of the American cohort seeking higher education is determined (and kept large) by a constant search for demands in society (in the form of potential students) and in the constant search for ways to meet those demands—the mass market producing democratic access. Unsurprisingly, there is an accompanying attitude that is both product and encouragement of this tendency. If Americans endorse the notion that higher education is a good thing per se, and if widespread college education thus meets a democratic standard, they also accept the view that competition is the best way to gain more of it and more variety within it, thereby endorsing a crucial role for the "educational marketplace."

Higher education suggests, then, that the four main themes running implicitly through all these essays—the four continuing characteristics of American culture—can indeed be found, most concretely, in one of the major applied realms of American society. American higher education is certainly a concrete embodiment of populism, individualism, democratization, and market-making, and especially of the conjoint presence of those four grand characteristics. In turn, because they are so deeply embedded in the American system of higher education, that system must provide a further, powerful means of transmitting them from era to era.

In a different sense, of course, higher education is only one of the public policies of the United States, albeit a major one. In that light, higher education also emphasizes how an effectively "public policy" can result from a decision to leave one or another policy realm to the marketplace or, even more commonly in the American context, from a decision to *mix* attention to any given realm not just among various (sub)governments but also between various governments and various private sectors. Indeed, the United States appears to be leading evidence for the proposition that an inclination to have less direct governmental provision is not necessarily an inclination to have less of the intended policy product, as, most dramatically, in the case of higher education.

The Fortunes of American Exceptionalism

Approaching the notion of American exceptionalism through four main conceptual themes not only locates the analysis at a level where it appears, theoretically, it ought to be. This approach also offers a sufficiently precise focus to prevent arguments over the actuality of American exceptionalism from slipping into ambiguity. Such an approach has three other closing virtues, over and above the virtues inherent in validating these four grand characteristics as diagnostic features of a continuing American experience. First, this approach permits American exceptionalism to be addressed without having to resolve every associated substantive puzzle. Second, this approach still allows the analyst to drive back toward higher levels of abstraction. And third, such an approach establishes an initial focus for subsequent returns to the question of American exceptionalism.

In the first of these additional virtues, an approach to the American experience by way of these four organizing concepts allows substantial generalizations and arguments without having to resolve all the substantive questions that have been appended to the issue of American exceptionalism. For example, one of the persistently asserted peculiarities in the evolution of American society is the manner in which the United States is the model for development and modernity in some regards, while resembling consensually underdeveloped and unmodern societies in others. In religion, to take one such instance, what has struck many observers as exceptional is the fact that the most economically developed society has not been powerfully secularized in the process of development.

A whole series of hypotheses could follow from this perception alone. This might, of course, be what makes the United States truly exceptional, in the sense of defying the full "normal" development curve. Alternatively, because the United States is not particularly distinctive from the world as a whole in many respects, the peculiarity may lie with the countries of northern Europe and Scandinavia, which, in their exceptional evolution, skewed scholars' perceptions about a dominant model. Or perhaps all "developing" societies adhere to one general model and all "stabilized" societies to another, with the United States being exceptional only in the sense of being consistently misclassified into the second rather than the (appropriate) first category.

Approaching the question of American exceptionalism in the manner done here, by way of a small set of central concepts that gather numerous individual findings and span large societal realms at the same time, escapes the need to resolve that question. If what makes the United States distinctive is the central and continuing place of populism, individualism, democratization, and market-making—and especially their conjoint and reinforcing character—then that is the basis for sustaining an argument about American exceptionalism. Moreover, it constitutes such a basis quite apart from any "normal" developmental trajectory or Scandinavian model. This is not to say that how these dominant empirical themes interact with (and support or challenge) these other hypotheses is uninteresting or unworthy of further investigation. Rather, it is merely to say that the essence of American exceptionalism does not require the resolving of this (related and interesting) set of arguments before it can be asserted.

A quite different virtue of this approach is that it not only escapes being trapped in certain prior, specific, substantive arguments. It also permits moving on to a considerably higher level of abstraction. The major themes of populism and individualism, democratization and market-making, appear to both continue across American history and cohere within the realms that they, in effect, link. Their mutual and continuing distinctiveness thus makes its bid as the central datum for arguments about American exceptionalism. Yet it is certainly possible to drive them further. For example, it is entirely reasonable to argue that what these themes really add up to, most fundamentally and at that higher level of abstraction, is one particular version of what has come to be known as "civil society."

Such a society features substantial resources, along with substantial activities, that are not just outside the realm (and even the reach) of the state but can intentionally be turned to restraining or disciplining it. The notion itself emerged in a (European) context where it stood in obvious theoretical contraposition to the notion of a self-conscious national state. By contrast, American history unfolded in a context where the notion of "the government" (effectively "the government of the day") was common enough, but where that of "the state" was not. The nation thus developed for much of its history in general ignorance of, and without any felt need for, some further distinction between state and society. Indeed, if the nation was frequently antistatist, and if governmental programs moved back and forth between levels of government and even between government and the marketplace, notions about the state and its alternatives seemed largely beside the point.

Nevertheless, the United States is, at bottom, not just a generic civil society but perhaps the archetypal one. It is not just that the United States has shown a preference for antibureaucratic responses to those problems for which government must inevitably provide the solution, nor even that the United States has shown a preference for devolving policy solutions onto the marketplace rather than government whenever possible. Rather, those who want to understand the latest developments in American life are well advised to look to the society, not the government, in seeking answers.

Forcing a generalization to this level has costs as well as benefits. Classifying the United States as a civil society should not be a substitute for noting the central and continuing place of four other, somewhat less abstract themes. Calling the United States a civil society does not imply, either logically or empirically, that civil society in turn requires populism, individualism, democratization, and market-making, together, for its existence. In theoretical terms, that combination is so distinctive that its requirement would, in effect, radically devalue the notion of civil society as an analytic category. More concretely, it appears possible to retain far greater use of the market than of government, along with far more emphasis on society than on the state, without requiring the introduction of, for example, populism.

In the end, the distinctive and organizing themes remain the "big four"—populism, individualism, democratization, and market-making. Their historical persistence appears impressive. So does their contemporary reach—across societal sectors, back to culture itself, and forward to applied policy realms. An argument about American exceptionalism, then, can certainly be mounted around these conjoint themes, and any such argument is likely to partake (at least implicitly) of their substance. What remains is only the question of where these themes are likely to be in another generation or two. Hidden inside that question, of course, is the further issue of whether they will continue, by that time, to look as distinctive.

Where will the substance itself go? There seems to be no point in trying to answer in detail. The detailed worlds of the federal, the Jacksonian, the Progressive, or the postwar eras—to skip across the surface of American history—were all noticeably different. So, presumably, will be the world of the twenty-first century. A major factor uniting these other periods, however, was the possibility of reinterpreting period details around four grand and continuing conceptual themes. That means, at a minimum, that these themes should still serve as an initial organizing framework, and that the search for their detailed incarnation in a new historical era should serve as an initial simplifying device. The four themes have arguably surfaced in every one of those preceding eras. Their place in the twenty-first century will at least be the first analytic item for investigation.

But will these themes themselves, in their mutual presence, linkage, and reinforcement, seem as distinctive in another generation as they (still) do today? Again, if a detailed answer to the first question cannot reasonably be hazarded, a directly supportable answer to the second is impossible, except, perhaps, for those who answer on the basis of extended historical continuities, on the basis of the continued resurfacing of major themes from particular (and otherwise strikingly varied) historical contexts. For them, the answer, or at least the hypothesis, is likely to be yes. If larger differences fade, lesser ones are likely at least to blur. Yet if other nations move toward this peculiar conjunction of traits, the United States too will surely continue to evolve. What these four grand themes implied, in their operational detail, was different in the late nineteenth century than in the late twentieth, even though thematic continuity was their most striking implication. Why should what they imply in the early twenty-first century not be different, at least in its details, as well—thereby sustaining, by reinventing, an American exceptionalism?

REFERENCES

Abramson, Paul R. 1975. *Generational Change in American Politics.* Lexington, Mass.: D. C. Heath.

Abramson, Paul R., John H. Aldrich, and David W. Rohde. 1990. *Change and Continuity in the 1988 Elections.* Washington, D.C.: CQ Press.

———. 1994. *Change and Continuity in the 1992 Elections.* Washington, D.C.: CQ Press.

———. 1998. *Change and Continuity in the 1996 Elections.* Washington, D.C.: CQ Press.

———. Forthcoming. *Change and Continuity in the 2000 Elections.* Washington, D.C.: CQ Press.

Addison, Paul. 1994. *The Road to 1945: British Politics and the Second World War.* London: Pimlico Press.

Adeney, Martin, and John Lloyd. 1986. *The Miners' Strike, 1984–5: Loss Without Limit.* London: Routledge and Kegan Paul.

Adonis, Andrew. 1996. Britain. In *Postwar Politics in the G-7: Orders and Eras in Comparative Perspective,* edited by Byron E. Shafer. Madison: University of Wisconsin Press.

Adorno, T. W., et al. 1950. *The Authoritarian Personality.* New York: Harper and Row.

Ahlstrom, Sydney E. 1972. *A Religious History of the American People.* New Haven, Conn.: Yale University Press.

Alexander, Herbert E. 1984. *Financing Politics: Money, Elections, and Political Reform.* 3d ed. Washington, D.C.: Congressional Quarterly Press.

Alson, Chuck. 1990. Warning Shots Fired by Voters More Mood than Mandate. *Congressional Quarterly Weekly Report,* November 10, 3896–98.

Ambrose, Stephen E. 1990. *Eisenhower: Soldier and President.* New York: Simon and Schuster.

America's Christian Crusader. 1995. *Time,* May 15.

The Angst of Victory. 1993. *Congressional Quarterly Weekly Report,* Special Report, August 7, 2122–42.

Another Paradigm Shift. 1999. *The Economist,* November 20.

Apple, R.W. Jr. 1990. Invading Iraqis Seize Kuwait and Its Oil; U.S. Condemns Attack, Urges United Action. *New York Times,* August 3, A1.

Baer, Kenneth. 1998. Reinventing Democrats: The Democratic Leadership Council and the Attempt to Change the Public Philosophy of the Democratic Party, 1981–1996. D.Phil. diss., Oxford University.

———. 2000. *Reinventing Democrats: The Politics of Liberalism from Reagan to Clinton.* Lawrence: University Press of Kansas.

———. 2001. Clinton Held the Center All Along. *Los Angeles Times,* January 21.

Banfield, Edward C., and James Q. Wilson. 1963. Reform. In *City Politics.* New York: Vintage Books.

———. 1964. Public-Regardingness as a Value Premise in Voting Behavior. *American Political Science Review* 58 (December): 876–88.

———. 1971. Political Ethos Revisited. *American Political Science Review* 65 (December): 1048–63.

Barbour, Haley. 1996. *Agenda for America: A Republican Direction for the Future.* Washington, D.C.: Regnery.

Barnes, James A. 2000. It's All About Leadership. *National Journal Convention Daily,* August 5, 1.

Barone, Michael. 1990. *Our Country: The Shaping of America from Roosevelt to Reagan.* New York: Free Press.

Beer, Samuel H. 1982. *Britain Against Itself: The Political Contradictions of Collectivism.* New York: W. W. Norton.

Bell, Daniel. 1973. *The Coming of Post-Industrial Society: A Venture in Social Forecasting.* New York: Basic Books.

Bennett, Michael J. 1996. *When Dreams Came True: The GI Bill and the Making of Modern America.* New York: Brassey's.

Berger, Bennett M. 1960. *Working-Class Suburb: A Study of Auto Workers in Suburbia.* Berkeley: University of California Press.

Berke, Richard L. 1998. Clintons Seek to Repair Rift for Democrats. *New York Times,* July 19, 1, 15.

———. 2000a. The Ad Campaign: Democrats See, and Smell, Rats in GOP Ad. *New York Times,* September 12, A1.

———. 2000b. The Context: Debates Put in Focus Images and Reality. *New York Times,* October 19, A29.

Berman, Larry. 1982. *Planning a Tragedy: The Americanization of the War in Vietnam.* New York: W. W. Norton.

Bernstein, Irving. 1969. *Turbulent Years: A History of the American Worker, 1933–1941.* Boston: Houghton Mifflin.

Bevin, Aneurin, 1961. *In Place of Fear.* London: MacGibbon and Kee.

Binkley, Wilfred W. 1937. *President and Congress.* New York: Random House.

Birnbaum, Jeffrey H. 1995. The Gospel According to Ralph. *Time*, May 15, 26–33.

Birtel, Marc. 1998. House: The Scandal Recedes. *Congressional Quarterly Weekly Report*, October 24, 2873–75.

Black, C. E. 1966. *The Dynamics of Modernization: A Study in Comparative History.* New York: Harper and Row.

Bloomfield, Barbara, Gary Boanas, and Raphael Samuel, eds. 1986. *The Enemy Within: Pit Villages and the Miners' Strike of 1984–5.* London: Routledge and Kegan Paul.

Blum, John Morton. 1976. *V Was for Victory: Politics and American Culture During World War II.* New York: Harcourt Brace Jovanovich.

———. 1991. *Years of Discord: American Politics and Society 1960–1974.* New York: W. W. Norton.

Bok, Derek C., and John T. Dunlop. 1970. *Labor and the American Community.* New York: Simon and Schuster.

Bosanquet, Helen D. 1896. *Rich and Poor.* London: Macmillan.

Boudon, Raymond. 1982. *The Unintended Consequences of Social Action.* New York: St. Martin's Press.

Brooke, Stephen. 1992. *Labour's War: The Labour Party During the Second World War.* Oxford: Oxford University Press.

Brooks, Thomas R. 1974. *Walls Came Tumbling Down: A History of the Civil Rights Movement, 1940–1970.* Englewood Cliffs, N.J.: Prentice-Hall.

Brown, Seyom. 1968. *Faces of Power: Constancy and Change in U.S. Foreign Policy from Truman to Johnson.* New York: Columbia University Press.

Budget Making: That Was Then, This Is Now. 2000. *National Journal,* January 1, 24.

Buenker, John D. 1969. The Progressive Era: A Search for Synthesis. *Mid America* 51 (July): 175–93.

Bunzel, John H. 1962. *The American Small Businessman.* New York: Alfred A. Knopf.

Burner, David. 1968. *The Politics of Provincialism: The Democratic Party in Transition, 1918–1932.* New York: Alfred A. Knopf.

Burnham, Walter Dean. 1970. *Critical Elections and the Mainsprings of American Politics.* New York: W. W. Norton.

Burns, James MacGregor. 1973. *Roosevelt: The Soldier of Freedom, 1940–1945.* New York: Harcourt Brace Jovanovich.

Bush, George W. 2000. *Renewing America's Purpose: Policy Addresses of George W. Bush, July 1999–July 2000.* Washington, D.C.: Republican National Committee.

Butler, David. 1993. The United States Election of 1992. *Electoral Studies* 12 (June): 185–87.

Butler, David, Andrew Adonis, and Tony Travers. 1994. *Failure in British Government: The Politics of the Poll Tax.* Oxford: Oxford University Press.
Butler, David, and Dennis Kavanagh. 1979. *The British General Election of 1979.* London: Macmillan.
———. 1992. *The British General Election of 1992.* London: Macmillan.
———. 1997. *The British General Election of 1997.* Basingstoke, England: Macmillan.
Butler, David, and Donald Stokes. 1974. *Political Change in Britain: The Evolution of Electoral Choice.* London: Macmillan.
Cairncross, Alec. 1985. *Years of Recovery: British Economic Policy, 1945–1951.* Cambridge: Methuen Press.
Calder, Angus. 1969. *The People's War: Britain, 1939–1945.* London: Jonathan Cape.
———. 1992. *The Myth of the Blitz.* London: Pimlico.
Calleo, David P. 1982. *The Imperious Economy.* Cambridge: Harvard University Press.
Campbell, Angus. 1960. Surge and Decline: A Study of Electoral Change. *Public Opinion Quarterly* 24:397–418.
Campbell, Angus, Philip E. Converse, Warren E. Miller, and Donald E. Stokes. 1960. *The American Voter.* New York: John Wiley.
———. 1966. *Elections and the Political Order.* New York: John Wiley and Sons.
Cannon, Carl M. 1998. What Hath Bill Wrought? *National Journal,* November 7, 2621–22.
———. 2000. Even Pablum Has a Purpose. *National Journal Convention Daily,* July 30, 1.
Carwardine, Richard J. 1983. *Evangelicals and Politics in Antebellum America.* New Haven, Conn.: Yale University Press.
Cassata, Donna. 1995. Republicans Bask in Success of Rousing Performance. *Congressional Quarterly Weekly Report,* April 8, 986–1005.
Ceaser, James W. 1982. *Reforming the Reforms: A Critical Analysis of the Presidential Selection Process.* Cambridge, Mass.: Ballinger Publishing.
Ceaser, James W., and Andrew E. Busch. 1997. *Losing to Win: The 1996 Elections and American Politics.* Lanham, Md.: Rowman and Littlefield.
———. 2001. *The Perfect Tie: The True Story of the 2000 Presidential Election.* Lanham, Md.: Rowman and Littlefield.
Chafe, William H. 1991. *The Unfinished Journey: America Since World War II.* 2d ed. Oxford: Oxford University Press.
———. 1992. *The Paradox of Change: American Women in the Twentieth Century.* New York: Oxford University Press.
Chandler, Alfred D. Jr. 1977. *The Visible Hand: The Managerial Revolution in American Business.* Cambridge: Harvard University Press.

Charmley, John. 1996. *A History of Conservative Politics, 1900–1996.* London: Macmillan.

Chester, Lewis, Godfrey Hodgson, and Bruce Page. 1969. *An American Melodrama: The Presidential Campaign of 1968.* London: Andre Deutsch.

Clinton, Hillary. 1996. *It Takes a Village.* New York: Simon and Schuster.

The Clinton Budget: White House Faces Reconciling Its Goals with What Congress Is Willing to Give. 1993. *Congressional Quarterly Weekly Report,* Special Report, April 10, 885–904.

Clinton's Bold Gamble. 1993. *Congressional Quarterly Weekly Report,* Special Report, February 20, 355–86.

Cloud, David S. 1992. The NAFTA Fix: Squeezed by Democrats and Other Allies, Clinton Inherits Mexican Trade Deal. *Congressional Quarterly Weekly Report,* November 28, 3710–13.

———. 1993a. Free Trade Ethos: Clinton Forges New Coalition to Expand Nation's Commitment to Open Markets. *Congressional Quarterly Weekly Report,* November 20, 3174–85.

———. 1993b. Sorting out NAFTA: Rhetoric and Hyperbole on Trade Accord Debate over Pros and Cons. *Congressional Quarterly Weekly Report,* October 15, 2791–96.

Cloud, David S., and Beth Donovan. 1994. House Delays Health Care Debate as Leaders Plot Strategy. *Congressional Quarterly Weekly Report,* August 13, 2344–53.

CNN. 1998. Democrats Enjoy a Big Night After a Hard-to-Read Election. cnn.com/ALLPOLITICS/stories/1998/11/03/election/overview.

Cohen, Richard E. 1998. After the Riot. *National Journal,* November 14, 2700–6.

Cohodas, Nadine. 1984. Panel Proposes Senate Committee Changes. *Congressional Quarterly Weekly Report,* December 1, 3035.

Collini, Stefan. 1985. The Idea of "Character" in Victorian Political Thought. *Transactions of the Royal Historical Society,* 5th ser., 35:29–50.

Commission on Party Structure and Delegate Selection. 1970. *Mandate for Reform.* Washington, D.C.: Democratic National Committee.

Commission on Social Justice. 1994. *Social Justice: Strategies for National Renewal.* London: Vintage.

Contract with the American Family. 1995. *Congressional Quarterly Weekly Report,* May 20, 1449.

Cook, Rhodes. 1991. Bush's Gulf Triumph Stifles Talk of GOP Primary Challengers. *Congressional Quarterly Weekly Report,* March 9, 581–87.

Cox, Gary C., and Samuel Kernell, eds. 1991. *The Politics of Divided Government.* Boulder, Colo.: Westview Press.

Crewe, Ivor. 1985. How to Win a Landslide Without Really Trying. In *Britain at the Polls, 1983,* edited by Austin Ranney. Durham, N.C.: Duke University Press.

———. 1987. A New Class of Politics. *The Guardian,* June 15.

Crewe, Ivor, Neil Day, and Anthony Fox, comps. 1991. *The British Electorate, 1963–1987.* Cambridge: Cambridge University Press.

Crewe, Ivor, and Donald D. Searing. 1988. Mrs. Thatcher's Crusade: Conservatism in Britain, 1972–1986. In *The Resurgence of Conservatism in Anglo-American Democracies,* edited by Barry Cooper, Allan Kornberg, and William Mishler. Durham, N.C.: Duke University Press.

Crick, Bernard. 1964. *The Reform of Parliament.* London: Weidenfeld and Nicholson.

Crosland, Anthony. 1956. *The Future of Socialism.* London: Jonathan Cape.

Cross, Whitney. 1950. *Burned-over District: The Social and Intellectual History of Enthusiastic Religion in Western New York, 1800–1850.* Ithaca, N.Y.: Cornell University Press.

Crotty, William J. 1977. *Political Reform and the American Experiment.* New York: Thomas Y. Crowell.

Davies, Gareth. 1996. *From Opportunity to Entitlement: The Transformation and Decline of Great Society Liberalism.* Lawrence: University Press of Kansas.

Deciding on War. 1991. *Congressional Quarterly Weekly Report,* Special Report, January 5, 7–44.

Democratic Leadership Council. 1991. The New American Choice: Opportunity, Responsibility, Community. Washington, D.C.: Democratic Leadership Council.

Denver, David. 1998. The Government that Could Do No Right. In *New Labour Triumphs: Britain at the Polls,* edited by Anthony King. Chatham, N.J.: Chatham House.

Derber, Milton, and Edwin Young, eds. 1957. *Labor and the New Deal.* Madison: University of Wisconsin Press.

DeWitt, Benjamin P. 1915. *The Progressive Movement.* New York: Macmillan.

Diggins, John Patrick. 1989. *The Proud Years: America in War and Peace, 1941–1960.* New York: W. W. Norton.

Duncan, Phil. 1990. Budget May Shift Advantage in Congress' Closest Races. *Congressional Quarterly Weekly Report,* October 13, 3279–83.

———. 1993. Perot Gores His Own Ox. *Congressional Quarterly Weekly Report,* November 13, 3105.

Easterlin, Richard A. 1980. *Birth and Fortune: The Impact of Numbers on Personal Welfare.* New York: Basic Books.

———. 1998. *Growth Triumphant: The Twenty-first Century in Historical Perspective.* Ann Arbor: University of Michigan Press.

Edsall, Thomas B. 1998. GOP's Own Successes Weaken Its Draw, Strategists Say. *Washington Post*, November 25, A4.

Eidelberg, Paul. 1968. *The Philosophy of the American Constitution: A Reinterpretation of the Intentions of the Founding Fathers.* New York: Free Press.

Election 1998. 1998. *National Journal*, Special Report, November 7.

Ellison, Nick. 1996. Consensus Here, Consensus There, but Not Consensus Everywhere. In *The Myth of Consensus: New Views on British History, 1945–1964*, edited by Kenneth Jones and Michael Kandian. Basingstoke, England: Macmillan.

Elshtain, Jean Bethke. 1989. Issues and Themes in the 1988 Campaign. In *The Elections of 1988*, edited by Michael Nelson. Washington, D.C.: CQ Press.

Elst, Philip V. 1975. Radical Toryism. *Political Quarterly* 46 (no. 1): 69–71.

Elving, Ronald D. 1990. GOP Candidates Scrambling After Bush Tax Reversal. *Congressional Quarterly Weekly Report*, June 30, 2033–36.

Epstein, Edward Jay. 1973. *News from Nowhere: Television and the News.* New York: Random House.

Epstein, Edwin M. 1969. *The Corporation in American Politics.* Englewood Cliffs, N.J.: Prentice-Hall.

———. 1979a. The Emergence of Political Action Committees. In *Political Finance*, edited by Herbert E. Alexander. Sage Electoral Studies Yearbook, vol. 5. Beverly Hills, Calif.: Sage Publications.

———. 1979b. An Irony of Electoral Reform. *Regulation* 3 (May/June): 35–44.

Feldstein, Martin, ed. 1980. *The American Economy in Transition.* Chicago: University of Chicago Press.

Fenno, Richard F. Jr. 1973. *Congressmen in Committees.* Boston: Little, Brown.

———. 1978. *Home Style: House Members in Their Districts.* Boston: Little, Brown.

———. 1982. *The United States Senate: A Bicameral Perspective.* Washington, D.C.: American Enterprise Institute.

———. 1986. Observation, Context, and Sequence in the Study of Politics. *American Political Science Review* 80 (March): 3–15.

Forbath, William E. 1991. *Law and the Shaping of the American Labor Movement.* Cambridge: Harvard University Press.

Ford, Henry Jones. 1898. *The Rise and Growth of American Politics: A Sketch of Constitutional Development.* New York: Macmillan.

Francis, Martin. 1995. Economics and Ethics: The Nature of Labour's Socialism. *20th Century British History* 6 (no. 2): 220–43.

Franklin, Mark, and Matthew Ladner. 1995. The Undoing of Winston Churchill: Mobilization and Conversion in the 1945 Realignment of British Voters. *British Journal of Political Science* 25 (October): 429–52.

Freeden, Michael S. 1997. *Ideologies and Political Theory: A Conceptual Approach.* Oxford: Oxford University Press.

Freeman, Ralph E., ed. 1960. *Postwar Economic Trends in the United States.* New York: Harper and Brothers.

Freeman, Richard B. 1980. The Evolution of the American Labor Market, 1948–1980. In *The American Economy in Transition,* edited by Martin Feldstein. Chicago: University of Chicago Press.

Friedel, Frank B. 1947. *FDR and the South.* Baton Rouge: Louisiana State University Press.

Gaddis, John Lewis. 1972. *The United States and the Origins of the Cold War, 1941–1949.* New York: Columbia University Press.

Galbraith, John Kenneth. 1967. *The New Industrial State.* Boston: Houghton Mifflin.

Galston, William, and Elaine Ciulla Kamarck. 1989. The Politics of Evasion: Democrats and the Presidency. Washington, D.C.: Progressive Policy Institute.

Gamble, Andrew. 1994. *The Free Economy and the Strong State: The Politics of Thatcherism.* London: Macmillan.

Gaubatz, Kathlyn Taylor. 1995. *Crime in the Public Mind.* Ann Arbor: University of Michigan Press.

Germond, Jack W., and Jules Witcover. 1989. *Whose Broad Stripes and Bright Stars? The Trivial Pursuit of the Presidency.* New York: Warner Books.

Gillspie, Ed, and Bob Schellas, eds. 1994. *Contract with America.* New York: Times Books.

Gitlin, Todd. 1993. *The Sixties: Years of Hope, Days of Rage.* Rev. ed. New York: Bantam.

Glad, Betty. 1980. *Jimmy Carter: In Search of the Great White House.* New York: W. W. Norton.

Goen, C. C. 1988. *Revivalism and Separatism in New England, 1740–1800.* New Haven, Conn.: Yale University Press.

Goldman, Eric F. 1968. *The Tragedy of Lyndon Johnson.* New York: Alfred A. Knopf.

Gordon, Michael R. 1990. Bush Sends New Units to Gulf to Provide "Offensive" Option; U.S. Forces Could Reach 380,000. *New York Times,* November 9, A1.

Gorst, Anthony. 1991. Facing Facts? The Labour Government and Defence Policy, 1945–50. In *The Attlee Years,* edited by Nick Tiratsoo. London: Pinter Publishers.

Gosnell, Harold F. 1937. *Machine Politics: Chicago Model.* Chicago: University of Chicago Press.

Goulden, Joseph C. 1972. *Meany.* New York: Atheneum.

——. 1976. *The Best Years, 1945–1950.* New York: Atheneum.

Graham, Hugh Davis. 1989. *The Civil Rights Era: Origins and Development of National Policy, 1960–1972.* New York: Oxford University Press.

Granat, Diane. 1984. Unsnarling the Senate's Jungle of Confusion. *Congressional Quarterly Weekly Report,* October 6, 2436.

Greeley, Andrew M. 1989. *Religious Change in America.* Cambridge: Harvard University Press.

Green, Ewen H. H. 1988. Thatcherism: An Historical Perspective. Paper delivered at the Minda de Gunzberg Center for European Studies, Harvard University, January.

Green, Mark J., James M. Fallows, and David R. Zwick. 1972. *Who Runs Congress?* New York: Bantam/Grossman.

Greenblatt, Alan. 1998. Re-engerized "New Deal" Coalition Boosts Democrats for 2000. *Congressional Quarterly Weekly Report,* November 7, 2983.

Hadden, Jeffrey K. 1969. *The Gathering Storm in the Churches.* Garden City, N.Y.: Doubleday Anchor.

Hale, Jon F. 1995. The Making of the New Democrats. *Political Science Quarterly* 110 (summer): 207–32.

Hamby, Alonzo O. 1973. *Beyond the New Deal: Harry S. Truman and American Liberalism.* New York: Columbia University Press.

Hames, Tim. 1995. The US Mid-term Election of 1994. *Electoral Studies* 14 (June): 222–26.

Hammack, David C. 1982. *Power and Society: Greater New York at the Turn of the Century.* New York: Russell Sage Foundation.

Harris, Josie. 1977. *William Beveridge: A Biography.* Oxford: Clarendon Press.

Harrison, Brian H. 1994. *Drink and the Victorians: The Temperance Question in England, 1815–1972.* Staffordshire, England: Keele University Press.

——. 1996. *The Transformation of British Politics, 1880–1995.* Oxford: Oxford University Press.

Harrison, Cynthia E. 1989. *On Account of Sex: The Politics of Women's Issues, 1945–1968.* Berkeley: University of California Press.

Hartmann, Susan M. 1971. *Truman and the 80th Congress.* Columbia: University of Missouri Press.

Hatch, Nathan O. 1989. *The Democratization of American Christianity.* New Haven, Conn.: Yale University Press.

Hayer, George. 1990a. Defiant House Rebukes Bush; New Round of Fights Begins. *Congressional Quarterly Weekly Report,* October 6, 3183–88.

——. 1990b. One Outcome of Budget Package: Higher Deficits on the Way. *Congressional Quarterly Weekly Report,* November 3, 3710–13.

——. 1990c. Parties Angling for Advantage as White House Falters. *Congressional Quarterly Weekly Report,* October 13, 3391–98.

———. 1993. 1993 Deal: Remembrance of Things Past. *Congressional Quarterly Weekly Report*, August 7, 2130.

Hays, Samuel P. 1990. *Beauty, Health, and Permanence: Environmental Politics in the United States, 1955–1985*. New York: Cambridge University Press.

Headey, Bruce. 1978. *Housing Policy in the Developed Economy: UK, USA, & Sweden*. New York: St. Martin's Press.

Heath, Anthony, Roger Jowell, and John Curtice. 1985. *How Britain Votes*. Oxford: Pergamon Press.

Hennessy, Peter. 1986. *Cabinet*. Oxford: Basil Blackwell.

Herring, George C. 1979. *America's Longest War: The United States and Vietnam, 1950–1975*. New York: Alfred A. Knopf.

Hess, Stephen, and David S. Broder. 1967. *The Republican Establishment: The Present and Future of the GOP*. New York: Harper and Row.

Hobson, Barbara M. 1987. *Uneasy Virtue: The Politics of Prostitution and the American Reform Tradition*. New York: Basic Books.

Hoff, Joan. 1994. *Nixon Reconsidered*. New York: Basic Books.

Hofstadter, Richard. 1955. *The Age of Reform: From Bryan to FDR*. New York: Vintage Books.

Holsti, Ole R., and James N. Rosenau. 1984. *American Leadership in World Affairs: Vietnam and the Breakdown of Consensus*. Boston: Allen and Unwin.

Hosansky, David. 1996. Christian Right's Electoral Clout Bore Limited Fruit in 104th. *Congressional Quarterly Weekly Report*, November 2, 3160–62.

House GOP Offers Descriptions of Bills to Enact "Contract." 1994. *Congressional Quarterly Weekly Report*, November 19, 3366–79.

How to Win the Next Election. 1950. *Tribune*, March 3, 1–2.

Hunter, James Davison. 1983. *American Evangelicalism: Conservative Religion and the Quandary of Modernity*. New Brunswick, N.J.: Rutgers University Press.

———. 1991. *Culture Wars: The Struggle to Define America*. New York: Basic Books.

Huntington, Samuel P. 1968. *Political Order in Changing Societies*. New Haven, Conn.: Yale University Press.

———. 1981. *American Politics: The Promise of Disharmony*. Cambridge, Mass.: Belknap Press.

———. 1988. One Soul at a Time: Political Science and Political Reform. *American Political Science Review* 82 (March): 3–10.

Idelson, Holly. 1994. Clinton, Democrats Scramble to Save Anti-crime Bill. *Congressional Quarterly Weekly Report*, August 13, 2340–43.

———. 1995. An Era Comes to a Close. *Congressional Quarterly Weekly Report*, December 23, 3871–73.

Inglehart, Ronald. 1977. *The Silent Revolution: Changing Values and Political Styles Among Western Publics.* Princeton, N.J.: Princeton University Press.

Integrating the Sixties: The Origins, Structures, and Legitimacy of Public Policy in a Turbulent Decade. 1996. *Journal of Policy History* 3 (no.1).

Jackson, Kenneth T. 1985. *Crabgrass Frontier: The Suburbanization of the United States.* New York: Oxford University Press.

Jacobson, Gary C. 1990. *The Electoral Origins of Divided Government: Competition in U.S. House Elections, 1946–1988.* Boulder, Colo.: Westview Press.

Jacoby, Sanford M., ed. 1991. *Masters to Managers: Historical and Comparative Perspectives on American Employers.* New York: Columbia University Press.

Jeffreys, Kevin. 1991. *The Churchill Coalition and Wartime Politics.* Manchester, England: University of Manchester Press.

Jensen, Richard. 1971. *The Winning of the Midwest: Social and Political Conflict, 1888–96.* Chicago: University of Chicago Press.

——. 1981. The Last Party System: Decay of Consensus, 1932–1980. In *The Evolution of American Electoral Systems,* edited by Paul Kleppner et al. Westport, Conn.: Greenwood.

Jones, Charles O. 1965. *The Republican Party in American Politics.* New York: Macmillan.

——. 1988. *The Trusteeship Presidency: Jimmy Carter and the United States Congress.* Baton Rouge: Louisiana State University Press.

Kaplan, Dave. 1988. Arizona's Mecham: The Troubles He's Seen. *Congressional Quarterly Weekly Report,* January 2, 6.

Katz, Jeffrey L. 1996a. After 60 Years, Most Control Is Passing to the States. *Congressional Quarterly Weekly Report,* August 3, 2190–96.

——. 1996b. Clinton's Quandary: All Eyes Turn to White House as GOP Prepares to Clear Big Welfare Plan. *Congressional Quarterly Weekly Report,* July 27, 2115–19.

Kavanagh, Dennis. 1982. Still the Workers' Party? Changing Social Trends in Elite Recruitment and Electoral Support. In *The Politics of the Labour Party,* edited by Dennis Kavanagh. London: George Allen and Unwin.

——. 1997. *The Reordering of British Politics: Politics After Thatcher.* Oxford: Oxford University Press.

Kearns, Doris. 1976. *Lyndon Johnson and the American Dream.* New York: New American Library.

Kelley, Dean M. 1972. *Why Conservative Churches Are Growing.* New York: Harper and Row.

Kelley, Stanley Jr., Richard E. Ayres, and William G. Bowen. 1967. Registration and Voting: Putting First Things First. *American Political Science Review* 61 (June): 359–79.

Kennedy, David M. 1999. *Freedom from Fear: The American People in Depression and War, 1929–1945*. New York: Oxford University Press.

Keohane, Robert O., and Joseph S. Nye. 1977. *Power and Interdependence: World Politics in Transition*. Boston: Little, Brown.

Key, V. O. Jr. 1956. *American State Politics: An Introduction*. New York: Alfred A. Knopf.

———. 1959. Secular Realignment and the Party System. *Journal of Politics* 21 (May): 198–210.

———. 1964. *Politics, Parties, and Pressure Groups*. 5th ed. New York: Thomas Y. Crowell.

Kirkpatrick, Jeane J. 1976. *The New Presidential Elite: Men and Women in National Politics*. New York: Russell Sage Foundation.

Klein, Joe. 1997. Learning to Run. *New Yorker*, December 8, 53–59.

Kleppner, Paul. 1979. *The Third Electoral System, 1853–1892: Parties, Voters, and Political Cultures*. Chapel Hill: University of North Carolina Press.

Kochan, Thomas A. 1980. *Collective Bargaining and Industrial Relations: From Theory to Practice*. Homewood, Ill.: Richard D. Irwin.

Kochan, Thomas A., Harry C. Katz, and Robert B. McKersie. 1986. *The Transformation of American Industrial Relations*. New York: Basic Books.

Kogan, David, and Maurice Kogan. 1982. *The Battle for the Labour Party*. London: Kogan Page.

Lacey, Michael J., ed. 1993. *Government and Environmental Politics: Essays on Historical Developments Since World War Two*. Washington, D.C.: Wilson Center Press.

Ladd, Everett C. 1976–1977. Liberalism Upside Down: The Inversion of the New Deal Order. *Political Science Quarterly* 91 (winter): 577–60.

———. 1989. The 1988 Elections: Continuation of the Post–New Deal System. *Political Science Quarterly* 104 (spring): 1–18.

Ladd, Everett Carll Jr., and Charles D. Hadley. 1973. *Political Parties and Political Issues: Patterns of Political Differentiation Since the New Deal*. Beverly Hills, Calif.: Sage Publications.

Ladd, Everett C. Jr., with Charles D. Hadley. 1975. *Transformations of the American Party System*. New York: W. W. Norton.

Lee, Alton. 1966. *Truman and Taft-Hartley: A Question of Mandate*. Lexington: University of Kentucky Press.

LeGrand, Julian. 1982. *The Strategy of Equality: Redistribution and the Social Services*. London: George Allen and Unwin.

Letwin, William. 1955. Congress and the Sherman Antitrust Law. *University of Chicago Law Review* 23 (autumn): 221–56.

———. 1966. *Law and Economic Policy in America*. Edinburgh: Edinburgh University Press.

Leuchtenberg, William E. 1963. *Franklin D. Roosevelt and the New Deal, 1932–1940.* New York: Harper and Row.

Levine, Lawrence W. 1975. *Defender of the Faith: William Jennings Bryan, the Last Decade, 1915–1925.* New York: Oxford University Press.

Link, Arthur S., and Richard L. McCormick. 1983. *Progressivism.* Arlington Heights, Va.: Harlan Davidson.

Lipset, Seymour Martin. 1960. Working-Class Authoritarianism. In *Political Man: The Social Bases of Politics.* New York: Doubleday.

———. 1963. *The First New Nation: The United States in Historical and Comparative Perspective.* New York: W. W. Norton.

———. 1991. American Exceptionalism Reaffirmed. In *Is America Different? A New Look at American Exceptionalism,* edited by Byron E. Shafer. Oxford: Oxford University Press.

Lipset, Seymour Martin, and Stein Rokkan. 1967. Cleavage Structures, Party Systems, and Voter Alignments: An Introduction. In *Party Systems and Voter Alignments: Cross-National Perspectives,* edited by Seymour Martin Lipset and Stein Rokkan. New York: Free Press.

Lowi, Theodore J. 1971. *The Politics of Disorder.* New York: W. W. Norton.

———. 1981. *Incomplete Conquest: Governing America.* 2d ed. New York: Holt, Rinehart and Winston.

MacDonald, J. Ramsay. 1908. *Character and Democracy.* London: Charles H. Kelly.

Madison, James. 1961. The Federalist, No. 10. In Alexander Hamilton, James Madison, and John Jay, *The Federalist Papers.* 1787–1788. Reprint, New York: New American Library.

Magleby, David B. 1984. *Direct Legislation: Voting on Ballot Propositions in the United States.* Baltimore: Johns Hopkins University Press.

Manza, Jeff, and Clem Brooks. 1999. *Social Cleavages and Political Change: Voter Alignments and U.S. Party Coalitions.* Oxford: Oxford University Press.

Marini, Stephen. 1982. *Radical Sects in Revolutionary New England.* Cambridge: Harvard University Press.

Marsden, George M. 1980. *Fundamentalism and American Culture.* New York: Oxford University Press.

Marshall, T. J. 1950. *Citizenship and Social Class and Other Essays.* Cambridge: Cambridge University Press.

Masci, David. 1994. $30 Billion Anti-crime Bill Heads to Clinton's Desk. *Congressional Quarterly Weekly Report,* August 27, 2488–93.

Mason, Robert J. 1998. The New American Majority: The Challenge to Democratic Dominance, 1969–1977. D.Phil. diss., Oxford University.

Matusow, Allen J. 1984. *The Unraveling of America: A History of Liberalism in the 1960s.* New York: Harper and Row.

Mayer, George H. 1964. *The Republican Party, 1854–1964*. New York: Oxford University Press.

Mayer, William G. 1992. *The Changing American Mind: How and Why American Public Opinion Changed Between 1960 and 1988*. Ann Arbor: University of Michigan Press.

Mayhew, David R. 1986. *Placing Parties in American Politics: Organization, Electoral Settings, and Government Activity in the Twentieth Century*. Princeton, N.J.: Princeton University Press.

———. 1991. *Divided We Govern: Party Control, Lawmaking, and Investigations, 1946–1990*. New Haven, Conn.: Yale University Press.

McCallum, Ronald B., and Alison W. Readman. 1947. *The British General Election of 1945*. London: Oxford University Press.

McClosky, Herbert, and John Zaller. 1984. *The American Ethos: Public Attitudes Toward Capitalism and Democracy*. Cambridge: Harvard University Press.

McKibbin, Ross. 1994. *The Ideologies of Class: Social Relations in Britain, 1880–1950*. Oxford: Clarendon Press.

———. 1998. *Classes and Cultures: England 1918–1951*. Oxford: Oxford University Press.

McLoughlin, William G. 1959. *Modern Revivalism: Charles Grandison Finney to Billy Graham*. New York: Ronald Press.

Merriam, Charles E., and Louise Overacker. 1928. *Primary Elections*. Rev. ed. Chicago: University of Chicago Press.

Merton, Robert K. 1936. The Unintended Consequences of Purposive Social Action. *American Sociological Review* 1:894–904.

———. 1957. The Latent Functions of the Machine. In *Social Theory and Social Structure*. New York: Free Press.

Miller, James. 1994. *Democracy Is in the Streets: From Port Huron to the Siege of Chicago*. Cambridge: Harvard University Press.

Miller, Warren E., and M. Kent Jennings. 1986. *Parties in Transition: A Longitudinal Study of Party Elites and Party Supporters*. New York: Russell Sage Foundation.

Miller, Warren E., and Santa A. Traugott, comps. 1989. *American National Election Studies Sourcebook, 1952–1986*. Cambridge: Harvard University Press.

Millis, Harry A., and Emily C. Brown. 1950. *From the Wagner Act to Taft-Hartley: A Study of National Labor Policy and Labor Relations*. Chicago: University of Chicago Press.

Mills, Mike. 1992. Road Work Ahead? As Economy Rallies, Clinton Must Decide Whether Quick Stimulus Is Still in Order. *Congressional Quarterly Weekly Report*, December 19, 3884–89.

Mitchell, Broadus. 1947. *Depression Decade: From New Era to New Deal, 1929–1941.* New York: Holt, Rinehart and Winston.

Moran, Michael. 1979. The Conservative Party and the Trade Unions Since 1974. *Political Studies* 26 (no.1): 38–53.

Morgan, Kenneth O. 1984. *Labour in Power, 1945–1951.* Oxford: Clarendon Press.

Mott, Luther Frank. 1962. *American Journalism, a History: 1690–1960.* 3d ed. New York: Macmillan.

Mowry, George E. 1949. The California Progressive and His Rationale: A Study in Middle Class Politics. *Mississippi Valley Historical Review* 36 (September): 239–50.

———. 1951. *The California Progressives.* New York: New York Times.

———. 1958. *The Era of Theodore Roosevelt, 1900–1912.* New York: Harper and Row.

Moynihan, Daniel Patrick. 1969. *Maximum Feasible Misunderstanding: Community Action in the War on Poverty.* New York: Free Press.

NAFTA Crucible: Undecided Members Weigh Voter Fears as Trade Pact Showdown Approaches. 1993. *Congressional Quarterly Weekly Report,* Special Report, November 6, 3011–22.

National Election Studies. 1998. *The NES Guide to Public Opinion and Electoral Behavior.* http://www.umich.edu/7Enes/nes.guide.htm.

Nelson, Michael, et al. 1989. *The Elections of 1988.* Washington, D.C.: CQ Press.

———. 1993. *The Elections of 1992.* Washington, D.C.: CQ Press.

———. 1997. The *Elections of 1996.* Washington, D.C.: CQ Press.

———. 2001. *The Elections of 2000.* Washington, D.C.: CQ Press.

Noll, Mark A., ed. 1990. *Religion and American Politics: From the Colonial Period to the 1980s.* New York: Oxford University Press.

Norris, Pippa. 1998. The Battle for the Campaign Agenda. In *New Labour Triumphs: Britain at the Polls,* edited by Anthony King. Chatham, N.J.: Chatham House.

O'Brien, David M. 1986. *Storm Center: The Supreme Court in American Politics.* New York: W. W. Norton.

O'Neill, William L. 1975. *The Progressive Years: America Comes of Age.* New York: Dodd, Mead.

Overacker, Louise. 1932. *Money in Elections.* New York: Macmillan.

———. 1946. *Presidential Campaign Funds.* Boston: Boston University Press.

Pacelle, Richard L. Jr. 1991. *The Transformation of the Supreme Court's Agenda.* Boulder, Colo.: Westview Press.

Panel on the Electoral and Democratic Process. 1980. *The Electoral and Democratic Process in the Eighties.* Washington, D.C.: U.S. Government Printing Office.

Pareto, Vilfredo. 1980. *Compendium of General Sociology.* Abridged by Giulio Farina. Translated by Elizabeth Abbott. Minneapolis: University of Minnesota Press. Original edition, *Trattato di Sociologia Generale.* 3 vols. Florence: Barbera, 1916.

Patterson, James T. 1996. *Grand Expectations: The United States, 1945–1974.* New York: Oxford University Press.

Pelling, Henry. 1987. *A History of British Trade Unionism.* London: Macmillan.

Perot, Ross, with Pat Choate. 1993. *Save Your Job, Save Our Country: Why NAFTA Must Be Stopped—Now!* New York: Hyperion.

Phillips, Kevin. 1998. *American Political Report,* October 16. Bethesda, Md.: American Political Research Corporation.

Pimlott, Ben. 1991. Trade Unions and the Second Coming of CND. In *Trade Unions in British Politics: The First 250 Years,* edited by Ben Pimlott and Chris Cook. London: Longman.

——. 1996. *The Queen: A Biography of Elizabeth II.* London: HarperCollins.

Pious, Richard M., ed. 1981. *The Power to Govern: Assessing Reform in the United States.* New York: Academy of Political Science.

Polsby, Nelson W. 1983. *Consequences of Party Reform.* Oxford: Oxford University Press.

——. 1984. *Political Innovation in America: The Politics of Policy Initiation.* New Haven, Conn.: Yale University Press.

Polsby, Nelson W., and Aaron Wildavsky. 1991. *Presidential Elections: Contemporary Strategies of American Electoral Politics.* 8th ed. New York: Free Press.

Pomper, Gerald M., et al. 1989. *The Election of 1988.* Chatham, N.J.: Chatham House.

——. 1993. *The Election of 1992.* Chatham, N.J.: Chatham House.

——. 1997. *The Election of 1996.* Chatham, N.J.: Chatham House.

——. 2001. *The Elections of 2000: Reports and Interpretations.* New York: Chatham House.

Ponting, Clive. 1990. *Breach of Promise: Labour in Power, 1964–1970.* London: Penguin Books.

Pope, Charles. 1998. Hollow "Victory": A Chronology of Rebellion. *Congressional Quarterly Weekly Report,* November 14, 3062–63.

Potter, David M. 1954. *People of Plenty: Economic Abundance and the American Character.* Chicago: University of Chicago Press.

President's Commission for a National Agenda for the Eighties. 1980. *A National Agenda for the Eighties.* Washington, D.C.: U.S. Government Printing Office.

Price, Robert. 1980. *Profiles of Union Growth: A Comparative Statistical Portrait of Eight Countries.* Oxford: Basil Blackwell.

Pritchett, C. Herman. 1984. *Constitutional Civil Liberties.* Englewood Cliffs, N.J.: Prentice-Hall.

Pye, Lucian W. 1962. *Politics, Personality, and Nation-Building: Burma's Search for Identity.* New Haven, Conn.: Yale University Press.

Pytte, Alyson. 1990. A Decade's Acrimony Lifted in the Glow of Clean Air. *Congressional Quarterly Weekly Report,* October 27, 3587–92.

Rae, Nicol C. 1989. *The Rise and Fall of the Liberal Republicans: From 1952 to the Present.* New York: Oxford University Press.

Ramsden, John. 1995. *The Age of Churchill and Eden, 1940–1957.* London: Longman.

Ranney, Austin. 1975. *Curing the Mischiefs of Faction: Party Reform in America.* Berkeley: University of California Press.

———. 1981. *The Federalization of Presidential Primaries.* Washington, D.C.: American Enterprise Institute.

———. 1983. *Channels of Power: The Impact of Television on American Politics.* New York: Basic Books.

Ranney, Austin, and Willmoore Kendall. 1956. *Democracy and the American Party System.* New York: Harcourt, Brace, and World.

Rasky, Susan F. 1990. Accord to Reduce Spending and Raise Taxes Is Reached; Many in Congress Critical. *New York Times,* October 1, A1.

Ravitch, Diane. 1983. *The Troubled Crusade: American Education, 1945–1980.* New York: Basic Books.

Reed, Louis S. 1966. *The Labor Philosophy of Samuel Gompers.* New York: Kennikat Press.

Reed, Ralph. 1995. *Active Faith: How Christians Are Changing the Soul of American Politics.* New York: Free Press.

Reichley, James. 1985. *Religion in American Public Life.* Washington, D.C.: Brookings Institution.

———. 1992. *The Life of the Parties: A History of American Political Parties.* New York: Free Press.

Religion in America Today. 1985. *Annals of the American Academy of Political and Social Science* 480 (July).

Relyea, Harold C. 1975. Opening Government to Public Scrutiny: A Decade of Federal Efforts. *Public Administration Review* 35 (January/February): 3–10.

Richards, Peter G. 1945. The Labour Victory. *Political Quarterly* 16 (no. 4): 355–56.

Rieselbach, Leroy N. 1977. *Congressional Reform in the Seventies.* Morristown, N.J.: General Learning Press.

Riesman, David, with Nathan Glazer and Reuel Denny. 1950. *The Lonely Crowd: A Study of the Changing American Character.* New Haven, Conn.: Yale University Press.

Roche, John P. 1961. The Founding Fathers: A Reform Caucus in Action. *American Political Science Review* 60 (December): 799–816.

Rosenbaum, David E. 1990. And the Victor Is: Bush? *New York Times*, October 1, A1.

Rosenstone, Stephen J., and Raymond E. Wolfinger. 1978. The Effect of Registration Laws on Turnout. *American Political Science Review* 72 (March): 22–45.

Rosenthal, Andrew. 1991. Bush Halts Offensive Combat; Kuwait Freed, Iraqis Crushed. *New York Times*, February 28, A1.

Ross, J. F. S. 1955. *Elections and Electors: Studies in Democratic Representation*. London: Eyre and Spottiswode.

Rowner, Julie. 1988. Congress Approves Overhaul of Welfare System. *Congressional Quarterly Weekly Report*, October 8, 2825–31.

Rubin, Alissa J. 1994a. Health Care Post-Mortem: Divided Democrats, United GOP Killed Overhaul Effort. *Congressional Quarterly Weekly Report*, October 1, 2797–801.

———. 1994b. Uncertainty, Deep Divisions Cloud Opening of Debate. *Congressional Quarterly Weekly Report*, August 13, 2344–53.

Rudder, Catherine E. 1978. The Policy Impact of Reform of the Committee on Ways and Means. In *Legislative Reform: The Policy Impact*, edited by Leroy N. Rieselbach. Lexington, Mass.: Lexington Books.

Saloma, John S. III, and Frederick H. Sontag. 1973. *Parties: The Real Opportunity for Effective Citizen Politics*. New York: Vintage Books.

Scammon, Richard M., and Ben J. Wattenberg. 1970. *The Real Majority*. New York: Coward-McCann.

Schlesinger, Arthur M. Jr. 1950. *The American as Reformer*. Cambridge: Harvard University Press.

———. 1957. *The Crisis of the Old Order*. Boston: Houghton Mifflin.

———. 1959. *The Coming of the New Deal*. Boston: Houghton Mifflin.

———. 1986. *The Cycles of American History*. Boston: Houghton Mifflin.

Schlesinger, Stephen C. 1975. *The New Reformers: Forces for Change in American Politics*. Boston: Houghton Mifflin.

Schlozman, Kay L., and John T. Tierney. 1985. *Organized Interests and American Democracy*. New York: Harper and Row.

Shafer, Byron E. 1983a. *Quiet Revolution: The Struggle for the Democratic Party and the Shaping of Post-Reform Politics*. New York: Russell Sage Foundation.

———. 1983b. Reform and Alienation: The Decline of Intermediation in the Politics of Presidential Selection. *Journal of Law & Politics* 1 (fall): 93–132.

———. 1988. *Bifurcated Politics: Evolution and Reform in the National Party Convention*. Cambridge: Harvard University Press.

———. 1989. "Exceptionalism" in American Politics? *PS: Political Science & Politics* 22 (September): 588–94.

———. 1997. The American Elections of 1996. *Electoral Studies* 16 (September): 394–403.

———. 1998a. The Mid-term Election of 1994: Upheaval in Search of a Framework. In *The Republican Takeover of Congress,* edited by Dean McSweeney and John E. Owens. New York: St. Martin's Press.

———. 1999. The Partisan Legacy. In *The Clinton Legacy,* edited by Colin Campbell and Bert Rockman. Chatham, N.J.: Chatham House.

———, ed. 1991. *Is America Different? A New Look at American Exceptionalism.* Oxford: Clarendon Press.

———. 1996. *Postwar Politics in the G-7: Orders and Eras in Comparative Perspective.* Madison: University of Wisconsin Press.

———. 1998b. *Partisan Approaches to Postwar American Politics.* Chatham, N.J.: Chatham House.

Shafer, Byron E., and Anthony J. Badger, eds. 2001. *The Changing Contours of American Politics: Structure and Substance in American Political History, 1775–2000.* Lawrence: University Press of Kansas.

Shafer, Byron E., and William J. M. Claggett. 1995. *The Two Majorities: The Issue Context of Modern American Politics.* Baltimore: Johns Hopkins University Press.

Shaw, Eric. 1988. *Discipline and Discord in the Labour Party: The Politics of Managerial Control in the Labour Party, 1951–87.* Manchester, England: Manchester University Press.

———. 1994. *The Labour Party Since 1979: Crisis and Transformation.* London: Routledge.

Silbey, Joel H. 1991. *The American Political Nation, 1838–1893.* Stanford, Calif.: Stanford University Press.

Sitkoff, Harvard. 1978. *A New Deal for Blacks: The Emergence of Civil Rights as a National Issue.* New York: Oxford University Press.

———. 1981. *The Struggle for Black Equality, 1954–1980.* New York: Hill and Wang.

Skowronek, Stephen. 1993. *The Politics Presidents Make: Leadership from John Adams to George Bush.* Cambridge, Mass.: Belknap Press.

Smith, Tom W. 1990. Liberal and Conservative Trends in the United States Since World War II. *Public Opinion Quarterly* 54 (winter): 479–507.

Solomon, Burt. 1998. Bill and Monica Who? *National Journal,* October 31, 2542–46.

Soper, J. Christopher. 1994. *Evangelical Christianity in the United States and Great Britain: Religious Beliefs, Political Choices.* Basingstoke, England: Macmillan.

Statistical Abstract of the United States. Various years. Washington, D.C.: U.S. Government Printing Office.

Steffens, Lincoln. 1904. *The Shame of Our Cities.* New York: McClure, Phillips.

Stewart, Michael. 1977. *The Jekyll and Hyde Years: Politics and Economic Policy Since 1964.* London: J. M. Dent.

Stouffer, Samuel A., et al. 1949. *The American Soldier: Studies in Social Psychology in World War II.* 2 vols. Princeton, N.J.: Princeton University Press.

Strahan, Randall W. 1998. Party Officeholders, 1946–1996. In *Partisan Approaches to Postwar American Politics,* edited by Byron E. Shafer. Chatham, N.J.: Chatham House.

Sundquist, James L. 1968. *Politics and Policy: The Eisenhower, Kennedy, and Johnson Years.* Washington, D.C.: Brookings Institution.

——. 1973. *Dynamics of the Party System: Alignment and Realignment of Political Parties in the United States.* Washington, D.C.: Brookings Institution.

Taft, Philip. 1964. *Organized Labor in American History.* New York: Harper and Row.

Taylor, Robert. 1991. The Trade Union "Problem" in the Age of Consensus, 1960–1979. In *Trade Unions in British Politics: The First 250 Years,* edited by Ben Pimlott and Chris Cook. London: Longman.

Thelen, David P. 1969. Social Tensions and the Origins of Progressivism. *Journal of American History* 56 (September): 323–41.

Thomas, Gary. 1996. Unions Spending Big Money to Sway Elections. www.cc .org/unions.html, July 10.

Thomas, Hugh. 1986. *Armed Truce: The Beginnings of the Cold War, 1945–46.* London: Hamish Hamilton.

Thomson, Charles A. H., and Frances M. Shattuck. 1960. *The 1956 Presidential Campaign.* Washington, D.C.: Brookings Institution.

Thorelli, Hans B. 1954. *The Federal Antitrust Policy.* Baltimore: Johns Hopkins University Press.

Tomlinson, Jim. 1996. Inventing Decline: The Falling Behind of the British Economy in the Post-War Years. *Economic History Review* 49 (November): 731–57.

Towell, Pat. 1988. Hill Weighs Bills to Avert Procurement Abuses. *Congressional Quarterly Weekly Report,* July 16, 1875–1976.

——. 1993a. Campaign Promise, Social Debate Collide on Military Battlefield. *Congressional Quarterly Weekly Report,* January 30, 226–29.

——. 1993b. Nunn Offers a Compromise: "Don't Ask, Don't Tell." *Congressional Quarterly Weekly Report,* May 15, 1240–42.

Undy, R., V. Ellis, W. E. J. McCarthy, and A. M. Halmos. 1981. *Change in Trade Unions: The Development of UK Unions Since the 1960s.* London: Hutchinson.

Vale, Vivian. 1971. *Labour in American Politics.* London: Routledge and Kegan Paul.

Verba, Sidney, and Gary R. Orren. 1985. *Equality in America: The View from the Top.* Cambridge: Harvard University Press.

Verbatim Report of 93rd Conservative Party Conference. 1976. October.

Vogel, David. 1989. *Fluctuating Fortunes: The Political Power of Business in America.* New York: Basic Books.

Von Drehle, David. 2000. Reality Check on a Decidedly Positive Day. *Washington Post,* August 1, A1.

Wald, Kenneth D. 1992. *Religion and Politics in the United States.* 2d ed. Washington, D.C.: CQ Press.

Walker, Jack L. 1991. *Mobilizing Interest Groups in America: Patrons, Professions, and Social Movements.* Ann Arbor: University of Michigan Press.

Waltz, Kenneth N. 1979. *The Theory of International Politics.* Reading, Mass.: Addison-Wesley.

Ware, Alan J. 1985. *The Breakdown of Democratic Party Organization, 1940– 1980.* Oxford: Oxford University Press.

West, William. 1985. *Administrative Rule-making: Politics and Process.* Westport, Conn.: Greenwood Press.

White, Theodore H. 1969. *The Making of the President 1968.* New York: Atheneum.

——. 1982. *America in Search of Itself: The Making of the President, 1956–1980.* New York: Harper and Row.

Whyte, William H. Jr. 1956. *The Organization Man.* New York: Simon and Schuster.

Wickham-Jones, Mark. 1997. Right-Turn? A Revisionist Account of the 1975 Conservative Party Leadership Election. *20th Century British History* 8 (no.1): 74–89.

Wildavsky, Aaron B., and Nelson W. Polsby. 1964. *Presidential Elections: Strategies of American Electoral Politics.* New York: Charles Scribner's Sons.

Wildavsky, Ben. 1998. Monica and the New Democrats. *National Journal,* September 26, 2334.

Williams, Juan. 1987. *Eyes on the Prize: America's Civil Rights Years, 1954–1965.* New York: Viking.

Wilson, Graham K. 1979. *Unions in American National Politics.* New York: St. Martin's Press.

Wilson, Harold. 1964. *The New Britain: Labour's Plan.* London: Penguin Books.

Wilson, James Q. 1963. *The Amateur Democrat: Club Politics in Three Cities.* Chicago: University of Chicago Press.

——. 1973. *Political Organizations.* New York: Basic Books.

——. 1975. *Thinking About Crime.* New York: Vintage Books.

——. 1980. *The Politics of Regulation.* New York: Basic Books.

Wintour, Patrick, and Rick Rogers. 1979. The Life and Times of Margaret Thatcher. *New Statesman* 97 (April): 578–80.

Wolfinger, Raymond E., and Stephen J. Rosenstone. 1980. *Who Votes?* New Haven, Conn.: Yale University Press.

Yankelovich, Daniel. 1984. *New Rules: Searching for Self-Fulfillment in a World Turned Upside Down.* New York: Random House.

Young, Hugo. 1991. *One of Us: A Biography of Margaret Thatcher.* London: Macmillan.

Zieger, Robert H. 1986. *American Workers, American Unions, 1920–1985.* Baltimore: Johns Hopkins University Press.

Zuckerman, Jill. 1990. Democrats Put up Bill to Meet National Goals Set by Bush. *Congressional Quarterly Weekly Report,* March 31, 1001–2.

INDEX

343

Tax cuts, 40, 45, 46, 68, 70, 78
Tax increases, 93, 100, 101, 102
Tax reformists, 23, 59, 77, 229
Teen curfews, 42
Televangelism, 43, 176, 178, 295
Television, 295
Temperance movement, 178
Term limits, 70
Thatcher, Margaret, 230, 232, 235, 236, 237, 243, 260, 261
  and Ronald Reagan comparison, 231, 244
"Thatcherism," 260
Tories. *See* Great Britain, Conservative Party
Tort reform, 74
Truman, Harry S., 8
Trust-busting, 194, 200, 203–204

Unemployment, 40
  compensation, 217
  increase, 87
Unions. *See* Organized labor
United Auto Workers (United Automobile, Aircraft (Aerospace) and Agricultural Implement Workers of America), 185, 186(table)
United Brotherhood of Carpenters and Joiners, 186(table), 187
United Food and Commerical Workers International Union, 186(table)
United Mine Workers of America, 136, 186(table), 187
United Nations, 96
United Steelworkers Union (of America), 186(table)
Urban machines. *See* Party machines

Valuational conflicts, 57, 226, 227
Value added, 146(fig.)
Vietnam War (1964–1975), 17, 18, 21, 42, 57, 87, 226, 230

protests, 18, 21, 31, 57, 158, 161, 167, 200, 227
Voluntarism, 197
Volunteer political activists, 9, 217–218
Voter registration, automatic and universal, 212–213
Voting Rights Act (1965), 17

Wagner Act. *See* National Labor Relations Act; National Labor Relations Board
Wales, 232
Wallace, George, 20
Ware, Alan J., 168
War on Poverty, 18
War Powers Act, 95–96
Warren, Earl, 19, 124, 227
Waste disposal, 205
Watergate crisis (1973), 24, 37, 81
Wealth, 34
Welfare reform, 41–42, 64, 75–76
Welfare state, 24, 28, 37, 142, 243
White-collar
  class division, 28
  coalition, 9, 32, 84, 217
  conflict, 122–123
  growth, 34, 117, 162, 163–164(figs.)
  majority, 11
  See also Middle class
"White Paper on Full Employment" (Keynes), 222
Willkie, Wendell, 30, 153
Wilson, Harold, 231, 233, 241
Working-class, 246
  "authoritarianism," 32
  See also Blue-collar coalition
World War II (1939–1945), 27, 55, 166(table), 217, 238
  aftermath, 11–16, 183, 250, 263. *See also* Cold War; Germany; Great Britain; Italy; Japan